FLEET STREET.

(From a print in the Crace Collection.   T. S. Boys, del. and litho., 1838.

MASTERS OF ENGLISH JOURNALISM

A STUDY OF PERSONAL FORCES

BY

T. H. S. ESCOTT

GREENWOOD PRESS, PUBLISHERS
WESTPORT, CONNECTICUT

Originally published in 1911
by T. Fisher Unwin, London

Reprinted from a copy in the collections
of the Brooklyn Public Library

First Greenwood Reprinting 1970

Library of Congress Catalogue Card Number 74-98834

SBN 8371-3020-4

PRINTED IN UNITED STATES OF AMERICA

To

SIR EDWARD L. LAWSON

FIRST BARON BURNHAM, OF HALL BARN, BEACONSFIELD, AND OF FLEET STREET,

THE HEAD OF A FAMILY WHICH ORIGINATED, WHICH STILL
OWNS AND MANAGES THE EARLIEST AND GREATEST OF PENNY
PAPERS, TO-DAY THE OLDEST REPRESENTATIVE OF JOURNAL-
ISM AS A NATIONAL INSTITUTION, TO WHOSE FAMILY IT IS
LARGELY DUE THAT POPULAR JOURNALISM HAS ORGANISED
ITSELF AS AN HONOURABLE AND PROSPEROUS PROFESSION,
IS INSCRIBED WITH PERMISSION AND IN ACKNOWLEDGMENT
OF UNFAILING PERSONAL OBSERVATION AND KINDNESS
EXTENDING OVER FORTY YEARS OF NEWSPAPER WORK,
THIS RECORD OF THE JOURNALIST'S RISE AND PROGRESS,
BY HIS SINCERE AND OBLIGED

T. H. S. ESCOTT

PREFACE

THERE are several good histories of, or books mainly, about, newspapers. Some of these have not ignored the name and work of those who have written for them. The individual, however, in all cases has been subordinated to the enterprise. Primarily, and as far as possible exclusively, true at all points to its title, the present work deals with the personal agencies of which those newspapers are the result. Even in the dim light of the Middle Ages may be traced the individual outlines of the journalist's pioneers. Without any break in the succession, these figures, in their "habit as they lived," here pass before the reader's eye. From Marchmont Nedham in the seventeenth century to Mr. J. L. Garvin in the twentieth, there have, it is hoped, been few gaps in the varied and, from the chronological point of view, orderly procession. The idea of this book, as well as of its treatment in detail, was suggested to me by a famous journalist of the Victorian age, Frederick Greenwood, whom a forty years' intimacy, professional and personal, made me think a good authority on a matter of this sort. More than once during his last illness this earliest editor of mine, and lifelong friend, not only recurred to the subject, but in several letters indicated down to minute particulars the lines whereon it seemed to him indispensable that the work should be done. Its interest was, in his opinion, to be personal throughout. Thus one had to show the manner in which the men lived, suffered, or enjoyed themselves, as well as that in which they laboured. This task could not have been carried through but for the invaluable assistance given me more than generously both by my own contemporaries, as well as by many distinguished and kindly men belonging to an older generation than mine. The fuller presentation

7

of individual journalists could not have been attempted before the seventeenth and eighteenth centuries. From that date onward, about the same amount of space has been given to the earlier and the later of the English newspapers' makers. At their head, when the present volume first shaped itself, was Lord Glenesk, to whom from family accidents I had been known, as schoolboys say, "at home," and to whom directly, rather than to any monograph which his family may since have published, I am indebted for everything said about his ancestral, personal, journalistic relationships and doings. His successor and doyen of the English press, Lord Burnham, has similarly enabled me to ensure accuracy in my remarks concerning the *Daily Telegraph's* earlier days, as well as concerning the men most conspicuous in the Fleet Street system, somewhat before my own day. Scarcely less have been my obligations to many others, who have grudged no pains to help me in verifying oral tradition and to make me independent of what has elsewhere been published about newspaper workers, universally accessible, as such records are, and not the less interesting or valuable though the latest phases of journalistic actuality and consequent novelty in handling did not come within their writers' scope. Here I must name Mr. E. J. Goodman, formerly of the *Yorkshire Post* first, the *Daily Telegraph* afterwards, Mr. T. E. Kebbel, Mr. Sidney Low, the late Mr. Edward Spender, or rather those who represent him to-day, Mr. Thomas Catling, Sir Edward R. Russell, of the *Liverpool Daily Post*, Mr. G. W. E. Russell, equally distinguished in Fleet Street and Paternoster Row, and Mr. Justin McCarthy, the oldest as well, perhaps, as the most illustrious among the ornaments of my own craft. After having observed me throughout my entire course, from the inexhaustible stores of his experience, with a courtesy and kindness not less great and unfailing than his knowledge, he has been good enough to supply me with touches and colour for episodes, and those who figured in them, beyond the reach of my own experience. There still remain unmentioned some to whom I owe it that there are not more vacancies in this gallery of journalistic portraits, and that in preparing them I have had the advantage of experiences more directly personal, and going back further than my own. My venerable and literally encyclopædic friend, Mr. John C. Francis, with the ties of a memory that never halts and a vigilance that nothing escapes, links together probably as many generations of journalistic and literary interest as were ever united by a single mind. His *Notes by the Way*, a treasure-house in themselves, have, so far as concerns me, been supplemented by many letters and conversations that have, I trust, helped me to throw some fresh personal light upon bygone newspaper episodes and their most important figures. These of course include Mr. Milner Gibson ; of him I have in another volume [1] placed some impressions on paper, formed from the recollection of juvenile days. The estimate of his personal and social services to the journalist, as given in the present pages, as well as of one or two more, is gathered from family letters addressed by him to relations of mine who were among his intimates. As regards other authorities, the usefulness of the best known newspaper histories, including Madden's work on the Irish press, has been little drawn on for the information regarding the journalist out of London, now, it is believed, given for the first time. The personal panorama unfolded in the present pages includes newspaper figures of mark on both sides of St. George's Channel, and of a calibre not less than variety justly proportioned to the position and power of the periodical pen in the great provincial cities of the realm. Here, as in many cognate matters, I have profited by the local experience of Mr. J. M. Tuohy, the *Freeman's Journal's* London representative, and the mellow universalism of Mr. McCarthy. That the present account of the Irish journalist at work correctly describes the men, their methods, their associations, and their results, is due less to my own acquaintance with the country, where I have been merely a visitor, than to the practical and minute knowledge long since accumulated by Mr. T. M. Healy, and in the most ready and handsome manner placed by him at my disposal. The personal method was, as I have said already, the essential condition on which Greenwood encouraged and desired me to take

[1] *Platform, Press, Politics, and Play* (Arrowsmith.)

the matter in hand. That method, easy enough of application to the greater figures of the English press, in
the case of men less well known, but scarcely less
influential, involves sustained reference to authorities less
accessible than the ordinary reference books. As regards
the personal forces secondarily active in forming the
Fourth Estate, I could seldom get more than disconnected
hints even from the *Dictionary of National Biography*.
That work, however, generally put one on the true
scent, and suggested the right quarters for discovering first one group of personal characteristics, then
another. The clue thus in the first instance obtained,
and patiently followed up, generally enabled me, often
in unsuspected corners of little known biographies or
memoirs, to equip myself with attributes and incidents
which at length supplied a key to the real character and
services of many of the less famous among those mentioned in this volume.

CONTENTS

CHAPTER III

CHAPTER IV

CHAPTER V

CHAPTER VI

CHAPTER VII

CHAPTER VIII

CHAPTER IX

CHAPTER X

CHAPTER XI

CHAPTER XII

CHAPTER XIII

CHAPTER XIV

CONTENTS

CHAPTER XV

Masters of
English Journalism

CHAPTER I

INTRODUCTORY

Thackeray on the public and "newspaper rows"—Nineteenth-century changes
caused by growing popular interest in the press—Increase in number of well-
placed journalistic amateurs—The anonymous system on the decline—
Nineteenth and twentieth century journalism contrasted—Modern newspaper
millionaires directly descended from the originators of the English press—
Ascendancy of the commercial aspect—Recent revolutions in the press caused
by financial considerations—Work of the journalistic profession—The English
newspaper the product of individual efforts—Ancient historical modes of influencing public opinion—Greek substitutes for the modern pressmen—*Tis*,
the drama, and the rhetoricians—Xenophon and Isocrates the first journalists
—Julius Cæsar and the *Acta Diurna*—Influence of the Roman satirists on
contemporary thought—The oracles of Greece and Rome.

"OUR governor thinks the people don't mind a straw
about these newspaper rows." Such, exactly sixty-two
years ago, was the indifference to the inner life of the
journalistic polity attributed by Thackeray's *Pall Mall
Gazette* proprietor, Bungay, to the readers for whom he
catered.[1] Disraeli showed a juster sense of the popular
attraction with which the enterprise and interiors of Fleet
Street had invested themselves, in a remark he made
not long before his death. He was going through
his last novel but one, published some dozen years
earlier, and stopped at the passage where Hugo
Bohun tells Lothair he should, as the "high mode
for a swell," take a theatre. "If," the author paused to
say, "I were writing this now, I should have put ' start
or buy a newspaper.' " Even Thackeray lived long

---

[1] *Pendennis*, i. p. 326 (1886 edition).

enough to see journalism in a fair way of becoming a
pursuit for scribblers of quality, when as yet there had
been observed no signs that the properties and personages
of Fleet Street might provide pastime or profit for
professional millionaires of British or foreign growth.
His particular friend Matthew Higgins (Jacob Omnium)
figured among the leaders of a movement which commended newspaper writing to the classes which looked
down on newspaper hacks, but which now supplied the
great editor J. T. Delane with some of his most
accomplished as well as most select recruits. During
the Grey Reform Bill period, Thomas Mozley was
received from Oriel into Printing House Square. In
1842 he was followed by another accession from
outside to the comity of journalism in the person of
Frederick Rogers, eventually Lord Blachford ; he
began by stipulating that his connection with the
Times should be kept a secret. Throughout most of
the nineteenth century the English newspaper remained
at least in theory anonymous. The editor's name
was whispered with something of almost religious awe,
even among the few admitted into the secret of his
identity. Wrapt in a cloud of mystery, the embodiment of the journalistic " we " had his daily interviews
with ministers and ambassadors ; after these he first
inspired and then revised the leading articles, in which
what the newspaper said to-day the nation thought to-
morrow. All this now belongs to the past. The entire
thoroughfare between Ludgate Hill and Charing Cross
is connected as by a whispering gallery with every point
of social meeting in the capital, and, indeed, throughout
the country. The collective expression of journalistic
policy known as the " leader " has been extensively superseded by the communication from the specialist or expert,
vouched for by the signature of an individual. The
processes, however, whose result is now described, are,
as will hereafter be shown, only a consequence and a
sign of the public's steadily growing occupation with
newspaper management, methods, and personages. In
all of these the end of the nineteenth and the beginning
of the twentieth century witnessed a change so striking
and complete as to have involved an entire transformation in every branch of Fleet Street's staple industry.

At the same time, amid all these innovations, there may be noticed a real consistency with the English newspaper's earliest precedents. At every turn, conditioned only by the law of supply and demand, each novelty successively introduced has been due to personal initiative and private enterprise. The policy and newspaper men in the twentieth century present many strong contrasts to those of their predecessors in the Victorian age. All this will be shown in detail on a later page. Here it is enough to point out that the capitalists, whether individuals or corporations, who, during the first decade of the present reign, have acquired almost a monopoly of the newspaper press, are the lineal descendants of the resolute adventurers, literary or commercial, who began to create that press even before the fall of the Stuarts and the freedom of speech following on constitutional kingship had made it possible quite to complete their work.

The bookseller who in 1702 started the earliest of English daily papers was no more of a philanthropist or less indifferent to quick money returns than the publishers who in 1868, following a provincial example, in the *Echo* endowed London with the earliest halfpenny paper, not, however, before journals resembling the *Echo* in size and cost had been established at Glasgow, Liverpool, and other provincial capitals. The *Echo* was followed by a now forgotten innovation, the *Penny a Week Country Daily Newspaper*, a single issue of which cost only a farthing. The beginning of Mr. Gladstone's last premiership witnessed the appearance in the *Leader* of the first halfpenny morning paper on the Thames. The *Daily Mail* came four years later. Since then opportunities have abounded of comparing the purpose and the system most characteristic of the twentieth-century press with the conduct and the objects that distinguish the newspapers of a less enlightened age. The newspaper, it has been said, has been from the first a commercial undertaking. Its promoters, however, often had other motives, such as the support of a party, the advocacy of a cause. This involved the dissemination of arguments and articles calculated to promote that end, not less than of news from every quarter. To-day political championship or attack is largely subordinated to improving the dividends of shareholders in the venture. With that end old-established journals are bought up to clear the way of rivals, new prints are started to anticipate attempts at occupying fresh territory. To collect and interpret news is the traditional business of a newspaper man, who to-day adventurously enlists each new agency for collection as it becomes known, but looks more and more to events for the interpretation. The popular interest in newspapers has at the present time been stimulated by the entirely novel kind of international agency which they may constitute. The function now referred to is not merely the reaction of newspaper writing, conciliatory or aggressive, upon the sentiments or the politics of different countries. The London Institute of Journalists has at least had the effect of making British and continental politicians better acquainted with each other.[1] Finally, in the summer of 1909 the Imperial Press Conference formed probably the first occasion on which, in its corporate capacity, the newspaper profession, not only in the Mother Country but throughout the Anglo-Saxon world, was recognised by the sovereign, through his representatives, as at once an employment and an interest whose opportunities, services, and aims placed its controllers almost on the same level with the men who directed his diplomacy, his armies, or his fleets. The method to be observed throughout these pages is prescribed by the most characteristic features of the subject. The English newspaper, in all its now familiar varieties, owes its existence, its form, and its authority to individual enterprise. Here, therefore, our concern is not with abstractions or generalities but with men.

To what extent, it may as a preliminary be asked, did the originators of the English newspaper profit from the earliest examples of an older civilisation in other countries? An answer to this question has been rendered possible by the wide learning and happy insight of one who, as a member of J. T. Delane's famous staff, might, had he desired, have been not less successful in journalism than he was distinguished in scholarship. In

---

[1] *E.g.* the recent interchange of hospitalities between those representing the English and the continental press.

the annual Oration, June 28, 1884, of Harvard University, in the Sander's Theatre, the late Sir R. C. Jebb set himself to answer the question whether the classical or a still earlier world, as regards the creation or direction of popular feeling, revealed any substitute for the influence, after centuries of struggle with interested prejudice and calculating opposition, at last won at the sword's point by the modern journalist. The newspaper man's motive power is public opinion ; he could, therefore, have had no precursor where, as in the East, that force did not assert itself. There the opinion of the nation normally meant the thought and performances of the king. As for these royal authors, the stone records accompanying their images or symbols still preserve their literary style, generally to this effect : :" He came up with chariots. He said that he was my first cousin. I impaled him. I am Artakhshatrá. I flayed his uncles, his brothers, and his cousins. I am the king, the son of Daryavash. I crucified two thousand of the principal inhabitants. I am the shining one, the great and the good." In the dawn of Greek civic life, the popular narrative supplied by the Homeric poems shows a national genius whose most marked traits constantly recur in the ripest age of the Greek republics. For Achilles and Ulysses always remained popular ideals. But in the political system of the *Iliad* there is as little place for public opinion as would be found under the ancient despots of the farthest East. Not only legislation but discussion is confined to the king in consultation with his nobles and elders. So far the popular assembly is practically unknown. On the other hand, in the social life of the community public opinion is represented as constantly on the alert, shrewdly observant of whatever is said or done, ever ready fearlessly to express itself with as much freedom as in a constitutional State. The chorus of the Attic stage has been said to convey the views of the ideally right-minded and well-informed spectator. The public opinion of the Homeric writings is personified in the indefinite pronoun *Tis*. The views and verdicts of the average man thus indicated are as little to be neglected in the domestic circle as in the market-place. The collective courage and wisdom of the army are in serious debate.; the low-born

Thersites, whose scurrilous tongue and mean person formed the index of a meaner mind, takes up his parable unasked.; Ulysses fetches the intruder a blow in the back which brings tears to his eyes and sends him back to his seat. *Tis* is delighted, and thinks that Thersites is not likely to try it on again. Elsewhere *Tis* appears in the similitude of Mrs. Grundy, mortally dreaded by the fair embodiment of girlish innocence, Nausicaa, because of the malignant construction sure to be placed by *Tis* on her being in the company of a strange man without any one to play " gooseberry." The closest, as indeed nearly an exact, equivalent for the modern newspaper to be found in ancient Greece was the theatre, as it existed in the Attic capital. Many thousand Athenians swarmed to the performance of plays whose authors were Euripides, Sophocles, or Æschylus. Every one of these spectators was a member of the popular assembly. He therefore made his own contribution to, and exercised a distinct influence on, the decisions which determined the State policy at home and abroad. On the day following the theatrical performance the playgoer might be voting on an issue of peace or war. If not this, he might, in the law court, be taking his share in adjudicating on matters involving the principle of property or the structure of the social system itself. The newspaper writer of our day tells his readers whom or what to support ; he thus at least tries to influence the numbers of a parliamentary division or the course of a general election. The Attic dramatist had exactly the same opportunity ; he was not less prompt to use it. Thus in the *Eumenides* Æschylus now exhorts his fellow-citizens that they should enforce their claim to certain disputed territory in the Troad, now makes a magnificent and irresistible appeal that they would allow no tampering with the powers of the Areopagus. Similarly two tragedies of Euripides, the *Heracleidæ* and the *Supplices*, are traversed throughout by an instructive vein of unmistakable allusion to the political intrigues arising out of the Peloponnesian War. Indeed, all the writings of this dramatist abound in remarks, political, social, and moral, such as to-day would find a place in a newspaper leader, a monthly magazine, or a quarterly review. Descending to modern Europe, pre-revolutionary France shows the tragic dramatist as the journalist's elder brother. Between 1694 and 1778 freedom of the press was not more unknown in Paris than were the modern appliances of the printing office in the city of the violet crown. Even so late as this, though the newspaper indeed existed, its modern functions were still performed by the stage. On the eve of the French Revolution thunders of applause from the courtier audience in the theatre at Versailles greeted the lines : "I am the son of Brutus, and bear graven on my heart the love of liberty and the horror of kings " ; and in his short history of French literature Mr. Saintsbury traces the popularity of Voltaire's tragedies generally to the adroitness with which he insinuates the popular opinions of the time. The closest analogy, however, to the journalist of modern times afforded by Athens of the fifth century B.C. is to be found in " the old comedy " known now from its greatest master, Aristophanes. Here is a writer who, before aspiring to stage representation, had studied the social and political conditions of his own time as patiently and profoundly as is done to-day by the best sort of newspaper men ; he redeemed the comic drama from the reproach of scurrilous buffoonery, he brings upon the stage the men who are making the social or political history of the time, with the forces which they control or by which they may be overmastered. A Tory of the old school, he casts back many regretful glances on the old days before the demoralising sophists had been so successful with their pernicious teaching that a credulous democracy believed there might not after all be much difference between evil and good, falsehood and truth. Grote and Thirlwall are agreed in attributing slight influence on current political thought to Athenian comedy. That, upon the whole, may be true enough. The chosen home of Greek political satire, in the form of comedy, further resembled the English newspaper in basing its chief appeals to the public on the broadest principles of common humanity. The death struggle of Athens and Sparta was draining the resources and exhausting the patience of both when in the *Acharnians* Aristophanes satirised the Athenian " Pro-Boers " personified by Dicæopolis. Four years later, however, he changes his note to much practical purpose, and, at heart ever a hater of war, contributed by his *Peace* to bring about the truce effected by Nicias. In one place Aristophanes, indeed, with mingled satire and entreaty, sways his audience on the side of clemency towards those suspected of complicity in the revolution of the Four Hundred. He scrupulously avoids the chance of making political capital against the hated demagogues by pursuing the contrast between the assured tranquillity of the ancient order and the perilous turbulence of the new regime. What in modern phrase would be called the virtuous sympathies of the mob are the powers which largely, in general terms, he tries above all to enlist on his own side. On the other hand, the Attic comedy, like the English newspaper, finds itself most effective when directing public attention not to measures but to men. In nineteenth, if not twentieth century England, cartoons like those of Sir John Tenniell or Sir F. C. Gould, and the best political writing by prose satirists in the weekly journals have produced impressions closely akin to those that Aristophanes made it his business to create.

But a nearer parallel even than the Athenian drama to the modern journalist was presented by the Attic precursor of the English pamphleteer. The rhetoricians, ready of tongue and easy of principle, in the fifth century B.C., made a livelihood by advocating any cause in the law courts, or supporting in the popular assembly the political party which paid them best. Within fourscore years of the Battle of Marathon, the ingenious Athenian who lived by his wits and his phrase-making found he had a better paymaster in the public which bought what he had written down than in those who hired him to argue for them in the assembly. When they relate to public affairs, such of these compositions as have come down to us are exposures of democratic folly and socialistic fallacies or are elaborate treatises on finance. Xenophon, the prototype of war correspondents, was also the earliest of Tory journalists ; as such he has left us some remarks on the Athenian polity, foreshadowing with curious closeness alike Gifford's diatribes against democracy in the *Quarterly*, and, in our own day, the *Spectator's* onslaughts upon the " new Whigs." The men now spoken of were, at a very long distance, the followers of Isocrates, who, both from his tongue and pen, has left us perfect models for the modern journalist or pamphleteer. His subjects, his treatment of them, and his whole tone of mind combined to make him the most essentially modern of Attic writers. His essays and addresses not only served as models in his own age and country. Since then, and throughout modern Europe, especially in England during the early period of our prose literature, they have been studied for patterns of construction and expression by the best writers for our newspaper press. Many among the most telling pieces of Isocrates are the shorter speeches which, never delivered nor intended for delivery, are in effect leading articles. As such they were widely read on their first appearance. They deal with all the topics of the day ; they are sometimes satirical descriptions of social degeneracy, sometimes stirring appeals to patriotic sentiment on behalf of a sagacious or spirited domestic and foreign policy. Here Isocrates had a rival in another rhetorician, Alcidamas. All these men bore the professional name of rhetoricians ; their appearances in the public assembly and the law courts gradually became more infrequent till they entirely ceased, and the advocate or the orator merged himself altogether in the pamphleteer. This precedent supplied by classical Athens has become the familiar experience of our own Fleet Street. The barrister, weary of waiting for briefs that do not come, at last chiefly looks for business, not in Temple Chambers but in newspaper offices. The rhetoricians were followed or rather overlapped by the sophists. " The sophists of modern life " is a well-known description of our own journalists, so far as these seek to influence public opinion in the columns of the weekly or daily paper. They are thus entirely distinct from the providers of the news on which the paper's policy is based. The want of constraining principles or deep convictions alleged, as Grote and others hold, unjustly against the Athenian sophist, has been found to have a parallel in the unscrupulous versatility of the English journalist. The resemblance does not go beyond the fact that the success both of the Greek sophist and the English journalist implies the same condition of unlicensed liberty in expression as in thought. High play, strong drink, general want of serious interest in life, and enervating self-indulgence of every kind seemed to Isocrates the growing curse of Athenian youth. These are the vices and failings lashed by him with a severity that, more than two thousand years afterwards, was to be emulated by the Dean of St. Patrick's in his *Project for the Reformation of Manners under Queen Anne.* Isocrates had many rivals, especially in his capacity of writer. The keenest competition was between himself and the already-mentioned Alcidamas, the point at issue in the literary war which engaged these and others being whether or not Athenian patriotism should consent to the restoration of Messene's independence by the military power of Thebes. During the latter part of the fifth century B.C. great improvements took place in the methods of publication. Copies were multiplied with unprecedented rapidity and distributed, not only in a shorter time, but over a larger area than had ever been attempted before. Such conditions could not but result in a fresh encouragement to the Attic equivalent for journalism as a substitute for oratory. Athens, moreover, now possessed an exact forerunner of the journalist in one who had never gone through the stage of orator. This was the Athenian Tory squire, Xenophon, whose discourses on politics and finance from the strictly conservative point of view, issuing in quick succession from his country house, exactly presaged the English pamphlet of the eighteenth century as the leading article's immediate predecessor.

Classical Rome abounded in rhetorical schools and professors; it possessed, at least in Tacitus and Sallust, two trained rhetoricians each of the material from which first-rate newspaper writers are made. Neither of them, however, has left us such genuine specimens of the leading article in its pamphlet stage as Xenophon's shorter pieces. As a war correspondent, the Athenian Xenophon has his Roman successor in Julius Cæsar. The author of the *Commentaries,* however, might also claim to be regarded as a newspaper man, not only because he was a great writer, but because he organised the earliest great news service which the world had then seen. The *Acta Diurna* were begun at Julius Cæsar's special order and under his personal supervision in his

first consulship in A.D. 61. These records formed a
daily chronicle, curiously full and interestingly minute, of
all that passed in the capital. Their circulation throughout the Latin world was arranged by the conqueror of
Gaul with a thoroughness that would have done credit
to a modern press agency's manager. Mommsen, in
his *History of Rome*, vol. iv. p. 607, reproaches Cicero
with being essentially a journalist. Cicero, however, complained of the literary worthlessness of these *Acta*, and
tells a correspondent who condenses their contents into
his notepaper that what he wants are letters with something worth reading about the course of events, and
not a bald compilation. *Compilatio* in such a context
might almost be translated " newspaper." Of journalism,
however, on its literary side, there was much less in the
Italian than in the Hellenic capital. The third century
B.C. did indeed witness an attempt by the poet Nævius
to reproduce the Greek comedy in his native city, but the
Roman respect for authority and order would not tolerate
a State personage being held up to ridicule on the
public stage. The plebeian Nævius produced his play
to create a feeling against the usurpation of popular privileges or rights by the aristocratic senate. His satire
seems to have been innocent even to tameness. It raised,
however, no applause ; the caricatures of eminent individuals which illustrated it fell flat. The piece drew to
its close amid such a storm of hisses that no revival of
the old Greek comedy seems afterwards to have been
tried. As an organ of popular opinion the one Roman
equivalent to the Attic drama was the satire. In this
kind of composition crude efforts had been made by
Nævius, who, attached to the Roman General Servilius
Geminus, had served as special correspondent during the
first Punic War.[1] The earliest satirist to have much
in common with the journalist is Lucilius ; the main
objects of this fearlessly outspoken writer's attacks were
the high-born statesmen, who thought they could blunder
with impunity and shelter themselves against criticism
behind their rank. Next he has nothing but bitter
contempt for the servile imitation by rich Italian parvenus
of Greek modes in social manner, in literary expression,

[1] See Professor Sellar's *Roman Poets of the Republic*, p. 55.

and in personal costume. This subject is also dealt with
at greater length and with deeper feeling by Persius,
the last of the satirists, resembling in many respects
Lucilius, the first, more than he resembles either Juvenal
or Horace.   Another classical agent for influencing
opinion was common both to Greece and Rome.   The
oracle not only determined the actions both of communi-
ties and individuals, but occasionally made itself felt
as the organ of a political party ; for did not the old
Athenian nobility bribe the Delphian priests to publish
responses insisting on the expulsion of Pisistratus? And,
indeed, upon topics of less momentous, of domestic as
well as personal import, the oracular utterances
judiciously edited by the priest presiding over the shrines
presaged with tolerable accuracy the " Answers to Correspondents " which have not yet quite gone out of
fashion with some newspapers.   So, too, even in our
own day, letter-writers to the editor of the *Times* are
but the oracle questioners of a later day.   But enough
has been said to show that the enterprise of individuals
in the old classic civilisations effectively fulfilled functions
broadly speaking comparable with those performed by a
later product of individual ingenuity, courage, and resource.   This is the English newspaper of to-day.   Its
quickness in seeking and supplying information, its
vigilant appositeness of comment, its electric sympathy of
social feeling—many at least if not all of these qualities
are now shown to have been active in the two most enlightened capitals of ancient Europe from five to seven
centuries before the Christian era.

CHAPTER II

THE JOURNALIST AND THE JOURNAL

The journalist before the journal—A typical news-writer of the fifteenth century—War on the "unconscionable newsletter-writer"—The journalist displaces the jester—And is employed by the State—Nathaniel Butter's career—Three "fathers of the English newspaper"—John Birkenhead the royalist—Marchmont Nedham the parliamentarian and political chameleon—Right about face—Defiance of the press censorship—Another "sharp curve"—A Commonwealth man once more—Collapse of fortunes at the Restoration—Birkenhead's reappearance—Experiences during the Interregnum and after—He becomes press censor—Retirement—The third "father"—Roger L'Estrange's family—A loyal subject of the King—Work for the cause with sword and pen—Condemned to death—Reprieved—Renewal of literary labours—His opinions on licensing laws—Some ingenious suggestions—Promotion to the press censorship—Impudent formation of newspaper monopoly—Origin of the *London Gazette*, L'Estrange's only rival—His connection with the press cut short by the Revolution of 1688—End of the press censorship—The first daily paper—Mallet's foreign news—His successor on the *Courant*—Samuel Buckley's enterprise—The coming of Defoe.

THAT the journalist is older than the journal, and existed independently of it, has been already shown by the instances taken from classical Athens and Rome. The same truth, it will now presently be seen, may be illustrated from the experiences of mediæval England. Before the invention of printing, in the fifteenth century, during the Wars of the Roses period, the precursor of the modern newspaper man is found in an indefatigable news collector and distributor named Fenn. A careful search of the Paston Letters fails to furnish any details about this notable forerunner of those who were eventually to assist in the foundation of the English press. Ben Jonson, however, in the *Staple of News*, and his contemporary dramatists are profuse in their satirical caricatures of those who, like Fenn, personified what, for the sake of brevity, may be called the journalistic enterprise of their period. Than Fenn there can have been no better specimen of the newswriter, who in the fullness of time was to make way for the newspaper reporter. A pushing, fearless, irrepressible spectator, where that was possible, of events, he forced his way past sentries and warders, now by mere pertinacity or bodily strength, now by persevering cajolery or some of the silver pieces carried in a leather girdle round his waist. On or near every battlefield, when he could not himself be there, he was represented by some of the numerous staff whom he had trained to observe accurately and report promptly. He had offices or correspondents in nearly every town and in most of the less obscure or inaccessible village centres. None but regular subscribers received the manuscript records, which he forwarded once a week or even oftener as opportunity served. Nor did he and his agents escape a process identical with that known in our own day as "nobbling the press." Experience had taught Fenn himself to see the newsletter-writer's best policy in honesty, and the attempts of interested persons to secure the suppression of inconvenient details, or the publication of *ex parte* statements, seldom seem to have been successful with Fenn himself. The real danger was lest his employees should prove less incorruptible ; for the commodity in which Fenn dealt passed through many hands on its way from the responsible head of the business to the customer. By Ben Jonson's time the business had organised itself with a completeness unknown, of course, a century or two before. In the already-mentioned *Staple* the chief personage bustles about amid surroundings which, for a long time both before and after this play had been witnessed, were those proper to the modern journalist's mediæval equivalent, and to his sub-editorial staff. The responsible purveyor of the newsletter sat in his own sanctum. In an outer room were his clerks docketing and alphabetically arranging the intelligence of all kinds as it poured in from north, south, east, and west, sent by touts from the battlefield or by key-hole listeners at the council door.

The name is as yet an anachronism ; but there exists official evidence of the sixteenth-century journalist having become an inconveniently active and all but irrepressible person. He was, indeed, between 1485 and 1509, the subject of a prohibitive proclamation by Henry VIII. For any lasting result, the sovereign might as well have tried to check by a royal frown the Thames in its encroachments on the Westminster shore. The "unconscionable newsletter-writer" not being one whom monarch or minister could suppress, it remained for them to make the best use of him they could. The reigns of the last Tudor and the first Stuart witnessed also the State recognition of the first journalist. The truth is that before the end of the seventeenth century the jester as the paid retainer of great families had gone out, and the journalist had come in. In Shakespeare's time persons of quality sported their private theatres beneath their London or country roofs. A little later no household or individual of quality was complete without some literary Autolycus, always, wherever he might be, ready to snap up trifles, unconsidered and considered, as a preliminary to dishing them up readably for his patrons. Of this class the best known specimen appears in a certain Rowland White ; so successful was this forerunner of "our own correspondent" in penetrating behind the scenes of social and political life, that a family no less considerable than the Penshurst Sidneys salaried him to send them, during their foreign travels, everything about divisions in the Council and intrigues at Court. Before the seventeenth century the newspaper man of the period received a striking tribute to his growing power. Queen Elizabeth had herself "tuned the pulpits." Her great minister began to inspire and doctor the newsletters for his own ends. The contemporary records with which Rowland White furnished the Sidneys helped to colour and shape the opinion on subjects of the day held by that noble family and their influential friends. Why not extend the process, and use the professional penmen generally in the Government's interest? To put it differently, the existence of the journalist in embryo was a fact neither to be ignored nor unmade. He had not yet set up his presses ; none the less he coloured and created popular feeling about the home and especially the foreign policy of the Crown. In future Burleigh determined that these writers should take their cue from his office, and square the accounts they sent out with his purposes. He began by trying his hand on Rowland White, but soon exchanged that obstinate scribe for one more pliable and docile, whose name has not come down to us.

In Ben Jonson's *Staple of News* one of Cymbal's staff is addressed as Nathaniel. The name would have had a familiar sound for the audience. To the seventeenth-century public it conveyed the same kind of meaning as to modern ears might be done by the words Harmsworth or Pearson. From the shadowy crowd of his fellow-craftsmen Butter stands out in strong and clear relief, not only as the most resourceful news collector and commentator of his period, but as one who, in advance of his colleagues or rivals, foresaw the journalistic possibility of the future and realised the proportions in which a judicious compound of authentic intelligence and sagacious criticism would make the newspaper a mighty leverage for influencing action and guiding thought. For that he saw there must be co-operation between the best minds concerned in a single enterprise. Hence his conception of a corporate policy, and his use for the first time of the editorial " we." So keen was his instinct of newspaper management and of the punctuality essential for its success that he again and again apologises in his broadsides for an uncertainty in his dates of issue, which he is sure posterity will mend.[1] Butter is a landmark rather than a personage ; he indicates the stage in the transition from the newsletter-writer to the newspaper-writer ; though he himself would be called a news pamphleteer more correctly than a newspaper man. This because his productions lacked continuity. Any event such as might to-day seem to warrant a special or extra special newspaper edition caused Butter to put forth a commemorative and not seldom a roughly illustrated sheet. After one of these specimens has seen the light, Butter draws his blinds and makes no sign till there happens something else which he sees his way profitably to turn into copy. His real functions, however, were those, not of an editor nor even of descriptive reporter. He was rather a sub-editor on a great scale, fertile in resource,

[1] The *Weekly News* was Butter's favourite title for his prints, though the same style does not seem to have appeared in more than two or three consecutively. In each case their external appearance resembled that of the ballads then hawked about the streets.

who not only knew but could create his opportunity, with a nose for news in unlikely places, as keen as that with which a trained dog scents truffles in a park whose owner has never dreamt of possessing such subterranean wealth. To literature he made no pretence ; he describes himself as a transcriber of books first, and as a printer afterwards. None the less he deserves a foremost place among the newspaper pioneers who shrunk neither from danger, toil, nor expense in their trade of providing foreign news for the benefit of home-staying Englishmen. The business offices of Nathaniel Butter and his professional brethren whether, like Bourne and Archer, his colleagues, or, like Newberry and Sheffard, his partners, seem to have been close to the Royal Exchange. This was the first structure of that name, built during Elizabeth's reign in 1570, and lasting till the Great Fire of 1666. The entire district in the seventeenth century preceded Fleet Street as a literary thoroughfare ; [1] the chief forerunners of Fleet Street newspaper personages between 1620 and 1640 had their shops or offices at such spots within this area as Pope's Head Palace, Pope's Head

---

[1] From Sir Walter Besant's *London*, at various dates during the fifteenth and eighteenth centuries it would seem there had begun the preparations for making Fleet Street pre-eminently a literary thoroughfare. The original booksellers' quarter was in St. Paul's Churchyard, Paternoster Row, Little Britain, and Moorfields. After the Great Fire (1666) the bookstalls and bookshops began to gravitate towards Fleet Street. The settlers here who did not sell books generally represented the licensed victualling interest. For more than two hundred years Fleet Street contained thirty-seven taverns. Most of these were approached by a long passage or court. The oldest of these places were the "Marygold," the "Horn on the Hoop," the "Bolt in Tun," the "Black Lion," the "Devil," and the "Mitre." In 1787 the "Devil" was pulled down, and a row of houses, Child's Place, built on the site. About the same time the original "Mitre," approached by the alley called Cat and Fiddle Lane, made way for Hoare's Bank, which still occupies its exact ground. Between 1728 and 1765 there had sprung up, close to where the Bank now is, a "Young Devil" tavern. Here throughout the period just mentioned the Society of Antiquaries held their yearly meeting, after which came an adjournment for dinner at the "Mitre." Fleet Street, moreover, had been fashionable or popular before it became literary. From 1558 to 1603 it had been the favourite haunt of showmen and their most modish customers, ready equally to admire the exhibition and the thoroughfare itself, picturesque with its many gable-ended houses, its decoration of quaint carvings, of plaster stamped in patterns, and the countless signs, glorious in their gilding or ornamented by strange devices, hanging above the shopfronts.

Alley, at the Sign of the Star, and under St. Peter's Church, Cornhill. Even at this early date the smaller sort of transcribers or printers found a grievance in the competition of capitalists who created a " corner " in the news trade. These for a time occasionally contrived to make the whole business their private monopoly. Under the Tudors Butter escaped molestation by the authorities ; he, however, suffered heavily from the severer press censorship of the Stuarts. Early in the reign of Charles I. (1639) he almost abandoned his occupation in despair. But he took heart of grace, and in 1640 a short relaxation of the licenser's tyranny revived his hope that he might still carry on his work. Yet a little later the State coercion proved too strong for the sanguine and courageous newsmonger. Butter could no longer observe a constant day every week with his subscribers, and in 1641 he and his broadsheets disappeared. Could Butter but have kept himself afloat a little longer, he might have been tided into the smooth waters of prosperity. Amongst the men who urged him to continue and placed their purses at his disposal were Sir Edward Dering, the first Sir Henry Vane, and John Pym. The good offices with the licenser of these and others had produced great results. During one or two years the press was practically free. But though the Long Parliament went some way towards making that free press an institution, it could not, when put to the test, save Butter. The newspaper man on the whole has owed as little to Whigs as to Tories ; Butter is the first instance of a journalist actively backed by the great political leaders of his time.

The man who had done more than any other individual towards crushing out the early broadsheets was Archbishop Laud. By one of those strange ironies in which history abounds, with Laud's name now associates itself that of the man who, coming after Butter, is given by Isaac Disraeli a place among the triumvirate comprising the " fathers of the English newspaper." In this group John Birkenhead, though as regards years slightly the elder of the two, and Marchmont Nedham may be called contemporaries ; while Roger L'Estrange belongs altogether to a later date. Between 1643 and 1660 Birkenhead and Nedham were by far the two most active and notorious newspaper men then at work. Birkenhead's journalistic course received solutions in its continuity from which Nedham's was free. For this reason, as well as because of certain details in the matter of dates, it will be convenient to follow Nedham's progress before considering Birkenhead. At the same time the labours undertaken and the vicissitudes experienced by each of these men were so closely connected, or reacted so visibly and immediately upon the fortunes and performances of the other, that the retrospects cannot be kept entirely distinct. Thus Birkenhead began as a writer in high favour at the palace. He founded, indeed, a royalist organ whose Latin title [1] may be Englished as the *Court Journal*. Such principles were well suited to a paper whose conductor's antecedents were those of its founder ; for, while private secretary to Archbishop Laud, Birkenhead had become tolerably well acquainted with the daily round of life at St. James's and with the chief figures among the courtiers of Whitehall. These never took him seriously ; but he had a pleasant turn for anecdote and epigram. The institution of a licensed jester ceased to exist with Charles I. ; it had, in fact, begun to decay before that sovereign's death. The position of palace fool, thus empty, was now filled by the vivacious writer whose political faith was summed up in the divine right of kings to govern as they chose, and whose loyalty to that principle remained unshaken through good and evil report. Birkenhead's success with the Court moved Nedham to try what might be made out of the general public. The *People's Paper*,[2] in Latin words to that effect, was the designation he chose for his venture. Kings and princes had in their pay literary hirelings condescending to purvey no intelligence except about foreign Courts, capitals, and the doings of great people beyond the four seas. Were the British masses at home, the sinews and the defence of the realm, to have no chronicler of their own ? Never, came the answer from Birkenhead's rival, should that be the case while pen, paper, and printing press remained at the disposal of Marchmont Nedham. Here, as that personage boasted of himself, was a true son of the

---

[1] *Mercurius Aulicus.*
[2] *Mercurius Britannicus.*

people, untrained from infancy in those arts of duplicity
which the Primate had taught his former private secretary, an honest plain dealer, with or without the pen
in his hand, devoted heart and soul to the well-being
of those masses from whom he himself had sprung.
Unlike Birkenhead, he had never been associated with
the multitude's oppressors in Church or State. Brought
up from an early age to earn his living in an apothecary's
shop or at a scrivener's desk, he was now henceforth
to concentrate his energies upon the instruction and
service of his countrymen through the printing press.
These duties he began to fulfil by letting his patrons,
high or low, enjoy the pleasure of seeing their friends
abused in his columns as impartially as their enemies.
Nedham's consciousness of his great abilities had been
embittered by the treatment meted out to him first as a
junior master at Merchant Taylor's, afterwards as a
lawyer's clerk in Gray's Inn.   His newspaper course,
therefore, was that of an Ishmael, with a pen nibbed
against every one.   Infamous scurrilities, as all agreed
to speak of them, were the literary commodities in which
he dealt.   Unmeasured abuse from every quarter and
unbounded popularity went together.   " A rascal whose
ears ought to have been cropped long ago, and who
would be too comfortably housed at Newgate."   So said
the guardians of public decency.   On the other hand,
the masses whose idol he had become hailed him as the
" one man in this courtier-ridden country who with the
knowledge combined the fearlessness and the literary
faculty for describing courtiers and statesmen as they
really were."   Nedham's literary methods, for their most
effective exercise, required the   stimulus of personal
hostility and resistance.   Here he showed himself of the
same temper as Defoe and Swift, as Cobbett, Fonblanque,
and Jerrold.   He found the opposition required for the
exercise of his faculties in the Court journalist of the
period, the already-mentioned Birkenhead.   That Birkenhead had made himself the champion of Charles was
reason   enough   for   Nedham's   supporting   Cromwell.
Nedham's literary broadsides raked the remotest corners
of the country.   Enthusiastic Roundheads, with some
little confusion of metaphors, applauded him as a Goliath
of freedom, with for spear a pen that, by the side of

other pens, was as a bulrush to a weaver's beam. A free lance like Nedham, despising conviction as pedantry, and shunning principle and consistency as superstitions, could not but sooner or later unpardonably offend even Puritanism, whose foes he cudgelled. In 1647, therefore, Nedham ratted to the Crown. Personally introduced to the royal presence at Hampton Court, he humbly knelt before Charles I. to implore and to receive the King's pardon. Nedham now rounded on his old patrons and friends. No sneers at the airs and fashions of the cavaliers had been so effective as Nedham's. In a minute the tables were all turned, and the Royalists were convulsed with laughter at Nedham's pen and ink caricatures of Independent or Presbyterian ministers, first sending whole congregations to sleep by their homilies against the man of sin, droned out through their noses, and then finding their ministrations had had the effect of converting the adherents of Oliver into enthusiasts for the Stuarts. In all this, Nedham showed himself a type not only of the seventeenth-century newspaper man, but of the seventeenth-century politician as well. Both of these passed from king-worshipper to republican, and then, for a time at least, back again to royalist as by a natural process not of transformation but of development.

Nedham's newspaper work was spread over some twenty years, from 1643 to 1660. Long before his death, in 1674, he had not only united in common detestation of himself all those whom at different times he had attacked or supported with his pen ; he left behind him a monument of his malignant activity more practical and permanent than any of his literary triumphs or defeats. This monument was nothing less than the press censorship, which had been created in 1647 by the Commonwealth with the personal purpose of checking Nedham's intolerable license of abuse. Quick changes of his residence and of his printers enabled the resourceful Nedham to treat with contempt the restriction thus imposed on his craft. Number continued to follow number, or, to speak more correctly, pamphlet was succeeded by pamphlet in almost regular sequence till the date of the King's execution in 1649. A certain American editor, notorious for his warm support of the South during the Civil War, on the settlement

of peace secured by a stroke of luck from the winning
side a promise of some valuable advertisements for which
he had been long fishing. The condition was his execution
of a literary right about face. Would he accept
the terms? To that question an immediate telegraphic
answer must be sent. Quick as thought the wires flashed
his reply : " It's a sharp curve, but I'll take it." Of
that editor Marchmont Nedham showed himself the true
prototype. This Proteus of the pen had successfully
eluded or defied the office of whose establishment his
own versatility of universal vituperation had been the
cause. He next proceeded to show that so far as concerned himself, the censorship, always futile, had become
unnecessary. In the long run, he shrewdly saw, the
Parliament must win. The services, therefore, which he
had placed at the feet of Charles, he now tendered to
Oliver. Monarchy or Republic, Protector or King, it
was all one to this father of the press, by comparison
with whom the eel was adhesive and the British climate
constant. The Restoration became inevitable. Nedham,
scenting it from afar, looked up the royalist plumes
he had so long laid aside, and polished up the epigrams
and periods which had delighted the satellites of Charles I.
He had now become a European personage. Losing
his London employment after Oliver Cromwell's death,
he retired to Holland for a short time, though long
enough for the citizens of Amsterdam to become familiar
with his "tall, gaunt figure, perpetually stooping from
shortness of sight, his hook nose, and the two rings
' dangling from his pierced ears when not in pawn ' " ;
before, however, Nedham had obtained any Dutch
celebrity, Charles II. had recrossed the Channel for
England. The one regicide lightly dealt with by the
re-established prince was Marten : " One cannot send
such a scamp as Harry to the block." Marchmont
Nedham certainly had as good a claim to the King's
description as Marten himself. The royal hero, however, of Monk's *coup d'état* did not throw away a thought
on the journalist, who, having boxed the compass of
time-serving perfidy, now found his life to all appearance scarcely worth a week's purchase. Still he contrived to scrape together as much money as secured him
backstairs interest enough to obtain a pardon under the

Great Seal for his past assaults upon the monarchy. As a periodical writer Nedham found his occupation gone. Fortunately for himself, and unlike many of the same calling after, if not before, his day, he had studied medicine as well as English composition in his youth. The spirit of practice returned to him now, and he soon succeeded in securing patients enough to keep him comfortably till his death.

Nedham brought his journalistic calling, as well as himself, into favour with the smart society which began under the Restoration. Among the newspaper men that followed in his steps were Giles Dury, of whom nothing is known beyond his name, and Henry Muddiman, who figures in the pages of Pepys as something of a scholar and a good deal more of a scamp. After Nedham, however, the most considerable person in the seventeenth-century newspaper system was undoubtedly his contemporary and rival Birkenhead. Nedham's connection with the official press of his period lasted through the Commonwealth ; that press, at· the Restoration of 1660, became of course royalist. The highest position on it naturally, therefore, now fell to Birkenhead. In comparison with Nedham, Birkenhead was and had always been a pattern of propriety in print, and a model of uncalculating firmness in politics. These qualities were recognised and rewarded by Charles I., who compelled the University of Oxford to make the man possessing them a D.C.L. and to accept him as professor of modern philosophy. His academic connection was only short-lived. In 1648 Birkenhead was first ejected from his chair and afterwards deprived of his All Souls' fellowship by the Presbyterians. At the age of thirty-three he was thrown loose upon the world. Penniless, but still adhering to the monarchy, he took his way from the Isis to the Thames. Persistent refusals to prostitute his pen in defence of republican usurpation kept him in dire poverty and often brought him to jail. He could, however, turn himself to any kind of literary composition ; he contrived to pick up a precarious livelihood by writing for young gallants about town " sonnets to their mistress's eyebrow," which they passed off as their own, by helping the same customers with their love-letters, or by now and then doing any odds and

ends of translation he could get from the booksellers.
Personally Birkenhead was more ill-favoured than
Nedham, and without the fashionable vogue which
Nedham sometimes enjoyed ; his manners were not winning, his presence lacked dignity, his snub nose compared
disadvantageously with Nedham's eagle beak, his
irregular features were unrelieved by any agreeable expression, and his eyes seemed to revolve in their sockets
as on a swivel. He was charged, and perhaps truly,
with forgetting in his prosperity those who had stood
his friends at his sorest need. In that age of short-
lived political dispensations, of sudden revolutions and
counter-revolutions, of precarious patronage and skin-
deep loyalty, the only form of gratitude, practicable or
known, was that represented by a lively sense of favours
to come. The only men who took life seriously were
a few theologians or recluses. Birkenhead never made
any pretence to religion ; he was compelled by his daily
necessities to live in not the most reputable section of
the bustling world. But cynicism prevented his being
a hypocrite ; loyalty to the Crown always raised him
above the charge of time-server. If he did not, therefore, often rise above the moral standards of his period,
he seldom fell below them ; while in not a few respects
he set his contemporaries an example which it would
have been to their credit to follow. As a writer he
magnified his apostleship, and reflected credit on his
craft. He seldom wrote a paragraph which had not in
it something of the quality that tends to bridge over the
void separating journalism from literature. He had found
time for wide reading, as well as for its careful digestion ;
he knew how to give an epigrammatic ring to the few
sentences of comment which served for links connecting
the paragraphs of news. He was absolutely the earliest
to reflect in his writings the diction that had then begun
to mark the debates in Parliament. John Eliot had
died in 1632 ; John Pym lived on till eleven years afterwards. Both men before they passed away had the
satisfaction of seeing their respective parliamentary styles,
in their origin Greek rather than Latin, become the
accepted models of oratory at St. Stephens. Their terse,
telling, crisp, well-poised sentences, emphasised by adroit
antithesis that never expanded itself into verbal conceit,

have influenced the language used by speakers at Westminster from that day to this.   In the middle of the
nineteenth century, the most telling political articles in
the *Times* had often something of a Palmerstonian echo in
their phrasing and their argument.   Those who, after
following an important debate at St. Stephens, skimmed
what Birkenhead might have to say about the incidents
of the hour, often seemed to hear the reverberations of
sentences and sentiments to which they had listened a few
days or hours before in the long, narrow, dimly-lit
chamber where the people's representatives then trans-
acted their affairs.   In addition to the University distinctions secured for him by the first Charles, Birkenhead
had been the earliest newspaper man, as, in the fourteenth century, Chaucer had been the first poet, to become
a member of the House of Commons.   Under Charles II.
journalism afforded a means of living scarcely less uncertain than ballad-mongering ; these, indeed, were sister
employments, for the latest intelligence was hawked about
the streets by the newsvendors quite as often in the form
of the doggerel rhymes which easily fixed themselves in
the popular memory as on the prose broadsides containing the germ alike of the pamphlet and the leader.
The prudent Birkenhead, therefore, after two years' experience of St. Stephens, and, at the same time, of the press
censorship, retired from public life on a knighthood and
the Mastership of Requests.   This, in addition to a snug
salary, gave him unlimited perquisites.   On the whole,
therefore, this founder of the newspaper system made a
tolerably good thing out of paper and ink.   His Government post enabled him to dispense with any further
share either in the active production or in the control
of news sheets.

His successor in the licensing office was the third
member of Isaac Disraeli's journalistic trio.   Roger
L'Estrange is the earliest known instance of a man born
to aristocratic, wealthy connections deliberately making
periodical literature his career.   Of the old and at times
opulent family to which he belonged, one branch had
settled in Ireland ; the other for generations was identified with Norfolk.   Both lines of this house on either
side of St. George's Channel are still flourishing to-day.
The East Anglian L'Estranges had always stood for

the King. Roger himself, while little more than a boy, had received a cornet's commission in Rupert's Horse. He was thus destined to form an early instance of the union between sword and pen, subsequently so conspicuous and fruitful in our periodical literature. From a promising cavalry officer, after the wreck of the Cavalier fortunes at Dunbar, as a writer he displayed to the fallen cause the same intrepidity which he had shown in his soldiering days, and a devotion, heart, soul, and conscience, not less unswerving than that given by Birkenhead, as well as far more active. The end justified the means. No stratagem or falsehood was to be stuck at if only it might lure the Roundheads to their ruin. Born at Hunstanton (1616), he knew every nook and corner of the country between that and King's Lynn. This latter town, in the preceding century the scene of Ket's rebellion, had in 1643 been taken by the Parliament from the King. The next year Roger L'Estrange organised, and was preparing in person to lead, a conspiracy for its restoration to the Royalists, when his seizure by a Puritan sentry brought him to trial for high treason, followed by a sentence to the block. That doom was commuted to four years' imprisonment in Newgate. On his release he went abroad. The year which saw Charles II. established at St. James's Palace restored L'Estrange to Fleet Street. In 1663 he took the opportunity of impressing the sovereign with the power for good or evil exercised by the profession to which he belonged, as well as of his own personal capacity for making the newspaper writer a security instead of a danger to the throne. In a clever, shameless, and slashing composition he set before the King the perils threatening him and his House from the impunity given to journalistic licence. The sovereign, he said, would not be settled or safe on his throne till there had been fitted to treasonable and seditious pamphleteers a bridle more severe than they had yet been made to feel. Should his Highness inquire as to a man apt for such a task, the writer, though painfully conscious of an undue disposition towards lenity in himself, might by the Court's favour find the energies that the business required. The Licensing Act of 1662 was, L'Estrange admitted, admirable in its design. Its feeble administration made it, however, almost a dead letter. Every one, he continued, knew the late rebellion to have been actuated by hypocrisy, scandal, malice, error, and illusion. The spirit of all these abominations had still to be crushed out ; it was now working not only by the same means, but in many cases by the same individuals. To exorcise this demon a short way must be taken with all concerned in producing or selling the printed infamies which were a foul shame to literature and a dire menace to the Crown. The offenders included joiners that set up presses, stitchers, binders, stationers, hackney coachmen, and mariners concerned in their circulation. Not that he would err on the side of excessive severity. Sometimes he would not enforce the death penalty, but would allow for its substitute mutilation, lifelong imprisonment or exile, corporal pains, disgrace, pecuniary mulcts. As regards humbler accomplices in the crime, the Mercury women and children who hawked the peccant prints, he would be so lenient as to insist on nothing' more than their wearing some visible mark of ignominy, a halter instead of a hatband, headgear stamped with some legend of infamy, or a stocking of different colours on each foot. The ingenuity of these suggestions tickled the fancy of the careless but ready-witted and not unkindly King ; it was, he at once saw, only a little piece of self-advertisement on L'Estrange's part. " We will," he characteristically said, " give the dog what he wants." The warrant was accordingly prepared. Within a few months of his having satisfied his conscience by warning the Court of its snares and pitfalls, L'Estrange became supreme licenser of all printed matter, with plenary authority to search the premises of any suspect writer or printer. L'Estrange discharged his duties in the true spirit of the bravo and the bully, who was the social and political commonplace of the Restoration. This also was the temper which had personified itself in the palace ruffians who slit the noses and broke the bones of M.P.'s like Sir John Coventry if they presumed to reflect on the escapades or the money necessities of the King. L'Estrange's official corruption and ferocity combined made his position and himself names of disgrace and dread to all law-abiding citizens and to all respectable Cavaliers. The murderer of a child's two

parents, who does not absolutely starve the orphan to
death, may call himself the father of the fatherless.
Only in some such sense as this does there belong to
L'Estrange the patriarchal relation allotted to him by
Disraeli to the English newspaper. L'Estrange first used
his official opportunities to crush all existing prints out
of existence. In their place he started his own broadsheets ; some of these were made up of news without
comment, others consisted of comment without news.
Whichever they might be, they constituted the only
records of the world's history from day to day or week
to week legally sanctioned in the greater portion of
the reign of the second Charles. This despotic and
shameless newspaper monopolist was not, however, without some of the journalist's most essential qualities.
Even under his royal patron, L'Estrange's authority experienced occasional checks from Court caprice. In the
autumn of 1665 the plague had sent Charles and his
retainers to Oxford. "Odd's fish," exclaimed the
monarch, "there are no newspapers here. If we are
not to be cut off from all the world we must have one,
and if we import L'Estrange's from London we shall
bring the plague here with them." Hence the foundation by the University printer, Leonard Litchfield, of
the still existing *Oxford Gazette*. But the fashionable
newspaper public liked to read on the Thames what
their crowned chief had served up to him on the Isis.
For the benefit of such readers, an old Commonwealth
printer, Thomas Newcombe, was allowed to reproduce
in London the sheets published for the royal exiles at
Oxford. L'Estrange was furious at this interference with
his prerogative ; without reference to the King, under
the shadow of Christ Church dome, he set up a rival
to the *Oxford Gazette*. The Court, however, continued
patronising the local print that had been started for its
convenience. The plague had cleared off, the King
returned to Whitehall. In his train there followed one
or two Oxonians whose cleverness with their pens had
recommended them to Charles—among them a certain
fellow of Oriel named Perrot. This importation from
the Isis to the Thames was the earliest precursor of
the innumerable cases in which since then Oxford
dons have, like Thomas Mozley, exchanged the calm

irresponsibility of college chambers for daily or
nightly attendance at London editorial rooms. As for
L'Estrange, he soon died out of periodical literature.
On being removed to the capital, the *Oxford Gazette*
became the *London Gazette*. L'Estrange, however, had
nothing to do with it ; indeed, he entered into competition with it. As good a classical training as his age
and his exceptional advantages of station could supply
had not made L'Estrange a man of letters or even trained
him to a correct taste. He could express himself clearly
or forcibly enough with an idiom which owed much of
its raciness and vigour to the free use of contemporary
slang. He had, however, in the first instance, taken to
journalism as a trade. In 1675 he met the *London
Gazette* of his former Tory associates and royalist patrons
with a trade organ of his own, issued from an office
in Holborn [1] ; there was no attempt at literature here ;
it was all commerce, consisting chiefly or entirely of
business matters, in its lighter columns presenting something like a presage of the twentieth-century *Exchange
and Mart*. This combination of shrewdness and resource
kept L'Estrange afloat throughout the Stuart period, and
even enabled him to feather his nest. He had so
used the licensing power as to extinguish every one
of his smaller rivals. The *London Gazette*, being the
official organ, could not be snuffed out. It was, however, the only other journal, except his own *City Mercury*, in which Londoners read the news of their time
during the six years that separated the founding of
L'Estrange's *Mercury* from that of the paper by which
he is best known, the *Observator*. This latter print
survived till the Revolution of 1688, when L'Estrange
finally disappeared, and the licenser's office, now doomed
and already indeed practically obsolete, was given by
William III. to a laborious and learned literary drudge,
known as Catalogue Fraser. With the press censorship
L'Estrange was the last man of great notoriety to be
associated. The appointment itself continued to be made
so late as 1695. By this time its prerogative had
become obsolete. The position ceased to exist by the
simple process of no fresh nomination to it being made.
 The earliest quarter of London to be appropriated by

[1] The *City Mercury*.

the newspaper men appears from the experiences of Nathaniel Butter to have been the district near the Royal Exchange. Two generations passed. The centre of journalistic gravity shifted towards the thoroughfare which in Samuel Johnson's day custom had allotted to newspaper enterprise. Close to the site of the existing *Times* offices, and, as the place was then described, next door to the King's Arms Tavern at Fleet Bridge, three days after Queen Anne's accession, Edward Mallet set up his presses for the *Daily Courant*. The man himself has been variously described as coming of a well-known Somersetshire family of his name and as connected with the same foreign stock whence sprang the Mallet Du Pan that, visiting England during the French Revolutionary epoch, founded a family whose members still supply the Crown with accomplished servants. The Mallet who in 1702 gave London its earliest daily journal lacked the advantage of birth and education possessed by some of his newspaper predecessors, notably L'Estrange. As a stationer's and printer's son, bred to his father's business and inheriting his father's plant, he came from the class which, in the person of Mallet's greatest contemporary, Daniel Defoe, produced the man who, by his force of character, courage, and literary faculty combined, first endowed English journalism with its tradition of intellectual distinction, of social and political power. A great newspaper figure of the nineteenth century, to whom due space will be given hereafter, Frederick Greenwood, was wont to emphasise during his editorial career the paramount importance to the public of publishing foreign intelligence with as little accompaniment as possible of personal bias on the correspondent's part. More than a hundred and fifty years before Greenwood's time, Mallet had recognised the same necessity, and had done his best to fulfil the conditions on which he insisted. Occurrences and feeling abroad formed the staple of the single folio page that formed the eighteenth-century progenitor of the daily newspaper press. No pretence of private information would, Mallet declared, tempt him to " impose feigned circumstances " on his accounts of events ; he would abstain from comments or conjectures of his own, would relate only matters of fact, crediting his readers with sense enough to make reflections for themselves. This was a hit at those who, like Defoe and Tutchin among the Whigs, or, on the Tory side, writers of smaller calibre and less notoriety than these, had not only introduced the leading article into their respective columns, but who had acquired the art of exploiting or doctoring their news in the interest of the faction or the party they desired to help, as well as, it might be, of illustrating and confirming the views and arguments set forth in their literary columns. Mallet's energies or capital soon began to fail. He would, indeed, scarcely have brought his paper to the close of its first year without assistance derived from another pushing and prosperous member of his own craft. This was Samuel Buckley. At the sign of the Dolphin in Little Britain, he carried on a perfect manufactory of literary wares, issued at tolerably fixed intervals, to suit all tastes of the rapidly growing public. With his capacities for various departments of literary trade he united an accomplished and effective pen. He possessed also an acquaintance with foreign languages, probably at this time almost unique in accuracy and range. Nearly all his work was done by himself. He was his own news collector, editor, chief writer, as well as on an emergency not only publisher but printer. No country in those days had a greater wealth of newspapers than Holland, whose capital was then one of the chief diplomatic centres in Europe. Buckley, however, did not trust entirely to the Dutch journals for his cosmopolitan intelligence. He had gained for himself the *entrée* of the British Embassy at the Hague. Among his regular correspondents were the political, financial, and social wirepullers of Amsterdam. One of his chief features was a daily letter from the French capital ; this was manufactured out of the shapeless paragraphs, though containing all he wanted, in the *Paris Gazette*. The development of his enterprises proceeded without a check. The number of newspapers he successively acquired made him the predecessor of the journalistic pluralists of our own time. The *Daily Courant* was brought out by Buckley till 1714, when his acquisition of the *London Gazette*, requiring all his attention, brought the *Daily Courant* to an end. The best proof of Buckley's excep-

tional capacities in all departments of his business was
that, in 1711, Addison first consulted him about his
Spectator, and then decided that at any cost he must be
secured for its publisher. But incomparably the greatest
of Mallet's contemporaries was Daniel Defoe. He,
rather than any of those already mentioned, was the real
creator of the English newspaper. His career, his work,
and its lasting results of various kinds will be considered
in the next chapter.

CHAPTER III

THE FATHERS OF JOURNALISM, FROM DEFOE TO ADDISON

Defoe's contemporaries—John Tutchin, an early press martyr—John Dunton—
Daniel Defoe's childhood—" No Popery ! "—Joins the Monmouth rebellion
—Flight from England—Foreign travels—Return—Commencement of long
term of political, personal, and domestic solitude—Failure of business and
settlement at Bristol—Publication of the *Essay on Projects*—Improving
fortunes—The foremost political writer of the day—The *Legion Memorial*
—*True-Born Englishman*—Defence of William III.—Reception of the
Shortest Way with Dissenters—Establishment of the *Review of the Affairs
of State*—A forerunner of the Spectator Club—Defoe the favourite of Court
and people—Work for the Union of England and Scotland—Imprisonment
for his *Shortest Way* — Release—Political labours — New features in his
broadsides—The *Review's* share in the Tory defeat of 1705—Rise of
Addison—Politics before literature—Evolution of the "leader"—A prosperous
newspaper man — Satire on journalistic romancing — Steele receives the
mantle of Defoe—The journalist and the tavern—Steele and Addison contrasted—Individual publications—The quarrel—Addison's death—Influence
of the two men on contemporary thought and literature.

UNAPPROACHED by any of his contemporaries as regards
the magnitude of his work, the varied, the far-reaching
vitality of his influence, the strength and keenness of perception which he showed in estimating the English newspaper's future possibilities, as well as in the genius that
enabled him to divine the literary requirements of the
multitude and of the age, Daniel Defoe was the master
spirit of a vocation and a period that produced several
men, alternately his colleagues or opponents, all, indeed,
of smaller calibre than himself, yet not without personal
importance, entitling them to notice here. The most
prominent amongst these, John Tutchin, differed in
politics almost as much as did Daniel Defoe from Roger
L'Estrange. Yet he may in a sense be called L'Estrange's
successor, because Tutchin's *Observator*, exactly coeval
with Mallet's *Daily Courant*, revived the title of
L'Estrange's best known newspaper. That, however, was

not the broadsheet whose conduct, by its bold assertion of English liberties, secured for Tutchin the imprisonment, the public whippings, and the mutilations entitling him to a place among the earliest newspaper martyrs. Tutchin may or may not have been as impracticable and quarrelsome as Defoe represents him. He did, however, for choice, fish in troubled waters ; he was perpetually flinging down challenges, and indiscriminately to friends and foes alike belonging to his own craft. Defoe's known admiration for William III. sufficed to inspire Tutchin's assault upon that prince in *The Foreigners*. This composition in turn produced Defoe's reply, *The True Born Englishman*, a string of rhymes that, without pretending to be poetry, caught the popular ear by its jingle, and reminded its readers, who comprised the entire nation, of the degree to which British glories came from our being the most variously mixed race in the world. Another writer of this epoch, alternately Defoe's associate and opponent, was John Dunton, noticeable here if only because he foresaw and practically encouraged a newspaper tendency which had set in even then, which has continued ever since, and which was never more marked than at the present hour. In other words, he was the first to notice and to help forward the growing assimilation by the daily newspaper of the most attractive and therefore profitable features previously regarded as exclusively proper to literary miscellanies having for their object less current information than general entertainment. Here at one and the same time Dunton not only rendered the sincerest form of flattery, imitation, to Defoe, who, as will presently be seen, was adopting an exactly similar course during the same period, but was also profiting by the ideas with which Steele's creative genius fertilised the mental soil of English journalists—of none more so than his most illustrious colleague, Addison himself.[1]   Never rivalling

---

[1] The journalistic relations of these two men are examined in a later page. Here it is enough to say that Steele undoubtedly surpassed Addison in what would be recognised to-day as the essentially journalistic instinct, and especially in journalistic mechanism, suggesting, as undoubtedly to Addison he did, the whole notion of the Spectator Club, of Sir Roger de Coverley, and of other characters (*cf.* Mr. Austin Dobson on Steele in the *Dictionary of National Biography*).

Defoe or perhaps even Tutchin, he still founded a newspaper tradition, and, at least better than most of his day,
understood the secret of magazining as a department in
the periodical writer's trade.

The modern journalist's true progenitor, Daniel Defoe,
was in all things the genuine product of his period.
He passed through youth to manhood amid popular incidents of mutual contrast more striking and significant
than perhaps had ever jostled each other during a single
reign before. Within the palace the rule of the " saints "
had been succeeded by the dispensation of gamesters,
harlots, and pimps. Outside no one could be a good
subject unless he was a bad Protestant. Three thousand
Evangelical clergymen of the National Church were
turned out of their livings in a single day, and sent
penniless upon the world, in no case for any other offence
than the refusal actively to promote or mutely to accept
the reversal of the religious and political settlement
growing out of the Reformation, or to make themselves the tools of the Popish Court, whose head, as
Charles II. put it, had now discovered that not only
Presbyterianism but Protestantism also was no fit religion
for a gentleman. A true-born son of the people, Daniel
Defoe was fortunate in his father. This well-to-do
Cripplegate butcher, a wise, grave, devout man, from
the educational work accomplished in Scotland by John
Knox, had learned to appreciate the acquisition of knowledge at its true value ; he spared, therefore, neither time
nor money to give his son the very best schooling within
a London citizen's reach. In after years Daniel was
taunted by his literary rivals, Browne and Tutchin, with
his meagre and mean Dissenter's book-learning. Filial
gratitude and Presbyterian pride were united in his reply.
Granted he was not qualified to match with Dr. Browne
the accurate, or Mr. Tutchin the learned ; if he were
a blockhead it was nobody's fault but his own. As a
fact his father had placed and kept him at the best
school of his day. That was the Newington Green
Academy, conducted by a famous Oxford graduate,
Charles Morton, who, afterwards driven across the
Atlantic for religious heterodoxy, became Vice-President
of Harvard in New England. Under Mr. Morton he had
learned in theology something more than the mere rudi-

ments, had been even grounded in mathematics, natural philosophy, logic, moral, mental, and political science. In addition to Latin and Greek, Defoe had mastered French and Italian. There was also another tongue not generally taught at our colleges or universities. This was English, in which Morton had made him perform all his declaimings and dissertations. To such a pupil no training could have been more exactly suited. Not till long after he had laid the literary foundation-stone of the English newspaper and won national fame as a journalist did Defoe perhaps do full justice to his early training Between the years 1719 and 1722, after, that is, he had passed his sixtieth birthday, Defoe wrote *Memoirs of a Cavalier, History of the Plague,* and his masterpiece, *Robinson Crusoe.* To the literary grounding, above all to the intellectual discipline, and to the habits of accurate observation brought by him away from the Newington Green school, scarcely less than to his native genius, was Defoe indebted for his power of making the things that were not seem as if they were, and of setting forth the pictures, the personages, and events of his own imagining with a verisimilitude which caused Samuel Johnson to mistake Defoe's accounts of the Parliamentary wars and of the Plague for the original documents of history. In one language, Defoe admitted he had attained no proficiency. This was the vernacular of Billingsgate, of which his revilers, Tutchin and Jonathan Swift, showed such command. There were two other things he had picked up at Newington Green : so thorough a use of his fists as to win him the title of the " English boxing boy," and a resolution never broken not to strike an enemy when he was down. To a nature, however, like Defoe's, the most valuable teachers and disciplinarians were the events which as a boy he lived through, and the conversations concerning them heard from the shrewd, serious Presbyterians among whom he was nurtured. Charles II.'s Declaration of Indulgence, ostensibly intended to relieve impartially all outside the Church of England, really aimed at crushing out all that was Protestant both in that Church and in Non-conformity, to clear the way for Rome. Before he was fourteen, while still at the Newington school, Defoe would have witnessed his elders' indignation at the persecution of Richard Baxter, of Manton, and other leading Evangelicals. This was what the King and his friends chuckled at as "tightening the curb for the snufflers." As afterwards Defoe himself put it, the frauds and barbarities instigated by the Court provoked among the people the spirit of revenge which is a kind of wild justice, and which found brutal and bloodthirsty expression in the hatching, by Titus Oates, of the Popish Plot. Meanwhile the savageries of the Cabal Ministry against the Scotch Covenanters were at their height. His family and friends were struck with the fullness and accuracy of the information which, no one exactly knew how, young Defoe had acquired concerning the martyrdom endured by whole companies of Protestant worshippers beyond the Tweed. Those abominations first gave currency to the name of the political party with which, as writer and politician, Defoe throughout his life was identified ; in some of his reminiscences he describes how a squat figure, with a vulgar, drawling voice, and, right in the centre of his broad, flat face, a mouth of fit capacity for the huge lies it uttered (such were Titus Oates's chief characteristics), described his opponents and censors by the Irish name of Tories, meaning villains and thieves. On the other hand, the hunted and harried Cameronians, living on sour milk or whey, were contemptuously called Whigs. Not that the ardent youth had been schooled into intolerance even of " Papishers." It was all an accident of nurture ; had he been brought up among Romans instead of Presbyterians, professing their doctrines, he would have vied with them in their practices ; because he would then have believed their cruelties had opened for him the path to heaven. When about thirty years of age Defoe found himself so far interested in Descarte's broad propositions concerning the Deity and His relations to man as to publish a little treatise, *A Voyage to the World of Cartesius*, of which few copies now exist. He cared, of course, as little about metaphysics as about Arabic. In religion as in politics his standpoint was always that of the average Englishman's common sense. His faith rested on the necessity of the Bible for any kind of religion. Therefore he believed the later Stuarts seriously wished to take the Scriptures away from their subjects. He had not left school when his father found him copying out the Pentateuch against the time when there should be no more Bibles left. The performance of this task secured him the crown of a precocious martyrdom, and, before he was fifteen, led to his being hooted through the streets by a courtier mob for thinking more of the Gospel whined out through Presbyterian noses than of the command, not a whit the less sacred, to honour and, if needs be, to humour, the King while fearing God. Broken crockery and curses, he faced them all without flinching, and with no other companion than an oaken cudgel. This he called his Protestant flail. Nor could any of William's Hessians have given him surer protection. Fleet Street, then beginning to be the haunt of newspaper men, was also infested by ruffians. As Defoe went from Fleet Bridge into Whitefriars, two or three fellows sometimes set upon him together. They had scarcely come within his reach when they got a knock " which not only caused them to dance, but which made them so humble as to kiss the ground at his feet, sometimes even descending to the kennel."

All this, however, was play in comparison with the experiences awaiting him soon after reaching man's estate. Charles II. lived long enough to draw up his *Reasons for disagreeing with Protestantism*, which the Popish Duke of York exhibited as a kind of title before succeeding to his brother's throne in 1685. Defoe dipped his pen in the ink of Protestant disaffection, and in article after article implored his readers to hold themselves ready for welcoming an anti-papal champion. Brave, beautiful, excelling in all manly exercises and games, the son of Lucy Walters had been admiringly watched by Defoe while he was stealing the hearts of the people from his uncle, their unlawful King. In Monmouth's train, conspicuous by the skill of his horsemanship and the completeness of his equipment, rode Daniel Defoe. That he came out of this adventure with a whole neck was due to his not having taken part in the fatal Sedgemoor fight. Moreover, before Jeffreys had opened his " Bloody Assize," Defoe had promptly placed the English Channel between the Court sleuth-hounds and himself. Inheriting with his father's money the business foresight and clear head of that opulent City tradesman,

Daniel Defoe had invested his very considerable savings to great advantage in Spain and in other foreign countries. Thus, on the hue and cry being raised against him, a few hours' voyage sufficed to place him in a safe and comfortable retreat. After doubling repeatedly he at last took ship for Lisbon. His pursuers were cursing their luck, themselves, and him for having lost the scent in England. Meanwhile, beneath its glorious cork-trees, Defoe was revelling beyond the reach of risk in the unclouded suns of his peninsular refuge. All this while at home his hosiery business, superintended by him through the post, went on as usual at Freeman's Court, Cornhill. Before he appeared at his counter again he had made the grand tour, and had covered most of the ground between Madrid and Moscow. He had left the shores of Britain a raw youth ; he returned to them a seasoned man of the world with a knowledge of foreign politics picked up on the spot, and with his natal patronymic improved into Defoe. His bodily dangers were for the present at an end. The long season of his mental, moral anxieties, perplexities, and sufferings was about to begin. James II. had used the dispensing power generally to place himself above the laws, and especially to re-establish Roman Catholicism. The persecuted Nonconformists were largely disposed to buy religious liberty at the price of civil freedom. The folly, the cowardice, and the danger of doing this formed the subject of Defoe's maiden effort at journalism. This piece of writing merits more than mere mention not only because it shows that there had come to him by nature that simplicity, directness, and force of style which caused him to found a school of newspaper writers, just as Eliot and Pym had introduced into the debates at Westminster the oratorical qualities that made them Parliamentary models for all time, but because it had the effect of isolating him from his fellow religionists. There thus began for him the life of literary as well as political, personal, and domestic solitude, which fate had ordained that he should lead almost to the end, and which made the narrative of Robinson Crusoe's lonely years on his island the allegorical account of his creator's newspaper course. Thus in Defoe's first newspaper piece of real impor-

tance was struck the keynote which sounded throughout the innumerable articles and tracts that were to
follow from the same hand. The Dissenters were
grovelling before the Court while they bolted the bait
of a trap into which a knavish prince lured them for
their ruin. On the other hand, the Anglican clergy,
who set the example of the loyal addresses that the
Nonconformists followed, were all blindly playing the
part of Judas to their sovereign.

Meanwhile there had been prepared for Defoe rough
vicissitudes of personal fortune fraught with two far-
reaching consequences. First, from this time forth he
became the most prominent public character among the
journalists of his time ; secondly, business reverses were
to be instrumental in providing the leisure necessary
for maturing and completing his whole scheme of newspaper operations. Experience had given Defoe the true
philosopher's stone ; he had, that is, formed the habit
of finding material for his pen in every experience and
so profiting by the sweet uses of adversity as almost
instinctively to pluck the precious jewel even from
the ugly and venomous toad's head. It was a bad time
for trade throughout the City, and, indeed, throughout the
country. The hosiery business in Freeman's Court, Cornhill, had for some time done little more than just pay. An
attempt to retrieve his fortunes by a new venture mis-
carried. The bailiffs came in ; the shutters were put
up. A jail, said Defoe, pays no debts ; perpetual imprisonment is nothing else than murder by law. For
some time he preserved his liberty by lurking among the
bankrupt sanctuaries of Whitefriars and the Mint.
Sickened with the moral and physical stench of these
places, he fled to the provinces ; he reached Bristol
safely, even though throughout his journey he could
never count on being quite out of the bailiffs' sight.
The change from the Thames to the Avon did not
enable him to dispense with strict personal precautions.
His walks abroad were confined to the first day of
the week ; his appearances then in a handsome suit
of clothes caused him to be known as the " Sunday,
gentleman."

Born journalist as he was, Defoe met with no losses
or sufferings which he could not and did not, at a
moment's notice, turn into capital " copy." His per-

sonal experience had sounded all the infamies, social
and spiritual, of which the metropolitan bankrupt
sanctuaries, described in Scott's *Fortunes of Nigel*, were
the scene. On the strength of what he had thus
learned he set to work in his newspapers on Insolvency Law Reform—with such effect that several
of the worst abuses had been swept away while
William and Mary yet reigned. The sojourn at Bristol
would have been sufficiently eventful if for no other
reason than that it secured Defoe the necessary leisure for
thinking out and partly writing the most important of
his early contributions to journalism, embodying as that
piece of work did a newspaper programme which was
to be developed by him during the next few years in
an effective series of shorter pieces. What, not so much
in politics, as in social, intellectual movements of all
kinds, in commerce and trade, in literature and morals,
were the tendencies of the age? How was progress
in each of these departments of activity and thought likely
to be affected by the new freedom brought in by a
Constitutional Monarchy? Such were the questions to
which Defoe addressed himself in the *Essay on Projects*,
entirely composed during the years he passed at Bristol,
though not published till quite the end of the seventeenth or the beginning of the eighteenth century. Practically or in detail to deal with the schemes mentioned
in this composition was beyond the power of Defoe or of
any other individual publicist. The chief importance of
the essay lies in the fact that for a long time to come it
provided a succession of newspaper writers with a chart
for their literary course, at once warning them against
the dangers of which they must beware, indicating the
points at which they were to aim, and acquainting them
with the spirit in which they were, for success to approach
the various topics catalogued in what was, in effect,
Defoe's journalistic testament. It thus contained not
merely material for essays and articles innumerable, but
for pamphlets entire, and even for a host of separate
newspapers. A glance at its chief heads shows this
statement to be literally true. The Revolution of 1688,
by securing civil and religious liberty to every class and
individual, had already given a fresh impulse to trade,
as well as to all commercial or industrial projects and
adventures. That formed the proposition from which

Defoe started. The first step towards promoting these ends was to connect the more important provincial centres by an improved system of roads. That done, banks in every country town would be a chief feature in a thorough reconstitution of the banking system. With the banks there would come also savings banks for the poor, to be supplemented afterwards by facilities for small investments in sound securities, calculated to encourage the virtue of thrift. Concurrently with these, there would be offices for insurance against every kind of accident, benefit and friendly societies subject to government or expert inspection, safeguarded for their members by the most stringent and practical guarantees against fraud. More than a generation in advance of Ralph Allen with his post office and road reforms, Defoe insisted on the need of quickening the transmission of letters, and, to that end, among others, of making the King's highway reasonably safe from John o' Groat's to Land's End. Allen's road improvements for postal convenience are only one instance among several of the immediate effect produced by the *Projects* essay. Ship insurance had existed in Italy between 40 and 50 A.D. ·That, however, was all. In England, the burning of the City in 1666 brought one or two fire insurance offices into existence. But life insurance was unknown till 1706, some years after its first advocacy by Defoe. His experiences in both relationships enabled him to outline wholesome changes in the law of debtor and creditor. The creditor's rights were to be secured by severe measures against dishonest debtors, but he was to lose his opportunities for depriving of their liberty those guilty of no other offence than inability, from causes beyond their control, at once to settle the debts which they had no thought of evading. From popular reforms dreamt of by no newspaper writer before him, Defoe turned his attention to high finance. William III. was firmly seated on the throne vacated by his father-in-law's flight. What Augustus had been to the muse of Horace or Virgil, that his adopted country's deliverer from royal absolutism and papal priestcraft had become to Defoe. The wars undertaken by William for the freedom of Europe must be brought to a successful end. Defoe overflowed with suggestions for raising the necessary ways and means. He received his reward in a piece of State patronage that delivered him from his counter in the Cornhill Court, and made him, between 1694 and 1699, accountant to the commissioners of the glass duty. The first to make the newspaper felt as a national power, Defoe was also the first to make the journalist's vocation respectable in the eyes of City men. His official promotion was, indeed, largely due to the good offices of a leading West India merchant, Dalby Thomas. At the same time he embarked upon a well-conceived private business of his own, some tile and brick works, occupying, he had satisfied himself, the very ground at Tilbury on which Queen Elizabeth had delivered the famous address to her people. Both in his accountantship and his brickyard were gathered experiences which left their mark upon his literary work. The Thames flowing past Defoe's kilns and brickfields also conducts its waters through much of his writing. The same attraction possessed for Defoe by the Thames with its longshore life and characters was felt by another great writer in whose popular fibre, simplicity, force, and realism Defoe would have seen his literary descendant. Within sound, if not within sight of the Thames, Charles Dickens fixed his country home. The river's banks witnessed the most tragic among the closing scenes in *David Copperfield*. Different sections of the river in other of its reaches or its shores formed the effective backgrounds in novels that, like *Our Mutual Friend* and *Great Expectations*, show the master's hand, since the Copperfield period, to have lost little of the skill in the realistic delineation whose rudiments he had first studied in Defoe himself. Rough characters abounded on the river banks in the days of both writers. Defoe's *Robinson Crusoe* and the Abel Magwitch of *Great Expectations* both had their originals in some of the Thames longshoremen of the different periods. Defoe's great narrative was deliberately planned as a kind of autobiographical allegory. The solitariness of his position in politics and literature was deepened by the trying conditions of his home life. Mrs. Defoe had no sympathy with literary pursuits of any kind or with books. The place, she complained, was in a state of everlasting litter from pens, papers, and rubbish of that kind. Why did not the man stick to his hosiery trade at the old shop, instead of writing what nobody wanted to read, or what, when it was written, only got him into prison or into the pillory? Defoe kept his temper, and refused to be provoked into any reply, or, indeed, to open his mouth at all at the domestic hearthside. The silence thus begun was continued for twenty-eight years, just the time of Crusoe's lonely sojourn on his island.[1] A severe illness brought the obstinate fit of taciturnity to a close. With speech and health regained, Defoe entered on the last portion of his strange and strenuous life, during which he wrote not only *Robinson Crusoe*, but all the other books on which his immortality rests.

Meanwhile, like Tutchin, Dunton, and most other leading spirits in the journalism of that day, Defoe passed for a Whig. The truth, however, is that his temper toward and his treatment of all matters concerning Church and State were consistently marked by entire independence of party connection. Parliament, he held, was in duty bound to secure good government for the whole realm, and to every individual subject the right of such religious worship as he preferred. So long as this was done, and a strong and wise executive personified itself in the King, it mattered little what Parliament men were in power. A Tory House of Commons had disgusted Defoe and those who thought with him by its violent impeachment of the Whig Ministers. Defoe therefore, in 1701, looked for the true sense of the country in the Whig House of Lords ; he thus agreed with the Kentish Petition, and himself wrote the *Legion Memorial*. The combined effect of these documents was to enable the King to recall his Whig Ministers, to increase his army, and to take up the scattered or broken threads of the Grand Alliance. Defoe's share in producing those results represented the exercise of an influence as great and as direct on politics as by his *Essay on Projects* he had already exerted upon social progress. It also deeply recommended Defoe personally to William, and secured for the literary Teniers of his day, as Defoe may well be called, the same personal favour as the Prince of Orange had already extended to the artist whose brush had done for Holland something of the same service as was rendered by Defoe's pen to Great Britain. To the

[1] For an exhaustive account of the details connected with this subject see the *Life of Defoe*, by Thomas Wright (Cassell & Co.), p. 27.

year (1701) which produced the *Legion Memorial* and in it established Defoe's fame as the first of political writers, belonged also his satire the *True-born English-man*. This ridicules the English claim to purity of descent, and reminds the railers at the Dutch and new-come foreigners that they themselves were descended from successive swarms of foreign conquerors and refugees. Truly then, is the general conclusion of the argument, a true-born Englishman is but a metaphor invented for expressing a man akin to all the universe. During this period, too, largely no doubt as a result of his close and constant conferences with William III., for the benefit not only of his immediate readers, but of all who might take it upon themselves to instruct their generation with the pen, Defoe defined the origin and the significance of the relations existing between Crown, Parliament, and people. To Defoe, William III. personified a principle greater and more permanent than either of the legislative chambers at Westminster. Power of every kind, whether royal or Parliamentary, had the people for its source. For their good it must be exercised. His mere acceptance of the invitation to the English throne left empty by the flight of James showed, as Defoe held, that William accepted the popular source of kingly power as the first principle of British monarchy. His conduct since his accession had convinced Defoe and those who thought with him that, in such a sov-ereign's hands, national rights and liberties were safe. Nothing, Defoe believed, could ever put the English people out of love with monarchy. And this because men never willingly changed for the worse, and the English people enjoy more freedom in their regal polity than any people in the world can do in a Republican. William was at once the King of the people and the people's King. To him, so long as he continued in his present temper, allegiance was due. No such claim could be made by the King's Parliament, Lords or Com-mons. Both, indeed, might serve for useful instruments of the royal administration. Such were the ideas which, nine years before *Robinson Crusoe* appeared, Defoe began to impress on the public in his weekly *Review of the Affairs of State*. From the newspaper office to the prison it has always been but a step. The connection between the two places commenced with Defoe ; it was continued, as will be shown hereafter, almost to our own time. Defoe, as has been seen, planned the *Essay on Projects* (1698) during the retreat from his creditors to Bristol, while a pack of bailiffs outside besieged the house in which he plied his pen. *The Shortest Way with Dissenters* (1703), mostly written at Steyning, in the house of Sir John Fagg, one of the Sussex members, was at first taken for a recantation of his earlier pleas for religious liberty. On being seen in its true character as a grim piece of sustained irony,[1] it secured him a year in Newgate. During that time he planned and completed all preliminary arrangements for bringing out the *Review*. This began by appearing once in every seven days. Its success soon caused its issue on Tuesday, Thursday, and Saturday. Defoe united in himself the functions of editor, publisher, political writer, social and literary critic. Whatever his preoccupation with national affairs, he always showed himself keenly alive to the fact that a newspaper's success must depend on its popularity with readers who cared·little or nothing for politics. The citizen who bought the *Review* in Fleet Street, and talked over its tidings and its comments with his acquaintances at the coffee-house or tavern, carried it home to his wife and daughters that they might instruct or amuse themselves with social and miscellaneous causerie containing the germ of those essays that, some ten years later, were to delight the town in the *Spectator* of Addison and Steele. The machinery employed by Defoe for social discussion was that of a "Scandalous Club." Before this tribunal a husband complains of his wife. Having had a hearing, he is asked : "Have you given

---

[1] The nature of this satire, which is exactly in the same vein as Swift's *Argument to Prove the Inconvenience or Abolishing Christianity*, may be seen from a few specimen sentences : "We can never enjoy a settled uninterrupted union in this nation till the spirit of whiggism, faction, and schism is melted down like the old money. To secure the Church we must destroy her enemies, though perhaps not necessarily by fire and faggot. Still they must be rooted out if ever we would live in peace or serve God. If the gallows or the galleys instead of mere fines were the reward of going to a conventicle there would not be so many sufferers." "Hear, hear," applauded the University common rooms, one of whose members, a Cambridge fellow, pronounced the *Shortest Way* an excellent treatise, and, next to the Holy Bible and the sacred Comments, the most valuable he had ever seen.

any just ground for offence?" His inability or refusal to answer makes the club pass a resolution to hear no complaints against a bad wife who is virtuous from a good husband who is vicious. As a journalist, Defoe prepared the way not only for Addison and Steele in his own century, but, in the subsequent period, for Cobbett, Cobden, and the newspaper champions of free trade. Defoe was a free-trader born out of due time. This is how he writes on the subject : By our impolitic restrictions we think to plague the foreigner. In reality, he argues, we do but deprive ourselves. Then comes an illustration : " ' If you vex me I'll eat no dinner,' said I, when I was a little boy : till my mother taught me to be wiser by letting me stay till I was hungry."

Defoe's personal interest and importance in English journalism are due much more to specimens of shrewd foresight like these, combined with force of phrase and character, than to his work as a party or even a political writer. That does not prevent his having been the most powerful publicist yet possessed by the Whigs ; in that capacity he is said to have made his first un-doubted hit in a Whig publication when replying to one of L'Estrange's Stuart diatribes. Defoe's rejoinder to the Court scribe bears the curious title of *Speculum Crapegownorum*. Beginning with a statement of the true principles for English foreign policy, it proceeds, like many other of Defoe's writings, to condemn the notion of helping the Turks in their war against the Empire on the ground that if Protestantism had an interest in checking the influence of the Catholic Power, it must be far more deeply concerned to oppose a Moham-medan Power. Defoe had already firmly established himself as the idol and the oracle of the masses. The English Teniers of the pen, as the Dutch William hailed him, now became a steady favourite at Court ; here he made himself the most effective of general utility men. In the morning he was talking over with King William, and receiving royal hints about, a forthcoming newspaper series. In the afternoon he was giving Queen Mary the benefit of the varied horticultural knowledge he had picked up in his foreign travels and practically instruct-ing her how to lay out the gardens of all kinds at Kensington or Hampton Court Palace. All this time, too, he was in the closest and most constant communication with William about the coming union between England and Scotland. Of this, indeed, the earliest idea had been thrown out in the conversations held by the sovereign with the journalist. Nor was it only with a newspaper-man's pen that more was done in furtherance of this project by Defoe than by any other individual subject. Appointed secretary to the Commissioners for carrying out the Union, he received from the reserved Godolphin an acknowledgment of the indispensable services rendered by him to the scheme. Thus, over twenty years before Bolingbroke and Pulteney brought out the Dean of St. Patrick's on the *Craftsman*, the Whig Defoe had stood as high in the confidence of his party chiefs as was ever done by Jonathan Swift in his intercourse with the men by whom the Tories, were led. Whatever might be his other engagements, he never ceased to be a newspaper man first and an official afterwards. During the Union negotiations his *Review* distinguishes itself by the entirely novel and necessary work of removing English prejudices against the people who lived beyond the Tweed. These, with many instances, he showed, were admirable for their love of liberty, their deep religious feelings, their undaunted perseverance, and their unfailing hospitality. The Scotch soil abounded in the kindly fruits of the earth ; it was favourable for every sort of manufacture. But while liberty and trade had made England rich, tyranny and its deadening influences on industry [1] had left Scotland poor. Not only was Defoe the most characteristic prototype of the English journalist ; the startling rapidity and the dramatic completeness of its vicissitudes make his

---

[1] Among other things, to counteract the evils from which Scotland suffered, but primarily no doubt to promote a better feeling between the two countries now about to be joined under one crown, Defoe started the *Edinburgh Courant*. This paper, transformed from a Whig into a Conservative organ, associated itself with many well-known names in nineteenth-century journalism. James Hannay was at one time its editor with T. E. Kebbel and J. P. Steele among his leader writers. One of its latest editors was James Mure, son of Colonel Mure of Caldwell, the accomplished Greek scholar. In 1886 came the final split in the Liberal ranks over Home Rule. The *Scotsman*, made by Alexander Russel the first of Scotch daily papers, sided with the Unionists, and performed all the essential functions of a Tory organ. The *Courant*, which had long been in a languishing position, now died quite out.

life a mirror and an epitome of the journalist's most distinctive experiences. In 1701 the *True-born English- man*, in the manner already seen, had indeed recom- mended Defoe in the highest quarters. Two years later his *Shortest Way with Dissenters* had laid him by the heels in Newgate, but in 1704 the Tory Harley, a patron of letters, had joined Godolphin's Government, spoke a good word for the poor prisoner, and was desired by his chief to find out what could be done for Defoe. The prisoner's reply was an adaptation of the New Testa- ment petition : " My lord, that I may receive my liberty." Liberty was the one, or at least the first, thing which Defoe desired and which, thanks to Harley and Godolphin, he at once secured. From the dungeon, Defoe thus became the man-of-all-work of a King and the spy and tool of the Minister whom it paid him best to serve. Of party loyalty Defoe made no profession, and only looked to see which way the cat jumped. At this stage of his career much of Defoe's journalism was done in the intervals of politics. On short notice he was perpetually sent on a secret business abroad to those capitals or countries whose people and whose language he had first studied when, from one end of Europe to the other, he was pursued as a rebel by the officers of the second James. From these missions beyond the sea, Defoe landed at Dover only to work off heavy arrears of home affairs. On the eve of the elections which broke down the Tory majority in the Lower House, he rode on horseback as many miles throughout the country as had been done by Hampden and Pym when they were beating up recruits for the Long Parliament. While in the saddle, he struck out the most effective couplets for his *True-born Englishman*. That compo- sition, appearing in 1701, had won an immediate and extraordinary success. Twelve editions and the eighty thousand copies sold in the streets brought the author a little fortune, as well as spread his fame throughout the land. If doggerel rather than poetry, it was at once effective in itself and a capital preparation for the writing of good prose. Its best known couplets about God's house of prayer and the devil's chapel, at once popular on their first appearance, are curiously suggestive of George Herbert's " No sooner is a temple built to God,

but the devil builds a chapel hard by."[1]   It also gave
a hint to a nineteenth-century versifier for some clever
lines now no longer too familiar for quotation here :—

> " In a church that is furnished with gurgoyle and gable,
> With chancel and reredos, with mullion and groin,
> The penitents' dresses are sealskin and sable,
> The odour of sanctity's eau de Cologne.
> But only could Lucifer, flying from Hades,
> Gaze down on this crowd with its perfumes and paints,
> He would say, as he looked at the lords and the ladies,
> 'O where is All Sinners, if this is All Saints?'"

In his most poetical moments Defoe never dreamed
of throwing into them the earnestness animating " holy
Mr. Herbert's " lines, or aiming at the lilt and polish
of the more modern versifier.   That, as has been seen,
did not prevent their catching the ear of the crowd, and
opening to their author the palace doors whenever he
chose to enter them.   Always thrown off with ease and
rapidity, and jotted down at odd moments, his rhymes,
if never rising to poetry, so improved with practice that
his nearly unknown poem, the *Diet of Poland*, contains
stray verses not without something of Churchill's ring.
These metrical exercises, moreover, proved an excellent
discipline to him as a writer of prose.   From the year
of the *True-born Englishman* (1701), to the terseness
and clearness which had always marked his political
pieces were added a finish and an epigrammatic flavour
such as till then the publicist had hardly displayed.
Now, too, he introduced into his broadsides fresh and
lighter features greatly contributing to their commercial
success.   Defoe was the earliest editor to give his readers,
though not always at the bottom of the page, a regular
feuilleton.   What the novel is to the twentieth-century
newspaper, the column of sensational and, for the most
part, supernatural incident was to Defoe's *Review*.   Unrivalled by his contemporaries for the quickness and
accuracy with which he judged the popular taste of
the moment or forecast its coming tendencies, Defoe
had long since seen that the materialism of the Restora-
ion period would provoke a reaction and bring the
supernatural into fashion.   By way of verifying this

[1] *Works of Rev. G. Herbert* (Routledge), p. 385.

estimate, he galvanised into life, by his sprightly preface
and by his account of Mrs. Veal's appearance from the
grave to her friend Mrs. Bargrave, a deadly dull treatise,
Drelincourt on Death. In a twinkling the printer sold
off the copies which he had hitherto looked upon as
wastepaper, and Defoe satisfied himself that he might
advantageously mingle some flesh-creeping paragraphs
with the political matter which formed the staple of
his *Review*. Whatever he really believed about the
relations between the visible and invisible universe, he
found, like the editor of the *Westminster Gazette* in 1894,
that the spooks would be a good card to play with his
public. It was all done with an air of seriousness.
After much thought and experience, he had, he said,
come to the conclusion that the Creator had posted an
army of ministering spirits round our globe to execute
His orders and serve on extraordinary occasions as His
express messengers to men. For himself, like Socrates,
he firmly believed in having for his constant companion a dæmon or good spirit, wisely counselling him
in all perplexities. That assurance, however, did not
prevent the sense of a never absent solitariness. Indeed,
the growing burden of perplexity and toil deepened with
Defoe into the gloom of periodical despair. Not that
he would ever allow to his own soul a real loss of faith.
Daily and nightly, like a second Jacob, he wrestled with
Heaven in prayer. At last came relief and an abiding
conviction of Divine guidance and protection. These
caused him, while at his desk, to break forth in a
Te Deum; they also left a sense, which never deserted
him, of a help on which, while walking humbly with his
God, he might, whatever the extremity, count. Nor, he
insisted, was his own a unique experience. All who live
in the practice of real devotion may receive unheard and
unseen notice of mischief or disaster in time to shun the
evil before it arrives. The mystic's familiar spirit sometimes proved practically useful to the journalist. On
Anne's accession the burst of Tory enthusiasm spread
from the Court throughout the kingdom. The House
of Commons was High Tory to a man. Better, said
Defoe to himself, confess the failure of his hopes at
once, and give up all thought of overthrowing Nottingham, the Tory chief. The inward voice whispered that

the case was not hopeless ; he redoubled the energies of his pen. By the spring of 1705 the Tory majority in the Commons had melted away. A split in the Tory Party had brought about the coalition between Harley with St. John on the one side, and Cowper with Halifax and Somers on the other. This result was due to Defoe's articles in the *Review* more than to any other single cause.

That was the first great victory won by the seventeenth-century newspaper man, who, more than any other among his predecessors or contemporaries, personified a great editor's and a great writer's most essential qualities. Such are the gifts and such the actual achievements constituting Defoe's claim to be considered the chief seventeenth-century creator of the English newspaper. By his permanent influence upon the political machinery of the time and on its social or literary conditions, Defoe did more than this ; he created Addison. For neither as journalist nor politician would Addison's distinction and success have been possible apart from the Whig ascendancy secured by Defoe's pen and the periodical writer's improved position, largely consequent on Defoe's literary example and personal success. Two years after the Tory discomfiture at the polls, so largely brought about by Defoe's pen, Joseph Addison, as Under-Secretary for State, accompanied Charles Montague, Lord Halifax, on a Garter mission to the Electoral Prince of Hanover. Addison's newspaper course is distinguished from that of others by the fact of his best journalistic work being done subsequently to his establishment in social and political position. At Oxford, indeed, as Demy of Magdalen first and Fellow afterwards, he had written some short prose pieces, but especially several exercises in rhyme complimentary to the House of Hanover, for the most part on grand State occasions. These marked him out to the Whig managers as a youth of promise to be looked after ; but he had become a considerable official of State before his pen made much social or political mark in the press. Like Defoe, and, for that matter, Swift, as well as others of the time, Addison had begun in metre. From the first the most vigilant observer of rising talent, as well as the best versed in literature, Halifax had kept his eyes on Addison, and knowing something privately of him as well as of his connections, had resolved to give him a chance. It was Halifax who secured Addison the commission to commemorate Marlborough's victory at Blenheim in *The Campaign*, and who showed his approval of the way in which the task was executed by taking the poet, three years later, on the continental errand already mentioned. Addison's literary style deserves all the praise given it by Bulwer-Lytton for perfection of workmanship and delicacy of art. Those, however, were the qualities elaborated by him in the *Spectator*, and so comparatively late in his literary course. As a thoroughly equipped man of letters and scholar, he rose to the first place in his vocation, but in his capacity of newspaper writer he owed his party effectiveness to the intimacy of his association with Halifax. This sagacious observer of the newspaper's growing importance generally, and of Addison's qualifications in particular, had convinced himself that the day of the pamphlet was nearly gone. For the future, he said to his companion during their joint sojourn at Hanover, at least as much prominence must be given to news as to comment. Instead of laboured dissertations upon the topic of the time, there must be well conceived and concise observations, of a length proportioned to the importance of the theme, upon each fresh batch of intelligence as it comes in. This, in effect, though not in words, was a hint to Addison that, if he wished to serve his party, he would do well to cultivate the composition of something midway between the tractate and the paragraph, in other words, the leading article. Not in the *Spectator*, but in other broadsheets with which he had earlier to do, and afterwards most conspicuously in his own *Freeholder*, of which something will presently be said, Addison acted on the advice of Halifax. Without any such counsel, Defoe had already written many leaders in his *Review*. The example was now systematically followed by Addison. From his time it began to be understood that it was not the pamphlet nor the dissertation in any shape which would be instrumental in guiding popular opinion, in making and unmaking Cabinets. Meanwhile, Addison's father, Dr. Lancelot Addison, from being Rector of Milston, Amesbury, in Wiltshire, had, in 1683, become Dean of Lichfield. To him, or to other members of his influential family, Addison had owed his first acquaintanceship with Halifax, as well as the comforting assurance that, amid all possible vicissitudes of party or even changes of dynasty, he would never lack well-placed friends to push his interest and to replenish his purse. Addison was thus from first to last a prosperous man, in a position, while admonishing his colleague Steele to be more cautious, to help that improvident friend out of his difficulties by a loan of a thousand pounds, which, whatever Macaulay may insinuate to the contrary, Steele honourably repaid. Addison, therefore, was never out at elbows, or, like so many of his fellow writers, pressed to barter his independence for a patron and a bank note.[1] Not being in want of money, he got of course good prices from those who employed his pen. In addition to a substantial sum down, *The Campaign* secured its author a Commissionership of Appeals. As regards the rest of Addison's doings with pen and ink, the usual order of experience was reversed. Instead of journalism being a stepping-stone to place, he had been for some time a comfortably salaried placeman before his advocacy of the Whigs attracted any great amount of attention in the newspaper press. In 1708, while, as throughout his life he continued to be, M.P. for Malmesbury in the English Parliament, he began his career of office as Irish Chief Secretary during Wharton's Lord Lieutenancy. He next entered the Irish Parliament as member for the borough of Cavan in 1709. In that year, too, he could first describe himself as " an unworthy member of that ingenious fraternity, the journalists of Great Britain." Thus did he pleasantly describe a craft to which he was always more than half ashamed of belonging. In his *Love Tricks* (1625), the Elizabethan dramatist, Shirley, had satirised the professional newsmongers of his day. These, he said, were the men who wrote a battle in any part of Europe at an hour's warning, without setting a foot

---

[1] " Three things another's modest wishes bound :
My friendship, and a Prologue, and ten pound."
Pope, *Prologue to the Satires*, l. 48.

out of the tavern. They would also describe towns, fortifications, the enemy's leaders and strength, and yet face no danger except that of contradiction. Such were the taunts at his craft and fellow-craftsmen which Addison now made his own. To these he added the gibe of earthquakes and other prodigies being so familiar in print as to have lost their name. Chief among these dealers in portents was a certain Dyer, so famous for his whales that within five months he had brought three into the Thames, besides two porpoises and a sturgeon. Another of the inventive writers whom Addison calls his fellow-craftsmen was Ichabod Dawks, quite unrivalled in discovering plagues, famines, and convulsions of nature, which unpeopled cities and desolated continents. This piece of vivacious badinage appeared in an early number of the *Tatler*. That paper had been started by Addison's old contemporary at Charterhouse and Oxford, himself also, as editor of the *London Gazette*, filling a Government post. In the work of popularising the newspaper, the mantle of Defoe may be said to have fallen upon Steele. He had, indeed, taken Defoe's *Review* as the model for his own venture. The guns he carried were fewer and lighter than Defoe's, nor did he take Defoe's serious interest in the graver issues of current questions, moral or political. In his earliest journal he showed himself true to the name he had chosen for it. Adopting the pseudonym made famous by Jonathan Swift, Steele put forward Isaac Bickerstaff as the *Tatler's* editor.

The early eighteenth century witnessed on the part of the newspaper-writer an intimacy as various and close with tavern life as was to be claimed by his later successors with the smoking-rooms of clubs. The journalist's forerunner, the newsletter-writer, picked up much of his information at ordinaries like those described in the *Fortunes of Nigel*. A little later, between 1698 and 1736, *White's Chocolate House* formed a centre for fashionable chit-chat of all kinds. About 1750 *White's Tavern* was started as *White's Club;* the old Almack's became Brooks's. These two grew into the chief West End clubs. They were not, however, to provoke much imitation till many years later. In Steele's and Addison's day the public to which the *Tatler* largely appealed, as well as the source from which its intelligence came, was the tavern. The distinction between Whig and Tory taverns was not less clearly defined to the middle of the eighteenth century than that between Whig and Tory clubs in the following age. Addison, Steele, and their friends had their house of call at *Button's*. Here, too, Pope, Arbuthnot, Swift, and St. John (Bolingbroke) often dropped in, sitting after dinner over their wine or punch till the place closed or they were due at the theatre, frequently, too, returning to supper from the play, or perhaps a cup of tea with some hostess in Russell Square. The receipts of the chief taverns, if they could be examined, would throw light upon the fortunes of the newspaper men who were their chief customers. *Button's* long survived in the *Bedford*, Covent Garden, shorn, however, in that shape, of its former glories. In Hanoverian days the journalists, who were the creation and the pride of Queen Anne's reign, began socially to be at a discount. Their conversation had lost its freshness ; citizens and macaronis no longer bribed waiters to give them a seat near Steele, Addison, or those who worked for them. But neither Addison nor Steele would ever have become journalistic forces in their own age and transmitted their influence to posterity if, during most of the eighteenth century, the gentlemen of the press, with an eye to picking up what they could at *George's* or *Garraway's*, had not, at both these haunts, attracted the most select among the patrons of the place. *George's*, in our own day the George Hotel at the top of Devereux Court, opposite St. Clement's Church, was once or twice visited by Sir Robert Walpole, though more frequently by some of his understrappers, to whisper in the journalist's ear something the Minister wished to find its way into print. Sometimes the coffee-house and the tavern were distinct ; but frequently they were combined beneath the same roof, the rooms only being separate. Steele and Addison, however, with all their colleagues, had many another point of social or convivial rendezvous than those already mentioned. To begin with, there were the two great gathering-points for wits, scholars, literati of all degrees at *Will's*, near Temple Bar, and the *Grecian*, a little further west. At the back of St. Clement's Church,

in, as it was then called, Butcher's Row, the two colleagues of the *Spectator* feasted at *Clifton's* off the best
mutton chops in London. When the present writer in
1865 first dined at the *Cock* in Fleet Street, Tennyson's
plump head waiter told him he remembered Dr. Johnson
well, and pointed out the box where he used to sit.
So some one else knew very well Lemuel Gulliver, and
found his biographer, Jonathan Swift, only incorrect
in not saying enough about his residence at Wapping.
Occasional appearances were also put in by the fathers
of journalism at the *Mitre*, then as now lying between
King's Bench Walk, at the east end of the Temple, and
Fleet Street. *Dick's*, Thackeray's favourite resort,
flourished in the mid-Victorian era, just as it had
done when, in 1709, Steele took to dine there some
country friends, who proved so punctilious about pre-
cedence that he had a difficulty in getting them from
the narrow crooked passage into the coffee-room. Further
eastward in the City the poet Cowper, when keeping his
terms at the Temple, used, at *Batson's*, to take his modest
repast, thinking all the time what he should say in the
next of the articles that, signed "Villager," were then
appearing from his pen in the *Connoisseur*. Hard by
Batson's, in 1710, Addison and Swift for the first time
dined together at *Kivat's Ordinary*, the landlord obliging
them with some good wine at seven shillings a bottle,
considerably, he said, below the usual price.

Such were the favourite resorts of the newspaper men
with whom is now our immediate concern, as well as of
the readers addressed by the *Tatler* or by the sheets
which followed it. Addison, Steele, and their comrades
of the better sort had their days and hours at the places
now mentioned, less that they might pick up the talk of
the town than that the social atmosphere of the tavern
might suggest to them some new and attractive feature
for putting into their broadsheets—some novelty, social
or political, like those for which Defoe had ever been
on the watch. This was how the journal grew in favour
with the wives and daughters who pored for hours over
the print which the head of the family, when he did
not live above his place of business, brought home with
him to Bloomsbury or to one of the new northern suburbs
by way of entertainment or instruction for the ladies of

his household. Neither by Addison nor Steele were fresh notions struck out in the same sense and to the same extent as by Defoe, the one great teacher of both in every phase of the co-operation that continued actively till within a month or two before Addison's death, after a sharp quarrel which served to bring out in strong relief the difference between the temper as well as the genius of the two men. Addison, as we already know, made himself a newspaper man not in the hope of winning political office, but of confirming in power the political friends who had made his fortune. Without further lifting of the journalist's pen, he would probably in the natural order of things have reached the Secretaryship of State that fell to him in 1717. As a fact, however, two years before that promotion he had performed his chief work as a pure journalist in the *Freeholder*. This was exclusively his own production, before which Addison's contributions to periodical letters were those of the essay writer rather than of the party publicist. That did not prevent Addison, in the opinion of himself and his friends, from having always served his party even more as a social than as a political writer. The *Spectator* refined and educated the middle classes. Surely to have done that was to have reflected not less public credit on the Whigs to whom this journalist belonged than if the *Spectator* influence had affected to the Whig advantage a division in Parliament or an election in the country. Steele, on the other hand, though, like Addison, he sat upon the Whig benches in Parliament, and as editor of the *London Gazette* was a Whig placeman, had always been a free-lance, as much at home with St. John and Harley as with Cowper or Halifax. He supported, indeed, the Whigs for choice, and with zeal so long as their conduct provided good material for his pen. But to a degree of which Addison knew nothing, Steele ever looked beyond the politicians who praised his writings to the readers who bought them, for instruction or amusement, as the case might be. The question ever present to Steele was, What does the public want, and what, during the longest period, may it be trusted to buy? And again, When can my paper improve its prospects by playing the part of candid friend to the Whigs rather than by being merely their champion? The reckless Steele believed in strong writing rather than in deep thinking. The decorous Addison, on the other hand, thought more of winning one Whig proselyte than of filling columns with pungent paragraphs. As journalists, Addison and Steele were both equally concerned, and equally contributed, to make their vocation, as well as those who plied it, independent of the patron. Each had a share in producing incomparably the most popular sheets which up to that time had appeared. Their broadsides, by their political, as by their miscellaneous contents, might or might not gratify the Whig managers. As to that neither cared so long as their subscribers and casual purchasers were pleased. Nevertheless, throughout most of their course the two men worked together, and remained necessary to each other. Macaulay's exaltation of Addison at Steele's expense has been sufficiently exposed by John Forster.[1] It is enough here to point out that, so far, as Macaulay says, from Steele never having succeeded without Addison's help, Addison's ventures never prospered so much as when he had the co-operation of Steele. Thus the *Spectator*, which in 1711 had superseded the *Tatler*, flourished just so long as Addison was supported by the keen, inventive, practical, and inexhaustibly resourceful Steele : that is, up to December 6, 1712. A year and a half later (June, 1714), Addison revived the *Spectator* by himself. The resuscitated print, now that Steele's pen and management were withdrawn, survived only for six months. In 1715, while Scotch Jacobitism was at its height, Addison produced the *Freeholder*, entirely a ministerial organ. Steele praised its literary style, but protested its writer, instead of playing on a lute, ought to have blown the trumpet. To show what Addison ought to have done, Steele actually launched a journal of his own, *Town Talk*, followed by the *Crisis* and one or two other short tracts. These lived about as long as the *Freeholder* ; they rendered, however, nothing like the same service to the new dynasty. Addison's *Freeholder* lived for just six months, from December, 1715, to the following June ; it was followed by his *Old Whig*. This had been

---

[1] *Quarterly Review*, April, 1855, reprinted in *Forster's Historical and Biographical Essays*, vol. ii. p. 105.

started to answer Steele's attacks in the *Plebeian* on
Sunderland's *Peerage Bill* ; when that episode was over
it ceased to exist, and with it there died the memory of
Addison's final attack on his old friend. It also brought
to a close Addison's long course of newspaper work.

Addison's early attacks upon the members of his own
craft began, as we have already seen, in his first
contribution to Steele's *Tatler;* continuing to the end,
they found their way into the *Freeholder's* initial issue,
at the place where contempt is heaped upon " Grub
Street patriots." These are the men who, if the Government be preserved, have nothing to hope for ; and if
overturned, nothing to lose but an old inkstand.[1] Another
Freeholder article apostrophises William not only as lord
and master of the realm, but as the true parent of his
people. Here his tone is an echo of that ringing throughout the pages of Defoe. " Once more and at last we
have a king, too good to desire any power except so
far as it enables him to promote the welfare of his
subjects, and to give proof of his sovereign virtues."
This composition is a panegyric upon William's whole
course ; from his prowess in the field against the enemies
of Christianity, begun in Hungary, in Germany, in
Flanders, and in the Morea, and continued to the day on
which he established a claim on British gratitude for
insuring to his subjects here the national blessings which
ought to be dear and 'valuable to a free people. This
is not the only vein which traverses the *Freeholder;*
for much space is given to satirising the artifices
and tricks that manufactured the recent rising for the
Pretender, when, as a fact, the kingdom only desired to
preserve a settled and tranquil loyalty to the House of
Brunswick.

In the hands of Defoe, the English newspaper first
earned its conventional title by becoming, in reality as
well as in name, a Fourth Estate. Defoe's *Review*,
supplemented by his other broadsheets, exercised a supervision over the national administration and expenditure
more close and more trusted by the masses than the
control of their representatives at Westminster. The
daily or weekly journal, as conceived by Defoe, supplied

[1] In the original the word is "standish," but this is what it means.

the initiative and leverage for all movements of political progress or social reform. For Addison and Steele it was reserved, while organising public opinion in support of the slowly accepted Revolution Settlement, to allay the animosities mutually embittering against each other, not so much rival factions in politics as competing orders and interests in society. The abominable system of funding—in other words, the investment of money in public securities rather than in land—had been declared by the country gentlemen to portend ruin to the nation and deadly danger to the Crown. The Sir Roger de Coverley of the *Spectator* lived like a patriarch among his tenants and a host of retainers whose well-being was his first care. In the Middle Ages the younger sons of county families had sought their fortune in trade ; as in modern phraseology it would have been expressed, they had gone into the City. All that had now fallen into disuse, or at least discredit. Addison had owed to Steele his acquaintance with a Yorkshire baronet's younger son, Thomas Morecraft, who figured in the *Spectator* as Will Wimble. This elderly young gentleman of between forty and fifty lived very comfortably at home on his elder brother, acting as a sort of head gamekeeper. Extremely well versed in all an idle man's little handi-crafts, he makes fishing-rods or ties May flies for the young sportsmen of the whole countryside, with the same skill, readiness, and good-nature as he knits pairs of garters for their mothers or sisters. Will Wimble is but a typical case of the junior brothers who had rather see their children starve like gentlemen than thrive in a trade or profession beneath their quality. Such persons as these helped to fill several parts of Europe with pride and beggary. Not that Wimble, as the typical stay-at-home cadet of his family, had always been above earning a livelihood in town like his social inferiors ; he has, indeed, tried physic, law, and commerce. None of them suited him, so he returned to the family acres.[1] In these pen-and-ink sketches Addison's object was not satire, but the promotion of a better feeling between the territorial order in all its degrees and varieties and the upper middle classes in towns. Once, he argued, let those of

---

[1] *Spectator*, No. 108.

Will Wimble's occupation and rank note the spread of a gentleman's feeling, taste, and breeding among the better sort of urban people, the two orders would soon learn to respect, to appreciate, and even like each other.

In Addison's day, little more than half a century had passed since the era of the Restoration. The bad taste, left by the journalism it encouraged, had to be taken out of the mouth of respectability. That was an accomplishment which, in conjunction with the peacemaking services to society at large rendered jointly or individually by the two men, made the newspaper in Addison's and Steele's hands a purifying as well as a reconstructive force. The eighteenth century was really a period not more of analysis or disintegration than of building up. From it dates the England of to-day, with all its characteristic fusion of aristocracy and plutocracy, both in some measure refined and spiritualised by the instrument of culture into which the *Spectator* men helped to transform the newspaper. Throughout the Stuart epoch, the reading class had been chiefly drawn from the titled aristocracy. That order long afterwards continued to supply the patron, who was as necessary to the writer as the bookseller. One good result of Addison's efforts at removing class antagonisms in the way already described, and organising an intelligent public opinion equally contributed to by all social orders, was that the well-to-do City merchant who lived in Russell Square began to vie with the nobility of Mayfair in their encouragement to writers of all kinds, not excepting the newspaper men and other varieties of the long despised " political hacks." In 1753 Edward Moore, long noticeable for his versatility and thoroughness in all kinds of literary task work, started *The World*. Among his patrician volunteer contributors was Lord Chesterfield. His pen and name together did much towards raising the periodical press in fashionable consideration. Under Queen Anne and George I., therefore, a variety of personal performances, of very different kinds, combined to win recognition for the nascent newspaper. No department or interest of daily life was too complex or commonplace for journalists of the *Spectator* type. The earliest royal edict against the corruption of the stage had been issued in 1697. But only a small minority of the public showed signs of being in earnest in the matter. The clergy were fearful lest the expulsion of grossness from the theatre should mean the return of Puritanism to the Church. By shirking their duties as guardians of the public morals, they unconsciously contributed to the fulfilment of Defoe's prediction more than a generation earlier, that the time was soon coming when the services which the pulpit owed to the community and ignored would be effectively performed by the press. Of this prophecy Defoe lived to see the verification. The *Spectator* for May 15, 1711, contains Steele's protest against a theatrical dispensation under which no modest woman entered a playhouse without first hiding her face beneath a mask. The play that called forth these literally accurate remarks were Sir George Etherege's *The Man of Mode*. No characters appear in this drama, writes Steele, but what are low and mean. The hero Dorimant, intended as the fine gentleman of the piece, is a direct knave in his designs and a clown in his language. The foremost lady, Mrs. Harriot, laughs at obedience to parents, at purity in womanhood, and at loyalty in marriage. The whole piece is a perfect contradiction to good manners, good sense, and common honesty. This protest might have produced no or little effect but for the earlier efforts of Addison's conciliatory pen, which now ensured its address to a homogeneous public, whose chief and, at the beginning, mutually discordant elements, the rural, the urban, the moneyed and the landed men, had, largely by the *Spectator* essays, been consolidated into a unity both of sense and sentiment. Before Johnson, if not before Addison and Steele, had disappeared, they and their fellow-labourers, even in the embryonic stage in which it then existed, had given the newspaper a reputation and an authority that made its alliance courted not more by the politician than by the philanthropist or divine. Joseph Addison and John Wesley had been contemporaries at Charterhouse ; they overlapped each other at Oxford. Wesley had been among the first to recognise the beauty of Addison's religious poems as well as the elevating tendency of his more serious prose. He now exhorted his followers to secure Addison's support for those movements, social or religious, for giving practical effect to the principles on which Christianity itself was based.

CHAPTER IV

THE EVOLUTION OF THE LEADER. FROM JONATHAN SWIFT TO PHILIP FRANCIS

THE earliest example of the journalist's encouragement or even recognition by the statesman was, it has been seen, set by Lord Burleigh under Elizabeth and James. The Queen openly tuned the pulpits ; discreetly stationed in the background, the Minister inspired the press. Of Addison's service in the Whig cause in Parliament and press, enough has been already said. The journalist chiefly associated with the Hanoverian dynasty's establishment is a man whose performances, literary and journalistic, give him a place next to Addison. Not, indeed, that the author of *Tom Jones* stood in the same relation to Sir Robert Walpole as the creator of Sir

Roger de Coverley had stood towards Halifax, Godolphin, and the other Whig chiefs of his day. Fielding, indeed, wrote leaders in the *Champion* to help Walpole. He was never, however, one of the many writers regularly kept by Walpole, who had then at his call, stationed at different points between Whitehall and Blackfriars, relays of hack pamphleteers, each pen in hand ready to be called up. Walpole's method was to supply the selected scribe with a copious and minute brief. With his own hand he wrote down all the details necessary for an exact understanding of the situation and the issues. Next the Minister set forth, in their exact order of importance, the arguments which should, he thought, be deduced from the facts in support of his case. Then followed the objections which his antagonist might raise, the answers which would dispose of them, or the statements by which they might be anticipated. When, therefore, Walpole used the " reptile " pressmen of his period, he left, it will be seen, little enough to their ingenuity, and trusted them only so far as he could rely on their being his exact mouth-pieces. Frequently he contrived to avoid a personal meeting with the Grub Street drudge, and managed through his secretaries not only the individual writers, but the collective newspapers in his pay. He controlled and salaried the anonymous editor of the *Daily Gazetteer* ; that print formed the centre of an entire newspaper system. In connection with it were some dozen journals. To those offshoots of the parent stem the *Gazetteer's* managers passed on the word of command from White-hall. When, therefore, Walpole called the press unanimous in his support, it only meant that he had bought up every newspaper which seemed worth his money.

If the price thus paid brought the Whig Administration a substantial return, on the other side, during the twenty-one years of the Tories' exclusion from office (1721-42) the journalist was life and soul of the Opposition ; for Walpole's assailants drew from the *Examiner* first and the *Craftsman* afterwards the organisation and the spirit that animated the series of movements leading up to his fall, and so preparing the way for Granville and the Pelhams. The political influence conferred by twenty thousand a year did not prevent the Tory leader, Pulteney, from courting the addition to his authority that might come from the *Craftsman's* editorial control. At this time no reports were published of the speeches made in Parliament by the men who governed the country. The opinions and arguments of the people's representatives on points of State policy at home and abroad were often best gathered from the essays and articles into which their ideas had been distilled. Halifax, we have seen, had insisted to Addison on the importance of curtailing his observations on passing events. In other words, he was to write not even short pamphlets but short articles. Instructions like those of Halifax to Addison were impressed by the editor King, after due conference with his political chiefs, on all contributors to the *Examiner* (1710). Sixteen years later, they were reiterated by Pulteney to the contributors of the *Craftsman*. The work thus produced, as regards length, arrangement, and number of paragraphs, closely conforms to the modern " leader " pattern. Atterbury, Bolingbroke, and Swift, therefore, produced in the *Examiner* a Tory print arranged and managed in much the same way as, nearly a hundred and fifty years later, was to be exemplified by the *Press*, conducted by Benjamin Disraeli and an editorial committee, with Mr. T. Kebbel as literary adviser and aide-de-camp. The *Examiner's* first editor was Dr. William King, who did his work so well that the Tory chiefs, on regaining power, secured him the principalship of St. Mary's Hall, Oxford. King performed an editor's first duty by writing nothing himself, but by skilfully pointing the gun which his contributors were to fire. His staff included Arbuthnot, St. John (Bolingbroke), and Swift. Pulteney's contest with Walpole was fought out even more in the columns of the *Craftsman* than on the floor of St. Stephens. The *Examiner's* or the *Craftsman's* editorial conferences gradually became indistinguishable from Opposition Cabinets, determining as they did not only on the policy of a paper, on articles and their writers, but on an entire party's control. The ninth volume of Mr. Temple Scott's edition of Swift (Bell & Son) contains the " terrible Dean's " best contributions to this paper. They all of them show Swift, not as an essayist addressing readers of leisure, but as the article-writer whom the man of business wants. Thus, throughout Sir Robert Walpole's

long reign, the centre of Tory gravity had been withdrawn from Parliament and, by Bolingbroke and Swift
more than by any two others, fixed in the press. The
Fourth Estate, indeed, had now made itself part of the
machinery of State, and its official representative, King,
may be considered to head the list of Carlyle's " able
editors." Even Pulteney's literary skill and taste and
Swift's genius required for full efficiency King's technical
discipline. In the nineteenth century the forgotten
Peelite *Morning Chronicle* was the training school for
the clever writers who began to make the *Saturday
Review*. So, under Queen Anne and the early Georges,
the most effective members of the *Examiner* and *Craftsman* staffs were grounded in the journalistic rudiments
by men who actually had or might have been the pupils
of Defoe. Thus, among the Tory editors who came after
King, Applebee, the originator of a journal bearing his
own name, had been much associated with Defoe, and
as a consequence profoundly influenced by him ; for
though Defoe traditionally bears the Whig label, as a
journalist he never wore the Whig livery,[1] and was quite
as ready to serve Harley as Godolphin when he thought
the Tories had a better case than the Whigs. In 1709
Sacheverell's impeachment drove Defoe openly to the
Tories, and kept him with them exactly so long as office
gave them patronage. But long before then he had been
quite as ready upon occasion to do their work as that
of the Whigs. In fact, Defoe's frequent secret missions
abroad were made as often for a Tory paymaster as a
Whig. The result of his association with Applebee was
the evolution of a journal more closely resembling the
twentieth-century society weekly than anything till then
known. Of the Defoe-Applebee sheet, the chief features
were early intelligence of State affairs at home and
abroad, relieved by lighter talk from the *coulisses* of
continental diplomacy. Readers must be introduced to
the company and conversation of fashionable drawing-
rooms, as well as admitted behind the scenes of states-

---

[1] Defoe's vindications of his complete independence as a writer of either party
are more wordy and less felicitous than might be expected from so clever a man.
They amount, however, to a declaration that he is equally against extremists on
either side, and that, like Augustus Tomlinson in *Paul Clifford*, he intends
definitely to settle down as a Moderate Whig.

manship. Above all, no class of readers must be bored and so estranged by undue space being allotted to any class of subject. Therefore the comments must be kept short, so that the appetite may be piqued rather than satiated. Upon Applebee party ties did not sit so loosely as on Defoe, but kept him throughout consistently loyal to the Tories. In this he presents a marked contrast to another Tory journalist of the time—Nicholas Amhurst, first editor of the *Craftsman*, best known by his pen name, Caleb Danvers. Amhurst was a type of the journalistic adventurer in the period to which he belonged. He had begun with pasquinades against the Tories in the Oxford *Terræ filius*. He is next seen coming cap in hand to Pulteney for employment on the latest Tory sheet. The literary committee then, as has been seen, conducting in the press their war against the Whigs, put Amhurst into the *Craftsman's* editorial chair ; Pulteney, however, trusted him no further than he could see him, and never relaxed his control over the paper. At the same time Amhurst, beyond doubt, made himself particularly useful to Bolingbroke, and invented for him the literary machinery which gave originality and strength to the denunciations of Walpole. Among the articles in which Bolingbroke profited by Amhurst's ideas was one called the *Occasional Writer* ; in this the introduction of a literary hireling, as one of the Prime Minister's pen-and-ink brigade, provides an opening for a dialogue deriving its novelty and point from personal epigrams against Walpole condensing into themselves the gall of Bolingbroke's bitterness, but receiving their literary finish from Amhurst's master touch.[1]   Notwithstanding the misconduct which caused his expulsion from Oxford Univer-

---

[1] Walpole did not receive these literary attacks without sometimes being stung into answering with abundant spirit and violence, but with little of the finish which Bolingbroke's invective owed largely to Amhurst's editing. There seems to be no reason for such a supposition, but it is conceivable that Amhurst, in some sore extremity, may have earned a literary wage from Walpole. That would explain expressions in Walpole's rejoinder like the following : " You are an infamous fellow, perjured, ungrateful, unfaithful," &c. Among the latest authorities on this subject, Mr. Churton Collins and Mr. Temple Scott have been at issue. Mr. Scott takes the view adopted in the present footnote. Mr. Churton Collins, on the other hand, agreeing with older writers on the subject, believed the *Occasional Writer* not to have appeared in the *Craftsman*, but to have been an independent pamphlet.

sity and all the infamous charges made against him, Amhurst, beyond any press personage so far mentioned in these pages, had the special gift of editorship. He not only knew what would " take " with the public ; he was extraordinarily skilful in adding those touches which turned a moderately good but commonplace into a first-rate and striking article. In *My Novel* the out-at-elbows, tipsified Bohemian, John Burley, writes pamphlets which make Cabinet Ministers famous. In the case of the *Craftsman*, Amhurst's was often the clayfield out of which their bricks were really made by the Tory leaders in statesmanship and letters. Even Pulteney's work for the *Craftsman* and his occasional pamphlets owed only less to editor Amhurst than did Bolingbroke.

Jonathan Swift, whose life and work are interwoven so closely with Bolingbroke's, had much less, if indeed anything, to do with the *Craftsman* under Amhurst than he had sixteen years earlier with the *Examiner* under King.[1] The differences, as well as the resemblances, between Bolingbroke and Swift are reflected in their literary styles. Both wrote about State affairs with an air of authority befitting men whose natural place was behind the scenes, who belonged to, or lived in intimacy with, the men who created events and made the history of the world from day to day. Like his longer pieces, the *Essay on History* and the *Patriot King*, Bolingbroke's contributions to the *Examiner*, and still more to the *Craftsman*, are the work of a writer always in full dress. His youthful ambition was still at its height when he stopped short at self-advertisement and called it fame. His admirers had named him the English Alcibiades. To complete the justice of the compliment, he proceeded in profligacy even more than in philosophy to model himself after his Athenian prototype, summoning to his confidence Swift by way of the best substitute he could get for Socrates. From that time

---

[1] The most active years of Swift's newspaper life closed with his promotion to the Deanery of St. Patrick's. His relations with the *Craftsman* are explained by Swift himself in his *Answer to the Craftsman* (1730), under these circumstances. Walpole's Administration had given to French recruiting in Ireland what the Tories called unpatriotic opportunities. These were, of course, denounced by the *Craftsman*. In his little tract Swift, while not committing himself in all things to the policy of the *Craftsman*, expresses his general sympathy with it and strongly approves it in this particular instance.

the lines of teacher and pupil, patron and client, present something of a parallel as well as more of a contrast to each other. Bolingbroke desisted from parading his debauchery when he had done with its uses as a bid for notoriety. He then travelled in high state abroad, only, however, associating with the aristocracy of rank or intellect. Thus he never condescended to that notice of his inferiors in European countries which would really have sent him back to England a wiser and a better informed man than when he left it. The one possession he acquired during these years was such a mastery of the French language that Voltaire acknowledged the English visitor's critical acquaintance with the language spoken in the salons of Paris to be greater than his own. It was with his literary accomplishments as with his social experiences. Mixing only with the rich and great abroad, Bolingbroke reappeared among his allies of the *Craftsman* a more impressive master than ever of the grand style. He was of course confirmed in his indifference to the tastes of the "vulgar." Even Pulteney's diction could on occasion blend with periods of classical mould an infusion of the Anglo-Saxon vernacular. That formed the element which, ignored by Bolingbroke but carefully cultivated by Swift, and improved in his case through personal contact with his humblest fellow-travellers, won for Gulliver's creator the ear of thousands who knew nothing about the *Letter to Sir William Windham*. Always intelligible to a careful reader, Bolingbroke considered a certain grandiloquence, or something closely approaching to it, a part of the *senatorius decor*, to use a phrase he sometimes employed, proper to a speaker or writer whose genius for oratory and success in intrigue had brought him to a peerage. In such a work as the present, and for the general reader, the interest belonging to this remarkable representative of his age and class comes from the fact that, more impressively and effectively than had been done by the most gifted of his predecessors, he established a tradition of union between responsible statesmanship in its most ambitious aspects, and periodical letters in their most popular form, as the statesman's instrument and ally.

With this favourite of fortune, contended for by statesmanship, literature, and philosophy, decorating all that

he touched with his patrician hand, contrast the penniless
genius of English family who had come into the world
with the grievance of having, as he himself put it, been
" dropped in Ireland." Purely English on both parental
sides, Swift can have had in his brains nothing Irish
beyond what came from his school and college training.
The dependence which he cursed, first on his uncle
Godwin, then on Temple at Moor Park, afterwards on
Lord Berkeley at Dublin Castle, and even the poverty
which often drove him into strange or vile companionship,
were to develop the pitilessly searching insight into human
nature, the grim humour, the weird irony, and the power
not of epigram-coining but of giving strong ideas expression in direct and forcible English, that did more
than any of Bolingbroke's philosophic declamation, of
Atterbury's essays, of Arbuthnot's satire, or of Mat Prior's
witty whimsicalities, to make the *Examiner*, to say nothing
of other sheets, not only the delight of *Button's* and
Will's, as well as the favourite reading of fashionable
parlours and ante-rooms, but intellectual food such as
could be digested with ease and delight by the multitude.
No man of his day combined, with sound education and
an often unsuspected amount of miscellaneous knowledge, so quick or accurate a perception of the popular
taste, and so shrewd a knowledge when to gratify it by
broad touches of generalisation and when by the skilful
marshalling of elaborate detail. The secret of Swift's
power is that of a much later writer too, from whom he
differed in every possible respect. Charles Dickens made,
as in due place will be seen, several notable journalists
without being, like Swift, a great journalist himself.
He and Swift, however, resemble each other in that by
pen and ink they convey to paper not merely their
impressions and experiences, but their own selves. Thus
the satire and irony of Swift, the life and character
sketches of Dickens, are not only transcripts from reality
but do themselves quiver with feeling, throb and vibrate
with life. Does Swift wish to arouse the indignation
of his readers at the wrong inflicted on Ireland by
" Wood's halfpence " or Walpole's enrichment of himself
and of his stockjobbing friends by prolonging that war
with France which eats out the vitals of national well-
being ; he makes the reader feel he is himself a man the

hardly-won accumulations of whose industry have been sacrificed to the greed of the moneyed class. So the coarse realism with which he outdoes Fielding or Smollett in the descriptive passages, both of his articles and books, implies a reminiscence of those days when he sat below the salt with scullion boys and kitchen maids, and considered it promotion to be admitted to the housekeeper's room or the butler's pantry. In this way he collected the material for the bitter piece of homely satire, the *Directions to Servants in General*, and, as the sub-title specifies, particularly the domestic menials beginning with the butler and ending with the tutor and governess. Swift, with meaningless absurdity, has been called the prince of journalists. He filled, of course, a great place in the evolution of the English newspaper, but, even of his shorter compositions, the most effective, such as that just mentioned, appeared not in journalistic but in pamphlet form, the explanation being that Swift had a greater impatience even than Bolingbroke of anything like editorial control. Among his eighteenth-century contemporaries of the pen, Swift surpassed Smollett, as in the coarseness of his descriptions so in his intense bitterness against Whig statesmen, culminating in Swift's case in the detestation of Walpole, for whom, to please Bolingbroke, he invented the name " Sir Bluestring." [1] Swift also resembled the Tory Smollett, as, indeed, the Whig Fielding too, in not meddling with newspapers till his reputation in general literature had been won. Not till five years after writing the *Tale of a Tub* and the *Battle of the Books* did he make his first contribution to Steele's *Tatler*. The subject of his earliest piece was purely social, and might well have been taken by Addison himself for one of his own *Spectators*. It is, indeed, a little satirical essay about the superior ladies who, wearying of the world, professed an admiration for purely Platonic love. Incidentally the trifle is not without some historical value, because it hits off several of the smaller celebrities and most characteristic humours of the time not mentioned elsewhere. During 1710 the pen that six years earlier had produced two of the greatest satires in the English language first dipped itself into

---

[1] The reference being to Walpole's blue ribbon as Knight of the Garter.

the ink of politics. The paper itself had been started during August ; Swift's contribution was held over till the following October. L'Estrange's *Observator*, an entire generation earlier, excepted, the *Examiner* is the earliest instance of a paper entirely enjoying the confidence of the Ministry and run with the single purpose of supporting the Government of the day. Of party journalists, Swift was the first to perceive and act upon the truth that the only newspaper whose support can really help a public man or advance a policy is that which awards praise or blame on the ground of public merit or the reverse. His method, as he himself put it, was to refer special acts of policy to first principles of statesmanship and, having done this, to arrive at the conclusions justifying the Tories and proving whatever the Whigs did or intended to be wrong.

Swift, it has been seen, though rightly considered a great journalistic force in his day, was really himself less of a newspaper man than of an essayist or pamphleteer. Whatever he may be called, the great fact to remember is that the independence which gave his pen its political value contributed in the same proportion to reflect fresh credit and influence upon the whole class of writers for the periodical press. Mere accident like that of having been born in Ireland had caused Swift to start as a Whig. Hating popery, he detested or despised James II. and all the Stuarts as its adherents. Directly, however, he saw the Church of England might look for more from the Tories than from their opponents, his connection with the Whigs ceased. Before Swift no political writer had shown such indifference to patronage or employment by political chiefs. His superiority to such considerations first raised him above the level of party hacks, and then proved instrumental in lifting Swift's branch of the writing profession to a higher plane. When Swift began on the periodical press, the journalist's status may be judged from the fact that Samuel Johnson had been commended for bracketing the scribbler for a party and the Commissioner of Excise as the two lowest of all human beings. Fielding's co-editor of the *Champion*, of which more will be said presently, James Ralph, was originally a merchant's clerk in America. He was held to have degraded himself when he took to journalism, as other ne'er-do-wells take to drink. The notes to the *Dunciad* state that James Ralph, though rating himself above Mr. Addison, was really illiterate and ended " in the common sink of all such writers, a political newspaper." Yet many a newspaper man of the time, with no more of education and ability than Ralph, managed to do tolerably well. Sir John Hill had such success in inducing editors and publishers to take him at his own estimate as in a single year to make fifteen hundred pounds. Between 1731 and 1741 Walpole distributed more than fifty thousand pounds among his penmen. Still the newspaper man's vocation seldom brought him into creditable notice before Swift's genius had elevated the calling. The fairness as well as the ability of Swift's pen won him the ear as much of those he attacked as of those he praised. His handling in the *Examiner* of the Duke of Marlborough explains better than any other single composition both his popularity with the crowd and the absence of serious resentment on the part of many criticised in his lighter vein. The sonorous Billingsgate, whose floods the *Examiner* and *Craftsman* opened against Walpole, was the joint work of Amhurst and Bolingbroke rather than Swift. Swift's influence upon newspaper diction has shown itself continuously from his own time to the present day, and, as will hereafter be seen, particularly affected three nineteenth-century journalists of repute : F. Greenwood, W. H. Mudford, and H. D. Traill, but always as a simplifying and condensing agency and never as a stimulus to rhetoric. To resume Swift's literary treatment of the great captain. Let Crassus, as Swift apostrophises Marlborough, go among the common people of Rome ; let him walk about his own camp, to hear at every tent every mouth censuring, lamenting, cursing this vice of infatuation for gold. Let not his flatterers prevent him from thus increasing his self-knowledge. Then will come a cure for his fatal greediness. He will be a truly great man, even though there may still remain imperfections enough to remind us he is not a god. Till Marlborough, to whom Swift grudges no glory, should act on this advice, the nation would continue to groan under the intolerable burden of those who sucked her blood for their own gain. In other words, we shall be doomed to carry on wars that we may fill the pockets of stockjobbers. For what shall we have revised our constitution, and have secured our Protestant succession? —why, only that we may become tools of a faction who arrogate to themselves the whole merit of what was a national act. Even already we are governed by upstarts who are unsettling our social system's landmarks, and are displacing the influence of our landed gentry by that of men who find profit in our woes. Really, exclaims Swift, the art of government is not the importation of nutmegs and the curing of herrings. Rather is it the political embodiment of the will of a Parliament freely chosen without threatening or corruption, and composed of landed men. That last expression gives the keynote to Swift's writing in the *Examiner*. With the disputes of Whigs and Tories as rival claimants for power he is comparatively unconcerned. His first, and indeed almost his only care is to uphold those whose interests, being in the soil, make them at one with the interests of those who live on the soil. A territorial Tory aristocracy was from Swift's point of view the only antidote to the bane of the plutocratic oligarchy which had been the mushroom growth of the foreign wars. Here Swift was not so much echoing Bolingbroke as putting in language, more effective because more universally intelligible, ideas that Bolingbroke was afterwards to incorporate in his political philosophy. Dressed in phraseology varied to suit the time, such utterances were to constitute one of Swift's most vital though least acknowledged legacies to political thought. For it was Swift's presentation in the Anglo-Saxon vernacular of Bolingbroke's fine and high Tory aphorisms in the *Patriot King* which, with the necessary verbal alterations, became the " Young England " watchwords in 1842, and which, invested with fresh and attractive embellishments by Disraeli and Bulwer-Lytton, were to be the secret of the incomparable successes of the Primrose League. Long before then, however, the notions first struck out by Swift in the terse sentences already quoted had been echoed at Westminster by the most approved specimens of Tory eloquence in its more serious moods. A hundred and thirty years after Swift's contributions to the *Examiner* the Tory member for Oxford University, Sir R. H. Inglis, exemplified the orator's frequent debt to the journalist when he diluted Swift's sentiment into " I respect the aristocracy of birth, the aristocracy of learning, the aristocracy of intellect, but not the aristocracy of wealth." The truth, indeed, is that, as Socrates is known from Plato, so any popular acquaintance with the views of Bolingbroke in politics or philosophy comes mainly from Swift. Bolingbroke's pen would have sufficed to give the *Examiner* a fashionable vogue. Without Swift's it would never have touched or reached the masses.

The newspaper man who thus proved himself a popular power was no sooner courted and feared by the great than the possibilities of journalism began to show themselves in a light as favourable as it was entirely new. In all this one sees Samuel Johnson's meaning when he says that Swift dictated for a time the political opinions of the English people. With Addison Swift had first become acquainted in Ireland. The two always remained on good terms. In their capacity of writers for the press they were not, as a fact, pitted against each other. Even the clash of two papers by the same name, respectively employing Swift and Addison, did not bring the two men into personal collision ; for by the time that Swift began his work on the original, the Tory *Examiner*, its Whig rival of the same title started by Addison had come to an end.[1] Thus it was not Addison but Defoe who diversified one of his panegyrics on William III. by some depreciation of the *Drapier Letters*. Even the newspaper controversies raised by the negotiations for the Peace of Utrecht did not directly embroil Addison and Swift. During the August of 1710 the defeat of the Whig Ministers under Nottingham and Godolphin had brought in the Tories under Bolingbroke and Harley (now Earl of Oxford). If the new men were to keep their places, there must be an immediate end to the popular enthusiasm roused by Marlborough's victories, and the nation must be made to feel that the return of the Whigs would mean its own misery and

[1] The dates involved in the journalistic transactions now mentioned contain proof of the statement made. The *Whig Examiner*, started by Addison in opposition to the Bolingbroke-Swift *Examiner*, ceased to appear on October 8, 1710. That was three weeks before the beginning of Swift's connection with the Tor *Examiner* on November 2.

ruin. The country's one chance of salvation was to give those it had now placed in power a mandate for pushing on the peace negotiations with France and to refuse all overtures from the Whig vultures who throve on the calamities of an artificially protracted campaign. All the signs of the time were against the new Administration. In Parliament, though by a small majority, Nottingham had carried a motion dead against all peace projects. So far back as February, 1710, Swift's comparison mentioned above of Marlborough with Crassus had set the great General's reputation, and with it his popularity, tottering. At the same time Amhurst and one or two more of the Tory writers put it about that the commander, with his secretary Cardonnel, had received perquisites far beyond those which even a corrupt custom would allow. This was the moment chosen by Swift for his tract on the *Conduct of the Allies and of the late Ministry in conducting the present War*. This broadsheet, little longer than a modern leading article, produced so great and so immediate an effect that within six weeks Marlborough had fallen, and a creation of twelve new peers secured the way to the Peace of Utrecht. Nearly fifteen thousand copies were sold in half that number of weeks, and this, as Johnson says, at a time when we were not yet a " nation of readers."

On the Whig side, Addison's mantle, so far as it descended to any single writer, had fallen upon the author of *Tom Jones*. Henry Fielding's father, General Fielding, of Sharpham Park, Glastonbury, had served in the field under Marlborough, and had brought up his son with an admiration for his old commander which coloured the novelist's remarks upon the great captain when, in the *Champion* first and the *True Patriot* afterwards, he provided what was intended to dispel the memory of Tory attacks like those of Swift upon the conqueror of Blenheim. No newspaper man so far had come to his work with social and personal advantages equal to Fielding's. Born into the governing class, he had for his contemporaries at Eton Lord Lyttelton, Sir Charles Hanbury Williams, Henry Fox, the first Lord Holland, and two future leading Ministers, Chatham and Wilmington. Not less in his articles than in his novels he drew his characters and his arguments from everyday experiences of life.

Many of his newspaper writings, signed " Captain Hercules Vinegar," were the rough studies for the most effective passages of satirical description or comment in the novels whose " exquisite picture of human manners " caused Gibbon to say that they would outlive the palace of the Escurial and the imperial eagle of Austria. From the Hapsburg Counts, afterwards the Austrian Emperors, the Fielding family drew its descent. His illustrious lineage and connections did not prevent him, at the close of his Eton days, of a course at Leyden University, and of a ramble round Europe, finding himself almost penniless in London. Then, as now, the most remunerative opportunities to a clever writer were presented by the stage. As a playwright, while achieving no great success, Fielding did better than he expected. Bold, witty dialogue and spirited repartee were never his strongest points. His conscious weakness in these respects during his raw youth caused him some secret surprise that *The Fathers*, in which he had been helped by Garrick, and *A Provoked Husband* both escaped failure. Then followed a long tale of dramatic hack work, adaptation, and translation, including *The Temple Beau* in 1728. That was the year of his first marriage. His connection with the theatre came to a close ; the very tradition of it was perpetuated only by the label with which his last play provided its author, who became known in fashionable circles as " Beau Fielding." While visiting Rome, Fielding heard about the fifteenth-century cobbler, noted for his caustic remarks and bitter sayings. After his death the building that had been his shop became an emporium for the epigrams and satires of the time, known consequently as pasquinades. The Pasquin inspiration moved Fielding to prepare for the stage his two satirical burlesques, *Pasquin* first and the *Historical Register* afterwards. The gibes at the Government of the day, of which these pieces largely consisted, caused the authorities to interfere, and both productions to be withdrawn. The playhouse that had witnessed the representations was closed. The dramatist transformed himself into the newspaper-writer. In his capacity of journalist, Fielding, as has been already said, never took Walpole's shilling. His columns, however, were always brightest, and he himself at his best, when heaping contempt on the assailants of the Whig leaders and of the Hanoverian succession. In *Tom Jones*, Squire Western's abuse of " rats generally, and of your Hanover breed in particular," is only equalled in violence by his contempt for the Hanoverian politics which were personified in his sister, and which, by their nonsensical principles, have undone the nation. This outburst over, the Squire sent after his sister the same " holloa " which attends the departure of a hare when she is first started before the hounds. The next paragraph in the novel describes Western as a great master of this vociferation, with a holloa proper for most occasions in life.[1]   *Tom Jones* appeared in 1749. Most of the points in the caricature of the Tory squire now glanced at had done duty before then in the paragraphs contributed by Captain Vinegar to the *Champion*, the *True Patriot* or the *Jacobite's Journal* (1747). This, Fielding's latest newspaper venture, made more ferocious fun of Jacobitism in all its aspects than was done by the two earlier papers, or is seen even in *Tom Jones*. Fielding's Whiggism never secured him from his bitterest enemies the epithet of revolutionary. That was not so with a man belonging to a younger generation, who, like Fielding, had composed plays before he manufactured leading articles, Thomas Holcroft, author of the once popular drama, *The Road to Ruin*. Holcroft, too, was among the earliest newspaper men who carried their liberalism much beyond the furthest point reached by their predecessors, and, in several little sheets unknown to-day even by name, established the first republican organs on the English press. Fielding was not the only father of the English novel who has a place among the inventors of the newspaper " leader." Swift had never been a slashing writer. The first of Tory journalists to merit this description was Tobias Smollett, the novelist. A Tory and High Churchman, he brought in and made his own that variety of journalistic composition for which the Bungay of *Pendennis* said, " There's nobody like the capting." [2]   The true ring of Captain Shandon's " slasher " may be caught in the following sentences from Smollett's denunciation of a certain naval notoriety of the time, in the *Critical Review*. " An admiral without

---

[1] *Tom Jones*, Bk. VII. chap. iii. p. 313 (Bell's edition).
[2] *Pendennis* (1886 edition), vol. i. chap. xxxii. p. 344.

conduct, an engineer without knowledge, an officer without
resolution, and a man without veracity." The individual
thus stigmatised, Admiral Knowles, had made himself
the pet aversion of the Tory hangers-on at the Court.
Smollett's vituperation in the *Critical Review* called forth
many congratulations to Bute on the discernment shown
by him in importing such a master of abuse from Scotland to London. The attacks on his ministerial organs
which had made Bute call Smollett to his rescue were
delivered, in the bitterness of his heart and the emptiness
of his stomach, by the above-mentioned Holcroft. The
attacking paper was the openly republican *Monitor*, whose
directors presented a droll picture of eighteenth-century
newspaper life in its purely personal aspect ; for with
Holcroft there were Entick, an ex-schoolmaster whose
Reader and dictionaries lived into the Victorian era,
and Shebbeare, eventually the *Monitor's* editor, who, as
a boy, had forfeited his apprenticeship to an apothecary
by misconduct, had afterwards crowned his disgrace by
taking to pen and ink, and becoming a newspaper hack.
He ended, however, in the odour of respectability, if not
of sanctity. A short term of imprisonment for lampoons
on persons in power convinced him that republican
journalism did not pay. He did a suppliant's penance to
the Minister and the Court, found odd literary jobs about
the palace. He thus qualified himself for a pension of
£200 a year ; after which he was heard of no more.
Meanwhile, the man of the ministerial newspapers, the
special abomination of the Grub Street demagogues,
the novelist Smollett, was on the eve of a new journalistic
departure. Like Fielding, he had begun with play-writ-
ing ; but he had only avoided starvation by becoming
a surgeon on board ship. His wife's little fortune had
been swallowed up by law-suits, but his newspaper work
kept him afloat. In 1762 Bute gave him the most
remunerative and responsible employment he had yet
found in the *Briton*. This title, of course, suggests the
rival *North Briton* and John Wilkes. That, however,
forms an episode too familiar, in connection with the
political story of the time, for more than passing reference here. No journalist now passed for conspicuously
successful if he could not sting his enemies into organising a hostile imitation of his own devices and works.

Addison had been moved by Dr. King's hit with the Tory *Examiner* to run a *Whig Examiner*. In 1756 the Whig *Test*, under Johnson's biographer, Arthur Murphy, had no sooner made its appearance than it stimulated the Rev. Philip Francis, the father of " Junius," to follow it up with the Tory *Con-Test*, and so, a little later, as a reward of his services, to earn the chaplaincy of Chelsea Hospital. Again, till Bute brought out Smollett, the Tories had found no writer to do anything like Swift's work. In the natural order of things, therefore, Smollett's *Briton* was bound, as it actually did, to prove the signal for John Wilkes with his *North Briton*, born a few days after the *Briton* had been started. Wilkes himself began life not only with a grievance, but with a sense of desperation that dipped his maiden pen in gall, and gave him all mankind for his enemy. Born of well-to-do Dissenting parents, he was excluded by his origin from the English universities, then open to none but members of the national Church ; even could the clever lad have been smuggled into Oxford or Cambridge, the elder Wilkes would not long have allowed the risk of the young man's religious and political contamination by influences that might have tainted his nonconformist purity. The future editor of the *North Briton*, therefore, finished, as Fielding had done, his education at Leyden, then the most popular of foreign universities. Whatever may have been learned or not learned by him at school or college, he had profited by the example of the blows for freedom and against privilege which Defoe in an earlier generation, and, in his own, the men who made the *Monitor*, had struck with their pens in the press. This explains his resolution himself to become the newspaper champion of democracy. If Smollett in the *Briton* slashed with a broadsword, Wilkes in the *North Briton* retaliated with a bludgeon. As to the literary qualities displayed by either combatant, they seldom rose above the level reached in their duel of reciprocal abuse by rival Eatanswill journalists in *Pickwick*. The latest descendant of the novelist lived till nearly the close of the last century. Those who can recall the oratorical style of Patrick Boyle Smollett in the House of Commons, including a description of the Irish members as " talking potatoes," and who have read his ancestor's journalistic invective, will recognise a family likeness between the styles of the two men. Five years before, in 1762, he started the *North Briton*, Wilkes had achieved notoriety in the House of Commons. That he should have cared to supplement his parliamentary opportunities with any newspaper enterprise shows how powerful a rival in influencing public opinion Fleet Street had now become to Westminster. To the modern eye, the broadsheets of this period have a poverty-stricken and insignificant look, making it difficult to believe that they were ever a real power in the land. Their growing attraction for men like those now under consideration shows that to the hardest, shrewdest, and most ambitious spirits of the age, the newspaper seemed a means of winning distinction, power, and even wealth at least as promising as politics, diplomacy, or trade. The evolution of the leader has, in its earlier stages, been already followed. It was not to reach perfection till a date much later than that now reached. But the journalistic work done by Fielding, Smollett, and Wilkes shows each of these to have anticipated with much cleverness and effect the occasional note, the descriptive report, and other features looked upon as specially characteristic of the twentieth-century press. As for any alleged inferiority on the part of the eighteenth-century to the most modern journals, it seems enough to say that, from Defoe to Delane, the newspaper article has seldom failed to reflect the virtues as well as the failings of contemporary style. J. S. Mill and Macaulay have, perhaps, done more than any two other men to fix the standard of the best journalism of the present time. The sheets in which Smollett, Wilkes, and others exchanged Billingsgate, reflected the prevailing literary taste and temper of the time neither more nor less faithfully than the spirit of Macaulay and Mill was caught by the best writers for the press of the Victorian age.

A slight service at Smollett's instance rendered by John Wilkes to Samuel Johnson brings together, during the last years of the second George, three men equally prominent, after their very different fashions, in the periodical press, not likely to have been brought into any associations with each other either before or after this date. Johnson's black servant, Francis Barber, had, as Boswell relates, been pressed for the navy into the crew of the *Stag* frigate. At this date (1759) Middlesex had not brought its six times elected member to the later notoriety which made the great moralist remark that if he had his deserts he would receive a good ducking. Wilkes, therefore, readily used his influence, however he may have acquired it, with Ministers to secure Barber's release. Meanwhile Johnson had not only begun his journalistic course by writing for a local print in his native county the essays which first gained him notice, but had made his position in the London press by some work essentially of the newspaper kind, though published in a monthly magazine. This was the account in Cave's *Gentleman's Magazine* of the proceedings in Parliament, under the title of the "Senate of Lilliput." A certain speech of the elder Pitt's had been called by the Francis whose son became Junius, "superior to anything in Demosthenes." "That speech," said Johnson, "I wrote in a garret in Exeter Street." One of the functions discharged by Addison and Steele had been to purify and sweeten the journalistic atmosphere. In this direction of moral improvement Johnson, whose conscientious scruples caused him in 1742 to discontinue his imaginary records of parliamentary doings, went a whole stage further. The only resemblance borne by the *Rambler* to a newspaper of any kind was its appearance at stated intervals. Marked more than any other of his periodical writings by Johnson's sesquipedalian pomp of diction, it largely consisted of discourses on the cardinal virtues, so grave and earnest that they might have been delivered from the pulpit, of admonitions to spiritual perfection as devout, sometimes even as impassioned, as any urged by the lips or pen of Wesley, Doddridge or Watts. The ethical or even theological matter was varied by excursions into literature, by anecdotes, allegories, and apologues ; it formed, indeed, a specimen of the mixture that constituted the Sunday reading of strict households two or three generations ago. Of the two titles to fame with which Johnson is still popularly labelled, that of the great lexicographer was made good by the *Dictionary* in 1755. The distinction of the great moralist came from the *Rambler* in 1750-52. Nor was there much extravagance in Boswell's remark that in no writings whatever could there be found more bark and steel for the mind, as well as in his further claim for it of the same superiority to the rant of stoicism as the sun of Revelation possesses over the twilight of pagan philosophy. Not, indeed, that the *Rambler* appealed to professedly serious readers alone. Johnson lived for this world as well as for the next. He thought it equally his duty as well as his interest to provide for the spiritual advance and the social entertainment or instruction of his readers. The Passion Week compositions on abstraction, on self-examination, on penitence, on the placability of the divine nature, are preceded or followed by social sketches which for lightness of touch, felicity of characterisation, insight into the humours of daily life, might be Addison's. The *Rambler* is also distinguished from the host of miscellanies that jostled it in not meeting with more of favour from the general public than of attention from the literary class. Thus number fifty-five of the series contains a character, that of Suspirius, which gave Goldsmith his idea of Croker in the comedy of *The Good-natured Man*. In quickness of composition under pressure, in the readiness with which he turned from one subject to another, Johnson would have been noticeable among the journalists of any age. These eminently journalistic attributes were illustrated by him not less strikingly in the *Idler* than in the *Rambler*. Neither place nor time was allowed to interfere with his work. Once, between 1758 and 1760, while on a visit to Oxford, he suddenly remembered the London printer had no copy in hand. The post went out in half an hour. That was quite long enough for him to write and send off one of the short *Idler* essays. These compositions varied from one-third to two-thirds of a modern leading article in length. It was, therefore, quick work, surpassed neither in quality nor length by many writers since Johnson's time. In his compositions for the periodical press, the English lexicographer showed himself as miscellaneously prolific as he could, on an emergency, be swift. The subjects of the *Idler* pieces recall, in their freshness and diversity, the contents of Defoe's *Reviews*. Among the topics put down by Johnson for treatment is an English academy for literature, such as suggested itself about the same time to Jonathan Swift. Both writers

expected the realisation of that project in their life-
time. Instead, it was to be among the earliest official
acts of King Edward VII. For the rest, as well, it may
be said, as Addison and Steele, Johnson showed the
soundness of his newspaper instinct by devoting thought
and space to questions of domestic economy, of household cookery, of public health in towns and villages,
to regulation of the drink trade, to licensing reform,
to improved methods of teaching in schools and colleges,
as well as to suggestions for amending all that affected
the position of women in the community. Even the germ
of the Married Women's Property Act may be discovered
in more than one passage of the *Idler* essays. Than
Johnson, indeed, the members of John Stuart Mill's
" suppressed sex " had no sturdier champion, as is shown
not only by page after page, but by number following
number of the *Idler*. A lady's performance on horseback
inspires an idea for forming a female army. Should that
prove impracticable, it is explained how, in the management of charities and hospitals, the intelligence of
English matrons and maids of all degrees may be successfully enlisted for conducting war against waste, want,
and all kinds of preventable sickness. In the *Idler*,
by the choice of subjects, the simplicity, the ease, or the
playful satire of treatment, Johnson is an example of the
writer who first makes and then enlarges his public
by keeping his finger always on its mental pulse, by
interpreting and supplying its daily needs in every department of its corporate or individual life. Something
of the same kind, indeed, had already been done by his
predecessors or contemporaries from Defoe to Swift,
Addison, and Steele. All Johnson's periodical work,
however, if not universally original, is stamped with the
character of his own strong individuality. During the
second half of the eighteenth century the *Rambler*, the
Idler, and above all that masterpiece of Johnsonian
commonsense, biographical compression, and terse criticism, the *Lives of the Poets*, had begun to share with
the compositions whose central figure is Sir Roger de
Coverley the honour of being considered among the
healthiest, as they were also the longest-lived, models
for periodical writers. Amid innumerable differences,
the journalistic prose of Samuel Johnson's day reflects

itself in that of the period during which Lord Macaulay's arrangement of sentences and paragraphs largely formed the secret of the effect produced by the leading articles in the *Times*. A former high authority on English prose, Bishop Hurd, with the diction of his favourite Addison compared unfavourably a school of prose whose growth to popularity he watched with dismay. This was what Hurd called the pompous or swaggering style, introduced by Bolingbroke, continued or heightened by Junius and Johnson. However it may be stigmatised, the diction detested by Bishop Hurd was to form the foundation and the model for the best newspaper writers, not merely of Hurd's own day, but in the centuries which followed.

Among the periodical writers beginning with Defoe, continuing with Swift, Steele and Addison, and ending with Johnson, each has been shown to embody some characteristic portion of the eighteenth-century spirit ; about each enough is known to enable us distinctly to realise his person, his position, and his life's work. Equally close will prove the connection with their time in the case of the other eighteenth-century makers of the English newspaper still to be considered.

Samuel Johnson's connection with the periodical press is noticeable for another reason than the quality of the work he did for it. The essays that composed his *Rambler* appeared, for the most part, if not entirely, in separate form, without, that is, the accompaniment of any other letterpress. The *Idler* formed his contribution to a weekly newspaper, the *Universal Chronicle*, published every Saturday. From that time forth the column or two of original composition became a recognised feature in the new sheet, great or small, whether of weekly or daily issue. Johnson lived to see the example he had set followed in a manner and with results more memorable than had so far been experienced. His memory and imagination combined had helped him, on the strength of a very few hints, to enrich Cave's reports of the " Senate of Lilliput " in the *Gentleman's Magazine* with speeches such as Chatham might well have been supposed to deliver. Cave found a successor in John Almon, whose record of the doings at Westminster, if not such polished and stately pieces of imagination as Johnson furnished to the *Gentleman's Magazine*, were historically more valuable, prepared the way for the parliamentary reports of a later day, and involved their publisher in constant squabbles with both Houses for breach of privilege. That was the period during which the newspaper had other champions and martyrs than those who were actually its writers. The middle of the eighteenth century witnessed the rise of a family three generations of which were almost equally remarkable for their skill, courage, resourcefulness and judgment in all that concerned the business side of newspapers. Whether intelligence or comment, the Woodfalls from 1760 onward knew what the public wanted, and shrunk from no labour or risk in its supply. Thus it was that, on the accession of George III., the *Public Advertiser*, in existence from the days of Defoe, but fallen into discredit and obscurity, had been worked up by Henry Woodfall into the most widely circulated journal of the time. His son, Henry Sampson Woodfall, needs no other claim to perpetual remembrance among the literary makers of the newspaper than the circumstance of his having brought out in the *Public Advertiser* the many-aliased writer best known as Junius. This paper then held a position comparable with the *Times* at the height of its power, and was recognised as the official organ for announcements by the party leaders on both sides. Ten years earlier, by publishing his *Idler* essays in the *Universal Chronicle*, Johnson placed on record a conviction that the newspaper article had, even in 1758, begun to displace the periodical essay sheet or the pamphlet. This admission by the first man of letters in the generation to which he belonged was significantly reinforced when the greatest literary gladiator in the language chose, as the medium for his deliverances, personal and political, a new sheet owing its then unequalled circulation entirely to its accurate intelligence rather than to any signal wisdom disclosed by its counsel to the statesmen of the time. In the spring of 1757, it was a Fleet Street rumour that Henry Sampson Woodfall had held several secret meetings with a gentleman who, a generation later, was to attract the attention of Parliament scarcely more by his eloquence than by his presence. The voice, first heard at St. Stephens in 1784, was as sharp and distinct as it was sonorous ; the gestures, impatient, irregular, were expressive in every

detail of a powerful and restless intellect. " Bursting
with bile " was the impression produced by his appearance and manner upon a shrewd and entirely unprejudiced
observer, who was frequently his fellow dinner guest at the
Brighton Pavilion, where some years later Francis became
domesticated. Presenting, both as writer and speaker,
many points of resemblance to Burke, Francis in one
respect excelled him. Burke's passion and irascibility
constantly overcame his reason, and excited as much of
pity for the man as his eloquence did of admiration for
the orator. In Francis, on the other hand, the powerful
and unwearied brain generally co-operated with the re-
lentless will to restrain the humours of petulance and keep
back the outbursts of bitterness or passion. Between the
last of the Junius letters and the return of Sir Philip
Francis to Parliament, there elapsed an interval of twelve
years. That, however, was not long enough to remove
the impressions produced by the philippics of the *Public
Advertiser* from the Chamber which Francis entered in
1784. The reports of his earliest parliamentary speeches
contain much to suggest that his newspaper writings had
served as the full-dress rehearsals of his most telling
oratorical effects. Even as a rhetorician, Woodfall's
illustrious contributor was unsurpassed equally on the
platform and in the press. Whether with voice or pen,
the effects he produced resembled the organ performance
of a master-hand, whose genius and art combined extracts
from his instrument harmonies entirely denied to
operators of less consummate touch. In 1784 came
the debate, that on Pitt's India Bill, at St. Stephen's.
Francis then delivered a speech immediately recognised
by all competent critics as having the same ring that,
a generation earlier, had sounded through the *Public
Advertiser's* columns. A clause in the measure provided in certain cases for the abolition of trial by jury.
This brought Francis to his feet with an impassioned
appeal to the then Prime Minister's father, the great
Earl of Chatham, whom such a proposal would have
brought from his bed of sickness to the floor of the
House. " Alas ! " exclaimed Francis, " he is dead, and the
sense, the honour, the character, and the understanding
of the nation are dead with him." " So then," on the
Treasury Bench whispered Chatham's son to his friend

Long, " the voice of Junius himself is now heard." Here
it may be noticed that Francis had begun his articles in
Woodfall's journal with an attack upon the same statesman, the elder Pitt, whom, with equal power and pathos,
he was afterwards to apostrophise in Parliament. In
1766 Chatham became Secretary of State in the Cabinet
nominally presided over by the Duke of Grafton, and
containing Bute, so often and so bitterly denounced by
the very Chatham who thus became the Duke's colleague.
Not as Junius but Poplicola in the *Public Advertiser* of
April 28, 1767, the future Junius charged Chatham with
having brought to a climax his insolence and hypocrisies
by taking that favourite to his bosom, and making him
the only partner of his power, and by thus finding his
ally in " a notorious coward who, skulking under a petti-
coat, sacrifices the honour of a king, and makes a great
nation the prey of his avarice and ambition." If, as
has been said, Poplicola was not identical with Junius,
he anticipated the style of Junius with superhuman
accuracy. Here our concern is not so much with the
subjects handled by Francis in the different characters he
assumed as with the definite results which his pen
helped to produce, and with the justification they
constitute for the choice in the first instance, by a
consummately clever man, of the press rather than of
Parliament as his agency for influencing events. Nothing
can be more unlike the simple and concise exposition
of Swift than the pomp of rhetoric and the elaborately
antithetical periods of Francis. On some questions, however, the two men thought with each other, and expressed
themselves in almost identical terms. About the moneyed
men and the landed men, as Atticus in the *Public
Advertiser* of August, 1768, Francis echoes the opinions
put forth in the *Examiner* and elsewhere, more than half
a century earlier, by Swift. Such, it is stated, were the
dangers to property and finance involved in unfriendly
relations with France as well as a probable break with
our American colonies, that prudent persons found it
necessary to sell out of the funds and to invest in land.
Among the varieties of vituperative phrase with which
Francis labours this point, are some whose coarseness
seems like an imitation of Swift in his least refined
moments—*e.g.*, "our rulers, careless of everything

but their own pleasures, leave their country like a cast off mistress to perish under the diseases they have given her." The newspaper directed by Henry Sampson Woodfall, and having for its most sensational feature the articles of Sir Philip Francis, achieved or contributed to the subsequent production of two specific results. On March 25, 1771, the citizens of London were beside themselves with admiration at the scornful invective heaped by the *Public Advertiser* on the Parliament for its extreme measures against not only those who printed the unlicensed report of its proceedings, but those who, like the Lord Mayor and aldermen, upheld the perpetrators of the offence. " It was not," said the newspaper, " the offensive individual but the free constitution of this country, including its whole newspaper system, to compass whose destruction the estates of the realm have added a new crime to the Statute book." From the day of that declaration, the issue of the struggle for full parliamentary reports was never in doubt for a moment. The other point at which Francis affected the legislation of his day was the beginning of that movement brought to a triumphant close in 1792 by Fox. For without the impetus in the right direction first given to public feeling by the writer, the statesman would have lacked the force which overcame the opposition of the Lords, and which enabled him, in libel cases, to bring matters of law as well as of fact within the purview of the jury.

The details proving Junius and Francis to have been one and the same are too familiar for review here. One, however, worn perhaps less threadbare than the others, may be mentioned. Lady Francis, who was entirely in her husband's confidence, used to show her friends a little book, *Junius Identified*, a posthumous gift from her husband, and inscribed on the fly-leaf with the words : " I leave this book as a legacy to my wife." Here it may be convenient to bring together the various persons to whom the *Junius Letters* have at different times been ascribed. Taken in alphabetical order, these are Lord Ashburton, Hugh Macauley Boyd, Edmund Burke, Dr. Butler (sometime Bishop of Hereford), John Dunning, Samuel Dyer, Henry Flood, William Gerard Hamilton (" single speech "), Major-General Charles Lee, Charles Lloyd (a Treasury clerk, afterwards teller of the Ex-

chequer), John Roberts (another Treasury clerk, afterwards private secretary to Pelham when Prime Minister,
subsequently M.P. for Harwich, also a Commissioner for
the Board of Trade), the Rev. Philip Rosenhagen, Lord
George Sackville, John Wilkes. That no one but Burke
had it in him to be Junius was at one time the opinion
of Johnson, whose admiration for the literary quality
of the compositions did not prevent his crossing swords
with their reputed author, and severely denouncing him
in a pamphlet about the Falkland Islands in 1771.
So great a critic as Johnson should have seen that as a
writer Junius was as much below Burke as Wilkes was
below Junius. Mr. Abraham Hayward, quite unrivalled
for his knowledge about Holland House, its traditions,
its contents, and its personages at different periods, told
me in the last year of his life that the first Lord Holland,
who gave Francis his start in official life, had bequeathed
evidence of one kind or another which should satisfy
all sane persons as to the impossibility of Philip Francis
having been Junius, notwithstanding the agreement of
Lord Stanhope, Lord Macaulay, and Thomas De Quincey
that, if Francis did not write the *Junius Letters*, " there
is an end of all reasoning on circumstantial evidence."
From the first, the chief circumstances of his life had
prepared Philip Francis for the authorship of the letters.
After leaving the school kept at Dublin by his father,
the Rev. Philip Francis, who translated Horace and other
classical authors, he went to St. Paul's School in London ;
here he had for his class-fellow his future publisher,
Woodfall, and here, while still little more than a child,
invited on half-holidays to Holland House, he began
to make distinguished acquaintances which afterwards
proved of such use to his career. Thus it was that he
not only secured his first clerkship in the public service,
but became for a time private secretary to the great
Lord Chatham himself. This, rather than any training
or proficiency in academic subjects, formed the education
without which the *Junius Letters* could not have been
penned. These compositions attracted attention not
because of their literary form, but by reason of the social
and official assumptions that imparted to them colour and
tone. Here was a writer affecting to speak, not only
with authority, but with something like omniscience, on

the secret history of the moment, and on the highly placed individuals who made it. The first condition of success was to satisfy readers in a position to estimate the value of the information conveyed. No one recognised that necessity more keenly than did Woodfall, who, in relation to these writings, showed himself much more than a publisher—a tactful and far-seeing editor. Only, in effect said Woodfall, let Lord North and Mr. Burke stamp us with the mark of their notice, and the whole town in every quarter will insist upon reading what we write ; so that, however much against their will, other newspapers must reprint them from the *Public Advertiser*. These calculations were fulfilled in each minute particular. As a result, the greatest triumph which had so far fallen to the leader-writer's art was won. From the specimens of the knowledge actually given, and its verification by the passing incidents of the hour, the *Public Advertiser's* readers could appraise for themselves the opportunities commanded by the writer ; the man who guided such a pen must be, in the truest sense of the words, behind the scenes. His revelations not only gratified a legitimate curiosity, but were conveyed in such a manner as to leave an impression of strength and knowledge in reserve. However they had been obtained, the secrets of the prison house were now put into print with as much of accuracy as bitterness. Here was a daily commentator who, unlike his Grub Street brethren, had mastered his subject before he took up pen to treat it, and whose whole previous life therefore must have been in a sense a preparation for his present work. The writing itself was the very best journalese then procurable, and was marked by one or two features not less commendable than new. The periods of Junius, in their length and involution, were often after the Latin pattern. Occasionally, however, the effect was heightened by the judicious employment of the short sentence, and by adroit paragraph arrangements that at once pleased the eye and relieved the ear. Above all things, Junius succeeded in getting the public to take him at his own estimate of himself. In doing this, he not only showed that he had mastered the secret of the journalist's success as a commentator on the events of the time, but he encouraged all followers of his vocation to magnify their apostleship by a literary style whose tone of oracular assertion and narrative infallibility made it worthy of the editorial " we." Others had devoted their genius or knowledge to instructing the public. The first aim of Junius was to impress it ; and in this he made himself the model for the manufacturers of editorial comment in his own and in succeeding generations. The grand manner in the periodical press, or, as it has been irreverently called, the " big bow-wow " style, had been practised by a series of publicists, from Bolingbroke to Johnson. The method reached its climax of majesty and vigour in Philip Francis. The notoriety-hunting but essentially second-rate pen of John Wilkes, violent in words but miserably destitute of ideas, weak to childishness in reasoning, and polluted by the unsavoury associations of his character and life, had shown the journalist at his nadir in the *North Briton*. Wilkes's other venture, the *Middlesex Journal*, did little to retrieve the reputation, intellectual, moral, literary, or political, of its projector, and was relieved from something below mediocrity only by the occasional contributions of Thomas Chatterton, who deplored being handicapped by the circumstance that nothing but what was moderate or ministerial would go down with the public. The connection of Francis with the *Public Advertiser* came just in time intellectually to rehabilitate the newspaper commentator in the judgment of educated men. Before the eighteenth century had closed Burke, in a House of Commons speech, could call the newspaper system the Fourth Estate. This he could never have done—above all, he could never have cited instances that justified his phrase—but for the joint labours of the two former class-mates at St. Paul's School, Henry Sampson Woodfall and Philip Francis. And if, under the Hanoverian dynasty, Francis was the first to show the perfection to which the leader-writer's art might be brought, Woodfall deserves to be remembered as the earliest and not the least successful among those of whom Thomas Carlyle was afterwards to speak as " able editors."

CHAPTER V

THE WORK OF WILLIAM COBBETT

The man of the new age—William Cobbett's humble birth and scanty education—
From lawyer's clerk to private soldier—" Ruling the regiment " in Canada
—Return to England and discharge—Failure of his charges of malversation
against former officers causes sudden flight to America—Contemporary
politics in the States—Cobbett joins the fray—Birth of " Peter Porcupine "
—Finds America too hot for him—In England once more—The *Political
Register*—From Tory to Radical—Two years' imprisonment—The newspaper
man reaches the masses—A second flight to America—Cobbett's *English
Grammar*—Across the Atlantic with Tom Paine's bones—Reception at home
—The financial losses caused by the Six Acts and by an unsuccessful election
contest force Cobbett into bankruptcy—Renewed literary labours—Bottom of
the poll again—Reform violence—The rising tide—Cobbett, prosecuted
by the Whig Government, makes a clever defence and is discharged—The
Reform Act—On top at last—M.P. for Oldham—Closing years.

In each of the instances so far reviewed, the newspaper man only made himself a popular force after he
had begun by fixing the attention or exciting the alarm
of the governing classes. He never played to the gallery
till he had secured the boxes and the stalls. It was
with the Roman periods of Philip Francis as it had
been with the arresting and coercive Anglo-Saxon of
Jonathan Swift. The principle of patronage then permeated the entire polity of letters. In unconscious
deference to it, both men felt they must be approved
by Mæcenas and his circle before they could hope to
win or sway the plebs. Both also, by birth, culture,
and associations, belonged, like other writers of different
calibre and of various periods, to the well-to-do classes
whose support might be indifferent to the book-writer,
but was the very breath of life to the journalist. Thus
as regards his *Dictionary* Johnson did not set to work
before he had committed the complete plan to Lord

Chesterfield. His journalism, or the nearest approach to it with which he can be credited, was done during the period that his large acquaintance with what he called the middling classes, in the provinces as well as in London, had brought him into, and enabled him to maintain, the closest touch with the individuals and the families for whom his *Ramblers* and *Idlers* were primarily intended. A newspaper press thoroughly popularised and the patron of the old, stately sort could not indeed long exist together. Journalism organised itself into a potent and paying profession, with a tendency to flaunt its independence of the rich and great whom it had found essential to itself throughout the Stuart and even into the Hanoverian period. Daniel Defoe has been already described as the earliest newspaper man who, by the popularity of his topics, of his treatment, and by the universality of the interests to which he appealed, carried the entire country with him, gave the law to legislators, and made himself a personage at Courts. A generation after Defoe's death arose a man the meanness of whose beginnings, the force of whose genius, and the intractability of whose temper made him, as the idol of the mob, Defoe's first genuine successor, but prompted him also to use the newspaper in a spirit more bitter and subversive than was ever thought of by Defoe. The aristocracy must now be compelled to feel and confess the sovereignty of the people. Born in 1762 and living till 1835, William Cobbett owed nothing to the men who had written newspapers before his time, except, indeed, to Swift, whose *Tale of a Tub* had deeply impressed his boyhood, and gave him a distinct notion of strong, simple Anglo-Saxon prose. He was the grandson of one Surrey labourer and the son of another, sufficiently shrewd and successful to have improved his position into that of a small farmer and publican. William Cobbett was taught reading, writing, and arithmetic at home. That which afterwards brought him livelihood and fame, his knowledge of men and manners, was picked up in the course of wanderings guided entirely by his own will or whim. Aptly called by one of his biographers " the contentious man," [1] he

---

[1] Lord Dalling and Bulwer's *Historical Characters*, vol. ii. pp. 97 *et seq.*

had from his earliest years conceived for himself a mission which was to make his normal state one of often causeless war not only with all the conditions, social, moral, or political, of the time, but with most of the individuals whom, whether allies or enemies, he met in the course of his tempestuous march.   The faults of the man lay on the surface.   His combativeness was ever ready to blow itself into flame.   A ludicrous sense of his own importance was exaggerated to grotesqueness by the constantly growing conceit of the man who had been his own schoolmaster.   The imperfect sense of humour which generally accompanies an inordinate vanity betrayed him into countless blunders or ineptitudes.   In spite of all this, no one could have personified more instructively the most characteristic tendencies of the age of which he formed in so striking a degree the product. Cobbett was ten years old when the *Junius Letters*, on their cessation, left the press, in all political matters, a rival to Parliament.   But though members of both Houses detested in a general way the competing newspaper, the masses as yet had scarcely learned to see in it an agency for proclaiming their grievances or healing their wrongs.   For that the scrappiness and frivolity discrediting many journals of the period were largely to blame.   In country pot-houses like that which Cobbett's father had kept, and in market-town taprooms, the rumours and the scandals of the day deduced from paragraphs of news or comment helped to form and diffuse a public opinion about the failings and the incapacity of the official classes.   There thus sprang up among the working population a widely spread and deeply seated distrust of their rulers in Church and State, as in every branch, civil or military, of the public service. But since the great periodical writers of the seventeenth and eighteenth centuries so often mentioned already, the newspaper press had not produced any fresh leader whose genius or moral and intellectual weight made themselves felt through every section of the reading public.

The short time, less than a year, spent by the Surrey ploughboy in a lawyer's office quickened the suspicions ingrained into him by his early surroundings, added perhaps much of superficial sharpness.   It left him, however, with faculties as undisciplined and as entirely uninformed as

when, in 1783, at the age of twenty-one, he had run
away from Farnham, intending to go to sea, but, getting
no further than London, had kept himself alive by becoming office boy and copying clerk to a solicitor in Gray's
Inn. Something, no doubt, he learned during this period.
But the gnawing consciousness of capacity for better things
baffled by want of opportunity was developing in him
a discontent which embittered him against all more
fortunately situated than himself. His Surrey home was
hard by Sir William Temple's Moor Park, then over-
flowing with memories of Jonathan Swift. Hence
Cobbett's choice of the first book he ever bought, as
has been already mentioned, the *Tale of a Tub*, and
the consequent turn of his ambitions to pen and ink. His
enlistment in a regiment bound for Canada kept him
from starvation, gave him the chance of enlarging and
maturing his acquaintance with English grammar, composition, and, within certain limits, literature too ; it
also had the result of introducing him to the frugal,
honest, bustling body who made him an excellent wife.
He became corporal soon after joining the 54th. Two
years after reaching Canada he was raised to the rank of
sergeant-major. Military administration in all its departments was then scandalously incapable and corrupt.
During his term of service in Nova Scotia he found that
the adjutant, whose business it was to write the orders of
the day, scarcely knew how to handle a pen. As
sergeant-major Cobbett not only kept the regimental
accounts, but wrote the orders of the day for the illiterate
adjutant. There is no conceit like that of the half-
educated and entirely self-taught man ; with characteristic
complacency he observed he " practically ruled the
regiment." These distinctions, due, as he modestly
admits, less to any intellectual merit of his own than to
his habit of never losing a moment, may not have turned
his head. They added several dangerous cubits to his
mental stature when he measured his own mental endowments and acquisitions against those of the superiors
whom he calls the " epaulet gentry." In 1791-2 the
regiment's return to England gave him the opportunity
of obtaining his discharge, not without a strong testi-
monial as to character and usefulness from the major,
Lord Edward Fitzgerald. His retirement, however, did

not immediately sever his connection with the army. In 1792 he brought serious charges of malversation against his former commanding officers. There followed a court-martial whose venue, at Cobbett's request to the Prime Minister, Pitt, was transferred from Portsmouth to London. His nerve now failed him, or a survey of the facts, more calm and practical than he had yet given them, disclosed insuperable difficulties in establishing his case. At any rate, when his name was called upon to appear, he had put some portion of the English Channel between himself and the court. But he had descended on the French coast only to gather strength for a longer flight across the Atlantic.

Cobbett had come back from Canada with his regiment to England in 1791. He remained there about a year, during which he contrived to drink deep of the political and religious ideas of Tom Paine ; though sooner than he could have foreseen there was to come the complete and violent reaction from Tom Painism and Gallicanism, deepened by the conviction, growing out of his French experiences, that England must soon find herself at deadly war with her nearest continental neighbour. During the October of 1792, he disembarked at New York. A very short and superficial acquaintance with democratic institutions in the New World filled him with a furious loathing of democracy and all its works in general, of the French character in particular, and of all those writers or teachers who pandered to the democratic instinct, his chief indignation, scorn, and disgust being reserved for Priestley and his particular follower, the Dr. Price mentioned in Burke's *Reflections on the French Revolution*. Priestley, declared Cobbett, had wished England to follow the steps of revolutionary France. Well, those led to massacre, bankruptcy, and war. It therefore came to this. Priestley either foresaw the blood-stained catastrophe of the French upheaval which he wished England to imitate, or he did not foresee it. If he did foresee it, his counsel to his countrymen was that of a criminal ; if he did not foresee it, he had written himself down an idiot. In neither case could he possess the slightest claim to be called, as his partisans protested, the " friend of human happiness." Priestley himself appeared across the Atlantic two or three years after Cobbett had established

himself in New York. The literary products of the duel
between the two were read in England with amusement,
but with a very different feeling in the United States,
then divided into parties sharply opposed to each other
on the question of helping republican France against her
enemies in monarchical Europe. The New York
Federals, led by Jefferson, Madison (drawn by Cobbett
as a little bow-legged man, stiff, slender, and with a
sourness of countenance that might become disdain if
the features were not too skinny and scanty), and Monroe,
were anti-French, pro-English, and consequently backers
of Cobbett to a man. The Democrats, on the other
hand, unanimous in Priestley's favour, hating the Briton
even more than they loved the Gaul, were bent on brush-
ing Cobbett, as a noisome obstacle, out of Priestley's
way.

Such was the controversy, English in its issues, though
the battlefield lay beyond the ocean, which gave Cobbett
his first experience of polemical writing. His first essay
in pamphleteering was an answer to James Thompson
Callender's *Political Progress of Britain*, under the title
A Bone to Gnaw for the Democrats. This composition
might be described as a confused series of imaginative
episodes, argumentative allegories, and fancy visions of
William Penn, of the American secessionists from British
rule, of episodes in the life and after the death of
Louis XVI, uniting France and America in antagonism
to England. The American *Monthly Review* retaliated
with a counter-attack upon the Britishers of every variety.
This stung Cobbett into renewing the assault, and became
the occasion which gave him his best known pen-name.
A Kick for a Bite was his own title for the new indict-
ment, in preparing which he compared himself to
the porcupine which uses its quills as weapons of
defence against its adversaries. Henceforth Cobbett was
better known by his literary alias of Peter Porcupine
than by his own name. Under that *nom-de-guerre*,
he produced in 1795 a defence of the Federalists and of
the Anglo-American treaty, from a literary and argumentative point of view much ahead of anything that
he had so far written. Its success on both sides of the
Atlantic was immediate and lasting. All parties and
factions in each country agreed that the necessity of a

good understanding and of close commerce between the
two peoples had never been so convincingly and judiciously put. About this time, too, Cobbett was admitted
to have done his American hosts a good turn by reporting and publishing the debates in Congress, much after
the same fashion as he subsequently brought together
those records of the two Houses at Westminster which,
in the shape they are now known to everyone, constitute
the thirty-six volumes of our parliamentary history from
the year of the Norman conquest onward. During the
seven or eight years of his residence in the States,
Cobbett's incessant industry and far-reaching enterprise
largely identified his material interests with those of
the people among whom he lived. They did not prevent
his being always in hot water with his Yankee associates.
By 1796 a *Prospect from the Congress Gallery* had
proved a great success. Cobbett, to whom the idea seems
to have been due, fell out with his publisher Bradford.
The controversy that followed produced on both sides
pamphlets and articles remarkable, even in that age of
Billingsgate, not only for the ferocity but the foulness of
their language. This formed the last occasion on which
Cobbett or any other newspaper-writer distinguished himself by a vocabulary such as even Swift might have
rebuked for its coarseness. The truth is that periodical
writing, already to some degree purified by Addison,
from the end of the eighteenth or the beginning of the
nineteenth century showed itself amenable to the same
wholesome influences which, as has been pointed out
by Mr. Andrew Lang, between 1770 and 1800, had in
every kind of writing been making for decency. The
change of opinion about witchcraft, effected between 1680
and 1736, was not more complete than the transformation
of literary taste gradually but decisively effected during
the interval which separated the last letter of Junius in
1772 from the first delivery of Cobbett some twenty years
later. Thus, between 1760 and 1770, the reigning
novelists were Smollett and Sterne. The first decade and
a half of the nineteenth century saw Sterne and Smollett
replaced by Miss Edgeworth, Godwin, Miss Austen, Mrs.
Shelley, John Galt, and Sir Walter Scott. In the *Spectator*
Addison and Steele had both remonstrated against the
coarseness and lewdness, not of the stage only, but of

those popular romancists who took Mrs. Aphra Behn [1]
for their model. On his return to England in 1800
Cobbett recognised that newspaper-writers and the newspaper public generally had come under those better and
cleanlier influences which had already done so much
towards purging the popular drama and the fashionable
novel. Meanwhile his exploits with pen and ink across
the Atlantic had brought him into wide notoriety at
home. Every stage in his long exchange of stink-pots
with Bradford had been followed by the English public.
From these purely personal encounters of the pen had
arisen literary battles not the less fierce because their
issues were of national importance. To disgust Americans
of every class with the French Revolution in all its
aspects was the task which Cobbett had set himself,
and which, to some degree, he accomplished (February,
1796) in the *Bloody Buoy, thrown out as a warning to
the political pilots of the United States*. Under this
title, Cobbett brought together the atrocities committed
by the French Revolutionists, especially by the infamous
gangs acting under Carrier. Nothing that ever appeared
in print did more towards withdrawing any popular
remnant of English democratic sympathy from the French
Terrorists, or towards converting Anglo-Saxon tolerance
for outrages into active detestation both of the men
who committed them and of the national conditions under
which they were possible.

At this time Cobbett was eking out a livelihood in
Philadelphia by teaching the English language to refugees
from France. His pupils included Talleyrand, the diplomatist, who now passed for a merchant, who had nothing
but compliments for his teacher's abilities and accomplishments. Where could he have acquired such various,
accurate learning? Had Oxford, Cambridge, or, as a
Frenchman he naturally hoped, Paris University the
honour of having been his *alma mater*? Cobbett was
not to be caught by this kind of chaff ; he soon discovered that his new pupil was as well acquainted with
English as was his teacher. The suspicions thus aroused
were exchanged for certainty when Talleyrand insisted

---

[1] *A propos* of this writer, how many recall to-day that she anticipated
Mrs. Beecher Stowe in making a negro the hero of a story?

on paying him twenty guineas instead of the six dollars
that were his usual charge. The French Judas, as
Cobbett called him, while playing the spy on Cobbett's
desk and house, wanted to bribe him into writing against
the French no more of the pamphlets or articles with
the noise of which two continents were ringing. The
anti-Gallican pamphleteering went on, however, just the
same ; and the *Bloody Buoy* already referred to appeared
after the diplomatist's attempt to buy the journalist.
By this time the American bitterness against the renegade
from Tom Painism was expressing itself in weekly dis-
plays of literary or pictorial abuse.   The democratic
Aurora, instigated by his former friend and colleague
Bradford, described him as " so inured while in the army
to the cat-o'-nine-tails that horse-whipping could have
no terrors for him."   At the same time a caricature represented Cobbett trampling on Tom Paine and the *Rights
of Man*, and then as destroying a statue of Liberty to
receive a bag of gold from Satan. " We like," chucklingly
remarked Cobbett, " to hear the lion roar, for then we
know he is hurt."   Vilification of this sort was exactly
what he wanted, and advertised his writing as nothing
else could.   Since the Yankees took fire at his very
name, Tom Paine was evidently Cobbett's best card to
play.   Encouraged by the foul epithets thrown at him,
Cobbett in a new sheet, *The Censor*, contrasted Paine's
recent abuse of George Washington with the fulsome
flatteries of him formerly contained in the *Rights of Man*.
" Now," he wrote, directly addressing Paine, " atrocious,
infamous miscreant, I would call on you to blush, but
the rust of villainy has eaten your cheek to the bone."
All these flowers of rhetoric may be found in *Peter
Porcupine's Memoirs*, collected from the most notorious
of Cobbett's journalistic ventures in the States, the
Porcupine.   It was not only his attacks upon republic-
anism which set the New Yorkers against him.   They
soon resented, or professed to resent, quite as deeply
the language in which these attacks were made.   Transatlantic puritanism now affected the polish of a hyper-
sensitive politeness in all phraseological matters, and
was, indeed, already not far from the point since reached
at which Americans " retire " instead of " go to bed,"
and veil their furniture with frilled coverings to con-

ceal the indelicacy of legs. Ignored on reaching the American capital as an obscure stranger, Cobbett had no sooner attracted notice by his combative pen than his controversial methods and style gave offence to every class of the United States public. The nineteenth century brought with it an incident destined to have the effect of restoring Cobbett to his native side of the ocean whose breadth had for eight years separated him from Europe. Returned to London, he found not only much interest in his American experiences, and appreciation for his dogged tenacity, but a disposition, beyond anything he could have expected, to lend him material assistance in his newspaper enterprises. The five thousand dollars in which Cobbett had been cast for the libel suit brought against him by the American Dr. Rush had exhausted his resources as well as made New York too hot to hold him. Yet very shortly after his reappearance in Fleet Street he was placed in funds that enabled him to start a second *Porcupine* in the Tory interest. He soon discovered the Tories to be as bad as the Whigs. In 1802 the *Porcupine* was succeeded by the weekly *Political Register*. In this, the most famous of all his papers, he began and continued by impartially attacking public men all round ; he ended by creating an irresistible impulse for parliamentary reform. The Tories, under Addington, were in office. An Irish judge named Johnson had a grievance ; Cobbett encouraged him to ventilate it in his paper. The result was the infliction of a heavy fine both on the editor and the writer. That determined Cobbett to become a Radical. He soon found an occasion for dealing Toryism a heavy blow. Ever since his discharge from the 54th Regiment he had maintained his interest in army matters, and especially in all that concerned the condition of the private soldier. During his stay in the States his writings about the hardships endured by the rank and file at the hands of their officers had exposed him to the charge of inculcating seditious ideas. In the *Political Register's* earliest days a mutiny had actually occurred ; German soldiers had been called in to put it down first, and afterwards to administer the punishment of flogging to the ringleaders. The *Register* of course now came out with a furious attack on the War Office for sanctioning a foreign outrage on the bodies of

English soldiers. Castlereagh, then Secretary for War and the Colonies, was promoting the supply of regular soldiers by volunteering from the militia as well as by recruiting. Let all whom it concerned remember that those who needed fresh men to bear arms were holding out these hundreds of lashes as an inducement for volunteers to come forward. Cobbett's observations on this occurrence were in the same vein of irony as Defoe's *Shortest Way with the Dissenters*, or Swift's *Argument to prove the Inconvenience of abolishing Christianity*. " Ay," he exclaimed, " flog them ! flog them ! Lash them daily, lash them duly ! The German soldiers will make them take a flogging as quietly as so many trunks of trees." The Government felt itself placed on its honour to prosecute Cobbett. He was sentenced to a fine of £1,000 and to two years' imprisonment. Cobbett not only found himself a martyr and an idol when he had served his sentence ; he was received by the authorities at Newgate with something of the deference due to a prisoner of state. Some jurors, who had not themselves tried Cobbett, but who visited Newgate while he was a prisoner, entered his cell with a courtier's bows ; having asked whether he had anything to complain of, they were told " nothing but the being here." [1]   The dignified and even amiable composure displayed by Cobbett during this confinement shows him in a new and pleasant light. From his cell he conducted his paper, managed eighty-seven acres of land which he had bought near Botley, Hampshire, in 1808, and superintended with tenderness and wisdom the education of his children. Four years after his release in 1812, he introduced into his *Political Register* changes that brought it regularly into every cottage and hovel of urban and rural England. The journalism which he thus personified addressed itself, not to the sufficiently fed and dressed, but to those in whose ill-built, ill-drained dwellings sickness and want were guests all the year round. The notoriety and success of his paper were helped by other agencies than his own pen, now felt everywhere as a national force, or even the scandals with which the *Political Register* had become associated. Cobbett possessed far-seeing business shrewd-

[1] Crabbe Robinson's *Diary*, vol. i. p. 224.

ness as well as a pen that compelled attention. There already existed, he saw, and there would daily multiply, a public which, reached by low prices and held by effective writing, must make the cheapest newspaper pay best. Hitherto he had charged a shilling and a halfpenny for each number of the *Political Register*. On November 2, 1816, he brought it out at twopence with, for its chief feature, an address to the journeymen and labourers of England, Scotland, and Ireland. The paper now not only spread itself like wildfire into every workshop and college of the English reading world ; it was read, re-read, and stamped itself more vividly on the mind than any newly printed matter then known. Peasant subscribers filed it for study and reference. Village Hampdens declaimed at the ale-house its arguments and catchwords. Other journalists, from and before Swift or Defoe to Junius, had reckoned their readers by thousands, and thrown down challenges which neither the Court nor the Cabinet could ignore ; these, as has been already pointed out, addressed the multitude through the governing classes. To Cobbett belongs the distinction of appealing directly to the voteless and voiceless masses. By the application of a weekly irritant in his paper, he organised their refusal longer to remain the passive outlaws of the constitution. Sir Robert Peel was described by Disraeli as playing on the House of Commons as if it were an old fiddle. Cobbett had so thoroughly mastered all the tastes and humours of his public as to ensure his shots never going wide or falling short of the mark. And he achieved a twofold triumph, first by strengthening and sustaining the popular cry for reform, secondly by applying to the Whigs the goad of a compulsion without which they would have indefinitely postponed it. Otherwise than in coin of the realm, not only Cobbett but his readers were to pay for this success. Strongly worded newspaper articles would lead to as little practical good as monster parliamentary petitions unless the rulers of the State were made to understand that there were force and violence in the background ready for use. Cobbett had scarcely made this clear when Reform riots raged throughout the land, but it was the threat of suspending Habeas Corpus which caused Cobbett openly to advocate an appeal to brute strength.

The weekly *Register* made itself the organ of all those ready to rise against the Government ; it further found them a ringleader in a man named Brandreth ; he, with two others, was proceeded against for " levying war against the King." At the trial his counsel, Cross, declared his client's crime to be due entirely to the *Register*, " the most mischievous publication ever put into the hands of man." Nothing could ever counteract the *Address to the Journeymen and Labourers* in the first number of the cheap series. Cobbett's choice, in his own words, now lay between silence and retreat. To stay in England meant the dungeon, with deprivation of pen and ink. Freedom to write and usefulness to his generation could only be secured by another sojourn in America. While preparing for his second flight across the Atlantic, Cobbett, according to his account, was approached by an emissary from the Prime Minister, Lord Liverpool ; would he take £10,000 as compensation for losses he had sustained from prosecution, and with that sum retire to his farm at Botley, then, by-the-by, mortgaged for £16,000.[1] Supposing the offer to have been made, it would have been almost useless to Cobbett, who, in addition to the mortgage, was liable to arrest for £20,000 of other debts. By the middle of May, 1817, Cobbett therefore found himself once more in America, this time with his two sons, and able uninterruptedly to resume his *Political Register*. His satisfaction on this score must have been heightened by the fury of his enemies. These used Robert Southey's pen in the *Quarterly Review* to denounce the Tory Ministers for letting so incorrigible a miscreant slip through their fingers. At least, said Southey, on some plea or other Cobbett's departure should have been delayed so that he should have lost the boat at Liverpool. Then he would have been sent back to London with the loss of liberty for the rest of his life ; whereas all that he had now forfeited was his wardrobe and library, together with anything else not compressible into the single trunk which formed his luggage. His former sojourn in New York had shown

---

[1] For these figures, as for many other details in this chapter, I am indebted to Mr. E. J. Carlyle's *Cobbett* (p. 201), a book admirable for its accuracy and freshness.

him injustice and oppression as the inevitable outcome
of democracy. Now (1817) he exhausted the vocabulary
of grateful praise at being domiciled in the land of
freedom, fair play, peace, and plenty. To have stayed
in England would have meant to have ended his days in
a filthy Newgate cell, hearing no other voice than that of
churlish jailors, terrifying their victims with curses and
blasphemies when they could not deal them blows and
kicks. As it was, he had safely reached a smiling land
of plenty, where content and happiness beamed forth from
every countenance ; where was abundance to eat and
drink for all, where the tax-gatherer's hangdog face
was unknown, where no long-sworded and whiskered
captains escorted from town to town judges who could
only sit under guards of dragoons ; above all, where there
were no Castlereaghs, no Cannings, no Liverpools, and
none of that variety of pawnbrokers who swaggered about
as bankers. Cobbett's American impressions gathered
in 1792 had been as little complimentary as could be
given by any earthly inferno. The English experiences
which sent him a second time across the Atlantic in
1817 showed him a new world which was, by comparison
with the old, a social and political paradise. Yet at
the earlier date the visitor's vanity had been gratified
after a fashion altogether denied him upon the later.
Neither the fearless obstinacy with which he had con-
fronted State prosecutions in England, nor his panegyric
on the polity of the Stars and Stripes served to arouse
for him among his hosts any feeling stronger than
curiosity. His wounded vanity expressed itself in some
disparaging remarks on the guests who occasionally pene-
trated his seclusion beneath an obscure tavern roof on
Long Island or on his farm at North Hampstead. This
second sojourn, however, in the New World was marked
by much literary activity, and bore fruit in books once
as widely circulated and as long remembered as any of
his political pieces, or even as his *Rural Rides*. Samuel
Johnson's *Dictionary* contained few definitions more
humorously expressive of his views than were some of the
instances and examples provided by Cobbett for his
English Grammar. Johnson's conversational identification of the devil with the first Whig had no place in the
great work ; this, however, actually does contain such

terminological explanations as : *Tory* ; one who adheres to the ancient constitution of the State and the apostolic hierarchy of the Church of England. *Whig* ; the name of a faction. *Pension* ; an allowance made to anyone without equivalent, and in England generally understood to mean pay given to a State hireling for treason against his country. *Pensioner* ; a slave of State, hired by a stipend to obey his master. *Oats* ; a grain in England generally given to horses, but in Scotland the support of the people. *Excise* ; a hateful tax levied upon commodities, adjudged not by the common judges of property but by *wretches* hired by those to whom the excise is paid. *Grub Street* ; the name of a London street much inhabited by writers of small histories, dictionaries, and temporary poems, whence any mean production is called Grub Street. *Lexicographer* ; a writer of dictionaries, a harmless drudge. Cobbett's specimens of verbal exposition in his *English Grammar* might have been suggested by Johnson in his lighter vein ; such are the nouns of multitude, House of Commons, den of thieves. Borough tyrants, gangs of men more cruel than fiends and more ignorant than brutes. Participles : a working man is more worthy than a titled blunderer who lives in idleness. The *English Grammar*, however, includes much that is really sensible and useful, and shows the thoroughness with which, as a preliminary to composition, Cobbett had studied the rudiments, genius, and idiom of his native tongue. Here the creator of Radical journalism showed himself almost as strong a Tory as Johnson. Thus he is bitter against the romanesque relative " who " or " which " for " that." Cobbett also showed something of his own obstinacy or wrongheadedness in absolutely denouncing a common use of the expression " than whom," condemning as downright ungrammatical such expressions as : " The Duke of Argyle, than whom no man was more hearty in the cause " ; " Cromwell, than whom no man was better skilled in artifice." In each case, exclaims Cobbett, it should be " who," for it is nominative and not objective, and is, indeed, abbreviated for " no man, etc., was better skilled than he was." Milton, continues Cobbett, may have made the blunder classical in his " Beelzebub, than whom, Satan except, none higher sat."

But real responsibility for it as a colloquial form rests with our Parliament house ; its prevalence there is quite enough to make it presumptively incorrect.   Cobbett would have been on safer ground had he censured the gratuitous conjunction introduced before the relative. Thus, " A pretty Government to depend on, *and which* our stupid press is lauding to the skies."   Also a similar solecism more prevalent, perhaps, since Cobbett's time than during it, and reaching its height in the Disraelian disregard of the relative's full force : "——, not experienced in feminine society, *and who* found a little difficulty in sustaining conversation."   Self-taught men have often a weakness for fine words that they do not understand.   Not so Cobbett, who protests against ten shillings *per* bushel, instead of *a* bushel, because *per* is not English, and is to most people a mystical sort of word.   Criticism of this kind may seem carping.   But as the journalist who first directly addressed or profoundly influenced the masses, and who, whatever his more or less mercenary tergiversations, was perhaps the shrewdest man of his day, Cobbett formulated some sound advice to newspaper men in his instructions to his nephew.   "Sit down," he said, " to write what you have thought, and not to think what you shall write.   Write unhesitatingly, taking the words as they come, not pausing for choice of words.   To secure a good style, beware of self-con- sciousness, which is always the cause of mannerism and involution."   It was during his second stay in America that, on the eve of his departure home, Cobbett dis- interred Tom Paine's remains from their unconsecrated grave and brought them, together with his scanty luggage, across the Atlantic.   Byron's familiar epigram (January, 1820) is at once so profane and so pointless that its quotation may be left to Cobbett's full-length biographers.   The year after Cobbett's death, the auctioneer refused to include the bones in the effects offered for sale. Mr. Carlyle, who shares with Mr. Smith the honour of succeeding Huish and Sir Henry Bulwer as Cobbett's biographer, has succeeded in bringing down the story of these relics only to the year 1844.   On his release from prison in 1812, the chair at a dinner to Cobbett had been taken by Sir Francis Burdett.   For some time the wealthy Radical M.P. and the needy conductor of the *Register* continued to be cordial fellow-labourers in the cause of parliamentary reform. Cobbett's money obligations to Burdett, and a difference as to whether a sum of £2,000 had been a gift or a loan, produced the coolness that might have been expected. On Cobbett's reappearance (1819) Burdett cold-shouldered him, and would have nothing to do with another banquet. The feast of welcome was therefore presided over by Orator Hunt, whom Cobbett now supported in his candidature for Westminster against Burdett. Cobbett could show himself imperious as well as quarrelsome. The philosophic Radicalism of the men who made the *Westminster Review* was above his head ; he resented even the appearance of its acceptance with Burdett without himself having been consulted on the subject. Meanwhile Cobbett's personal finances were in as ill a state as his journalistic fortunes. In 1820 came the reactionary Six Acts. One of these measures was declared not without some excuse by Cobbett to be the weapon which Castlereagh had specially forged against the *Register*. Cobbett, in 1816, had been able, as has been seen, to secure for his *Register* a circulation as yet unheard of, and to make it a valuable property because of its exemption from the tax to which larger publications of the kind were subject. His circulation at the cost of twopence gave him, he calculated, a penny profit on every copy sold.[1] The repressive Tory measure of 1819-20 provided a rearrangement of the newspaper stamp duties which compelled Cobbett to choose between giving up his paper altogether or selling at a price prohibitive of a wide sale. From twopence he had to raise the price to sixpence. The newspaper duty and the cost of producing every copy left Cobbett without any margin of profit on his paper. Even could Cobbett have produced his paper for nothing, one of the Six Acts prohibited all periodicals, not being monthly publications, from appearing at a less price than sixpence. His choice therefore lay between turning the *Register* into a monthly magazine or charging sixpence for it as a weekly sheet. The war levied by the law against the newspaper men of Cobbett's time went further even

[1] Carlyle's *Cobbett*, p. 215.

than this. The Six Acts further required all newspaper publishers to give security in advance for any fines incurred by blasphemous or seditious utterances. That provision placed a fresh and severe strain on the resources not only of Cobbett, but of all other Radical journalists of the time, especially William Hone and the Hunts, of whom more will be said presently.

Neither Cobbett nor his comrades of the press had many friends in Parliament. Tierney, who advocated Cobbett's prosecution in 1810, denounced indeed, ten years later, the journalistic clauses as well as the other portions of the Six Acts. It was not the prospect of any cordial welcome at St. Stephens that had turned Cobbett's thoughts in that direction, but the spirit of the notoriety-hunter militant. The dissolution following the death of George III. in 1820 brought him forward as parliamentary candidate for Coventry. Some of the money necessary for that purpose could come from the Reform Fund which he had helped to start. Further sums were to be raised by an appeal for modest help to seventy gentlemen of fortune. He came out of the contest at the bottom of the poll, and narrowly escaped death from the violence of the mob. His sturdy defence of himself was only reinforced by one of his supporters in time enough to prevent his butchery near the polling booth. Cobbett's failure on this occasion was attributed by him to the immense sums his opponents spent in bribery, and to his own lack of means and inclination to follow their example. His account of the whole business in the *Political Register* is a mixture of abuse and incoherence showing but too clearly his disgust and mortification at this new discomfiture. Nor does he seem to have escaped any of the personal insults and indignities incidental to the election fights of that period. The landlord of the Bull Head, the inn outside Coventry at which Cobbett stayed, was threatened with the loss of his licence unless he instantly expelled the Radical candidate from his house. Radical voters were terrorised from going to the poll. Eventually the two seats were won by " Bear " Ellice and Peter Moore, an Indian nabob, the last of these defeating Cobbett by more than a thousand votes. This ill-starred contest completed Cobbett's ruin. He was sold up for the benefit of his creditors, some

of whom, like Sir Francis Burdett, refused to press their
claims upon him. One further blow Cobbett had provoked from destiny. Wright, from the first his business
manager and now his open adversary, brought against
him a libel action in which Cobbett cut a very sorry
figure indeed. And now, hunted from pillar to post,
Cobbett could not pay the paper-makers and printers for
bringing out his next *Political Register*. Even from
this desperate strait he found deliverance through the
good offices of a Southampton friend, George Rogers.
This gentleman had helped him before ; he now came
forward in time to save the *Register's* life. Neither
reverses, miscarriages, nor persecutions, not the loss of
friends and the successive failures, actual or threatened,
of his undertakings ; not gods and men leagued together
against him could turn Cobbett from the path he had
marked out for himself, or could extort from him the con-
fession of defeat at any single point. Penniless, friend-
less, worn in health, exhausted in spirits, he settled down
in 1821 to the cultivation of a small piece of ground
he had acquired in Kensington, varied by literary work
as severe and as unbroken as if the day of misfortune
had not dawned upon him. " They now," he told the
electors of Westminster, " boast of having sunk me in
good earnest. But in truth this is merely shipping a
sea. Like every other sinking I have experienced, it
will be at last a mounting." Certainly, the *Register*
never displayed more freshness, vigour, and variety than
when (January, 1821), in a cheap Brompton lodging,
family life with their children was begun again by Cobbett
and his wife with a total capital of three shillings for
the new start. His exemplary wife's cheering constancy
to her husband in his darkest hours is indeed the golden
thread traversing and often beautifying the succession of
tempestuous vicissitudes that constitute his strange career.

As an illustration of the tenses, Cobbett in the *English
Grammar* had written about the fourth George's unhappy
consort : " Queen Caroline defies the tyrants, has defied
them, and will defy them." In the *Political Register* he
now invented a letter from the Queen to her husband.
About the same time, by way of investing his paper
with more novelties, he put his attacks on Canning in a
dramatic setting. A coarse woodcut above the letter-

press showed in the background a haggard and famished multitude. "What complaint have you, Mr. Canning," asked the judge, "against these poor, worn, pale, ragged men, with padlocks on their mouths and thumb-screws on their hands?" "Can it be," was Canning's reply in accents of tremulous horror, "that you do not know these are Radicals, men, that is, who wish to destroy the throne, the peerage, with all property, and to obliterate morals and religion from the human heart?" "Where are your proofs?" inquired the judge. "Oh, they are too cunning to let me have any." "Then, sir," was the judicial reply, "it really means that Englishmen may not enter a room to hear speeches or lectures on government and political economy without offending against the laws." This, however, scarcely proved of flavour strong enough for the *Register's* readers. A fresh sensation suggested itself in an attack on the clergy. And here, without the compensation of any literary effect, Cobbett is betrayed into fallacies that the slightest exercise of the logical faculty would have enabled the most shallow free-thinker of the time to avoid. The Bishop of London was charged with saying that the French Revolution had been caused by the clergy knowing less about books than their people. Hence, the Bishop argued, a nation's spiritual teachers ought not only to have received the education of scholars but should be furnished with libraries, housed beneath comfortable roofs, and stately rooms equipped with every appliance for literary study. How, asked Cobbett, did this agree with the doctrines of Christianity, or with its Founder's example and words? Did He choose for His apostles men of great estates, with a retinue of indoor servants and their manor houses, and outside a regiment of gamekeepers? Or did he insinuate that for its success His word must be taught by men dressed in lawn, lolling in coaches drawn by six horses? Cobbett was of course far too clever not to know what pitiful clap-trap all this logical trash was. Cobbett does not seem to have tarred himself with the brush of Paine's infidelity. By way now of vindicating his orthodoxy, he published *Cobbett's Monthly Sermons*. These were among the most respectable as well as most successful things he ever did. The subject matter showed good taste, good temper, and freedom from offensive personal reference in its handling. The style had earnestness, dignity, and restraint. Sometimes, of course, he let himself go. Still smarting from the wounds inflicted by Castlereagh and the Six Acts, in *Naboth's Vineyard*, a discourse on the Carlile and Hone prosecutions, Cobbett returns to his old and most denunciatory form. Nothing, however, could be more wholesome and helpful than the hints in his *Cottage Economy*, written about the same time, for improving the homes and everyday life of the working classes. Among other suggestions till then undreamt of, this work anticipated several features in the programme of Young England's peasantry reform promulgated a quarter of a century later. In the specification of a porch, an oven, and a tank as indispensable for every home, Cobbett almost verbally anticipated Disraeli's most constant and characteristic recommendation. While Cobbett was still bringing out his *Register* in his Brompton lodging, Castlereagh, tortured to death by foul calumnies, committed suicide at Foot's Cray. In a congratulatory letter to his friend Joseph Swann, then imprisoned at Chester for complicity in the Reform agitations, "How base," remarked Cobbett, "not to exult at the suicide, since his life meant a mass of pauperism hitherto unknown, and the enrichment of his own family out of the people's labour." Cobbett's exultation over the tragic incident may not have been in the best taste. His words about the occasion are, however, high bred refinement itself in comparison with Byron's references to the subject both in *Don Juan* and especially in his Castlereagh *Epitaph*. At last the pressure exercised by Cobbett and one or two other newspaper men had made the Whigs pledge themselves to parliamentary reform. Cobbett's view of the situation, and of the agencies which could alone rouse Whiggism from its lethargy, had been justified at every step. In 1828 began the Duke of Wellington's Administration, which lasted till the formation of Lord Grey's Reform Cabinet. During most of that time there seemed no possibility of an enfranchising measure soon being introduced. Lord Althorp declared the English people had become perfectly indifferent to the question, and that he had no intention of moving in it again.[1]

[1] *Mirror of Parliament*, 1832.

Francis Place, the Charing Cross tailor, co-operated with Cobbett to keep Reform alive. But for these, it might have died out before the days of July (1830) in Paris made it a practical and pressing question in England. Throughout their dealings with and treatment of the Whigs, Cobbett and his allies did but practically illustrate the Tory as well as the Radical belief that Whiggism never moved without the application of the Radical goad. Having now impartially abused all politicians, leaders and followers alike, Cobbett turned to the clergy. The fire that he had reserved for them was contained in a *History of the Protestant Reformation* (1824-5). This work merely puts into homely language the attacks on the Reformation made by the popish historian Lingard. It never passed for more than a literary curiosity and is deprived of any value by its confusions and mistakes.[1] Cobbett's presentation of English ecclesiastical history seems to have been conceived purely in the spirit of mischief. It was a congenial task to describe the pretences on which the Reformation was effected as " base, hypocritical, and bloody " ; he had, however, no wish to see the work undone. With the passionate conviction of profound ignorance, he declared the Anglican clergy of various ranks personified the most malignant influences of the time. Yet, Protestantism being here, his mission began and ended with an exposure of the odious way in which it had come, but against the monarchy as the cause of Protestantism or as an institution he had little or nothing to say. Still he needed some new object of attack and, if he spared the Crown, what was there for him but the Church?

It was Cobbett's way never to recognise accomplished facts if they told against him. In 1825 nothing could have been more undoubted and complete than the wreck of his worldly fortunes. Yet this was the moment he chose, on the strength of Sir Thomas Beevor's support, for opposing at Preston the future fourteenth Earl of Derby, the " Rupert of Debate." All that he got by this was to send up the price of votes at Preston to a figure which caused the successful candidate, the future Lord Derby, an outlay of £15,000. It was only after a

---

[1] For instances of these see Carlyle's *Cobbett*, p. 243.

parliamentary quest of seven years that Cobbett found a
seat at Oldham. At one among the public meetings
which he attended during this time, a characteristic
glimpse of him was caught by Heine, then visiting
England. To Heine Cobbett personified the " spirit of
impetuous and undistinguishing revolt against political
institutions." Once only did the German poet see the
English agitator, at an uproarious " Crown and Anchor "
dinner, with his scolding red face, his Radical laugh,
in which venom of hate mingles with exultation at his
enemies' approaching fall. " He is," continued Heine,
" a chained house-dog, who falls with equal fury on every
one he does not know, and often bites in their calves
the best friends of the dwelling. Because of this incessant
and indiscriminate barking, the illustrious thieves who
plunder England think it no good to throw the growling
Cobbett a bone to stop his mouth. At this time Cobbett's
pen was for the most part innocently employed on the
purely social subjects of domestic economy in his paper.
His speeches, however, were political, and grew increasingly violent and provocative. The whole country seethed
with disturbance and discontent. Pillage, rick-burning,
and machine-breaking expressed the popular indignation
at the delay with parliamentary reform. The root of
the mischief was seen in Cobbett's monthly serial, on
Gifford's hint, called *Tuppenny Trash*. A Sussex
labourer, tried for rick-burning, alleged in defence that
he had been instigated to the crime by Cobbett's
writings. In July, 1831, Cobbett, once more prosecuted
for incitement to violence, made the conduct of his own
defence an occasion for denouncing the Whig Government.
That, he said, had done more to harass free speech in
seven months than the Tories had done in as many years.
His management of his case was also noticeable for the
adroitness with which he proved from Brougham's own
admission in the witness-box that the highest law officer
of the Crown, the Chancellor himself, even after the
incriminating articles had appeared and the prosecution
was decided on, in a friendly letter to Cobbett's son,
asked to see his father's latest writings. Brougham's
evidence was accompanied by like testimony and general
certificates of good character from Lord Melbourne, then
Home Secretary, and the then Earl of Radnor, Dr. Pusey's

cousin or uncle, who, as Lord Folkestone and a Liberal
member of Parliament, had been in personal touch with
Cobbett. Denman, the prosecuting counsel, amazed by
the appearance of all these great men in the witness-box,
felt no doubt of Cobbett's being acquitted without the
jurors leaving the court. "The truth is," perorated
Cobbett, "the Whigs are the Rehoboams of England,
scourging with scorpions where the Tories chastised with
whips." As it was, the dramatic surprises which Cobbett
prepared for the court had the effect of preventing the
jury, after being locked up for fifteen hours, from agreeing on a verdict. Cobbett was therefore released. The
whole episode marks an era in newspaper history because
it was the last instance of the State prosecuting a newspaper man for political offences like those alleged against
Cobbett.[1] His opponents had now so completely played
his own game that Cobbett might have had almost any
constituency created by the 1832 Reform Bill that he
wished. So confident, not without reason, of this was
Cobbett himself as to challenge contradiction when saying
that, if the Whigs wished to keep him out of Parliament,
they must carry a Bill against him through both Houses.
He chose Oldham rather than Manchester out of the two
seats definitely offered him because its smaller dimensions
rendered his return less troublesome and more sure. His
hatred of the Whigs had not prevented his supporting
through all its stages the Grey Reform Bill. Appropriately enough, therefore, he took his seat in the first
Parliament which the measure had created. Before a
session elapsed he had discovered that physical strength
and courage were more necessary for an M.P. than for a
soldier. Then, of course, came the inevitable grievance :
"Fancy," he growled, "only fifteen inches of space
allowed to each man." A manner quiet, deferential, and
even subdued, did not prevent his maiden utterance being
a failure. The debate on the Speech from the Throne
gave him the chance of moving the rejection of the
Address, with the result that he was beaten by a majority
of three hundred. A little later, in a thoroughly
characteristic spirit, he attacked Sir Robert Peel, on the

[1] The proceedings against some earlier partners in newspaper enterprise, the
brothers Hunt, had taken place in 1812. They were not mixed up with charges
of political agitation, and were, indeed, only libel actions.

pretext, indeed, that Peel, by re-establishing the gold standard in 1819, had made himself unfit to remain a Privy Councillor, but really for no other reason than Cobbett's own disgust at Peel's extraordinary popularity in his High Tory and Protectionist days. " Wordy and absurd " was Mr. Gladstone's description of this onslaught ;[1] its faults did not, however, prevent Peel's discomposure from throwing him into a perspiration which caused his shirt collar to be soaked and lie down flat upon his neckcloth. In the period of Cobbett's entering it, the popular Chamber was, or had recently been, scarcely less aristocratic in its composition and social prejudices than the hereditary House of our own time. Fairness was, however, then, as always, one of its characteristics. It could not welcome Cobbett, but saw in him a clever and representative new member entitled to be heard, and listened to him accordingly. The elderly, red-faced gentleman, in dust-coloured coat and drab breeches with gaiters, for some time excited only curiosity. By degrees he made himself a really good debater and, avoiding the sallies of vehement vituperation which at times marked his writings, had no difficulty, whenever he wished it, in catching the Speaker's eye.

Thomas Carlyle's essay on Sir Walter Scott has a passage about the eighteenth-century reaction from Wertherism, Byronism, and other sentimentalism, tearful or spasmodic, fruit of internal wind, in which British literature long lay sprawling. Of that healthier movement he takes for one of its instances Cobbett, the pattern John Bull of his century, strong as a rhinoceros, a most brave phenomenon, with singular humanities and genialities shining through his thick skin. This, in rather different words, is very much Heine's estimate of the man. Cobbett himself confessed to never having been of what he called an accommodating nature. The most skilful, perhaps, among his monographers, Henry Bulwer, eventually Lord Dalling, conveys the same fact when he treats him as " the contentious man " ; while Heine, in his reminiscence of the " Crown and Anchor " dinner already quoted, bears testimony to the same effect when seeing in him a man not to be liked but to be admired.

[1] Morley's *Life of Gladstone*, vol. i. p. 114.

Intellectual tastes and capacities above his station in life constituted the grievance with which Cobbett was born, of which, while a child, he became morbidly conscious, and the discouragement of which, by an untoward destiny, embittered him against all who, rightly or wrongly, were more fortunate than himself. At the age of eleven he went supperless to rest by a haystack in Kew Gardens that he might buy Swift's *Tale of a Tub*. Such was the literature which produced in him what he called a sort of birth of intellect. The revolt of the North American colonies woke in him the partisan of freedom and justice. By an untrained and untaught enthusiast these creditable sympathies were of course often extravagantly and coarsely expressed. That in no way detracts from, but rather renders more admirable and conspicuous, his success in making his native Anglo-Saxon the effective medium of strong, clear thought, clothed in words that still give Cobbett a place among the masters of English prose. His argumentative and controversial manner suited the audience to which it was addressed, but in literary quality falls far below the descriptive passages of the *Rural Rides* and the *Porcupine Letters*. For freshness, for felicity of touch, condensed suggestiveness of phrase, truth and originality of local colour, Cobbett's nature sketches stood quite by themselves in English literature till the appearance in 1878 of the *Gamekeeper at Home*, by Richard Jefferies. This was a man whose earliest experiences were much those of Cobbett, and who, while absolutely without any of his special views and characteristics in life or thought, resembled Cobbett in having perfected his knack of literary expression, not by literary study, but by feeding and training in the open air a genius for accurately observing the daily and nightly succession of rural nature's sights and sounds. Since the day of Cobbett, even of Jefferies, the agricultural labourers and journeymen, specially addressed by Cobbett in the first number of his *Register* sold at twopence, have wanted neither political champions under signatures like "A Voice from the Plough," nor picturesque describers of their home life. So far, they have found neither a second Jefferies nor, in the other aspects and interests of their existence, any among their social equals or superiors who has united, with a fraction of Cobbett's genius, the driving power which wrested freedom of utterance for the journalist and representation in Parliament for all taxpayers. Made of the same stuff as Defoe, trained for journalism chiefly by the study of Swift, there still stands alone in newspaper story Cobbett's lifelong display of the courage which leads a forlorn hope, combined with the strong patience unsurpassed by the cart-horses he tended in his boyhood, and the obstinacy which wins, not from a conviction that victory is certain, but from a resolve to ignore even the accomplished fact of defeat. His entire conduct of the *Political Register* was an unbroken war. Neither imprisonment, bankruptcy, nor even absolute ruin shook his endurance. The pen which was his sword he surrendered to no captain of any opposing force less than death. His work was fulfilled ; the results of his sufferings endure. Some of his phrases and nick-names still live, as, for instance, " Æolus Canning," the " pink-nosed Liverpool," " unbaptized, buttonless black-guards " (William Penn and his followers), and " the bloody old *Times*." These gems of vituperation, what-ever their literary demerit, answered their purpose at the time by sticking, and still gather up into themselves something of the history of the time. In the nineteenth century Jacob Bright never produced a happier effect in the House of Commons than when, referring to the family borough at that time represented by the Duke of Marlborough's second son, he spoke of Lord Randolph Churchill as the member for Woodcock. So no verbal device of Cobbett's proved more successful than his habit of addressing the eloquent Erskine by his second title of Lord Clackmannan.

CHAPTER VI

THE TWO HUNTS, PERRY, AND STUART

Leigh Hunt's boyhood—Appearance among the journalists—Launching the famous *Examiner*—Its founders' aims and methods—Some of its chief features—A model for later journalism—State prosecutions—The Hunts in prison—Contemporary estimates of *Rimini*—The *Indicator* essays—American criticism—Leigh Hunt's Skimpolism—Byron and Hunt on the *Liberal*—Ill-assorted yoke-mates—The Cockney and the nobleman part—James Perry and the *Gazetteer*—He buys the *Morning Chronicle*—And takes front rank among the "able editors"—Famous writers on the *Chronicle*—Perry as a social light—His influence on the journalistic profession—Struggles of his successor, Black, against successive misfortunes and disadvantages—Pott and Slurk in real life—"Pickwickian" insults—Daniel Stuart's enterprises and helpers—Sir J. Mackintosh—Course of the *Post* and the *Courier*.

THE greatest of Cobbett's eighteenth-century prede-cessors, Philip Francis, had, before going to India, been a clerk in the War Office. Of the writers who in Cobbett's time and on his side completed his work in building up the Liberal press, the most active and the best known, Leigh Hunt, was, like so many journalists of our own day,[1] a War Office clerk also, while regularly work-ing for a journal which gave him his earliest opening in print some time before his *Examiner* days. Born of West Indian parents, Leigh Hunt's father, Isaac Hunt, settled and practised as a lawyer in Philadelphia while it was still an English colony. His loyalty to the British connection brought him into odium with the New World patriots, and, after a narrow escape of being literally tarred and feathered, caused him to take refuge in flight. Coming to England, he settled at Southgate, and took pupils, one of whom gave a name to his second son,

---

[1] Such instances, to mention only a few, would be those of Tom Hood, son of Thomas Hood who wrote the *Song of the Shirt* ; Arthur à Beckett, as well as certainly one of his brothers, Albert, possibly another ; Clement W. Scott, son of William Scott, Rector of Hoxton, an early *Saturday Reviewer*, and E. Barrington Fonblanque, Albany Fonblanque's nephew.

Leigh. A school contemporary of Charles Lamb, Leigh Hunt was, like him, intended for Anglican orders. But he lived in a stirring time and among men in the habit of freely discussing its events and personages. Conscious of literary power, he had decided while yet a youth to become a journalist. So far as literary style can be conveyed by teaching, the best lessons in it, as in his general course of reading, were given by his father, who, in the musical voice that had gone to so many hearts, and with the grand manner which had made him so many friends, used, when they were seated together in the King's Bench Prison, to read the best passages of Barrow's, Massillon's, and Saurin's pulpit masterpieces to his wife and youngest son, stopping at points of special excellence to explain the art which made them beautiful and good. From Chaucer to Pope the English poets, from Homer to Lucian the great Greek authors, as well as the Latin, beginning with Livy and ending with Pliny, were the subjects of his solitary study, while his earliest essays were modelled on Voltaire. In the year during which he became of age (1805), his brother John, whom his father had set up in life as a printer, started a paper called *The News*, and gave Leigh a chance as his theatrical critic. Three years later the Hunts produced a paper destined to longer life and wider fame than their first venture. This was the *Examiner*. The title had received an earlier distinction from the Swift-Bolingbroke sheet started in 1710, itself suggesting Addison's ill-starred and transient *Whig Examiner* a little later. Among the Hunts' successors with the *Examiner* were Fonblanque and one or two more, all to be mentioned in their due place. The *Examiner* as a title only disappeared from the newspaper stalls in 1880. Leigh Hunt's personal appearance during his maturer years was closely reproduced by his son Thornton Hunt, a leading member of the *Daily Telegraph's* editorial staff during the sixties, on whom, as there will be occasion to mention him later, this is not the place to dwell. The West Indian origin of the Hunt family showed itself in the dark complexion and the jet black hair, the brilliant and variously expressive eyes which, together with figures noticeably straight and erect, his sons, Leigh included, had inherited from their father. Himself fond of connecting his personal peculiarities with, in his own phrase, the tropical blood in his veins, apart from the Middlesex birthplace, Leigh Hunt was not an Englishman ; from his mother, an Americanised Irishwoman, he inherited all the Celtic bitterness against Anglo-Saxon domination and the British Government.

Since Cobbett's hit with the *Political Register* launched six years earlier, there had entered no such force into the newspaper system as was imparted by the two sons of the newly created clergyman [1] and his wife in the *Examiner*. Its first number was brought out by the Hunts in the opening week of 1808. Except as regards absence of political connection with all corporate interests, factions, parties, and sects, the men who made the *Examiner* and the man who created the *Register* had little or nothing in common. By way of emancipating himself from all restraint upon absolute freedom of newspaper utterance, Leigh Hunt, having retained his War Office clerkship for about a year after he had begun to edit the *Examiner*, then, in all proper terms, sent in his resignation. A playgoer from childhood, Leigh Hunt, while, as has been already mentioned, theatrical critic for the *News*, had received Charles Lamb's warmest praise for the independence, insight, freshness, and originality which had marked his dealing with the stage and its ornaments from Siddons to Munden. As he had written about players, so he soon let it be seen he intended handling politicians of all parties,

[1] In his *Autobiography*, Leigh Hunt does justice to his father's pulpit eloquence, to the popularity always secured by his handsome presence and expressive delivery. The colonial lawyer had a university education both at Philadelphia and at New York. On settling in England, he was ordained by Lowth, Bishop of London. His first pastoral charge was at Bentinck Chapel, Paddington. Then, while living at Hampstead, he is spoken of as taking duty at Southgate. Here he had the good fortune to attract the favourable notice of the last Duke of Chandos (family name Leigh), whose title, going in 1789 to the Grenvilles, enlarged itself a generation later to the Duke of Buckingham and Chandos. With such a patron, Isaac Hunt must secure high Church promotion, probably a mitre. The Duke actually made him private tutor to his nephew, James Henry Leigh, whose entire style, patronymic and Christian name, was taken by Isaac Hunt for the baptismal appellation of his best known son. Eagle Hall, Southgate, was Isaac Hunt's house, and Leigh Hunt's birthplace ; but even a Duke's good offices could not keep an expensive ecclesiastic out of trouble. Leigh Hunt's early recollections were chiefly of a room in the King's Bench Prison, where his father was confined for debt, relieving his captivity by drinking claret and reading Horace.

whatever their achievements or rank. In his theatrical estimates, Leigh Hunt had escaped the imputation of interested motives by shunning personal acquaintance with any actor as, in his own words, " a vice not to be thought of " ; he was equally careful not to compromise his independence by accepting free admissions. Honestly prepared, as it cannot be doubted, to sacrifice much when necessary to a principle, he kept his judgment studiously free from all suspicion of external influence, of bias from above or below, by holding himself aloof from all political persons, by never accepting social invitations from party leaders or their hangers-on. Till Byron visited him in prison, he had shown no inclination to pass half an hour in any nobleman's society. He had defined the object of the *Examiner* as the production of parliamentary reform, general liberality of opinion, especially freedom from superstition, and a reproduction, in its plain business-like English, of graces coming from loyalty to the great masters of our national prose. Every item in this programme was fulfilled. Particularly in keen criticism of public affairs and personages, combined with finished phraseology and all qualities that raise journalism to literature, Leigh Hunt set a newspaper pattern which has been followed by succeeding generations even more systematically than by that which witnessed the *Examiner's* birth. Why, it was asked, should " Parisian writer " be a compliment and " literary Londoner " or " Cockney school " a term of reproach? Because, as Leigh Hunt was ready to answer, he and his friends, though differing much from each other in character and in direction of intellect as well as in literary manner, resembled each other in not cultivating what Cicero calls " urbanity." They could not have moved in a circle less small had they been inhabitants of a country town. That reproach against the Cockney penmen was little heard after the proof of what the best among them could do, given by the *Examiner*. Radical this paper gloried in being, but its Radicalism was no more that of Joseph Hume than of Gradgrind. It abhorred statistics and aimed, not at pushing Bills through Parliament or wrecking them, but at permeating classes and masses alike with sentiment and knowledge that would hasten and illuminate the day of democracy. Proud of his family's descent from the Puritan stock transplanted for freedom's sake from the Old World to the New, Leigh Hunt liked equally to connect his origin with some of the seventeenth-century Cavaliers. In Leigh Hunt himself Byron saw something of Pym or Hampden born out of due time. He was also particularly impressed by the austerity and, as he called it, the extraordinary independence of character which made Leigh Hunt hold most celebrities of the time at arm's length. To Burdett, though in a way his hero, Hunt had never spoken. On William Cobbett he had never set eyes. His own name-sake, Cobbett's later friend, Henry, otherwise " Orator " Hunt was unknown to him in everything but name. Leigh Hunt was, however, fond of tracing back family connection with Anglo-Saxon politics across the Atlantic in the following more or less humorous way. " Let us hear what brother Jonathan says " were the words in which George Washington showed the value he set upon the wisdom of the Jonathan Trumbull in whom Washington's confidence personified American common sense. Trumbull's nineteenth-century descendant came to England that he might study painting under West, was arrested, and might have been shot for a spy had not Isaac Hunt effectively intervened on his behalf. " That," as he recalled the incident Leigh Hunt would say, " is the extent of our family association with political people on either side of the Atlantic. How absurd, therefore, to talk of our paper being a political organ." The Hunts, indeed, refused all dinner invitations, private or public, rejected all personal overtures from party leaders ; they could, therefore, with perfect truth say that they had started and that they carried on the *Examiner* with no other views than those of promoting the public good and of earning a livelihood for themselves. Taking the public into his confidence, Leigh Hunt confessed, with an airiness as much a part of his nature as the strenuous gravity of the Commonwealth men observed by Byron, that he always thought more about getting his verses into print than raking his opponents with heavy political broadsides. " I galloped," he continued, " through my editorial duties, took a world of superfluous pains in the writing, sat up very late at night, and was a very trying person to compositors and newsmen."

The first hebdomadal calling itself the *Examiner* belonged, as has been seen in an earlier chapter, to the second decade of the eighteenth century ; it provided Swift and his friends with a means of animating and organising the opposition to Walpole. Addison's Whig sheet, with something like the same title, lived for too short a time to exercise much influence, literary or political. The second *Examiner*, therefore, having any claim to notice was that which made Leigh and John Hunt the first founders of the weekly journal, in its best and still existing form. The blood of the martyrs was the seed of the Church. State prosecutions, together with the abuse of the orthodox, made the *Examiner* during the first year of its life a commercial success, with a regular circulation of two thousand, still steadily rising. Naturally this prosperous journalistic hit provoked comparison with the luckiest and most famous of Cobbett's ventures, some half-dozen years before. It also suggested something in the nature of a personal coincidence between writers at all other points differing so widely as William Cobbett and Leigh Hunt. Among Hunt's contributors was an essayist, William Hazlitt, of whom something will be said later. Hazlitt, of Irish blood but of English birth, had been taken in his childhood by his parents to the United States. Long residence in or near New York had to some extent Americanised Cobbett as well as, was said by the Yankees whom he at times detested so cordially, taught him the art of newspaper writing. Both Leigh Hunt's parents were of transatlantic stock if, in their beginnings, of British origin. Hence the American claim, made by some among Hunt's keenest critics in the New World presently to be glanced at, that the Stars and Stripes had done much towards presenting the Old Country with its greatest newspaper men. Leigh Hunt's aim in the *Examiner* was to give his readers popular teaching not only in Radical principles but in the art of expression and intellectual culture. His own literary perceptions were always keen, if sometimes, in details, inaccurate. Here is an instance. The idea and, in the earlier parts, the execution of the Lady Elizabeth Hastings sketch in the *Tatler* were Congreve's. Reading this piece of pen-and-ink portraiture, Leigh Hunt was particularly interested and charmed by the words " to love her is a liberal education." Never doubting the author of the phrase to have been Congreve, " it might," he exclaimed, " have come from Steele." And here Hunt showed at once the readiness of his critical insight and the pardonable limitations of his literary scholarship. The truth is that both Congreve and Steele had a share in the picture of this female paragon ; it was the portion from Steele's, not Congreve's, pen that contained the gem of expression which, if it dazzled Hunt, did so without blinding his judgment. The political articles always furnished a strong attraction by the prospect of State prosecution which they opened up. Apart from these, the paper's two most paying novelties, each from Leigh Hunt's pen, were the paragraphs summarising the week's news on the first page and the theatrical criticisms. These were as iconoclastic as they were breezy and fresh. John Kemble was told in effect he could not properly pronounce his mother tongue, and generally stood in the way of other actors and actresses who could do better than himself. The political paragraphs created as well as gratified a newspaper taste lasting to, and never more marked than at, the present day, when the column and a half " leader " seems sometimes elbowed out by the pithy occasional note, by the character sketch, or by the signed communication from an expert on a question of the day. Some of these features had been introduced by Cobbett in the *Register*. In the *Examiner* the first attempt at their combination was systematically made. Isaac Hunt's sympathetic and animating instruction on prose rhythm and the means of producing the most telling effects language could convey, followed by the intellectual intercourse both with boys and masters which Christ's Hospital sometimes allowed, enriched for all time the periodical press with a model at once stimulating and instructive in the man who suffered fine and imprisonment for disrespectful remarks about George IV. in 1812.

Before, however, that offence, the *Examiner* had come into legal collision with the Government upon three different occasions. Of these the first was an exposure of military mismanagement under the Duke of York (1808). The next year appeared some highly exasperating recommendations to the Spencer Perceval

Cabinet of certain reforms, English and Irish, which they might undertake. Such good things, however, as the *Examiner* hoped for seemed more likely to come in another reign than that in which Perceval was Prime Minister. What an opportunity for the third George's successor to make himself the most popular monarch who had ever swayed the sceptre of Great Britain and Ireland. Where, gasped out Southey for the Government, would this Hunt's criminal audacity stop? To hint at the possibility of a better monarch than the sovereign actually regnant was declared by the Attorney-General to be a seditious libel. The *Morning Chronicle*, then under Perry, of whom more presently, had approvingly quoted the *Examiner's* words. That daily newspaper, therefore, was associated with the weekly *Examiner* in the proceedings before Lord Ellenborough in the February of 1810. " Not guilty " was the verdict which at once set all the defendants scot free. Some months later in the same year, the Hunts followed Cobbett's example in their denunciation of flogging in the army, though not under the special circumstances which had excited Cobbett's wrath. The usual State prosecution followed. Henry Brougham in his defence won fresh laurels for himself and his clients by the contrast he had no difficulty in drawing between the *Examiner*, written and edited by able, cultivated men, on many subjects the teachers of their generation, and the coarse, ill-informed " rags " never seen by respectable readers. John and Leigh Hunt were acquitted amid the cheers of the expectant multitude outside. The *Examiner's* fourth encounter with the law officers of the Crown, less fortunate in its issue than those already mentioned, is too universally familiar for more than passing notice here. In the February of 1811 the future George IV. became Prince Regent. Many disagreeable things were said. The *Morning Post*, horrified with the liberties taken with august names, ventured to assure His Royal Highness of respectful, profound sympathy, and implored him to treat with merited contempt the rude and unkind words of other journals. " The Mæcenas of the age, delightful, blissful, wise, honourable, immortal, and true," were the phrases which, applied to himself, the *Post* assured the deputy-sovereign did him only justice. Here was a text impossible for the man of the *Examiner* to resist. " A corpulent man of fifty, the subject of millions of shrugs and reproaches, a libertine over head and ears in disgrace, a despiser of domestic ties, a companion of gamblers and demireps, without one single claim on the gratitude of his country, or the respect of posterity ; such," wrote Leigh Hunt, " is the Prince Regent of reality, as contrasted with the Prince Regent of fiction."

The man with a grievance sometimes disturbs the public peace as a means of securing attention to his real or imaginary wrong. Hunt's transatlantic ancestors had risked all for the English connection, and had lost it. His mother, whom he loved, though of American birth, was of Irish family ; in the poverty or extinction of her relatives Hunt saw the Irish victims of English misrule. By way of avenging himself for the ruin by which those of his name had paid for their fidelity to the British Government, and denouncing a dynasty even though he could not come by his rights, Hunt created a fresh sensation with this tirade against a Sardanapalus, who he hoped might be taught to shake, in the very drunkenness of his heart and in the midst of his minions, at the voice of honesty. The public was amused, but the Hunts were laid by the heels. On this occasion Brougham's defence did not carry the court with it. The trial had begun in December, 1812. During the February of the next year, Ellenborough sentenced the two brothers to fines whose gross amount was not less than £2,000. With the fines went a two years' deprivation of liberty. John and Leigh Hunt's bestowal in different prisons did not prevent their securing the *Examiner's* appearance regularly throughout their captivity. Its force, variety, and freshness had indeed never been more marked than when the addresses of its proprietors were respectively Cold Bath Fields and Horsemonger Lane. Than such residences as these the paper could have had no more paying advertisement. The entire public was with the incarcerated journalists, the amount of the mulcts was subscribed almost without effort, the jail authorities, great and small, treated the two men, not as convicts undergoing a sentence, but as distinguished inmates who by a regrettable incident were separated for a while from the outside world, but whose seclusion

did not disentitle them to all personal respect and assistance in the daily services to the public of their pens.
Even Leigh Hunt's domestic life went on after a fashion
throughout his loss of freedom. Once for a short time
the mother of his children took them to the seaside,
but for the rest his wife, with their boys and girls,
remained peacefully and happily by the father's and
the husband's side. As for agreeable or distinguished
visitors, Leigh Hunt saw more of these in prison than
he would probably have done in the same time beneath
his own suburban roof. Charles and Mary Lamb, with
Barnes of the *Times*, Horace and James Smith of the
Rejected Addresses, Haydon and Wilkie the artists, Lord
Brougham, Sir John Swinburne, Hazlitt, Shelley, and
Jeremy Bentham, who came especially to play battledore
and shuttlecock with this versatile and irrepressible newspaper martyr. Of all the visits, however, received by
Hunt in prison, the most interesting and important in
their consequences to the prisoner's future life, as well,
in some sense, to his character, were those of Lord Byron.
The acquaintance thus begun was cemented by the dedication to Byron of the longest poem written by Hunt
during his captivity, the *Story of Rimini*, " a real good
and very original poem, sure to be a great hit. But for
the dedication to myself," said Byron, " I would have
got Tom Moore to review it in the *Edinburgh*." What
ever in that case the Whig periodical might have said,
the *Quarterly* in its actual notice of the poem was
sufficiently outspoken. " Note," it exclaimed, " the
vulgar impatience of a low man, labouring with coarse
flippancy to scramble over the bounds of birth, education,
and fidget himself into familiarity with a lord." The
Tory *Blackwood* two years later followed suit with " No
modest woman ever read it without the flushings of
shame and self-reproach." Meanwhile the healthy air
and repose of Hampstead were re-establishing Hunt's
health, which had been much shaken by confinement,
anxiety, and vexations. Once more he was actively at
work with the *Examiner*, writing, perhaps, less himself,
but indefatigable and inspiring in his suggestions to
his contributors. The record or the spectacle of Leigh
Hunt's natural resiliency amid the continual difficulties
and dangers of his vocation may well have suggested

to Dickens the buoyancy of temperament which he caricatured into egotism and improvidence in Harold
Skimpole. Among Leigh Hunt's personal associates
Dickens may have found the original of another *Bleak
House* character. John Jarndyce in the novel presents
a contrast to Skimpole not less complete than may be
seen in Leigh Hunt's eldest brother and journalistic
partner, John Hunt, to Leigh Hunt himself. John Hunt's
business qualities, sound and sober common sense might
have qualified him to give his kinsman counsel which
would have kept him out of many troubles, and were
not less essential than literary genius to securing the
Examiner that position in periodical letters which made
it not only the forerunner but the pattern of high-class
weekly papers like the existing *Spectator* and *Saturday
Review* of our own day.

Leigh Hunt's political articles were always smart and
sometimes strong. His special newspaper mission was
to adapt to nineteenth-century journalism, as social
" leader " or " middle," the essay which Addison and
Steele had introduced. Here his easy colloquial diction,
his wide, ready sympathies, his keen and picturesque
observation, won him a real success and a lasting literary
influence in the *Indicator*, which, beginning September,
1819, showed him for two years at his best as an
essayist, without indeed Hazlitt's pungent, piercing criticism, intellectual strength, or Elia's weird humour. But
his pure English and sound sense were not debased by
so much alloy of sentimentalism as to prevent them from
being safe models for some, though not all, writers, as
well as uniformly pleasant and at times impressive and instructive reading. However homely or simple the theme,
the treatment is kept some degrees above the level of
baldness or bathos ; while here and there the incidental
comments are as incisive and fresh as they are true.
As if by anticipation to answer Bulwer-Lytton and others,
" The Cockney school of poetry," he exclaims, " is the
most illustrious in England. How could it help being so,
since Chaucer, Spenser, Milton, Pope, Gray were all of
London birth, and Shakespeare alone among our immortal
bards came into the world outside the sound of Bow
Bells ? " After Cobbett, Leigh Hunt was the one writer
of his time simultaneously, and to an almost equal

extent, in demand on both sides of the Atlantic. His lighter discourses, in particular his literary causeries, found at least as many readers in America as in his native land. The critics of New York and Boston considered him at his best in his *Feast of the Poets* ; while the first authority of the time in American letters, J. R. Lowell, extolled Hunt's command over the " delicacies and luxuries of language," and compared the " rounded grace of his thoughts to the shifting lustre of a dove's neck." At the same time even Russell and others complained of his poverty in what they called the raw material, denying him the possession of solid judgment in literary matters, and calling him as a critic " merely saucy, lackadaisical, falsely enthusiastic, or pointedly conceited " ; his eulogies on Coleridge the Yankee Aristarchi stigmatised as absurd. It was his *metier*, so ran the general verdict, neither to apply a literary stimulant nor to refresh the jaded mind with the repose found in Addison's *Spectator*, whose style was pronounced the very antipodes of Hunt's.[1] Among the personal impressions of his various visits to England recorded by the American N. P. Willis were accounts of conversations with Leigh Hunt which greatly displeased his admirers in the New World. This will account not only for the disparaging comments that tempered the praise of the Boston press, but for a tendency, originating on the other side of the Atlantic, to question the quality of Leigh Hunt's intellect, to affect doubt whether he really deserved all the attention he had received, to hint that he had made his bricks out of other men's clayfields, and to allow credit for little more than adroitness and perseverance to the most thoroughly and variously trained newspaper man of his time, who had begun as " theatrical critic and censor general " of the *Traveller*, before, in 1805, filling the same position, as already mentioned, on his brother's *News*. In 1852 American criticism of Leigh Hunt's poetry, prose, and personal character was indebted for a revival to the already mentioned N. P. Willis. For this writer, to the annoyance equally of Leigh Hunt and Charles Dickens, started a discussion about the exact relations

[1] Edgar Allan Poe, *Marginalia*, vol. ii. p. 474. Black's edition.

in which the Skimpole of *Bleak House* stood to the editor of the *Examiner*. It is sometimes forgotten that Skimpole had a good and serious side to his character ; he deteriorated, not at once, but by degrees into thriftlessness. In his better days, his unselfish attributes might fairly be said to have reflected characteristics of Hunt. But for *Bleak House* the contrast wanted to Jarndyce was some one who could amuse. The Skimpole of the novel is, therefore, necessarily a caricature ; Dickens point-blank denied having borrowed any disagreeable traits from the reputed original. He said, however, nothing to contradict the idea of Leigh Hunt having suggested the sunny superiority to reverses of fortune that gives a charm to Skimpole and that was to be found in Leigh Hunt. Again Skimpole (*Bleak House*, chapter lxi.) wrote his autobiography ; so did Leigh Hunt. But the Skimpole memoirs represented their author as victimised by a combination on the part of mankind against an amiable child. Hunt's narrative throws a new light of real historical value on the political, the literary, the parliamentary life of his time, is generous towards a benefactor like Shelley, states, indeed, his own case in opposition to Byron's, yet without showing himself in the martyr's pose. Skimpole is to some extent a second edition of Micawber in a new setting, with perhaps not more about him of Leigh Hunt himself than of his father, the eloquent elocutionist who fascinated dukes and ladies of high degree from the pulpit or reading-desk, and who, in his son's description, when confined within the Rules of the King's Bench, contrived to enjoy the elegancies, physical and intellectual, of polite life, recited the most striking passages from favourite authors to his wife and children, and could awaken curious sensations in his son by the grace and vigour which he displayed in the racquet court. The truth is that Micawber and Skimpole both represent, not individuals or characters, scarcely even types, so much as elements in human nature. Micawberism and Skimpolism indicate a temperament which may not be without its usefulness, if properly checked, amid the difficulties and discouragements of daily life. Hunt may have carried his Skimpolism too far. Without it he would have gone under more than once at an early point of his course.

But for the besetting readiness with which he idealised mere acquaintances as well as tried friends, he would have avoided serious misfortune.

Of the two most controversial passages in Leigh Hunt's literary relationships, enough has already been said about the Skimpole-Dickens episode. Of the other, the Byron-Hunt co-operation, the chief points can be given in a few words. Thomas Moore's compliments on the *Story of Rimini* did not prevent his warning Byron not to have any connection with such a company as Hunt, Shelley and Co. But without, perhaps, intending finally to commit himself, Byron, in or about 1820, found he could not honourably withdraw from the project of a quarterly periodical in the democratic interest. That was actually started in 1822, and lasted a year. It gave Byron the opportunity of publishing his *Vision of Judgment;* this, reprinted in the *Examiner*, subjected John Hunt to a fine. Shelley, for whose sake Byron had gone into the matter, contributed some good verses and Hazlitt a bitter denunciation of monarchy. Hazlitt, indeed, never wrote more effectively than he continued to do in all his pieces for the *Liberal*, especially one on *Pulpit Oratory, Chalmers and Irving*. Without Byron's funds, the paper could not have come into existence, still less have lived through four numbers. Soon after the first appeared, if not indeed earlier, Byron and Hunt experienced a gradual but complete disillusionment in their opinions about and feelings towards each other. Shelley's good offices had brought Hunt to Italy in 1822, and with his wife and seven children, had quartered him on Byron for his host. Hunt's impecuniosity increased. His drafts on Byron grew heavier. The reciprocal enthusiasm which first united the two men was gradually replaced by mutual weariness and disgust. Byron now discovered that Hunt was no gentleman. Hunt found out that, as he many years afterwards told Lord Houghton, the poet-peer combined the conversation of a pugilist with the heart of a pawnbroker, and that not even at his best was he ever or could he ever have been more than a *poseur*.

Leigh Hunt's later periodical ventures, the *Week's Chat*, the *Tatler*, and the *London Journal*, presaged the seven-days prints whose paragraphs and short essays

make them the most flourishing of twentieth-century
journalistic growths. Meanwhile his Tory assailants
had expressed regret for the intemperance of their
earlier abuse. Wilson asked him to write for *Blackwood*. The *Quarterly*, indeed, made no such overtures,
but Hunt actually became an *Edinburgh* reviewer, notwithstanding the misgivings of the *Edinburgh* editor,
Macvey Napier, as to his new contributor's ability to
give his articles the requisite gentlemanlike tone. When
Southey's health began to fail, the future Lord Macaulay
used his best efforts for securing Hunt's succession in
the office of Poet Laureate. Thus the most varied and
vigorous performer in the department of *belles lettres*,
as his hair whitened and his strength failed, received
all the attention and homage due to one regarded by
friends and foes as the grand old man in the journalism
of his day.

At different points of his life's warfare, Leigh Hunt
was brought into relations with the men who were head
and shoulders above their contemporaries in the personal
achievements which made the daily press a national
institution. The first of these to be considered now
was James Perry, of the *Morning Chronicle*. The difficulties encountered by him in building up this enterprise
were complicated and formidable enough to have crushed
a man whose strong, keen intellect, resourcefulness and
business tact were not equalled by strength of will, in-
vincible courage, rare knowledge of character, and extraordinary insight into the public temper and taste. The
journal calling forth the triumphant display of these
qualities, the *Morning Chronicle*, had been started in 1769
by William Woodfall, brother of the Sampson Woodfall
who brought out Francis as Junius. Perry himself
had first been heard of in connection with the *Gazetteer*,
the daily sheet that Sir Robert Walpole owned or inspired,
and that conveyed his instructions to the countless newspapers in his pay. The *Gazetteer*, however, which in
1783 Perry was engaged to edit, had long outgrown
the functions that Walpole paid it to perform. It
had, in fact, become to the bookselling trade what the
Morning Advertiser afterwards was to the licensed
victuallers. Perry at once perceived that if it were to
pay its way it must at once be changed from a trade

organ to a thoroughly popular sheet of comment and news. In its new form it could not but come into rivalry with Woodfall's *Chronicle*. That paper had already begun to suffer in reputation and revenue from not keeping pace with the spirit or supplying the wants of the time. Perry's rehabilitation of the *Gazetteer* deprived it, in its existing shape, of any future. In 1789, therefore, the *Chronicle* was for sale. It was bought by James Perry partly with his own money, entirely with the sums raised by his personal efforts from private friends. The Whigs, indeed, cherish a tradition representing the Liberal press as, at all stages of its history, a special creation of their own. But for a desire to secure an organ of Whig sweetness and light, the *Morning Chronicle* would never have made for itself the illustrious record which, opening under George III., lasted into the second half of the Victorian Age. As a fact, the aristocratic Whigs gave newspaper men and their work less encouragement than was received from democratic Tories or from Radicals. The Whig leader, Charles Fox, cared little, did less for the press, and boasted that when abroad on a holiday he only opened a daily journal to see the racecourse odds. The sole person in authority on the buff and yellow side from whom Perry received the slightest help or encouragement was the Duke of Norfolk. He gave the *Morning Chronicle* an office in one of the unlet houses on his Strand property. Of the purchase money a substantial sum had been advanced by Ransome and Bouverie, the bankers. Other capitalists, great or small, who had lent a hand, were Bellamy, a Chandos Street wine-merchant, door-keeper and caterer to the House of Commons, for one of whose pork pies Pitt is said to have asked on his death-bed, and Gray, an assistant master at Charterhouse School, who had just come into a legacy. The money which he was thus able to find not only secured Perry the editorship of the *Morning Chronicle*, but gave him, as a principal proprietor, a decisive voice in its business management. Perry, the life, soul, engineer and director of the whole undertaking, found a fresh stimulus to his exertions in political antagonism to the *Times* and the " whole monstrous monopoly of the overweening tyrant of Printing House Square." As an editor he had but one fault—

he wrote too much himself ; for a literary team is handled with the best results when the holder of the reins leaves the actual work to be done by those whom he directs. The chief attraction of Perry's writing was not so much strength as brightness of thought and felicity of touch. In graver matters the master mind belonged to Gray, a man of first-rate intellectual power who, had his life been spared longer, would have taken higher and better known rank among the personal forces that created and controlled the English newspaper of the eighteenth and nineteenth centuries. As it was, in return for his investment of £500 he became assistant editor and, in the *Morning Chronicle's* more serious work at all critical times, he it was who pulled the labouring oar. As for Perry, the great qualities which had raised him to a position more commanding, perhaps, than had been won by any of his predecessors or contemporaries, went together with an inordinate fondness which he never quite outgrew for seeing himself in print, and a personal vanity never more gratified than when the public persisted in attributing to his inspiration, if not handiwork, all that was freshest, brightest, or best in any particularly striking issue. Perhaps the very brilliance and strength of his contributors increased a jealous anxiety to keep himself well in the foreground. His staff included R. B. Sheridan and Sir James Mackintosh. Mackintosh was more at home in the ampler space of pamphlet dissertation or *Edinburgh Review* article, but generally contrived to pack weighty matter pregnant with wisdom into the three or four paragraphs which he was allowed by Perry ; Sheridan, on the other hand, might always be trusted not to exceed a column of pointed and epigrammatic observations on the leading incidents and individuals of the hour. Of all Sheridan's *Chronicle* articles there was scarcely one in which the author of the *School for Scandal* did not stand revealed. Perry's theatrical critic was a future Lord Chancellor, John Campbell, who, however, when writing for the *Chronicle*, had not yet been called to the bar. This is a name which, it may be mentioned in passing, suggests a notable instance of journalistic heredity ; for Lord Chancellor Campbell's son, the Lord Stratheden and Campbell, who died in 1893, began to copy out, as well as study, Blue books while an Eton boy, and in later years to the close of his life was an inexhaustible letter-writer on the Eastern Question to every London paper. Another of Perry's leading article manufacturers bearing the Campbell name was Thomas Campbell, the poet, whose private letters about his work show that in 1793 the regulation payment for a leading article had become the two guineas which for many years afterwards it was to remain. The offices of the *Morning Chronicle* and Perry's fine and hospitable house in Tavistock Square were pervaded by a tiny little gentleman whose puffed, frilled shirt-front suggested the breast of a pouter pigeon, and whose dress, in the extreme of fashion, exactly reproduced that of the Prince Regent. There seemed something drolly consequential in the air of this duodecimo dandy as he strutted hurriedly from one room to another or walked up to Perry, whose shoulder he barely reached, that he might impart something to his private ear. This was the member of the *Morning Chronicle* staff specially charged with the fashionable part of the paper, Thomas Moore, Byron's friend and biographer, the tame cat of Holland House, of Bowood, and of half-a-dozen other great mansions, who, when not picking up odds and ends of society talk, wrote the *Chronicle's* poetry and sometimes, as on the Regent's restrictions, some uncommonly clever epigrams. His biographical notices were quite the best in the whole London press. Perry's dinner parties at the already mentioned Bloomsbury residence, as regards the quality both of the guests and the fare, were famous. Erskine Romilly, and Miss Mitford, among the earliest of lady journalists, were habitually at the table, while Luttrell and Tierney, the two wittiest masters of conversational satire, shone there more brightly than at Holland House. The talk, however, of the host himself was unsurpassed for brightness and variety. Perry was also a kindly-hearted man, ever ready to do a good turn, to opponents as well as friends. The late Mrs. Procter, who lived till 1888, often dwelt on the high-minded and open-handed services rendered to her husband by this newspaper potentate.

Parliamentary reports had found their way into print long before Perry's time. The reporters, however, had to crowd into the Gallery with other strangers, and might be told at any time that note-taking was contrary to the orders of the House.[1]   The newspaper accounts of debates could not, therefore, but be very imperfect ; though in 1775 there had been such improvements in reporting as to make Horace Walpole call the newspapers " now tolerable journals of the Commons."   At the same time, while unrecognised by any formal order, reporters were allowed by the Speaker and the Sergeant-at-Arms to use the back bench of the Strangers' Gallery.   In 1803 the recognition of reporters was completed by that position being, at the Speaker's order, reserved for their exclusive use.   Another improvement in the reporting system was due entirely to Perry's personal initiative. Hitherto time had not allowed the publication of the debates in the morning papers.   Perry stationed his stenographers in the Gallery by relays.   Thus a fresh man took his turn every twenty minutes, after the fashion still in force.   In this way, by the time the latest reporter's last slips had been written out for the printer, the earlier parts of the debate were actually in type. Perry would not have been a true representative of his newspaper epoch if he had been without experience of State prosecutions.   One of these, though the last in order of time, was his inclusion in the proceedings in 1810 against the Hunts already described, when, like them, he was acquitted.   The first proceedings instituted against him were for seditious libel in 1793.   Then, too, the verdict was not guilty.   Five years later he charged the House of Lords with refuting the charge of absolute idleness by a session for the special purpose of regulating opera dancers' dresses.   This piece of sarcasm produced a call to the bar of the Peers' Chamber, the infliction of a £50 fine, and three months' imprisonment.   The services rendered to his craft by this great editor and business man will be the better estimated if one contrasts the honour and authority secured by Perry for his vocation with the discredit and contempt in which he had first found it.   Throughout the eighteenth century, and indeed during part of the nineteenth, what Johnson had said in the bitterness of his soul about the newspaper-writer's lot was literally true.   " Away with

these blackguard newspaper scribblers from the parliamentary precincts," had been the pleasant cry throughout
the lobbies in 1798. No gentleman, it was said, could
stoop to the foul indignity of prostituting his pen to
payment at so much per column. The Benchers of
Lincoln's Inn excluded all who at any time had written
in the daily journals from being called to the bar. Robert
Southey, who had himself plied for journalistic hire under
Stuart of the *Post*, told Lord Liverpool that newspaper
men were pestilent nuisances who would destroy the
Constitution if they were not first exterminated themselves. In or about the year 1830, the Lord Chancellor
of the day got into trouble with his Cabinet colleagues
for asking the editor of the *Times* to dinner.

Perry's services to the newspaper profession generally,
as well as to his own journal in particular, were continued so far as circumstances allowed by the man who
followed him at the *Morning Chronicle*, John Black.
Had he succeeded to Perry's exceptional advantages,
Black did not want the qualities which might have enabled
him to rival Perry's reputation. Like Stuart of the
Morning Post, as well as like Perry himself, Black takes
his place among the Scotch founders of the London
newspaper. His wild oats had been sown during his
earliest youth while living from hand to mouth in Edinburgh. In 1810 he found his way to London, and
settled down to serious work on the *Morning Chronicle's*
reporting staff. His course might have been one of
unbroken prosperity as well as credit had he not been
trapped by a friend into marrying his cast-off mistress.
After that, one misfortune followed quickly upon another.
In a short time the lady's disappearance to some extent
unmade the ill-starred marriage. She still, however,
remained a source of misery and expense. Harassed at
home, Black was hampered and hindered in the conduct of
his paper by the proprietors. In business management as
well as in editorship, Perry was from the first his own
master. On his death in 1821 the paper had been
sold. Black found himself a paid servant, without voice in
its management, without share in its profits. Unrelieved
by the rest and solace of home life, Black found his editorial cares and difficulties aggravated by lack of public
spirit and intellectual interest on the part of those to

whom the paper belonged. Even though thus heavily handicapped, he showed himself a born editor and leader of men. Without Perry's gifts of style, humour, sympathy, he proved at least Perry's equal in gathering round him the first writers and thinkers of the day. Coleridge, Lamb, Mackintosh, and others whom Stuart had recruited for the *Post*, placed their pens at the disposal also of Black. Members of Black's team were united in admiration of the skill with which he handled both them and their articles. Jeremy Bentham, who was not prodigal of praise, called him the greatest publicist yet produced in Great Britain. Bentham's most illustrious disciple, James Mill, and his son, John Stuart, welcomed the platform given them by Black's columns for delivering their message to the world. The first newspaper critic of English institutions in detail was their description of their editor. Black's touch, however, literary or editorial, never acquired the lightness which had been the charm of Perry, and on which, in their weekly talks with their editor, both the Mills insisted as a condescension necessary to the temper of the time. Nor was it only that Black and his contributors were habitually writing above the heads of the public. In a progressive and enlightened sheet like the *Chronicle*, his Whig readers resented civilities to their Tory enemies, as well as certain inconsistencies in their editor's views. Why, for instance, these critics wanted to know, should Black lash himself into such a fury about the Peterloo massacre, and yet fail to see in Queen Caroline the injured wife whose only fault was the innocence which alone had made her the victim of a cruel conspiracy.? What, too, could be more obstinately wrong-headed than Black's declaration that a Tory might have brains and even genius? Byron had exclaimed of Pitt's most brilliant disciple and successor in the Tory leadership :

> "E'en I can praise thee—Tories do no more,"

and elsewhere :—

> "While Canning's colleagues hate him for his wit,
> And old Dame Portland[1] fills the place of Pitt."

---

[1] *A propos* of the Duke of Portland's premiership following, after Pitt's death, the "Talents" Administration.

Such a licence might be permitted to poets, but did Mr. Editor Black think the Whigs befriended him and his paper to hear eloquence allowed to an adventurer like Canning and the Duke of Wellington called anything else than a bungler or a bigot? And then, exclaimed the Radicals, the insolence of Black's discovery that Cobbett wrote and talked a great deal of nonsense in his time ! " The players and I are happily no friends." So Pope had boasted of himself. But the *Morning Chronicle's* sometime owner was Woodfall, who gave to the drama a prominence greatly increasing its circulation ; while Perry found his theatrical critic in William Hazlitt. Any indifference of Black to theatrical matters was, he might have said, more than compensated in his paper by such features as Brougham's slashing leaders and Tom Moore's happiest epigrams, one specimen of which is not too well known to be given here, the subject being the Regency Bills, 1788-1811.

> "A strait waistcoat on him and restrictions on me,
> A more limited monarchy sure could not be."

The Walter dynasty will receive due consideration on a later page. Some time, however, before the date now reached, the members of this remarkable family were making the *Times* the first paper not only in England but in Europe. Black's encounters with that great journal under various editors form too important an episode in his course to be ignored now. The abuse interchanged between Black and the gentlemen of Printing House Square is no more than echoed in the reciprocal fury with which the two Eatanswill editors in *Pickwick* fell upon each other. As a fact, the entire Pott and Slurk episode may well have been intended for a description of the thunders, to use his own word, rolled forth by Edward Sterling from Printing House Square, and the answering bolts that Black discharged from the Strand.[1] This, too, is quite in accordance with

---

[1] At 332, Strand were the *Morning Chronicle* offices ; beneath the same roof, on the floor above these, was John Black's private residence. In the same way, some of the Walter family or their representatives lived on the *Times* premises in Blackfriars ; while, throughout all his editorship, J. T. Delane had his own dwelling-house quite near, 16, Serjeant's Inn, Fleet Street.

Dickens's method. In the opening chapter of *Pickwick* he had described a quarrel between the founder of the Pickwick Club and a member called Blotton. This incident was undoubtedly suggested by a House of Commons scene in which Brougham and Canning were the chief figures (April 17, 1823). Brougham had described Canning's accession to a divided Cabinet as an incredible specimen of monstrous truckling for the purpose of obtaining office. Canning at once interrupted with the words " That is false." The two political rivals would have been committed to the Serjeant-at-Arms. Sir Robert Wilson, however, suggested the explanation that Brougham's offensive words were applied to Canning not in his personal but official character. Thirteen years afterwards, when *Pickwick* was at the zenith of its fame, Fonblanque, referring to the adroitness with which the disturbance had been quelled, commented : " In fact, Brougham and Canning only called each other liars in the Pickwickian sense, just as in the story Blotton says he had merely considered Mr. Pickwick a humbug in the Pickwickian sense."

Neither " Michael Angelo Titmarsh " nor " Boz " would have desired a place among the makers of the English newspaper. Both, however, were brought out in the *Morning Chronicle*, Thackeray as art critic, Dickens as parliamentary reporter. The author of *David Copperfield* was complimented by Black on being the best stenographer who had ever " taken his turn " for the *Chronicle*. By way of getting more regular newspaper work, Thackeray applied for the editorship of an evening edition which the *Chronicle* proprietors were bringing out. Thackeray's practical knowledge of newspaper work was at this time too slight to make it surprising that the preference should have been given to another candidate, Charles Mackay, the song-writer, Miss Marie Corelli's stepfather, who, if almost as inexperienced as Thackeray himself, had, so far as his age allowed, had some apprenticeship to the technical work of journalism. The disappointment irritated the novelist, and may explain the occasional bitterness of his remarks on newspaper writers and owners. Mackay was one of the few newspaper managers who ever helped a royal duke to write a leading article. His Grace of Sussex had long been a good platform speaker, able to deal with literary or social matters sufficiently well to pass muster. He had never tried his hand at a leader, but was ambitious to do so ; he found the work less easy than he had expected. Mackay was called in to correct the proof ; the affair passed off to Black's as well as to the Duke's entire satisfaction.

The first of the *Morning Chronicle's* great editors came from a Scotch province exceptionally rich, as will be seen at several subsequent places, in the journalistic ability of its natives, Aberdeen. Black, though a Scotchman too, was a Lowlander. The next notable journalist who pushed his way from beyond the Tweed to the Thames was Daniel Stuart, proud of his clan, the Perthshire Stuarts of Loch Rannoch, and prouder still of a connection, historical or legendary, with the Royal House of his own name. The grandfather had been out in the 1715, his father in the 1745. Accepting the Hanoverian succession, he had now become George III.'s most loyal subject. The Jacobite exodus to the South had been going on for some time. Daniel Stuart's brothers were already well started in a London printing business ; in 1778 Daniel joined them, and the family lived over their business premises in Catherine Street with their shrewd, kindly sister Catharine for housekeeper. That domestic arrangement was to have the effect of enlarging the journalistic activities of one who, if afterwards neither with the pen nor in Parliament he quite fulfilled his earliest promise, by his intellectual elevation, his learning, by the stateliness of his language, and his lifelong responsibility to conviction and conscience alone, reflected fresh honour and dignity on the English newspaper and on the work of writing for it. This was the illustrious man who, in 1804, became Sir James Mackintosh, and whose course, both before and after his marriage to Catharine Stuart, might be described as Odyssean in its varieties and vicissitudes. With a medical degree from Edinburgh he had come up to London in 1788 to practise as a doctor. He failed to do this as signally as another great newspaper man, Tobias Smollett, had failed in a like attempt at Bath. Towards the close of the eighteenth century took place the marriage with Catharine Stuart, followed by a wedding

tour in the Low Countries, with Brussels as his headquarters. He had, however, other objects for his journey
than enjoyment. His health needed repair ; he wished
to study foreign politics amid the actual scenes of the
disturbance still in progress. As an eye-witness he
watched the growth and progress of the quarrel between
the Emperor Joseph and his people ; while in France
the revolutionary movements were coming to a head.
Knowledge is power ; with Mackintosh it was to be
money also. The experiences now gathered formed the
capital on which, quickly returning to London, he could
set up as a newspaper-writer. In rivalry to the *Times*,
the *Oracle* had been started recently by John Bell.
Mackintosh soon became one of its regular staff. The
information brought back by him from the Continent
and the close connection he was able to maintain with
well-placed friends abroad qualified him for superintend-
ing and writing up all the *Oracle's* foreign news.
Meanwhile his brothers-in-law, Peter and Daniel Stuart,
had acquired the *Morning Post*. The Stuarts found this
paper moderately Whig. They proceeded to give it a
temperate Tory bias in dealing with social and political
affairs. How well Daniel Stuart at least, the chief
manager of the paper, knew his business may be inferred
from the fact that he bought the paper for £600, that
eight years after he sold it for £25,000, and that during
his proprietorship he worked up the circulation from
three hundred and fifty to four thousand five hundred.
Such a sale exceeded that possessed by any other paper
of this date. By the time of his becoming established
on the *Morning Post* Mackintosh had achieved fame
through measuring himself against Burke. His *Vindiciæ
Gallicæ* had been the first in a series of replies to Burke's
Reflections, which afterwards included compositions by
the third Earl Stanhope, Tom Paine, and last of all
Arthur Young. The *Vindiciæ* were enough to make Mackintosh rank as one of the *Morning Post's* most valuable
pens. Other writers were the " Lake Poets," including
Coleridge and Southey, then politically in a transition
stage, having broken with his revolutionary colleagues,
but not yet made much progress in the training which was
to leave him the reactionary Tory of the *Quarterly Review*
In the *Morning Post*, however, literary criticism rather

than disquisition on State affairs formed Southey's department.   Charles Lamb, another occasional contributor
to the *Post*, praises Daniel Stuart as the finest tempered
of editors, frank, plain, English all over, and so somewhat of a contrast to Perry of the *Morning Chronicle*,
for whom, Elia reminds us, he had worked as well as for
Stuart. Between 1795 and 1803 Southey made some
absences on the Continent, leaving temporarily his work
to Wordsworth, then only beginning to be known.
Southey's already-mentioned outburst to Lord Liverpool
against newspapers and those who wrote them belonged
to the year 1817. By that time, as the names already
mentioned here show, journalism had become not the
least distinguished department of letters. From Defoe,
Swift, Addison, and Steele, to Johnson, to Junius, and
so onward to the Hunts, the makers of the English newspaper were also the makers and the masters of English
prose. No more, as will duly be seen, in the nineteenth
and twentieth centuries than at any preceding period,
as regards either the method or the merit of the work
done, has there been or does there exist the much-
talked of antagonism between journalism and literature.

As ambitious of public influence as he was able, Daniel
Stuart followed up his purchase of the *Post* fourteen years
earlier by buying in 1799 the *Courier*. This was an
evening paper founded and owned by John Parry, now,
as he had already done for the *Post*, transformed by
Stuart from a strong Liberal into a moderate Tory
organ. In more respects than one Stuart proved himself
to possess the instincts, gifts, and methods as much
associated at the present day as in his own time with
newspaper success. He had a knack of discovering
literary talent, of engaging it on the most advantageous
terms. He also presaged the most characteristic tactics
of the nineteenth and twentieth century evening press in
arranging an indefinite sequence of editions following
each other with a rapidity undreamt-of before. With his
new journal Stuart repeated the success of his earlier
venture. The *Morning Post*, indeed, remains to the
present day the monument of his sagacity and shrewdness
in everything to do with paper and printer's ink ; probably
he never showed greater wisdom than in selling the
Courier after the peace of 1815, when newspapers began

for a time to be at a discount. The distinguished pens already a work for his *Morning Post* supplied Stuart with the literary labour he needed for the *Courier*. Charles Lamb is only one among several who has testified to Stuart's uniformly considerate or at least satisfactory dealing with his contributors. In so acting he certainly never inflicted injustice upon himself. This is a combination of qualities entitling him to be called a really great as well as successful man.

CHAPTER VII

THE WALTERS: THEIR WORK, WRITERS, AND EDITORS

The journalist's training ground—S. T. Coleridge as journalist—A cool offer—The dawn of the Walter dynasty—The *Times* under the first Walter—Skirmishes in Whitehall—Foreign news organisation under Walter the second—Famous members of his staff—John Stoddart—Some slaps at "Slop"—Thomas Barnes—His career before and during the *Times* editorship—Notable occasional contributors—Captain Edward Sterling, the "Thunderer"—The triumvirate of Printing House Square—William Combe—"Roving Rabbis" on the *Times*—Peter Fraser—Walter meets the Delanes—J. T. Delane in the chair of Barnes—Delane's staff—Remarkable events during his editorship —Mistakes of policy and fact—Thomas Chenery, Delane's successor—Lord Blachford's contributions.

OF two great London public schools, Christ's Hospital associates itself with great newspaper men in the first quarter of the nineteenth century not less prominently than Westminster is connected with the foremost figures in the nation's life, work, and thought at other epochs. Leigh Hunt, S. T. Coleridge and Charles Lamb were the most notable among the old " Blues " in the journalistic system of their period. Scarcely less conspicuous in his day was Thomas Barnes. He had been Leigh Hunt's schoolfellow ; he became his comrade in the fight for a free press, sharing his reverses as well as triumphs. Barnes contributed regularly to Hunt's *Examiner*. Most of Coleridge's newspaper work, however, was done for some of Stuart's papers already mentioned, both of them, like the *Morning Chronicle* also, memorable links between the better sort of journalism and the best kind of literature. Here he gave proof of intellectual aptitudes which, if not counterbalanced by moral and physical eccentricities or infirmities, would have fitted him to deal with political subjects. As things were, he was no more fitted to be a journalist than a dragoon—the career which,

under the name of Comberback, he had, when homeless
in London, for a short time essayed. When he wrote
under pressure his faculties were subject to a species of
moral paralysis. These sudden fits made it impossible
for any editor to count on Coleridge's work in the make-
up of his paper. When forthcoming, Coleridge's newspaper writing, like his conversation, was remarkable for
the way in which he brought to a focus an infinite
variety of subjects and information mutually, as it seemed,
the most disconnected in themselves, and the most impossible, as it might be thought, for one mind and tongue
intelligently to manage. In an essayist this would have
been interesting and even agreeable. As a leader-writer,
however, it made Coleridge rather impracticable. His
articles disdained the points, some of which ought to
be made in every paragraph. A newspaper article, to be
effective, must not only carry the reader from beginning
to end along with it, but must from point to point
enlighten and instruct on the collateral issues which the
central topic raises, and avoid all references which cannot
easily be understood. To such considerations as these,
Coleridge was, of course, far above paying any heed.
His peculiarities, personal and literary, were patiently
borne in the *Courier* and the *Post* by Stuart, who had
discovered and admired his genius. In other quarters,
appreciation of Coleridge was an acquired taste. Take
the result of his overtures to the *Times*. Nine years
before its owner's energies, the abilities of its editors,
its writers, and the steam press raised that paper to
greatness, in 1805, the second of the Walter dynasty
received from the poet of the *Ancient Mariner* a proposal
for service in Printing House Square. The terms were
at least specific ; if accepted, they would have made
the poet not only the paper's chief writer, but an active
controller of its policy. Coleridge offered to attend
daily at the office for at least six hours, and to write as
many articles a week as might be required. This was
to be on condition that the paper showed itself independent of the Administration, that it advocated the due
proportion of political power to property, but that it used
its influence to promote the free transfer of property,
as well as discourage its accumulation in large and growing classes by any single order of the community. As

might have been expected, Coleridge's newspaper record
at that date was such as to deter the sane proprietors
of the *Times* or of any other newspaper from engaging
on his own conditions even such a genius as himself.
His slight military experiences as a cavalry private were
enough to make him as bitter against the army authorities
as had been Cobbett himself. Recently he had given
vent to these feelings in an article denouncing the Duke
of York when Commander-in-Chief. This article was
written for but never published in the *Courier*. The
Treasury, indeed, in some unexplained way, got wind of
the poet's screed, not only after it was in type, but
after two thousand copies of the issue for which it was
intended had been struck off. Rather than face a Government prosecution, Stuart stopped the press. Coleridge
therefore escaped public identification with this assault on
the Government. The whole story, however, had been
gossiped about by Fleet Street, from Temple Bar to Blackfriars. Better a writer who is dull than one who is
dangerous formed the wise motto of the *Times* managers.
Nor is this the only case in which an illustrious child of
the muses has set a price upon his services which the
unsympathetic compilers of the world's contemporary
history from day to day have refused to entertain.

No details can be given concerning the men who
have co-operated with its owners to make the *Times*
the first newspaper in Europe, before some mention of
the family to which the journal belonged from the first,
and the part taken by different members of that family
in developing their literary property. Early in the
eighteenth century's second half, Robert Dodsley, who
had printed and published for Pope, Johnson, Goldsmith
and Chesterfield, received an apprentice destined to
become the founder of a great dynasty. This was the
John Walter who, born in 1739, learned his trade in
Dodsley's Charing Cross shop to such good result as,
some years later, first to become his old master's rival
in the bookselling business, secondly to start on an
entirely new industry for himself in Printing House
Square. The secret of the new business, known as logo-
graphic printing, was to set up type in whole words
as well as in single letters. In 1785 Walter turned this
innovation to practical account by employing it on a

broadsheet which he then called the *Daily Universal Register*, but which three years later he changed to the *Times*. There soon became traditional in the Walter line certain experiences which may well have warned them on the occasion already mentioned against employing so risky a writer as Coleridge. In 1789 the first John Walter's venture at paper and printing ink spoke its mind about the Duke of York. A State prosecution, of course, followed ; Walter was condemned to a fine of £50, to an hour in the pillory, to a year's imprisonment, and to give security for good behaviour for seven years afterwards. The pillory part of the sentence was remitted. The confinement at Newgate did not prevent Walter, any more than it had prevented Cobbett, or than a like incarceration had prevented Leigh Hunt, from managing his paper throughout his whole detention. Among Walter's staunchest friends and strongest backers was the Under-Secretary of State, Bland Burges, who first organised the Foreign Office in its modern shape and who found the means of ensuring that the founder of the *Times* should lose nothing by his Newgate sojourn. And this though, while he was serving his sentence, there were made against Walter fresh charges, involving additions to the original penalty. Eventually, however, after sixteen months of his cell, Walter was held to have expiated his libels upon the royal dukes, and returned to the newspaper office that was also his family residence. Invigorated by seclusion and partial repose, he at once used his regained liberty to improve the business arrangements of his paper. Perry's energy with the *Chronicle* stimulated him to fresh efforts. These included a small and rapid sailing ship ever in readiness to bring messages from his French correspondents as well as copies of any French newspapers, some of whose contents might be worth transferring to his own columns. That particular item in his arrangements had the effect of bringing Printing House Square once more into hostilities with Whitehall. Ever since the Duke of York imbroglio, the relations between the Government and the newspaper had been strained. At last, in 1804, matters came to a head. The *Times* then, with more vehemence than it had lately employed, accused Lord Melville (Henry Dundas), Pitt's particular friend, Treasurer of the Navy, of flagrant incapacity in administering his department. This naturally lost the Walters their business as printers to the Customs. The policy of their journal soon received complete justification from facts. The shock of his one confidant's impeachment may have hastened William Pitt's death. The proceedings sanctioned by Speaker Abbot's casting vote confirmed the charges of mis-management and corruption levelled by the *Times*, not only to the risk of its proprietors but to their actual loss, at the Admiralty. That, of course, only embittered official resentment against a newspaper which thus asserted its authority over a department of State. White-hall's ill-will survived the man who had excited it.

The founder of the *Times* had (1803) transferred the paper to his son when the reigning, otherwise the second, John Walter discovered that all packages for Printing House Square were stopped at Gravesend. Walter's complaint to the authorities brought him the reply that as a favour he might receive his continental despatches if he would promise a corresponding favour to the Government in the tone and spirit of his publi-cations. This condition was refused. Put upon his mettle, the second Walter strained his resources to secure early tidings from beyond the sea with such entire success that, in the ensuing rivalry, the newspaper again and again beat the Government hollow. Thus, during the Walcheren Expedition, the sole success, the English capture of Flushing, was known at Printing House Square four-and-twenty hours earlier than at the Foreign Office. Meanwhile the newspaper had marked an era in newspaper narrative by engaging the earliest of nineteenth-century special correspondents. This was Henry Crabb Robinson, the diarist, w' ι two years earlier, in 1807, the second Walter had sent out to Altona, not so much, however, to put on paper his impressions of European wartime as to pack an allotted space with the news and opinions of journals published in the actual scene of campaign. Robinson's travel sketches from the Elbe, Stockholm, and Gothenburg answered their purpose. His arrange-ments for a comprehensive foreign news service soon enabled the *Times* to distance its rivals in the race for early and accurate tidings from abroad. Robinson's work for the paper continued after the close of his travels as its representative. On returning to England, he began in 1808 in the capacity of foreign editor ; he was to attend at the *Times* office from five o'clock in the afternoon till as late an hour as his services might be required. He was thus a humble instrument in establishing the newspaper's credit for the European omniscience which formed one of the secrets of its power. Crabb Robinson, too, proved himself a useful servant not only by the work he did but by the stimulating example which he left. Nearly a generation after its alacrity in announcing the already mentioned fall of Flushing, the great journal, still during the second John Walter's reign, anticipated all its contemporaries in obtaining probably direct from the Czar's Government at St. Petersburg the Russian protocol recently accepted by the Duke of Wellington in the Russo-Turkish negotiations, then engaging our Foreign Office, about Greece.

No newspaper man ever stamped, in characters more distinct and durable, his personality upon his journal than was done by the second John Walter upon the *Times*. This remarkable man resembled his father in being not only the business manager but the actual editor of his great and growing broadsheet. That authority, however, he found it convenient titularly to share with some of those composing his literary staff. This staff contained several notable names, especially Peter Fraser, William Combe, and Edward Sterling, of whom more will be said later. The first chosen for this honour was, in 1810, John Stoddart. Educated at Salisbury Grammar School and at Christ Church, Oxford, he began his connection with the paper as a parliamentary reporter. On terms of personal intimacy with Coleridge, Southey, and others of the French Revolutionary or, as Byron called it, the pantisocratic school, he had been converted to Burke's loathing for French Jacobinism, had emphasised and amplified the recantation of his early heresies in the leading columns of the newspaper. Walter, however, wanted for his second in editorial command not so much a man who could write well himself as one who would be the cause of good writing in others ; he must also, in the great paper's interest, have a quick eye for rising journalistic talent in any quarter. Stoddart, though a good worker, hated taking trouble of any kind. The really irksome but, from his employer's point of view, the most essential part of his duties was systematically neglected. The inevitable dispute followed ; in 1817 Stoddart left Walter's employment and started an opposition sheet of his own. The paper to which he transferred his services, the *Day*, bore a title revived some half a century later for a daily print of Tory principles not exactly those of Stoddart, whose political creed became Napoleon on the brain, and who saw in the " Corsican fiend " the incarnation of evil. In 1818 Stoddart's *Day* rechristened itself the *New Times*. Here he failed equally as editor and writer. His pompous panegyrics on our great and glorious constitution won him the sobriquet of " Dr. Slop," as well as, in 1820, made him the subject of a pamphlet entitled *A Slap at Slop*. The journalist who provokes a quarrel with his employer commits suicide. Fortunately Stoddart had in his earlier days gone through some legal studies. These now qualified him for the justiceship of the Vice-Admiralty Court in Malta.

Stoddart's successor on the *Times* has already been mentioned among those forming the Christ's Hospital group of newspaper men so active and distinguished during the first quarter of the nineteenth century. Thomas Barnes went directly from school to journalism. At twenty-one he was writing occasional articles for the *Times*, as well as for his friend Leigh Hunt's *Examiner* The productions, however, that first brought him into notice appeared in the *Champion*, edited by Cyrus Redding. These papers, signed Strada, formed a lively and brilliant series of criticisms on English poets from Shakespeare and Milton to Campbell and Rogers, as well as of a few novelists, chiefly those belonging to the early nineteenth century, and in particular Mrs. Opie and Miss Edgeworth. In fiction, however, Barnes's favourite authors were Fielding and Smollett. Here are names recalling Leigh Hunt's discriminating remark ; when speaking of his old school-fellow he said : " Barnes might have made himself a name in wit and literature had he cared much for anything beyond his glass of wine and his Fielding." Indeed, their author's habits made his articles somewhat difficult for editors to get. Writing materials and reference books were near his bedside. He had the gift of waking at daybreak with a clear head, and of getting through his work while the printers who were to set it up still slept. For Leigh Hunt's *Examiner* Barnes furnished pieces of a very different kind. His early experiences in the Gallery had acquainted him with the manner and appearance of the men most famous in both Houses. His parliamentary character sketches in the *Examiner* formed the earliest specimens extant of the pen and ink photographs which, beginning with Barnes, have since, from hands not inferior to his, admitted whole generations to the inner life of both Chambers.

As editor of the *Times*, Barnes from the first avoided his predecessor's faults. Stoddart, it has been seen, showed himself jealous of literary ability in any of his staff, regarded his own writings with a complacency surprising in a really clever man, and practically refused to help Walter in securing fresh contributors. Barnes took infinite pains to enlist the ablest writers under him —whether they happened to live by their pen or not. Personally he had no liking for Brougham. He even occasionally crossed swords with him in matters affecting the conduct of the paper. In 1830, Brougham, as Lord Chancellor, had gone into the Upper House ; he took offence at the remarks made by the *Times* on the Duchess of Kent's absence from William IV.'s Coronation. One of the Chancellor's representatives called on the editor to inquire about the source of the knowledge shown in the article. Barnes was not to be pumped ; from that moment began the feud between Printing House Square and the Keeper of the Royal Conscience. As a fact, and as Brougham suspected, the editor's informant in this matter had been the Chancellor's particular aversion, Lord de Ros. This was not the only personal collision between the two men. Brougham, indeed, took the lead among the Whigs in resenting the newspaper's attacks on the Grey Reform Bill, and especially on Lord Grey himself. From whose pen had these onslaughts come? Some said "The young Benjamin Disraeli " ; others "Lord Durham." In 1834 the newspaper once more found itself at loggerheads with the Ministry over the new Poor Law Bill. The coming resignation of the entire Whig Cabinet did not prevent another assertion of his inquisitorial authority by Brougham, with no more result than the former, except a widening of the breach between Downing Street and Blackfriars. The personal forces that had established this early antagonism between the *Times* and the Whigs made themselves felt some way into the Victorian Age.   Barnes, a retiring man, who went as little into society as he could, rather than live with the Whigs, made no secret of his wish to live against them.

There is a general idea that the *Times* has, like the bishops, for the most part independently supported the Government of the day.   As a fact, the personal forces which, already mentioned, made the *Times*, were by choice always strong for the Tories, only giving the Whigs or Liberals a good word when they were carrying out a Tory policy or kept in office by Tory votes.   The paper may thus be said always impartially to have represented the innate Conservatism of the country ; it began to do so by being consistently Ministerial under Liverpool, Canning, and Wellington, as well as uniformly Oppositionist under Grey and Melbourne.   The great national reforms, however, prepared for under George IV., actually carried forward in the next reign, were accomplished not only without the newspaper's help, but in the teeth of its strong resistance.   This was the policy of Barnes, and, as will presently be seen, he did his utmost to secure its continuance by his successor Delane.   Yet before his frequent quarrels with Barnes, Brougham had been among the newspaper's most regular and highly-paid writers, furnishing a daily " leader " during the years in which much occasional verse appeared in the same columns from Thomas Moore and T. B. Macaulay ; but Macaulay, though his literary influences were afterwards seen plainly enough in Printing House Square, does not seem to have written articles or prose of any kind.

Among the makers of the most representative newspaper ever produced in England or in any other country, a place must be given to a man inferior neither as writer nor thinker to any of those already mentioned. When, in 1817, Thomas Barnes entered upon the control of the *Times*, he found that the second John Walter's discriminating energy had already secured for the paper

a man one of whose phrases supplied the *Times* with
an alias formerly as familiar as it is now forgotten.
" We thundered out the other day an article on social
and political reform," had been the words with which
Edward Sterling opened one of his attacks upon the
Whig Government. Hence the " Thunderer," subsequently to be supplemented as a nickname by the
" Organ of the City." Some of Leigh Hunt's characteristics as a newspaper-writer have been traced
back in these pages to his ancestral vicissitudes and
idiosyncrasies. In like manner Edward Sterling's slashing pen reproduced qualities of his swashbuckling fore-
father. That " Scottish Gustavus-Adolphus soldier," to
quote Carlyle's description, who sprang from the same
stock as the Scotch Stirlings of Keir, displayed personal
sympathies with the Duke of Ormond faction, which
separated him from his friends of the Parliament. This
Colonel Robert, after 1649 Sir Robert Sterling, personally recommended himself to Charles II. At the Restoration he became an Irish landlord of wide estate and
great consideration in Munster. His descendant, Edward
Sterling's father, was Clerk of the Irish House of Commons at the time of the Union ; then, to compensate
him for the loss of his position, he received a pension
of two hundred a year. Edward Sterling himself, born
in 1773, went through Trinity College, Dublin, was called
to the Irish Bar. In 1798 he joined a corps of loyal
volunteers raised by the Irish barristers for putting down
the rebellion. These experiences left him with a dislike
for law that caused him to quit the bar and with a
turn for soldiering gratified by a captaincy in the Lancashire Militia. In 1804 he married Miss Hester Coning-
ham. This lady not only made him a capable and
devoted wife, but transmitted many of her higher qualities, spiritual and intellectual, to the son of this marriage,
the Broad Church clergyman John Sterling, who had
Carlyle for his friend and Archdeacon Hare for his
biographer. The family settled near Cowbridge in
Glamorganshire. Here began the connection between
sword and pen which was to prove the starting-point
for the memorable connection with the *Times*. Captain
Edward Sterling had been appointed adjutant of the
Glamorganshire Militia in 1811 ; he at once wrote a

pamphlet on military reform, dedicated to the Duke of
Kent. A chance communication on a local subject with
Printing House Square introduced him to John Walter.
In 1812 began, under the signature of "Vetus," the
trenchant and emphatic letters on Napoleon, Catholic
Emancipation, national defence, the mutual and necessary hostility of England and France. "Bravo !"
greeted these compositions on every side. "Here is
some one not afraid to write like a man," approvingly
growled the "Iron Duke," then making arrangements
to smash Napoleon at Waterloo. His brother, the
classically-minded Wellesley, chuckled with delight.
"This," exclaimed Lord Lyndhurst, "is the sort of
writing which makes the editor of the *Times* the first
man in the country."

In 1815 the Sterling household had settled itself on
the Thames, close to the spot on which Blackfriars Station
now stands, and in a house near that afterwards to be
J. T. Delane's in the long since vanished Chatham Place.
Except for an autumnal holiday, Sterling remained in or
near London till his death in 1847. His *Times* salary
did not fall much short of an ambassador's or a Cabinet
Minister's wage, as that wage in Sterling's day was.
It sufficed not only for all his wants but, had he wished it,
for something of the state befitting the Olympian employment of which he was proud. His articles derived their
great effect from other qualities than the strength and
sting of their invective. They interpreted with great
felicity and skill the popular sentiment of the hour.
Reading them to-day, one is chiefly struck by the absence
from them of the heat and abuse that then weakened
much really good newspaper work. Some credit for
these virtues must be given to the moderating temper
of the second John Walter, who discussed the subject
of the day with Sterling before he wrote, and exercised
an editorial prerogative with the proof. Whether, after
1817, Barnes took a part in the preliminary consultations
is a secret of the prison-house. Sterling therefore might
well, as it was remarked he did, emphasise the editorial
"we," seeing that the policy of the paper, expressed
in his smart and vigorous sentences, was the product
of several different intellects co-operating with each other.
The first person plural is applied with no more affecta-

tion and at least as much accuracy by the leader-writer
as by the leader of the House when announcing the decisions of his Cabinet.   While thus stating his own
opinions, the *Times* under the second John Walter became the interpreter, which it long remained, of the convictions or prejudices, the partialities and the antipathies,
entertained by the upper section of the ten-pound house-
holders in whose hands political power was lodged by
the Reform Bill of 1832.   From Sterling's day onward,
in fact, the average Englishman of the better sort not
only read and pondered Sterling's and his successors'
leaders, but talked them too.

Meanwhile other pens than the original " Thunderer's " were contributing to establish its best and most
enduring traditions for the paper.   The Captain Shandon
of *Pendennis* wrote his prospectus for the *Pall Mall
Gazette* in the Fleet Prison, and there the printer's boy
used afterwards regularly to repair for the incarcerated
captain's copy.   Between the Sterling of real life and the
Shandon of fiction, there was not, as will be more particularly shown hereafter, the slightest connection.   The
Times, however, of Sterling's day occasionally printed
a column or less of lighter matter furnished by a " remarkably fine old gentleman with a stately figure and
a handsome face," who wrote under Shandon's conditions.
This was William Combe, of *Dr. Syntax* notoriety ; his
usual address was the King's Bench Prison, but he
sometimes contrived on an *exeat* to visit Printing House
Square.   Combe was a strange, shrewd man, keenly
observant, and of an experience extraordinarily varied
and wide.   His writing may not have been particularly
valuable to the paper, but there is no doubt that its
proprietor consulted him more intimately and frequently
than Barnes altogether liked.   Walter was prepared to
do more for Combe than Bungay had ever undertaken
for Shandon.   He would, that is, had Combe allowed
him, have settled all the money claims and restored him
to freedom.

Men long whispered Sterling's name as the supreme
forger of the literary bolts from Blackfriars.   He was,
however, only one among several writers who, in a degree
scarcely less important than the editors who directed
their pens, were instrumental in giving to the *Times* its

distinctive character. Printing House Square in its
earlier days had much attraction for young clergymen
unattached, often known on the premises as "roving
rabbis." One of these, by name Peter Fraser, the senior
by some years even of Barnes in his *Times* connection,
obtained his first employment on the paper less as a
writer than an out-of-doors "snapper-up of unconsidered trifles." The business of this newspaper
Autolycus was to collect less facts than opinions.
Wherever representative Englishmen were in the habit
of congregating, at places of business or amusement,
of profit or pleasure, in the public locomotive, at refreshment bar, in the eating-house, there it was the reverend
gentleman's business to be. There he stayed, alert in
body, with vigilant eye, quickly receptive ear, electric-
ally impressionable memory, and hair-trigger wits, till
the confused mass of what he saw and heard yielded him
evidence of the feelings which, on matters of the moment,
united the miscellaneous groups of human beings whose
study he had reduced to a science. This discovery made,
he was free to return with a report to his editor or to his
own room, that he might write. As vehement and vivid,
when occasion required, as Sterling himself, Fraser's
leaders were noticeable for the adroitness and accuracy
with which they reflected opinion as well as guided
and to some extent created it. Fraser knew the capital
better than he did the provinces. London, east or west
of Temple Bar, now saw in the *Times* a kind of Delphic
oracle, to be consulted in perplexity through the strictly
anonymous Fraser as its high priest. It was neither
the enterprise of a Walter, the comprehensive master-
fulness of Barnes, nor the cosmopolitan tact of Delane
which won for the *Times* the reputation of London infallibility that made foreigners call it the "organ of the
City." The articles in which Fraser held up the mirror
primarily to metropolitan but also to national life and
thought were probably among the earliest and certainly
the best known agencies that made the *Times* office
one of the sights of London, and in foreign eyes gave
its controllers the lion's share of an authority divided
by them with the Lord Mayor. The generation following
Fraser's also drew to Printing House Square its own
clerical recruits, but under a new editor, who had chiefly

to carry on the processes set in motion by Walter and Barnes. The House of Commons is wiser than its wisest member, a great newspaper greater than its greatest editor or writer. In the story of every broadsheet there comes a time when it is the journal which makes the man, rather than the man who shapes or sways the journal. So was it with Printing House Square by the middle of the nineteenth century.

The Delanes owed their connection with the Walters to the settlement in 1775 at Old Windsor of Cavin Delane, whom the good offices of the Villiers family had helped to become Serjeant-at-Arms to George III. Cavin Delane's son, a barrister, had a country home at Bracknell, four or five miles from Wokingham, near which, at Bearwood, John Walter the second, having consolidated his dynasty in Printing House Square, had founded a Berkshire family. During his parliamentary contests, which, in 1832 and 1835, brought him in for the county, he found supporters and active helpers in his Bracknell neighbour, W. F. Delane, and his second son (J. T.), then a student at King's College, London. Struck by the business aptitudes of this strenuously sympathetic neighbour, Walter made W. F. Delane his financial manager, destining also from the first to some position in his office the youth, J. T. Delane, whose zeal and industry had brought him many useful and uncertain votes. Before that opportunity came, Walter's editor-elect had finished his course at Magdalen Hall. He had entered on his twenty-fourth year when Thomas Barnes died. "A man who used the utmost power of the press without arrogance and without bitterness to any one, whose sudden and premature death was lamented by all." Such were the words in which the young Delane summed up the impression left on himself as well as on others by the editor whom he was to succeed, and of whose methods his early familiarity behind the scenes at Printing House Square had naturally shown him much. In addition to this, foreseeing his ultimate succession to himself, Barnes in some short memoranda impressed on Delane the expediency of supporting Lord Aberdeen, but of distrusting and opposing the party to which he belonged, Lord Melbourne, Lord John Russell, and the Whigs generally. That counsel, in all its broad features,

was systematically carried out. When, therefore, in the
fifty-second year of its existence, Delane followed Barnes
at the *Times*, he had simply to proceed on the lines laid
down by the experience and wisdom of his predecessors.
He established no new tradition and made no change in
an old policy. The one novelty in the journalistic record
of the Delanian era was the increase of the material
agencies at his command, and the periodical increase
of mechanical improvements unknown and undreamt of
before his day. The social position to which the new
editor had been born helped him in turning to better
account than may have been done by most before him
his editorial opportunities. In doing this, he was, moreover, but gratifying the social instincts that were as
marked in him as they had been entirely absent from
Barnes. Between Delane and his immediate predecessor,
there thus existed a personal contrast. That, of course,
may have reacted on the work of the two men ; it did
not affect their editorial methods, which were the same.
His Oxford education and his family connections gave
Delane from the first many well-placed friends. Troubled
with none of the reserve that kept Barnes so much out
of evidence, he soon became, at the beginning of his
course, a welcome guest everywhere, culling his honey
from every flower. Even Barnes, however, in his latter
days, had expanded himself in club and drawing-room.
This was inevitable from the connections created for him
by his work. The same thing, of course, holds true of
all gentlemen charged with editing the *Times* or any
other even less considerable journal, and will for all time
be the case. Edward Stanley, Bishop of Norwich, his
more famous son, the future Dean of Westminster, then
signing himself in the paper " Anglicanus," George
Grote the historian, Jones Loyd, afterwards Lord Over-
stone the banker, began under Barnes the contributions
which some of them were to continue under his successor.
The chief influence which drew Barnes out of his shell
was that of Benjamin Disraeli ; his *Runnymede Letters*
(1836) secured Barnes his gratitude, and brought that
editor an invitation to join the Carlton Club in the
year of his contributor's election to it. The offer was
refused, but as Disraeli's guest Barnes soon became
no stranger in the establishment. The record of the

two-score years all but three (1840-77) of Delane's editorship is so much that of nineteenth-century England, and in various ways has been written so often as to make it a part of general rather than of journalistic history. About Delane's dealing with national or international questions, and about the quality of the knowledge he sometimes displayed, some details will presently be given. All these points, however, were illustrated by the attitude of his paper, 1845-6. Chronological order renders it proper now to say something as to those years. In December, 1845, readers of the *Times* were told of a decision taken by the Peel Cabinet to meet Parliament in the first week of the following January for the purpose of considering the Corn Laws, with a view to their total repeal. So far from this being the case, Sir Robert and his colleagues had made up their minds to resign.[1] They did so a little later, coming back soon afterwards because the jealousies between Grey and Palmerston made a Liberal Administration impossible. In reference to the whole Free Trade controversy, the *Times* began with sneering at Cobdenism as a kind of midsummer madness, but was forced by the anti-Corn Law demonstrations at Manchester to recognise in the League a great fact. The largest European event during the first half of the Delanian era was the Crimean campaign. Had Delane been not only the strong, shrewd man he of course was, but cast in the absolutely heroic mould, as sometimes described, he might not have been able to arrest the process ; but he would probably at least have found an occasion for a weighty protest against the fatal policy of drifting, instead of, as he did, adopting that policy for his own. Palmerston had become the idol of the man in the street. More and more abandoning all show of criticism, Delane made his paper frankly Palmerstonian also. And yet he had become a jingo in spite of himself. He had been dragged into putting, as Lord Salisbury afterwards phrased it, his money on the wrong horse. Palmerston had always headed for war ; Aberdeen, with whom the editor was most closely associated, had from the first drifted. Delane did exactly the same, which is but another way of saying

[1] Spencer Walpole's *History of England*, vol. v. p. 133, though at the time the mistake had been detected and exposed by A. W. Kinglake.

that, when the people's blood is up, great papers and great editors will follow and not lead. During the progress of the struggle, by his penetrating and comprehensive vigilance, Delane became a model for all future editors. Once satisfied of a leader-writer's or correspondent's judgment, sense, and trustworthiness, Delane let him, as much as might be, work out his subject on his own lines, though he did not, because he believed in his writers, scrutinise their work the less severely. Seeing everything that went into the paper, he showed himself specially happy in the finishing touches he occasionally gave. Thus to " Nick Woods' " account of the Heenan and Sayers fight he added the words : " Restore the prize ring? As well re-establish the Heptarchy ! " The judgment with which he chose his writers at the seat of war was shown not only in the dispatch of W. H. Russell, but in the choice of men less known at the time, though they proved them-selves not less effective, such as Thomas Chenery, as well as Lawrence Oliphant, correspondents with the Turks, and Stowe at Varna. To echo Kinglake's criticism that the accounts from headquarters commissioned by Delane kept the enemy acquainted with all that was going on, is merely to say that the satisfaction of the public demand for war news may have dangers as well as its refusal. Whether or not, as a rival peeress charged her with doing, the great Lady Jersey reported for the *Times*, Barnes had certainly received occasional contributions from drawing-rooms as well as from Whitehall offices or Pall Mall clubs. Delane not only continued but largely extended this precedent. A man of Society him-self, he used his paper in what he honestly believed to be Society's best interests. The social mixture which came in during the second half of his course was an innovation on the exclusive regime of early Victorian days from which he foreboded mischief, and on which he wrote largely with his own pen—so strongly did he feel on the subject—more than one warning article. Unlike some of his old friends whose exclusiveness proved less strong than the cosmopolitan associations of the turf for which they first lived, Delane never gave in to the earlier indications of the craze for democratic smartness ; such he shrewdly predicted as eventually must base the polite system not on birth or breeding but on wealth. If the *Times* had been robbed by competition of the political supremacy it once claimed, the loss was more than compensated by the immense access of power in social matters accruing to it from the line taken by its editor.

"He seems to me to be equal to anything" had been Delane's verdict on the doings of one of his men who had been told off for some particular duty. This gentleman, Thomas Chenery, more than any of his contemporaries, specially trained, moulded, trusted by Delane, deserved much of the credit, especially in regard to foreign affairs, generally given to Henry Reeve. When, after 1877, he filled the editorship, he soon gave a place on the staff to his own successor, the accomplished gentleman who now reigns in Printing House Square. Delane did not live to witness the proof of decline in the journalist's political power as forthcoming in the Unionist collapse of 1906, notwithstanding the united efforts for the contrary of, with a few exceptions, the metropolitan, and, a great extent, though in a less degree, of the provincial press. Or if, indeed, he suspected the political leader of exercising less power than formerly, not only he, but those who filled his chair after him, had observed the journalist's increased authority in the purely social sphere. Mr. Chenery, therefore, began by giving fresh prominence to non-political topics, increasingly in signed articles from popular pens outside the regular staff. So far, this precedent has been faithfully followed, and does not seem likely to go out of date. The charge against a newspaper of a mistake in policy is a matter of opinion. A charge of inaccuracy in fact may be brought to a practical test. Delane, it has been seen, showed no strength or originality of statesmanship in his treatment of the Crimean episode. As regards the American Civil War of the sixties, he only shouted with the biggest mob when, like all the publicists and most of the statesmen of the day, he supported the South against the North. An error of statement, into which he was betrayed some years earlier characteristically recalls his periodical brushes with Cobden, and was on this wise. During the fifties, the *Times* announced as a novelty Prussia's consent to join the German Zollverein, the fact, as Cobden was not slow to point out, being that this Customs league had been founded a generation earlier by Prussia herself. As a set-off against this rare case of editorial neglect, take this instance of his extreme care in verifying anything like a sensational statement even from a trustworthy quarter. Delane's Printing House Square period was coming to an end when, in 1875, his Paris correspondent, Blowitz, sent him news of the Prussian plan for reopening the war against France. Not till after a fortnight of the letter's arrival did its contents see the light. In the interval Delane had personally investigated the whole matter, had sent Chenery on a secret inquiry to Paris. The sensation known as the war scare of 1875 was thus only flashed upon the world when the editor and his aides-de-camp had sifted every statement in connection with it. A decade later, in 1886, under the then latest management, the paper was duped by the impostor Pigott into publishing the Parnell forgeries. Ten minutes' reflection, and the slightest practical use of table talk that would long since have reached Printing House Square, would have prevented this imposition's success. C. S. Parnell never wrote a line except under compulsion. It was simply inconceivable that he should have troubled to disguise his caligraphy in the laborious production of folios representing the work of many days.

With one of the significant editorial arrangements concluded during Delane's editorship in Printing House Square, Delane himself had nothing to do. Coleridge and Hazlitt's connection with it had not made journalism in the popular belief entirely respectable. In 1842 Lord Blachford, then Frederick Rogers, seeming to think he might, if he wished, be editor of the *Times*, consents to try his hand as a writer. Not, indeed, even this without sore compunction, and only when he has satisfied himself he can do just as much or little as he pleases, and that no one except his private friends will know. The duties, once undertaken, prove less voluntary than had been anticipated. The matter is only of importance so far as the air of condescension, that occasionally breathes out in Lord Blachford's reminiscence of the incident, shows journalism to have made no real advance in popular estimation between the thirties and the sixties. The

Times, of course, and one or two other papers were
exceptions, but during the third or fourth decades of
the nineteenth century even newspaper writers who were
winning fresh repute for their craft as well as themselves were compelled to accept payment at the rate
of ten shillings for a yard-long column of matter.

CHAPTER VIII

THE MEN WHO MADE THE PENNY PRESS

Peter Borthwick in Parliament—A terrible threat—He becomes editor oɪ the *Morning Post*—Succeeded by his son Algernon, who buys the sheet—Its policy and position in the public world—The *Post* at a popular price—Origin of the *Morning Herald*—A scurrilous print—The Baldwins—Rivalry with the *Times*—The *Standard* as an evening paper—The Baldwins' staff—Giffard—"Bright, broken Maginn"—Proprietorial changes—James Johnstone's enterprise—The *Standard* as a morning print—Reductions in price —Captain Hamber—Fighting editors—Hamber's writers—His summary dismissal—The Mudford era—Some audacious coups—Occasional contributors—The *Standard* in later years—Its unsuccessful rivals—Quick work—The Lawsons and the *Daily Telegraph*—Foundation of the penny press—The *Telegraph* writers—Dickens and the *Daily News*—The novelist-editor's ill-success — The work of the Dilkes — Famous correspondents of the *Daily News.*

PERSONAL influences, however, between the later forties and the sixties began to change the journalistic situation much for the better. Before dwelling upon these, something will at this point appropriately be said concerning another newspaper family, not less well known than the Walters, and connected during two generations with the oldest of all London dailies. Neither the *Morning Post's* superior antiquity nor its fashionable prestige was allowed to prevent its reduction of price in 1882 from threepence to the popular penny, with results that have fully justified the bold experiment. As member for Evesham (1835-47), Peter Borthwick made his mark at Westminster and became a personage in society. He had entered St. Stephen's as a rising hope of Conservatism. His maiden speech was listened to with the closest attention by the then Protectionist leader, Sir Robert Peel. His subsequent utterances were less successful, and were apt to provoke not so much cheers as yawns. That was a mode of reception which so tried him as to provoke a retort less felicitous than funny. " If," he said, " I am not allowed to conclude at my own time and in my own way, I am determined not to conclude at all." The deviser of this verbal quaintness transmitted not only his first-rate brains but his good looks, his olive complexion, his profusion of black hair, and in particular his roundness of head, to his son Algernon, the future Lord Glenesk. To him, rather than to his excellent biography by Mr. Lucas, the present writer is indebted for the personal details concerning Lord Glenesk's journalistic course to be given here.

The pedigree of Algernon Borthwick's paper, the *Morning Post*, has been fully given on an earlier page. Not till some time after it had passed out of Stuart's hands did there appear in it the eulogy of the Regent which excited Leigh Hunt's wrath, and his answer to which eventually lodged him in prison. At that date its chief owner was Tattersall, and among those who shared with him some interest in it was the Prince of Wales himself. Though it had been brought into fashionable repute, it had not yet overcome its business troubles. The paper-maker, a Lancashire manufacturer named Crompton, held a mortgage on the paper which eventually placed him in the position of sole owner. In or about 1850 the already mentioned Member for Evesham had left Parliament, and unsuccessfully applied to the Foreign Office for employment abroad. He now entered the *Morning Post* office as, to use his son's exact word, *gérant*, or perhaps general, political not less than literary, manager. His son Algernon, before going to King's College School, London, had (1841-3) been educated in Paris and could speak French like a native, as well as write in it, not only all necessary prose but some very passable verses, if some way after those in the same language written by another Paris correspondent, Frank Mahony (Father Prout), the *Globe's* representative on the Seine during later years of the same period. In 1852 Peter Borthwick's death was followed by his son's recall from the French capital to make himself generally useful at the *Morning Post's* London office. In no vocation more surely than in journalism do brains and knowledge mean power. From his place in the manager's department, Algernon Borth-wick's universal aptitudes reached the editor's room. By degrees the journal's supreme control and after-wards its proprietorship concentrated themselves in this comely, clever, pawky and pleasant-mannered Scot, who, in his own agreeable person, afforded, it was said, a fresh justification for the Caledonian boast that the London press was a Scotch creation, and that Flodden had avenged itself in Fleet Street. Chief among the moneyed backers who enabled Borthwick to buy up the Crompton interest in the paper was Andrew Montagu, the wealthy Yorkshire squire formerly known as a pro-tecting providence of the Conservative party in general and of the Carlton Club in particular. Mr. Montagu had been acquainted, not only with Mr. Peter Borthwick but with the family of the Yorkshire lady whom that gentle-man married. The political flavour imparted to the *Morning Post* in the eighteenth century by Daniel Stuart was brought out more strongly a hundred years later by the Borthwicks. Of these the father, besides being a Tory stalwart in the Commons, had organised a specific Conservative interest constituting him the life and soul of the territorial resistance to the abolition of West Indian slavery. High Tory in Church and State, Algernon Borthwick was himself the *Morning Post* to at least the same extent as J. T. Delane ever personified the *Times*. He became thus, during the Victorian age, the expositor as well as heir of those principles in states-manship at home and abroad first made by Stuart part and parcel of the paper. At the same time, he possessed the vitalising intellectual energy which enabled him to transmit these ideas of newspaper conduct to posterity, and so to insure the *Morning Post* as a penny paper against any solution of continuity in the social considera-tion and the political importance won by it in a more costly and exclusive state of existence.

In its threepenny days Borthwick had mirrored in his paper the prejudices of the Conservative voters who kept a nominally Liberal premier, Palmerston, in office. Borthwick and his men it was who daily reminded the Minister that he received this support on the condition of discouraging parliamentary reform, as had been done by his master Canning. As to foreign affairs, whether with the Spaniard or with the Turk, he was to employ men not less after Palmerston's own heart than Sir Henry Bulwer, and to show more decidedly than had been done by Canning that Britain's interest compelled her to have a voice in every continental settlement. The polite world looked at the *Post*, not for news but to see the whole mind of Palmerston, which often meant only the whole mind of Borthwick. But on one point the paper refused to go with the Minister. Palmerston's exercise of ecclesiastical promotion, dominated, as it seemed, by his relative Lord Shaftesbury, was consistently evangelical. That did not please the society in which Borthwick moved, and was therefore censured by the Borthwick paper. The *Morning Post*, in its criticisms of the Palmerston bishops, became the mouthpiece of Samuel Wilberforce or George Anthony Denison. Generally, however, Borthwick's personal preferences not only made the *Post* Palmerston's organ, but may be said to have given that statesman a place among its writers ; for the briefs prepared by Palmerston to direct the manufacture of " leaders " often proved full enough and finished enough for wholesale production in the " leader " columns. During that part of the fifties in which Walewski was French ambassador in London, the notorious intimacy of his relations with Algernon Borthwick and his staff, if not, as was alleged by Lord Malmesbury, his own statement to that effect, spread a popular belief that the newspaper's Napoleonic sympathies had been secured by a regular subsidy.[1] Lord Malmesbury's words on this matter may have been influenced, perhaps unconsciously, by personal feeling ; for in 1859 he complained of the *Morning Post's* having received orders from the French Emperor to attack him on every possible occasion, adding : " The paper is also Palmerston's, so the connection between them is clear." In any case, such an accusation must be received with much reserve. Exactly the same thing was said about other English papers of the same period, especially the *Standard*.

For only twelve years less than a century and a half, from, that is, Bate Dudley to Algernon Borthwick and

---

[1] *Memoirs of an ex-Minister*, vol. i. p. 362 (1884 edition).

his successors, the adroitest newspaper runners of their
times have succeeded in making the *Post* now spoken
of what it always was and what it now is. Whether at
the price of threepence or of the penny to which, as
has been seen, it was reduced in 1882, five years after it
became Lord Glenesk's sole property, the personal per-
sistence and opportunities of its managers has brought
the *Morning Post* so closely into relation with political
parties and their controllers as to constitute the paper at
once the answering echo and the inspiring oracle of the
statesmen favoured by the " upper ten." In the columns
once supposed to reflect Palmerston the first call is still
given for choice to writers of parliamentary or official
training. During the seventies and eighties the best
foreign policy " leaders " in the *Post* were those of
Mr. F. H. O'Donnell, once the Cavan M.P., written on
occasions chosen by Borthwick's singularly sagacious
editorial deputy and *alter ego*, Sir William Hardman.
Mr. O'Donnell's, too, was the pen which, when not
occupied with international matters, reflected in the paper
his own really instructive sidelights on the mutual connection of Irish Statecraft and Churchcraft. The
same tradition shows itself as active in operation as ever
during the twentieth century's early years. Imperial
defence and fiscal readjustments have become the
questions of the day. They are dealt with in the newspaper after a fashion whose fullness and accuracy of
expert knowledge has not only informed those who
dissent from some of its conclusions, but has con-
fessedly compelled them to reconsider their own
positions.

This is all demonstrably due to the silky-mannered,
silver-voiced, genially-cynical, suavely-shrewd, clear-
sighted, hard-headed Scot who, after a struggle both
long and hard, contrived in the manner already described
to make the oldest London newspaper exclusively his
own, and to stamp it in every paragraph with his own
idiosyncrasy. The *Post*, when sold at threepence, had
a large and, though a mainly fashionable, a most commercially paying circulation. He was, therefore, under
no pressure of circumstance to change the price. Had
that charge been raised instead of reduced, the buyers and
patrons of the paper would not have withdrawn their

support. No proprietor who did not combine Algernon Borthwick's literary training, newspaper experience, knowledge of human nature, and well-placed confidence in himself would have ventured on an experiment from which all his old subscribers persistently united to dissuade him. Nor had he ever a moment's doubt that the "organ of the classes" would flourish more rather than less when, at a popular price, he had made it the democracy's organ of the Monarchy and the Empire.

Other newspaper owners have rivalled or anticipated Borthwick's sagacity, courage, and prevision. Relying on their own sound judgment alone, they have successfully popularised, both as regards cost and contents, journals first started under conditions whose continuance would have kept prosperity beyond the reach of the penny press. Indeed, long before Borthwick's feat, another London Scot had already worked out the scenes of journalistic transformation afterwards to be effected by the future Lord Glenesk. Before the day of Daniel Stuart, here considered as the *Morning Post's* true founder, the paper had for its editors at least two unfrocked or retired divines. One of these, in 1775, was Henry Bate, less scurrilous of pen and unsavoury of life than the brother priest who was to be his successor, Jackson. A quarrel with his employer or his colleagues severed Bate's connection with the *Post*. In 1780 he contrived to start the *Morning Herald*, whose nineteenth-century offspring was to be the *Standard*. Bate prospered, as did his journal. A family windfall gave him a little fortune. An appreciative Ministry made him a baronet ; from April 17, 1813, till 1824, when he died, Sir Edward Bate Dudley was a notability of the period. This newspaper baronet was by no means the first journalist of title. In 1681 the same honour had been given to another Fleet Street habitué, George Wharton. The Bate Dudley style was clearly due to the good offices of the Prince of Wales in the Regency period. The man selected for the honour had long done duty as a kind of convivial understudy to Sheridan and Fox at Carlton House and at the Pavilion. It was supremely indifferent to him what he printed or wrote so long as it raised a laugh or sold a copy, especially if it withdrew a single reader from his hated rival, the

Morning Post. Buffoonery, scurrility, riskiness of language, reeking of scandal, and only falling short of the obscene, had formed the staple of the unregenerate *Morning Post* under Bate's editorship. These features were reproduced in the *Morning Herald* in its most ancient and least edifying period. Bate Dudley, indeed, had no other ideas than those which had already done duty in his earlier paper. His only notion of novelty now was, in proportion as the *Morning Post* which had left him became more respectable and less Whig, to make the *Morning Herald* more anti-Tory and less nice.

A succession of men less indifferent to the proprieties than Sir Edward Bate Dudley, and more energetic than those connected with him was, between 1827 and 1857, to give the *Herald* or other sheets issuing from the same establishment a noticeable place in the newspaper narrative of the period. The earliest among the *Herald's* later owners was Edward Baldwin, a thoroughly respectable not less than enterprising and enlightened trader in journalism, who, two decades after Dudley's death, bought the paper from the little group of fifth-rate capitalists to which it had then gone. He at once entered on a course of spirited rivalry to the *Times.* Printing House Square, however, set all its resources in motion to crush the new competitor. By this time the arrangements, originally due to the second John Walter's efforts, for securing foreign news had increased so much in cost that he had admitted the *Morning Chronicle* and the *Morning Post* to a partnership in this matter only with him. From that association he persisted in excluding Baldwin. The object of Walter's animosity soon proved not less equal to the occasion than, under similar trials, Walter had formerly shown himself. So excellently did his continental intelligence service work that, very early in his proprietorship, the *Herald* won European reputation for the promptitude, the accuracy, and the fullness of its dispatches from beyond the seas. By 1844 Palmerston had been twice Foreign Minister ; he was then in opposition and abroad, but was universally pointed to as the one man who would dominate the entire policy, domestic as well as international, of the next Liberal Cabinet. To him, there-

fore, Baldwin determined on giving a general but independent support.

Meanwhile another newspaper runner of his own name
had come forward. This was Edward Baldwin's son
Charles, who had recently started by the purchase of the
St. James's Chronicle. That evening expositor, dating
from 1760, of plain Whig principles, transformed itself
promptly, under Baldwin's dexterous touch, into a Tory
sheet. He carried his efforts in this political direction
much further by bringing out for the first time, on
May 21, 1827, another evening paper called the *Standard*,
the sum and substance of whose whole programme was
the support of Tory Protestantism and resistance to
Catholic emancipation. His political friends had supplied their astute propagandist with £15,000 for launching the enterprise. Edward Baldwin had imitated the
second John Walter in being, as regards the *Herald*, for
the most part, his own editor. Conscious perhaps of
literary inferiority to his father, the son had engaged
as his literary conductor and adviser Stanley Lees
Giffard, an Irish writer of much cleverness and notoriety,
who, from having begun as editor of the *St. James's
Chronicle*, now became responsible for the *Standard*.
In newspaper diction and politics Giffard foreshadowed
the best known qualities of his still happily surviving
son, Lord Halsbury. That venerable and vigorous peer,
in some of his most characteristic speeches, might, indeed, sometimes be thought to have taken his father's
most militant and inspiring articles for models. Not,
indeed, that Giffard allowed himself to be a regular or
even frequent writer for his own paper. He knew his
business too well for that ; the editor had at hand, when
he was not an inmate of the Fleet Prison for debt,
a contributor deservedly famous for facility and skill in
the composition of slashing " leaders." This was W. C.
Maginn ; born at Cork in 1793, and educated at Trinity
College, Dublin, he had no superiors, if, indeed, any
equals, among the gifted young Irishmen then hurrying
to try their fortunes on the other side of St. George's
Channel. His best biography is written in J. G. Lockhart's well-known epitaph on his death, at Walton-on-
Thames, in 1842. His brilliancy and thriftlessness are
personified in Thackeray's Captain Shandon, to whom

reference has been already made. " Genius, wit, learning,
life's trophies to win." Those, as Lockhart says, were
his. What he lacked was " the great lord or rich cit
of his kin," and the discretion to " set himself up as
to tin." The lines conclude :

> " Barring drink and the girls, I ne'er heard a sin :
> Many worse, better few, than bright, broken Maginn."

Maginn notoriously having been Captain Shandon's
original, by what confusion of probabilities, it was once
asked, did Thackeray, when describing Bungay's dinner
party, represent as on terms of intimacy with Shandon
Mr. Wagg, not less indisputably drawn from Theodore
Hook, who never consorted with out-of-elbows scribblers,
and who generally contrived to dine with a lord? The
answer is simple. The association was as much a reflection of realities as were the characters of the two men.
Hook had started *John Bull* in 1820 as a Sunday paper.
Three years later he projected, but did not accomplish,
a Wednesday edition of it. Eventually, however, the
idea was carried out. In 1823 Maginn began to edit
the week-day edition of the Sunday print whose conception and execution make Theodore Hook a figure
among the purely personal journalists of the Georgian
era. Hook, a typical society journalist under the
Regency, is described at once more briefly and more
vividly in the Wagg of *Pendennis* and in the Lucian
Gay of *Coningsby* than in Barham's *Life* or Lockhart's
famous *Quarterly* essay. When, as frequently happened, Hook left the printer in the lurch, Maginn could
generally be trusted to turn out the kind and the quantity
of the " copy " wanted. The best proof of Maginn's
really high standing with competent judges as a Tory
writer is the fact that he was suggested, among others,
as a possible editor for the second John Murray's *Representative* at the starting of that paper in 1826. The
Representative's editorship, formally offered to the com-
poser of Maginn's epitaph, J. G. Lockhart, Walter Scott's
son-in-law, was refused by him for two reasons, one
of which shows newspaper editorship even in 1826
not entirely to have outgrown its traditional stigma.
Such a position, Lockhart and his father-in-law,

Scott, both protested, would not only compromise him seriously with his polite acquaintances, but would interfere with his pursuit of the legal profession. Shortly after this Lockhart, who had long been a writer for it, took the editorship of the *Quarterly Review*. Evidently, therefore, his real motive in declining the earlier proposal must have been a fear that, in stooping to newspaper employment, he would seem to degrade himself as well as risk his prospects at the Bar. Here it may be added that the future Lord Beaconsfield, then known as Disraeli the Younger, was never recognised as the *Representative* editor. He, indeed, like a friend of his named Powles, agreed to find some £20,000 for launching the enterprise ; he also, in the second John Murray's words, plied that publisher with his unrelenting excitement and importunity to such effect that, against his better judgment, he consented to the venture. The chief leader-writers were Lockhart and one or two of his friends then distinguished in politics and letters, but now only the shadows of names. Benjamin Disraeli bustled over Europe in quest of correspondents and of capital, but seems himself to have written little or nothing. It is therefore a pure fable to say, as has been said, that after two months' existence the *Representative* died of a leading article written by its editor Disraeli, and beginning with " Seated the other night in our box at the Opera." Afterwards, as will be seen presently, Disraeli made good with his pen his claim to be considered a " gentleman of the press." A newspaper-maker, however, he at no time was. The whole of this episode, with the complicated relations it involved between Benjamin Disraeli, his father on one hand, and Murray on the other, irresistibly recalls the situation described in *Vivian Grey*, in which the hero of the romance essayed just the same part in politics as that taken in journalism by the future Lord Beaconsfield, when urging Murray on to the costly enterprise. Trained in these schools, Maginn brought to the *Standard* in 1828 a clever trick of hitting off character in a few strokes of his pen, and enough of desultory, perhaps, but useful and well-remembered reading to give his paragraphs a literary flavour which made his work a pleasant relief to a generation that had begun to think its leading dailies were becoming, whatever their theme, intolerably didactic and desperately dull. For many years and under various editors, the present writer, with occasional breaks from the sixties till late into the eighties, was intimately connected with the journalistic offspring of Maginn's paper, the *Standard*, constituting, as that paper does, a link of the most varied and picturesque interest between the journalism of the last century and the present day. At one time there was on the Shoe Lane premises a messenger named Jenman, who, as a small boy, had daily brought Maginn's articles from that very room in the Fleet where Thackeray places Captain Shandon while penning the prospectus of 'the *Pall Mall Gazette*. During my own membership of the *Standard* staff at the points now looked back upon, Maginn's contributions could be identified frequently on the *Morning Herald* file, less often or easily on that of the *Evening Standard*.[1] Here they were studied less as patterns than as curiosities by us writers, while waiting to see the editor for his instructions. During the earlier years of James Johnstone's ownership, presently to be dealt with in detail, the *Standard* had for its editor Thomas Hamber, who encouraged one of his writers, George Painter, in a vein more humorous than the paper generally indulged. Matthew Arnold had spoken in his essays about the " young lions of Peterborough Court." Painter's little burlesques of their style were headed the " Gaily Bellograph," and, as their writer flattered himself, reproduced something of Maginn's humour.

Edward Baldwin's death left to his son Charles the *Morning Herald*. Concurrently with that, he carried on the evening newspaper founded by himself, the *Standard*. Hence, till 1868, the issue from the same office of the *Morning Herald* and the morning, as well as evening *Standard*. Meanwhile the Baldwin dispensation had long since come to an end, and been succeeded by an entirely new regime. Johnstone, Wintle, Cooper, and Evans constituted a well-known firm of accountants. One of the

---

[1] No more, of course, than that of the present day was the *Evening Standard* of the sixties the *Standard* in which Maginn wrote, nor was there any complete series of Baldwin's evening paper constituting the original *Standard*. Still there seems no reason why the articles traditionally called Maginn's may not have been from his pen.

partners in this business, James Johnstone, had a remarkable turn for politics as well as for figures. Social accidents had acquainted him with and brought him under
the influence of a future Dean of St. Paul's, H. L.
Mansel, then an Oxford tutor, famed for his rhetoric
and wit, as well as the militant leader of conservatism
on the Isis. Baldwin's affairs had fallen into hopeless
confusion ; his papers had gone down. A sagacious
and honest friend, John Maxwell, who subsequently
married Miss Braddon the novelist, advised him to refuse
no reasonable offer for his newspaper property. When
the sale had been effected, Maxwell's expert counsel
proved as valuable to the new owner as it had been to
the old. In truth, however, James Johnstone was clear-
headed and strong-minded enough to need no other counsellor than himself. He had secured a manager from one
of his partners in the accountancy firm, D. Morier Evans ;
to him the entire business department was entrusted.
The first step taken was on June 29, 1857, to bring out
the *Standard* as a morning paper, the price being reduced
from fourpence to twopence, and the quantity of matter
being doubled. Next year, February 4, 1858, the cost
was reduced still further to a penny, the *Morning Herald*,
though under the same management as the *Standard*,
continuing to be sold at fourpence. Two years later,
in 1860, the penny morning *Standard* published an afternoon edition also priced at a penny, and known as the
Evening Standard. James Johnstone placed in the same
hands the editorship of his two morning papers and his
evening one. The morning *Standard* and the *Morning
Herald* gave the same news but different leaders. If an
article struck the editor as a little over the heads of the
penny public, it generally went into the fourpenny *Herald*,
but was often lifted from that to do duty also in the
Evening Standard. At the beginning of its penny period,
the *Standard's* record gained a certain picturesqueness
from the thin, spare, but manly and handsome figure
which filled its editorial chair. Among the City persons
with whom Johnstone's business had brought him into
contact was a certain Insolvency Court official named
Hamber. This gentleman's son, with a turn for writing
and an instinct for politics, had been at Oriel while
Lord Goschen was still an undergraduate of the same

College, and during the same period that, among other Cabinet Ministers who were to be, the ninth Lord Salisbury and Ward Hunt, the future Chancellor of the Exchequer, were keeping their Oxford terms elsewhere. After that, Thomas Hamber served in the Swiss Legion during the Crimean War. On entering journalism he was known as Captain Hamber. Throughout the sixties and seventies he remained as familiar a personage in Pall Mall as in Fleet Street. Hamber in his best days united great intellectual quickness with many political opportunities, with wide social popularity, and with a certain personal magnetism which made him a leader of men. Never, perhaps, on the parliamentary staff, he had regularly attended the parliamentary debates about which he was to write articles. The two great *Times* editors already mentioned had been men of physical prowess. Barnes, at Cambridge, not knowing who he was, once prepared to square up to Tom Cribb himself, only to hear that master of fisticuffs murmur, with sleepy scorn, " I'm Cribb." Delane, while keeping his terms at Magdalen Hall, had not come off second best with another professional pugilist, the " Chicken of Wheatley." Had Johnstone's first editor had the same opportunities as Barnes or Delane for showing his pluck and prowess, he need not have feared comparison with them. With the help of a tact and temper equal to his other remarkable qualities, he might have retained his position throughout the Johnstonian period. Of the writers who, under him, helped to make the *Standard* newspaper in its new, that is, its now long familiar form, one, George Painter, has been already mentioned. The paper's many personal friendships if not interests abroad called for special wariness, knowledge, and tact in dealing with foreign affairs. With the unerring rapidity which he then seldom lacked, Hamber found the men exactly cut out for this particularly delicate and responsible work, a practised writer trained on the *Morning Chronicle*— Burton Blyth, and a future Poet Laureate. Mr. Alfred Austin had before this been connected with the *Daily Telegraph*. He was, however, best known by his first satirical poem, *The Season*, and, among an inner literary circle, by a clever and audacious attack on the *Saturday Review* and its editor in a pamphlet entitled a *Letter*

to Cook. The *Saturday* reviewers having been severe
on his verses, Mr. Austin ironically addressed their chief
as "evidently one of those genial, unceremonious,
thoroughly good fellows, who would be hurt if approached in a more formal manner." Of Roman Catholic
birth and education, Mr. Austin had lived much abroad,
especially in Italy, after leaving Stonyhurst, before being
called to the Bar in 1857. Continental politics were only
one of the subjects he had made his own. In 1870 he
won real distinction for the *Standard* as well as for
himself by the exhaustive circumstantiality with which,
almost immediately on its appearance, he refuted in
several columns Mrs. Beecher Stowe's *Lady Byron Vindi-
cated.* Often at headquarters during the Franco-Prussian
War, whether as correspondent abroad or leader-writer
at home, he personified in himself the better and popular
Standard which Johnstone had created just as the public
saw the threefold intellectual power that made the *Daily
Telegraph* in Edwin Arnold, George Sala, and Felix
Whitehurst. Mr. Austin's intimacy with the Trollope
family after he himself had ceased to travel for the
paper gave him the opportunity of putting the novelist's
elder brother, Thomas Adolphus Trollope, as Italian
correspondent, in the same relation to the *Standard* as
that to which, by Bulwer-Lytton's good offices, Antonio
Gallenga had been promoted on the *Times.* The then
Lord Robert Cecil contributed a few political slashers
under Hamber, but most of the hard hitting in this
department was done by Percy Greg, W. R. Greg's
clever son, and H. E. Watts, formerly editor of the
Melbourne Argus, who, in each of the Shoe Lane papers,
consistently and emphatically advocated Colonial Preference and an Imperial Tariff, while as yet Disraeli had
not meditated speaking in that sense, and long before
the ideas were officially recognised at any of the Conservative headquarters. Before or after his Crimean
spell of soldiering, Hamber had been much in Paris
and in several German capitals. The waiting-rooms
in Shoe Lane were in his day filled with foreign refugees
of all nationalities, seeking employment as translators
or with early and exclusive news from Continental
Embassies and Chanceries to sell. Such persons in the
sixties abounded in most newspaper offices ; they imposed

upon no one less than upon Hamber. Of Napoleon III.
and his personal surroundings Hamber's first-hand
knowledge equalled Borthwick's, and so of course gave
rise to the rumour that the *Standard,* as well as the *Post,*
was in the pay of the Tuileries. In the case of the
Standard this was as ancient a legend as it was in the
case of the *Post* ; for when in Baldwin's day it had been
an evening paper, it was currently spoken of as existing
mainly on a Napoleonic subsidy. During the Franco-
Prussian War, 1871, the *Standard* in its comments held
the balance equally between the two combatants, and
was mainly distinguished by its success in securing
Sir Henry Brackenbury to write his diary in the war, as
well as, on one or two occasions, to watch for it the
progress of the struggle from the battlefields themselves.
Then, as at such other times, it was chiefly represented
on the theatre of strife by G. A. Henty, while the eldest
brother of the present Lord Knollys, Major W. W.
Knollys, most frequently wrote the military " leaders."
Nor did any other editor of his time surpass Hamber
in attracting to his journal writers who professionally
showed themselves equally at home with the sword and
with the pen. Well thought of by Benjamin Disraeli,
whom he frequently visited in his London house at
Grosvenor Gate and in Buckinghamshire at Hughenden,
Hamber, before threatening cloudspots on his horizon
were discovered to be presaging a certain fall, was
admiringly pointed to by the wirepullers and minor
scribes of his party as a model Conservative editor of
the most militant and chivalrous type. Between 1861
and 1865, with the more demonstrative spirits of the
Carlton Club, approval of this editor was transfigured
into enthusiasm by his daily " leaders " maintaining the
Southern cause in the American Civil War, and yet
more by the letters, even more fiercely anti-Federal still,
signed " Manhattan," which sent up the circulation of
the paper by leaps and bounds. Neither Delane's unshaken ascendancy with the *Times,* nor the triumphant
advances of the Levy Lawsons, with the *Daily Telegraph,*
to the " largest circulation in the world " materially
impaired the personal prestige won by Hamber. In
1868, the collision between the two Houses over Gladstone's Irish Church Bill gave him the signal for re-

opening, with fiercer demands than ever of no quarter to the enemy, the war against Gladstonianism. The reckless rank and file cheered till they were hoarse. The judicious, however, began to shake their heads. Some of Hamber's own writers hinted to the proprietor the doubts they had long felt about a policy which chiefly consisted of charging a granite wall. Moreover, it was adroitly instilled into James Johnstone's mind that while Hamber won cheers by the constant raising of impracticable war cries, he also had his own axes to grind. If the paper were to render to the party services as valuable as undoubtedly were in its power, its conductor must take counsel with the party managers as well as ask for information from them. Great improvements in the *Standard* buildings were then going forward. It began to be whispered that when the new premises were further on their way to completion, a new editorial regime would begin. Hamber point-blank refused the proposal of anything like supervision by, or even co-operation with, any Conservative official from Parliament Street. The Carlton Club men were horrified at his audacity, and declared he would speedily find he had reached the end of his tether. No one, therefore, felt really much surprised when it became known that Johnstone's solicitor one October morning in 1870 had called upon Hamber at his Chiswick home with an intimation of his services being no more required. The dismissed editor carried off the crushing sentence with resigned and even cheery composure. He rallied his energies to fight against the ruin falling upon him ; he found a good friend in Morier Evans, the *Standard* manager. The two men combined their efforts. The result was a rival to the *Standard* in the shape of the short-lived *Hour*, about which something will be said presently. James Johnstone followed Hamber's dismissal from the *Standard* by overtures to the Conservative headquarters for cementing the traditional connection between the party and the paper. The arrangement decided on made James Johnstone's son nominally editor with Sir John Gorst to supply the defects of his political experience and Mr. A. P. Sinnett and Mr. Burton Blyth to read his proofs. So things went on until after 1874, when Sir John Gorst's criticisms of Lord Carnarvon's colonial policy brought about first his dismissal and then the end of the whole provisional regime. All this time, however, the shrewd owner of the *Standard* had his eye upon one of his Gallery staff, who, in 1867, had acted with great success as Jamaica correspondent during the Eyre-Gordon riots. This was W. H. Mudford, a member of a well-known journalistic and literary family. His father had been editor of the *Courier*, about which so much has already been said ; his mother had written novels, and his brothers, if not W. H. Mudford himself, had a share in more than one Kentish newspaper. The new editor made almost a clean sweep of the remnants of the old staff, the most notable exception being Mr. Alfred Austin. The then Laureate elect wrote through most of the Mudfordian epoch the same articles, both as to subject and quantity, which he had begun to furnish under Hamber. The uniform success attending his work made James Johnstone on his death name Mr. Mudford in his will not only editor in perpetuity, but manager with a substantial share in the paper's profits. The will at the same time provided that the *Standard* should always be conducted upon Conservative principles. Sir John Gorst, it has been said, had been got rid of for his audacity in criticising a Conservative Minister's dealings with the colonies. Placed beyond the possibility of sharing Sir John Gorst's fate, Mr. Mudford employed his omnipotence in Shoe Lane in openly showing a slightly contemptuous indifference as regards the instructions or the menaces, the prejudices, sensibilities, and threats of the Tapers and Tadpoles, in a word the whole tribe of " twelve-hundred-a-yearers," as, using Disraeli's phrase, he called the Tite Barnacles of the Conservative headquarters. Not one of the paper's arrangements, political, literary, commercial, mechanical, did Mr. Mudford neglect or fail permanently to improve. As good at organisation as editorship, he perfected all the arrangements for a Continental news supply. The daily Paris wire and other facilities provided by him for his French correspondent, Hely Bowes, made the *Standard*, for the first time in its life, in the matter of world-embracing news, commercial not less than political, a formidable competitor not only with the *Daily Telegraph* but with the *Times*. The editor of that paper, indeed, as for many others so for Mr. Mudford, had become a model, followed by him in details as well as generalities, down even to the headline of a side paragraph. Mr. Mudford's great strokes were due to the courage and resourcefulness enabling him alone among the journalists of his time to forestall in his columns the publication equally of important books and Government papers. In 1880 he gave the public Mr. Gladstone's forthcoming Irish Land Bill while it was yet in the Government printer's hands ; a little later he published a detailed account of Lord Beaconsfield's *Endymion*, at least a week before the earliest review copy of that novel had been sent out.

One of Delane's examples most successfully adopted by Mr. Mudford was the publication of headed articles, occasionally even leaders, from the pen of writers not belonging to his regular staff. Among these were Sir Clinton Dawkins, then in the India Office, who during the eighties enabled the *Standard*, in advance of the whole daily press, to publish full details concerning the creation of a reserve corps for the native army, and the maintenance of the Imperial Service Troops, paid and officered by the native States, but under British supervision, and available for general service under the Indian Government. These troops were, of course, distinct from those kept up by the States for purely local use, and practically for honorary and ceremonial purposes rather than for fighting. Colonel Stirling, then of the Scots Guards, also contributed many interesting and valuable paragraphs, a selection of short pieces embodying the latest news of the hour, and started by Mr. Mudford as an entirely fresh feature in the paper. For some quarter of a century he devoted his strong brains, energies, and opportunities to modernising or rather recreating the journal that, started by Charles Baldwin in 1827, had been in existence exactly two years less than three-quarters of a century when, in 1900, Mr. Mudford, on his retirement, handed it over to his second in command, George Byrom Curtis. This sure-footed, steady-paced, and most capable journalist had long taken charge of the paper in his chief's occasional absence, and had done all the night work. He was thus Mr. Mudford's only possible successor. The dispensation established in Shoe Lane since then has been one not of revolution but development. Under Hamber the *Standard*, it has been seen, advocated Colonial Preference. Its policy under Mr. Pearson has, therefore, marked a reversion to that whose keynote was first sounded during the second half of the last century.

Before passing to another order of newspaper makers, something may be said about the several gentlemen whose careers as newspaper projectors, inspired in some cases by the success of the Shoe Lane celebrities, left a wholesome and enduring mark on the journalism of their day. In 1874, with money found by his loyal Shoe Lane colleague of other days, D. Morier Evans, and by a few more friends, Tom Hamber started the *Hour*. Its speciality was to be the ultra-Protestant Conservatism whose headquarters were the National Club, Whitehall. It brought out several clever writers who have been heard of since. Chief among these were Sir Spencer Walpole, the historian, Mr. W. L. Courtney, while these lines are being written editor of the *Fortnightly Review*, and Mr. H. de B. Hollings, then fresh from Oxford, where as Fellow of Corpus, he had crowned a brilliant course with what Benjamin Jowett pronounced to be the best English essay which had won the Chancellor's Prize since J. A. Symonds', six years earlier. On the death of Hamber's tried and trusty ally, D. Morier Evans, under the auspices of a Presbyterian clergyman, the Rev. J. R. Badenoch, the *Hour* was kept alive by money doles at first from Colonel MacDonald and other gentlemen, chiefly Scotch, of whom Lord Balfour of Burleigh is to-day probably the one survivor. After several subsequent vicissitudes, Mr. MacDougall financed it for a time as the organ of his opposition to Baron Albert Grant. But in 1876 there came a day when, as he afterwards said to Hamber, Disraeli "heard with a pang that the *Hour* was no more." So ended the second and the last attempt at organising an opposition to the *Standard*. The first of these efforts belonged to the year 1866-7, the period of the abortive Russell-Gladstone and the successful Derby-Disraeli Reform Bills. Edited by James Hutton, in 1867 the *Day* had begun as the organ of the Conservative dissidents from the Reform ideas with which Derby and Disraeli were both credited, and of the more philosophic politicians who believed in proportional representation. Afterwards the *Day* accepted the Disraelian view—not that a democratic franchise was in itself desirable, but that, inasmuch as it had become impossible to avoid it, the wisest thing would be to end the controversy by resting the Constitution on the bed-rock of household suffrage. Before that, however, the support, political, literary, and financial, of the Adullamites, with other party malcontents on both sides, had put the paper in a fair way of flourishing, even of becoming permanently and prosperously established by the capable and instructive writers who vigorously represented in its columns a school of political thought till then inarticulate in the press. Indeed, some reference to the Museum file of Hutton's paper will always be necessary for the writer who is to take his readers behind the scenes of the period, or vividly to bring before them the shifting scenes in the drama of plot and counter-plot, the twists, the whirls in the political undercurrents, with the personal agencies at work, and the methods pursued by the men who either directed them or were carried along by them. Not less noticeable were the services rendered to the penny public by Hamber and his literary supporters on the *Hour*, more particularly Spencer Walpole, Colonel F. Cunningham, one of Allan Cunningham's sons, great on the old English dramatists, a sometime *Saturday* reviewer, and the formerly well-known vigorous Madras ex-law officer, John Bruce Norton. The writers now mentioned excelled not so much in leading articles as in social and political essays of real literary flavour, containing much illustration and knowledge then made accessible for the first time.

Of newspaper-writers who, on the other side, stamped their personality in lasting characters on the press, something will presently be said. Here it may properly be pointed out that, the literary and intellectual traditions of Whiggism notwithstanding, with only a few breaks, from the Bolingbrokian to the Disraelian era, there has been a closer alliance between journalists and generals on the Tory or Conservative than on the Liberal side. Of that fact a memorable instance had been afforded during the Crimean War. In 1853 the newly started *Press* had become the weekly mouthpiece of the Conservative party, then led by Disraeli. Samuel Lucas, subsequently the brightest and best informed of *Times* reviewers, and

David T. Coulton were, at different times, its editors. A subsequent personal link between the party heads and the paper was the already mentioned Mr. T. E. Kebbel. The management of the *Press* had vested itself in a committee whose meetings were regularly attended by Disraeli himself, especially throughout that season when the paper had concentrated all its energies on turning out the Coalition Ministry for its Crimean blunders. On one of these occasions the article, which was to be the opening feature of the week, struck the assembled judges as below the necessity of the hour. Disraeli at once undertook to replace it by another of his own composition. He went to the next room, and returned in an hour with the complete copy ready for the printer. " A better leader," said a Liberal journalist of the day, " never appeared in print."

The old rivalry of the *Morning Herald* first, of the *Standard* afterwards, had been with the *Times*. The journal against which, of more recent years, the *Standard* has pitted itself has been the *Daily Telegraph*. For several reasons the personal associations of this paper mark an epoch in journalistic history. Its foundation by a man about town, living not for business but enjoyment, suggests that newspaper projection was in a fair way of becoming fashionable. Further, but for the abolition of the Stamp Duty in 1855, it could not have been sold at its original price of twopence. Its reduction to a penny in September of the same year by the new owners who, in the second month of its existence, had bought it from its founder, made it the pioneer of the penny press. A distinguished member, now the head, of the family who had become its possessors, the present Lord Burnham, while still Mr. Edward L. Levy, gratified his theatrical tastes and improved the property by dramatic notices which at once gave the paper a vogue with play-going London. But the journalistic instinct and genius were strong in all generations of his relatives. None of them but knew at a glance the exact sort of writing wanted by the public of their day or the exact men who, in their plastic hands and moulded by their training, could be trusted to supply it. The experience of the Victorian age repeats itself to-day. Mr. H. L. W. Lawson, Lord Burnham's heir, is but the twentieth-century proof of the newspaper faculty being innate and hereditary in the house of which

he some day must be the chief.   The Walters, the Borthwicks, the Levy Lawsons make the great family
journalistic trio of the Victorian Age.   If Printing House
Square led, Peterborough Court or even Shoe Lane paid
it the compliment of promptly following.   Earlier in
the nineteenth century the competition for Cabinet place
among the great political families still remained keen.
This at the point in the Victorian Age now reached was
replaced by what, even in the absence of all private
animosities, could not but be a war of the great journal-
owning families.   The incidents in this struggle are too
much inwrought into the general history of the time to
be closely followed here.   The fight for deliverance from
the " taxes on knowledge " began over the issue of the
newspaper stamp abolition in 1855.   This the Walters
at once made a personal matter, describing the measure as
one for " restricting the circulation of the *Times*, raising
up an inferior and piratical press, and sacrificing a
revenue of £200,000 a year." [1]   As regards paper
duty repeal six years later, the opening note sounded
from Printing House Square was very different.   The
muster of the rival clans did not prevent the house of
Walter's acknowledgment that the proposal for withdrawing the time-honoured impost was inevitable in itself,
and even might not be entirely mischievous in its results.
It was, however, inopportune.   And so on and so on.
Thus from day to day the Walter writers were occupied
with qualifying and hedging against what had been said
a little earlier.[2]   Meanwhile the Walters enjoyed the
compensating satisfaction of seeing their competitors
practically acknowledge that, in respect of enterprise,
expenditure, contents, and even arrangement, they had
established a journalistic type to which, if they were to
secure any hold on the public, the new broadsheets for
the masses must conform.   The " organ of the City "
was really popular during the autumnal holiday, when it
began to be relieved of long parliamentary reports and
became, in a word, pleasant family reading.   The
" gentlemen and widows " described by Kinglake in a
memorable passage as forming the small fry of the

[1] The *Times*, March 20, 1855.
[2] See the *Times* file for February and March, 1860.

Printing House Square proprietorial body,[1] had submis-
sively but successfully appealed to Mr. Walter that he
might think well of increasing their little dividends by
somewhat lightening his columns when Parliament was
not sitting. Accordingly, when that period came round,
two of the most pointed and accomplished pens ever in
the Walter employ, John Oxenford, the theatrical critic,
and John Davison, who afterwards married Miss Arabella
Goddard, the pianist, and who did the music, were permitted freer and fuller play in their brilliant and popular
notices or retrospects of opera, concert, and stage. Pro-
portionate space was allowed to the two best experts in
current literature, George Dallas and Samuel Lucas.
Thus, then, did the Walter family provide a stimulating
exemplar for the legion of new rivals, led by the Levy
Lawsons with the *Daily Telegraph*. This paper had
passed from its founder, Colonel Sleigh, into the
possession of his printer, Mr. J. M. Levy, who, quick-
witted, clear-sighted and enterprising, laid the foundations
of success that two years less than half a century afterwards was to be crowned by the creation of the Burnham
barony. On its purchase by him the paper consisted
of a single small sheet ; a few months later he doubled
its size, and reduced its price to a penny. By January,
1856, the new proprietor had secured a daily sale of
twenty-seven thousand. And it had needed less than
four months to take this long step towards that
" largest circulation in the world " which soon became
the journal's popular synonym. It was, too, a literary
as well as commercial success. The Oxford Professor
of Poetry might have his jokes about " the whole
earth being ennobled every morning by the magnificent
roaring of the young lions of the *Daily Telegraph*,"
but the public generally, and members of the newspaper
craft in particular, knew that it meant as much to be in
the employ of Peterborough Court (then the *Telegraph's*
headquarters [2]) as to write for the weekly whose owner

---

[1] *Invasion of the Crimea* (cabinet edition), vol. ii. p. 233.

[2] The statement that the *Daily Telegraph's* original offices were in Catherine
Street, Strand, is pure fable. The earliest offices were opposite St. Clement
Dane's Church, in the Strand, where Samuel Johnson once worshipped ; a few
doors from Carr's Restaurant, where Charles Dickens and George Sala used to
dine. Thence was the removal to the present site in Fleet Street, involving the
purchase of a paperhanger's freehold from the Ecclesiastical Commission.

was Mr. Beresford Hope, and whose editor had his offices in the Albany. Mr. Levy had, indeed, got together a staff which combined the freshest and most serviceable brains of their own day with the best traditions of an earlier epoch. Such, pre-eminently, was Thornton Hunt, Leigh Hunt's son, who tempered his father's fervour by his own cool head and practical knowledge of newspaper management. Meanwhile the author of *Pickwick* had in 1850 begun to make his earliest magazine, *Household Words*, a singularly effective training-ground for the rising generation of newspaper-writers. The Levy Lawson family, as at another time the proprietors of the paper whose first editor had been Dickens himself, found some of their most useful pens among the pupils of a master who was not only the most popular novelist of his time, but quite the best instructor in the rudiments of literary production. On none of this school was the Dickens mark stamped with better result than on G. A. Sala, who, in the hands of the present Lord Burnham and Thornton Hunt, developed from a desultory essayist into the creator of the social and miscellaneous " leader," so symmetrical in form and telling in its points as soon to become a model for the popular journalist. Sala was, too, a correspondent who served the paper well in all quarters of the globe. Not France only but Europe agreed to see another literary incarnation of the *Telegraph* in the pen-and-ink impressionist, who sent it by every mail his vivid sketches of the Paris world or half world, of the imperial Cabinet's doings, and of a whole continent's diplomatic or political *coulisses*. Felix Whitehurst was at home equally with his subject and his public. If his descriptions of fêtes at the Elysée and the Tuileries represented the sky as brighter than was actually the case, his invention of the " *Daily Telegraph* moon " only made him more popular with his readers. Never were the social genius, the glare, the glitter, and the local colour of the second Empire transferred so vividly to paper. Politicians used to consider themselves made as soon as their caricatures appeared in *Punch*. Whitehurst was in his prime, and his newspaper had recently christened Mr. Gladstone " the people's William," when Charles Austin's smart article in the *Saturday Review*, *Jupiter Junior*, gave the paper a sobriquet soon to become as familiar as, but more euphonious and complimentary than the Mrs. Gamp and Mrs. Harris long applied to the *Morning Herald* and the *Standard*. The *Daily Telegraph*, however, played upon the public with heavier guns than those just mentioned. A chance sight of Mr. Levy's advertisement in 1861 had brought an ex-scholar of University, Oxford, a Newdigate prize-winner, of Poona, in India, to Peterborough Court. Perhaps, indeed, Edwin Arnold, rather than Sala, should be called the original inventor of the genuine *Daily Telegraph* " leader." For the best part of a generation he continued the prose, as well as, upon occasions, the poetical laureate of the paper, often combining editorial work with his writing. Round him there gathered the keen metaphysical and political intellect of James Macdonell, brought from Russel's staff on the *Scotsman* in Edinburgh, Edward Dicey, Jeffery Prowse, Herbert Stack, J. M. Le Sage, George Hooper, scarcely less good a judge of military strategy than of political movement. H. D. Traill did not come on till 1882. Some years later still was Mr. W. L. Courtney, who, supplementing his ripe Oxford knowledge of philosophy and classics with a genius for dramatic art, was qualified for theatrical criticism as well as political or general discourse in the " leader " columns. Throughout these years, Bishop Samuel Wilberforce was only one among several impartial and ·competent critics who were struck by the paper's additions in its natural history and historical articles to the popular stock of educating knowledge. The great hits of its special correspondents were, in 1874, H. M. Stanley's completion of the African explorations made by the Dr. Livingstone whom three years earlier he had discovered for the *New York Herald*, George Smith's successful search among the Nineveh ruins for the cuneiform account of the Deluge, Sir H. Johnston's ascent of Kilimanjaro and researches in 1884, and Lionel Decle's march from Cape to Cairo in 1900.

The newspaper house of Levy Lawson is one of the comparatively few which enjoys the satisfaction of seeing its property uninjured, and its own prestige unimpaired, by the competitors whom its success with the *Daily Telegraph* has naturally raised up. The founder of the family fortunes, Mr. J. M. Levy, as may be inferred from what has already been said, was himself liberally gifted with the real journalistic genius. That faculty has descended to his grandson, Mr. Harry Lawson, who to-day represents those of his kin and name in the active management of, to use the obsolete name, the Peter-borough Court business. The connecting link between the two generations, the first Lord Burnham, united with singular charm of manner and subtlety of intellect not only high literary power but an extraordinary editorial faculty, the more effective because of the unconventional method of its execution. Standing on the hearth-rug or walking up and down the room with hands deep in his shooting-coat pockets, and a cigar of inspiration in his mouth, he gave forth in emphatic and homely sentences the points which he wished the writer he was addressing most forcibly to bring out. By the time the oral brief had been fully delivered, the contributor who was to execute the work found that the " leader " had practically written itself in the tersely suggestive and idiomatically phrased instructions of his chief. Since then, from the sixties to the present time, the experiences that, at the earlier day, may have been those of Edwin Arnold, Edward Dicey, Herbert Stack, or H. D. Traill, with Edward Lawson, have been repeated on other scenes in the case of newer men. But in his day the twentieth-century Lord Burnham had no superior and few rivals in stimulating, after the fashion now described, his able men to do the most successful and the best work that was in them.

In 1844 Charles Dickens, whose novels now brought him high prices and world-wide fame, renewed, as an occasional writer, his connection with the *Morning Chronicle*, in which, ten years before, he had begun as a reporter. He wanted comparative rest and foreign change. Would the paper commission him to send sketches of European travel from such particular places and at such particular times as he should find convenient? Editor Black had now been succeeded by Andrew Doyle ; he, after consultation with his proprietors, found himself compelled to decline the offer on the ground of expense. Dickens went off in a huff, and never entered the *Chronicle* offices again. The wound inflicted on his self-love refused healing, and would, indeed, give him no rest till he should have started an opposition to his old paper. His special counsellor, John Forster, now called in, arranged a meeting with his publishers, Bradbury and Evans ; these at once entered into the proposal. No definite or practical decision, however, was to be taken till Dickens had refreshed himself with the long-coveted holiday abroad. By January, 1846, all this had been done. The novelist had returned thoroughly reinvigorated to command the hostile movement now organised against the *Chronicle*. This took final and public form in the *Daily News*. How Dickens as editor led off with a characteristic statement of its mission ; how its opening number appeared, January 21, 1846 ; how its first " leader " was written by William Johnson Fox, the paid speaker of the Anti-Corn Law League, who showed his unique power with the working classes by the audiences he held spellbound at the National Hall, Holborn, and who, as a writer, was the first critic to popularise Robert Browning ; all these things have been related by the well-informed pens of Mr. Justin McCarthy and Mr. John Collins Francis. The capital found for the paper by the printers, Bradbury and Evans, was largely increased by contributions from the novelist's personal friends. First among these came Sir Joseph Paxton, whom he knew through his acquaintance with the Duke of Devonshire and his frequent visits to Chatsworth. Other shareholders were Sir William Jackson, at different times the local leader or parliamentary champion of Midland or North of England Liberalism, and, most important of all, Sir Joshua Walmsley. Before entering Parliament in 1847, Walmsley had lectured and written in Lancashire and Leicestershire on the democratic aspects of the characters and the scenes described by the novelist, hailed by him as the best friend to progress and reform yet seen in English fiction. It was he whom Cobden looked upon as the best Liberal organiser of his party, and to whom, in 1849, he specially entrusted the bringing of the borough registers under the control of men favourable " to our policy and to the four points." [1] Walmsley did even better work than this in bringing

---

[1] Lord Morley's *Cobden*, vol. ii. p. 57.

together middle-class people and Chartists without setting them by the ears. That, too, constituted from the first, in its editor's view, the *Daily News* policy. All those now mentioned were influenced personally by Dickens to support the paper. Without his name the necessary funds would not have been forthcoming. The *Daily News*, therefore, seemed to him a thing of his own creation, to be dealt with exactly as suited his convenience and whim. He had done his part when he gave the start and drew up the programme, pledging its support to the principles of progress, improvement, of civil and religious liberty, and of equal legislation. That done, in the exercise of his paternal right, he put it out to edit just as, in his novel, Oliver Twist had been put out for an apprentice. Genius resented the drudgery of editorship. Not without a touch of his own Harold Skimpole spirit, Dickens complained to Forster of Fleet Street's monotony and fog, and sighed for a renewal of his acquaintance with Southern skies and sunshine. After four months Forster became, in title as well as in reality, the editor of the *Daily News*. For its earliest fair start, however, the paper was indebted to Charles Wentworth Dilke, the late Sir Charles Dilke's grandfather, equally eminent in literary criticism and newspaper business capacity. Undertaking its management at the decisive point in its destiny, with his son's co-operation, he prevented the newspaper from settling by the head. The two at once matured a most effective system for the paper's circulation through the provinces soon after its appearance in London. Their first great triumph came in 1848, the year of European revolutions. Space was then beginning to be precious, and had to be economised accordingly. " Miracles of faithful compression ! " exclaimed the newspaper experts, when morning after morning they scrutinised the complete, telling, and terse pen-and-ink panorama of European disturbance, from which no essential detail was omitted, presented under Mr. Dilke's personal supervision and at his instance. The *Daily News* was on the eve of publishing its first number when its prospects were discussed at a dinner-table round which had assembled, among other leading literary Liberals, Eyre Crowe, subsequently Dickens's great leader-writer, Dickens himself, John Forster, Henry

Reeve, not then the *Edinburgh* editor, but only the Privy Council Registrar, and Dilke himself, whose critical essays and successful management of the *Athenæum* had combined to confirm him in the rare reputation already described. Dilke and Reeve walked home together. " I foresee," said Reeve, " your knowledge will some day be invoked to remedy the mischief done by Dickens's genius to this new paper." Dilke not only made the *Daily News* ; he established for it a tradition of full and early information, unbroken loyalty to which has been the secret of its success. Proprietors, editors, managers, changed. The lines laid down by Dilke were never departed from. The tact and spirit of his administration transmitted themselves to his successors till, in the middle of the last century, the paper was owned by a group of men so strangely assorted with each other, forming such a heterogeneous group as, to mention a few representative names, Mr. Henry Oppenheim the financier, the cheeriest and kindest of Mayfair hosts, Mr. Samuel Morley, the evangelical philanthropist, and Mr. Henry Labouchere, both before and after he had become editor and proprietor of *Truth*. Those were the days of Frank Harrison Hill's editorship and of Sir J. R. Robinson's management. Between the two men that, at different dates, made the *Daily News* a commercial success, Charles Dilke and J. R. Robinson, a personal link appears in the " she-Radical," in flaying whom the Rigby of Disraeli's novel had admittedly no superiors. This was Harriet Martineau, during the fifties, the writer of an almost daily article for the paper while living at the Knoll, Ambleside. To a later generation belonged the accomplished and happily still surviving writer Justin McCarthy, who, by his political articles and even more by his personal estimates of celebrities, contributed, in as conspicuous degree as Miss Martineau herself, to form the *Daily News* style. Most of this happened under the editorship of Thomas Walker, a blameless, rather colourless journalist, justly rewarded for his Liberal loyalty by the editorship of the *London Gazette*, and of the caustic political philosopher, Frank Harrison Hill, the editor during most of Robinson's time. Robinson's first great managerial achievement came in the early seventies. Archibald Forbes, wishing to write about the Franco-Prussian War, but turned away from the *Morning Advertiser*, transferred himself to the *Daily News* office, where Robinson's quick eye for a good man at once caused a bargain to be struck. A week or two later began, from the headquarters of the Franco-Prussian campaign, the most famous war correspondence published in any newspaper since W. H. Russell's letters from the Crimea. After Miss Martineau, the most earnest of the *Daily News* workers for Liberalism was P. W. Clayden, who lived into the new era of his paper. That was to be adorned by Sir H. W. Lucy ; he revived in the *Daily News* the parliamentary sketches originated, as has been seen on an earlier page, by Thomas Barnes in the *Examiner*, and continued elsewhere by W. White and E. M. Whitty.[1] To this later dispensation have belonged also the freshness and fun imparted by the brilliant Oxford band, including Mr. Herbert Paul, Mr. G. W. E. Russell, and led by Mr. Andrew Lang, who first revealed himself to the *Daily News* readers as master of a humour and scholarship blended with such delicate skill and in such nice proportions that the ingredients always seem really as new as the mixture itself is enjoyable.

> "Most can raise the flowers now,
> For all have got the seed."

In other cases, perhaps, than those already mentioned, it may be that the *Daily News* men were the first to provide the seed of the journalistic flowers now of ubiquitous luxuriance.

---

[1] The collections of White's and Whitty's parliamentary impressions, published by Mr. Fisher Unwin in 1898 and in 1906 respectively, take the average reader behind the scenes at St. Stephen's and at Downing Street more effectively, and at the same time more entertainingly, than has been done by any book covering the same period, the Greville diaries not excepted.

CHAPTER IX

THE TEACHING MINISTERS OF THE PRESS

Educational forces in journalism—The great quarterlies and their editors—
William Gifford's remarkable career—The weekly newspaper—E. F. S.
Pigott—Publication of the *Leader*, a forerunner of the *Saturday Review*—The
Leader writers—E. M. Whitty—Vizetelly and the *Observer*—An unheard-of
feat—A presumptuous journalist crushed—Birth of the illustrated press—
Among the Bohemians—Robert Brough and James Hannay—The *Illustrated
London News*—Herbert Ingram's work—The close of the *Chronicle* and
birth of the *Saturday Review*—John Douglas Cook—A fiery editor—The
Saturday reviewers—Lord Salisbury among the journalists—The men
who followed Cook—The *Saturday's* rivals—The *Examiner* under Fonblanque and others—The *Spectator*—Its policy, past and present.

THE foundation of the penny press by the men whose
careers have been already traced occupied nearly thirty
years, from 1855 to 1882, of the Victorian Age. It had
not begun when the organisation and expression, elsewhere than in newspapers, of the best thought on political
or literary subjects generated a force that became of
much service to newspaper development on its literary
side. A fair working definition of a journalist would be
a man who seeks to influence public opinion in a given
direction by periodical writings published at short
intervals. The instrument chiefly employed for that
purpose is the leading article ; the successors of the
pamphleteers, who now manufactured that newspaper
commodity, were to find new teachers of their art in the
elaborate compositions issuing from different companies
of literary workers famous in the first decade of the nineteenth century. The earliest among the great leaders of
two rival bands were Francis Jeffrey and William Gifford.
In the eighteenth century, with Bolingbroke, Pulteney
and Swift for its writers or managers, the Tory
opposition to Walpole, as has been seen above, was kept

alive by the press when languishing, exhausted, or practically dead in Parliament. A hundred years later a like service with similar literary instruments was, chiefly at Sydney Smith's instance,[1] arranged for the Whigs by a company of clever young men, mostly in or training for the law, assembled in Francis Jeffrey's Edinburgh residence on the third floor of 18, Buccleuch Place. The projected and promptly started periodical was to appear once in every three months. Sydney Smith, as the first editor, showed his writers how they might co-operate to make first-rate party capital in print out of the rich opportunities offered them by the Tory tacticians of the day. Such were Perceval's and Canning's "no surrender" attitude as regards parliamentary and social reform, and their unscrupulous readiness to screen or justify their nominees in the perpetration of gross blunders or crying scandals. By this time Fox had been in his grave four years ; but the penetrating power even of his oratory was surpassed by the popular effect visibly resulting from the terse and cutting analysis of the early *Edinburgh* reviewers. Some of these—for instance, Brougham—had fleshed their pens in newspapers ; all of them in the *Edinburgh Review* showed a spirit and a brilliancy they had never approached in the daily print. Between 1797 and the date now reached (1802) there was witnessed an efflorescence of generally insignificant periodicals. These, for the most part, exemplified by Godwin and Priestley in the *Monthly Magazine*, were Whig or democratic organs, deriving alike their inspiration and success from the enthusiasm excited among English Radicals by the earlier stages of the French Revolution. On the other side, William Pitt's second in command and successor, George Canning, constantly emphasised to his chief the importance of securing effective representation in the newspapers, and in 1797 had himself shown what might be done in that direction by starting the *Anti-Jacobin*. Canning's views on this subject became known in the year after Pitt's death to Byron's "Anak of publishers," the second John Murray. Curiously enough,

[1] Sydney Smith's account is : " I remained in Edinburgh long enough to edit the first number, and afterwards gave it over to the stronger hands of Jeffrey and Brougham " (preface to one volume edition of Smith's *Works*, Longmans, 1858).

as it may now seem, Murray's name had in that year
(1807) appeared on the title-page of the *Edinburgh* ;
for at this date the connection of the coming *Quarterly's*
proprietor with the publishers Constable brought him
into touch with the *Edinburgh* reviewers ; these then
included Sir Walter Scott. A difference between the
Constables and their earliest representatives, the Longmans, had caused the Edinburgh house, from which the
Edinburgh Review originally issued, to transfer their
London agency to Murray. The second of the Albemarle
Street dynasty had, therefore, naturally heard of the quarrel
with Jeffrey which was about to withdraw Scott from
the *Edinburgh* reviewers. This explains Murray's letter
to Canning (September 25, 1807) proposing in effect a
Tory rival to the Whig *Edinburgh* ; that *Review's* conduct, wrote the Tory publisher to the Tory Foreign
Secretary, was marked by unquestionable talent.   Its
principles, however, were so radically bad that their
diffusion could not but produce much mischief unless
their dangerous tendency were counteracted by some
equally popular means. At the same time, without the
authority or encouragement of the party leaders, Murray
could do nothing. That Canning wished to give the
publisher support and help is clear from a visit paid
by his cousin, Stratford Canning, to Albemarle Street
early in 1808. Upon that occasion, indeed, all the preliminaries were settled ; the date of publication was
fixed, and an editor was found in one who, born in a
workhouse, serving as a boy on a Brixham fishing smack,
apprenticed next to an Ashburton cobbler, had now
become the most famous satirist and the first literary
critic of the time. In this amazing triumph over circumstance he had received the indispensable help of a
Devonshire doctor, William Cookesley ; to him Gifford
owed the Bible clerkship at Exeter College which brought
an Oxford training within his reach. The benefactor
preserved a family memorial of his kindly action by giving
his son his protégé's name, and Disraeli's particular
friend among the Eton masters [1] of the last century was

[1] From Mr. Cookesley himself the present writer heard that Disraeli, when
consulting him about the Eton scenes in *Coningsby*, was advised to see the boys
at breakfast. After the accident on the Thames, which narrowly escaped being
fatal, C . . . . y is said by Henry Sydney to have "behaved like a
trump" ; in the earliest edition the name Cookesley was printed at full length.

known as William Gifford Cookesley because of his father's share in making the first editor of the *Quarterly Review*.

The most valuable part, for himself and his literary posterity, of Gifford's education came not from college or school, but from the acquaintance with society and the world acquired while travelling tutor to Lord Grosvenor's son. The introduction given him by such a patron, and the authorship of the *Baviad* and *Mæviad*, some ten years before concluding the engagement with Murray had made him one of the London season's literary lions. The satires prompting Byron's exclamation, "Why slumbers Gifford?" had, indeed, already, in 1797, secured him the notice of Canning and the editorship of the *Anti-Jacobin*. Some of the articles that created the greatest stir in the early *Quarterlies* were written almost entirely by Gifford himself. Others were dictated by Canning during the intervals of his absence from office and taken down by Ellis. The most effective of these compositions often did not much exceed in length the daily "leader," as it was to be known a few years later. For closeness of argument and variety of illustration daily journalists soon found themselves taking these pieces for models. The abundance of opportune information upon subjects of the day condensed by the *Edinburgh* or *Quarterly* reviewer into a few pages told the newspaper writer more than he could learn from carefully following the parliamentary debates, as well as saved him precious time in hunting up authorities and references not easily accessible. In 1824 another quarterly, the *Westminster*, was to accumulate the stores of learning and philosophy which were carefully assimilated by the writers who, after 1856, successively under Samuel Lucas, Justin McCarthy and Leicester Buckingham,[1] formed the staff of the Manchester School organ, the morning and evening *Star*.

---

[1] Leicester Buckingham, Silk Buckingham's son, remained during most of the sixties a conspicuously handsome presence among Fleet Street celebrities; Buckingham, Thomas Hamber, mentioned some little way back, two Houldsworths, each, I think, connected with the *Times*, and Burton Blyth of the *Standard*, were famous beyond their fellows for the pointed brightness of their talk and their encyclopædic knowledge in the assemblies of the Arundel Club, Salisbury Street, Strand, then a favourite journalistic haunt. The short connection of Lord Morley of Blackburn with the *Star*, long after Buckingham's day, did not identify him with any fresh or marked development of the paper.

The organising and educating services of the great reviews to the press were supplemented in the nineteenth century's second half by other influences for good, individual or collective. Of these, one among the very earliest, if the least familiar and not the least unjustly forgotten, was E. F. S. Pigott. For several years before his death, Pigott was known, if at all, as the dramatic licenser. Previously to his appointment to a place in the Lord Chamberlain's office, he had made his mark as a political and general writer in the *Daily News*, where, together with P. W. Clayden and Justin McCarthy, he sometimes " took charge " during the editor's absence, and acquired such influence on that paper that subsequently he contrived to clear the office of an editor whose appointment he did not approve. The Coleridge and Wordsworth associations of his Brockley home in the Clevedon neighbourhood gave him as a boy a bias towards a literary career. Well-connected, well-to-do, he had no sooner come up to London than he found himself in the thick of all that was most interesting and animated in its social or intellectual life. At Milner Gibson's well-known corner house in Brook Street, the chief managers as well as supporters of the then rising penny press were the most regular guests. Mrs. Milner Gibson's evening parties were looked upon as the chief link connecting the cheap newspaper with the world of fashion or even of respectability. Milner Gibson himself had taken the lead in the 1861 paper duty repeal, and being a newspaper reader almost as omnivorous as Shirley Brooks himself, did much towards dispelling the wide and deep prejudice against the low-priced prints whose purchasers often seemed half ashamed of them. At the Milner Gibsons', Pigott soon became more at home than anywhere else. Nominally by profession a barrister, he had no domestic or business ties to London. Much of his time was soon passed in Paris under the Orleanist monarchy, where literally, like the Vavasour of *Tancred*, he " dined with Louis Philippe and gave dinners to Louis Blanc." Going on to Florence, he found many old Eton or Balliol as well as London friends. Amongst these, during one of his many Florence visits, the most interesting was Charles Lever, the most venerable and illustrious was Walter Savage Landor ; with Landor, however, he chiefly became intimate during his stay in the capital of Pigott's native county, Bath. Lever he saw also at many other points of his British or continental wanderings, and in the palmiest of the novelist's most cosmopolitan days. Close study of *Galignani's Messenger* during a week of incessant rain at Pallanza on Maggiore gave Pigott his first idea of a weekly journal which, unlike *Galignani*, should give no special reports of particular events, but which should condense into its articles and paragraphs as much of original information as of comment. When he returned to London he brought with him the first of Walter Savage Landor's denunciations of United States slavery for the *Daily News*, and a tolerably complete scheme for a new weekly, which he intended to start himself, and almost entirely with his own capital. In every capital and at every Court between Madrid and Moscow Pigott had well-placed friends with whom he had arranged to act as his correspondents. The new venture was to be called the *Leader*. An entire novelty in all its departments, it lived long enough to entitle its projector to the distinction of having been among the first to create the taste which was more fully gratified a little later by the *Saturday Review*. The best literary talent of the time, serious or light, was represented in Pigott's columns. Its philosophy, social or political, was done by Herbert Spencer. The physical science articles, which were one of its chief features, came from G. H. Lewes, who, also in Pigott's paper, showed himself, Miss Martineau not excepted, the best writer of short biographies then existing. It was a *Leader* article by Lewes that contained the germ of a work admitted by the most critical compatriots of its subject to be a success. This was the *Life of Goethe* ; for some hints in writing it he was indebted to Herbert Spencer and to the future author, then Marian Evans, of *Adam Bede*. Other hints equally useful came from Pigott. The theatrical interest and knowledge of these two men, and the joint articles on dramatic matters which were their outcome, really marked an epoch in the mutual relations of journalism and the stage. At Oxford Pigott's taste had been for scholarship rather than philosophy. As editor of the *Leader*, he suggested certain literary notices which would give Lewes a chance of demolishing, in his slap-dash manner, the processes and conclusions of *a priori* reasoning from Plato to Cudworth, and of showing that, after the juvenile attraction of metaphysics had worn off, no sane man could rest except in the haven of positivism. The laurels won by Pigott's county friend and neighbour in the West of England with *Eothen* were, during the fifties, still fresh. In some very irregularly delivered, pithy, short, and most happy pieces, A. W. Kinglake rehearsed for the *Leader's* benefit some of the literary effects he was afterwards to produce in his *Invasion of the Crimea*. Amongst these was the touch in the account of Napoleon III., attributing his studied taciturnity to long association in England with the " grave, silent men of the turf."

Pigott also made the *Leader* an opportunity for introducing to the London public a Liverpool writer of much freshness and ability, Edward M. Whitty, whose bright extemporaneous flippancies lightened, at the *Leader* office, the conversation which, if habitually irreverent in its tone, was often turned by Lewes, Spencer, and Pigott to lofty themes. Of London birth but Irish extraction, he began on the provincial press. Coming to London when only nineteen, he wrote from 1846 to 1849 the *Times* parliamentary summary, and first made his mark in the *Leader* with some pen-and-ink portraits, *The Governing Classes of Great Britain*, in a vein not unlike that afterwards to be hit on by Grenville Murray. Whitty's novel, *Friends of Bohemia*, though it once passed for a clever protest against the literary dandyism of Bulwer-Lytton, leaves a disagreeable taste in the mouth, and is deformed by the introduction of a character designed, as the family believed, for a caricature of the author's father. The end of this really gifted but undisciplined man was the more sad because unhappily typical of the clouds amid which so many bright intellects then employed on the press went down. Enfeebled by the physical results of his Bohemian courses, he received from his friends a passage on a temperance ship to Melbourne, where employment might have awaited him on the *Argus*. The vessel's doctor, however, had a large supply of spirits on board. To these Whitty obtained access. This was his last break out, for shortly after landing he died. Whitty, however, had lived long enough to enrich Pigott's paper with not only the personal sketches already mentioned, but with a series of articles that broke soil then entirely new, and that in one passage invented the phrase for which, long afterwards, a much more famous writer than himself was to obtain credit as original. " 'Tis the gondola of London," in Disraeli's last novel but one, exclaims Lothair, as he hails a hansom. Poor Whitty, however, had struck out the epigrammatic simile decades before it appeared in the pages of a Prime Minister's romance. For the rest, the pieces of literary impressionism that to-day form a feature in every journal were first known as Whitty's specialities in the *Leader*. His peculiar gift in this direction, with a more prudently ordered life, might then have secured him not only fame but fortune ; for Delane and the Walters, appreciating his really original gifts, only asked that he should " live cleanly and leave sack " as a condition of regular and well-paid employment in Printing House Square. Whitty's observations of Parliament men have been collected and recently published. Those who look into the volume will be struck by a remarkably accurate prognostication of the exact position, national and parliamentary, long afterwards to be filled by Gladstone. Whitty also was the first newspaper man to " spot " Robert Lowe, when entirely unknown to the outside public, and not, perhaps, universally appreciated at the true value of his intellect in the House of Commons.

The particular department of the periodical press with which Whitty's name connects itself was, shortly after his time, to attract the enterprise and energy of men not less essential to the newspaper system as it exists to-day than any of those whose acquaintance has been already made. Till late in the nineteenth century, the Strand and Fleet Street knew no figure more commanding or familiar than the tall presence of Henry Vizetelly, always thin and spare, with something of gauntness about him that suggested the Knight of La Mancha, but vigorous and active in old age, with nerves of steel and muscles of iron, and thus presenting a picturesque contrast to his brother Frank, whose stout, square figure had in it a suggestion of Dirk Hatteraick as well, perhaps, as of Falstaff. He had been with the blockade runners in the American Civil War, acted as special correspondent in all parts of the world, and was said only to have died during the operations against the Mahdi in the Soudan. The Bill for the repeal of the newspaper stamp was still going through Parliament when Henry Vizetelly undertook the editorship of a paper that brought out, all at the same time, several young men of characters and capacities very different, but each destined in after years to stamp his personality, in a fashion not yet effaced, upon the journalistic system. Seventeen years before that, while on the staff of the *Observer*, Vizetelly had performed an unheard-of feat. At Queen Victoria's coronation in 1838 he had been the first newspaper man to obtain, in any public ceremony, a press pass from the police. As he approached the Abbey, he encountered ladies with nodding plumes on their heads, dainty white satin shoes on their feet, embarrassed by long trains gathered up in their arms. These, together with the gentlemen in Court and full dress, had foreseen the hopelessness of reaching their destination in carriages, and were calmly proceeding thither on foot, laughing at the curiosity they excited in the crowd. Henry Vizetelly had no such misgivings. Onward he strode to Westminster, saw every detail of the ceremony, and wrote the best account of it in the press. Here he was more fortunate than his chief ; for the editor of the paper had asked the Duke of Wellington's permission to view the procession from the roof of Apsley House. In reply the Duke acknowledged a letter signed " Vincent Dowling," added he had no knowledge of anyone by that name, nor interest in the person possessing it, nor in the *Observer* newspaper ; that Apsley House was not a public building but the Duke's private residence, to whose roof he would certainly admit no stranger of any kind. Apt with his pencil as well as pen, Vizetelly had made many sketches. These grew into a panoramic drawing of about twelve feet in length. The artist afterwards sold the pictures of which it consisted to an engraver named Tyas at the rate of from half a crown to half a guinea per foot. For at least a generation after this Henry Vizetelly found abundant exercise for his energy and inventiveness in newspaper enterprise, as for his native amiability in doing newspaper-writers a good turn. The earliest and most productive of these ventures was the most spirited opposition put forth to the *Illustrated London News*.

In 1855 the *Illustrated Times*, owned by David Bogue
and edited by Henry Vizetelly, became a school for
several journalists destined to later distinction in various
departments. It sowed in the journalistic soil of the
middle Victorian Age the seed of ideas that were to
become powerful growths a little later and whose fruit
is still being gathered in the twentieth century's present
years. Vizetelly's writers, to take them alphabetically,
included Robert Brough, Edward Draper, Henry Sutherland Edwards, James Hannay, Augustus Mayhew and
Edmund Yates. Some of these will be mentioned
separately later in connection with the more important
undertakings of their maturer years. Edwards united
a light literary touch with a turn for neat phrases, as
when, *à propos* of the growing popularity of Paris, he
said : " The Lutetia of the Ancients has become the
Lætitia of the Moderns," and humorously doubted
whether he ought not to have entitled a novel he had
written, *The Three Louisas, Unlimited Loo*. This was
the little trick of words which, in earlier life, had caused
Albert Smith to ask about him : " Who is that young
man making thin remarks through a ragged moustache ? "
Subsequently, as occasional critic of music and opera
under John Davison for the *Times*, on the *Pall Mall
Gazette*, and last of all on the *Standard* during the
latest performances of Eleonora Duse, he did much
towards raising the standard of musical taste, as, indeed,
has been publicly declared by George Grove, the
organiser of the Crystal Palace concerts, in his *History
of Europe*.

When they first began to work together these men
formed a kind of family party. The region in which
they laboured and lived belonged to the vanished province
of Bohemia, wherein is laid the scene of so many
chapters of Thackeray's *Pendennis*. In modern times
Bohemia, from a locality, has become a phase, an aspect
of social existence not confined to any single class, equally
shared in by the leaders of fashionable smartness and
their highly respectable suburban or provincial imitators.
The Bohemia of the days now looked back upon was
peopled by persons who never moved or thought of
moving outside its limits. It kept late hours ; its industry
was by fits and starts ; there were times when, for a

week or even month or two together, it lived, as it liked to put it, at the rate of several thousands a year. It was rich in characters that were then at least as original as, in the present retrospect, they are amusing. The Bohemianism that was a reproach of so many periodical pens during several decades of the Victorian Age resulted from the newspaper-worker's irregularly-paid and altogether insufficient wage. Hence a chronic condition of impecuniosity and of social insurrection. There did not exist the means for cultivating the graces and refinements of life. Consequently many vigorous but deeply-wounded minds were provoked into an affectation of despising them.

Most conspicuously was this the case with Robert Brough. Of a Liverpool family, he had, while yet a boy, awoke the echoes and given plenty of talk to the scandal-mongers of his native city with the cracking of his witty whip. He lampooned alike himself and his fellow-citizens in a novel called *Maston Lynch*. In the few numbers of the *Liverpool Lion* that appeared, he showed exactly and completely what he could do. Bright wit, strange fancy, alternately wierd and droll, went together with the real journalist's quickness in fastening on the topics of the time, and presenting them in the most effective dress. Coming up to London, he had his best time while co-operating with Edmund Yates, under Vizetelly, in preparing some burlesques, both prose and verse, containing among other things the earliest published parody of Edgar Poe's *Raven*. Poverty, ill-health, and an inability to resist temptation distorted and jaundiced his views of life. Intellectually much above the average of his class, Robert Brough in other respects was a true representative of the Bohemianism which, during two-thirds of the nineteenth century, was as plentiful in Fleet Street as its taverns. With better brains, he united deeper feelings than belonged to all his brethren of the pen, those brethren of whom he used bitterly to say : " Yes, all of us regular Cains and Abels." Conscience had been silenced, remorse took its place, and, with Brough, expressed itself in a rancorous hatred, first of all the successful and well-to-do, secondly of every class and every individual born to those gifts of fortune, whether rank or wealth, which,

except by sight, he never knew himself. Not that, with
some such pen-name as Gracchus or Publicola, he ever
bespattered, as may have been done by some other Alsa-
tians, the governing classes with the cheap and coarse
abuse then current in portions of the Sunday press.
The vindicative hatred of rank and wealth, that formed
the collective sentiment of the coteries whose idol and
oracle he was, found expression in his witty and fierce
talk, or condensed itself into lines [1] that, first appearing
in the *Illustrated Times*, were on many lips in the old
Savage Club more than a generation before it could
have been dreamt that an institution of that name would
have had for its guests premiers, proconsuls, judges,
generals, even prelates and keepers of the Sovereign's
conscience that were to be. The animating cause of
Brough's demagogic outbursts was his resentment at
the assumption of superior culture and authority by a
new school of writers, who, as he thought, offensively
flaunted in the press those academic attainments which,
as he put it, " enabled them to turn the Ode to Thalia-
chus into halting English verse, or to imbue with a few
classical allusions their bitter political essay or flippant
literary article "—in other words the *Saturday* reviewers,
concerning whom what is necessary will presently be
said.

Even, however, among Brough's boon companions and
literary fellow-labourers were men who had very different views of writing and thinking. Some of these
glorified the principle of birth and of hereditary fortune
or greatness as hotly as Brough ever assailed it ; and
at least one made his first literary mark with a novel
redolent of the social civilisation which Brough despised.
Before Brough had run his course, his social intimate
but out-and-out political antagonist, James Hannay, had
founded a small literary apostleship of " blood and

> [1] " There is a word in the English tongue,
>   Where I'd rather it were not :
>   For shame and lies from it have sprung,
>   And heart-burns fierce and hot.
>   'Tis a curse to the land, deny it who can,
>   That self-same boast ' I'm a gentleman,' " etc.

—From *Songs of the Governing Classes*, by Robert B. Brough (Vizetelly & Co.
Henrietta St., Covent Garden, 1890).

culture." The novelist was Edmund Yates, to whose newspaper work I must revert, and of whose clever stories the earliest, *Broken to Harness*, appeared in 1854. The companionship to which Brough belonged was rich in character to an extent that can scarcely be conceived in these more decorous days. Hannay was the English Pierre Loti of an earlier day, and had not a little of the French writer's grace and skill in reproducing with pen and ink the colour and the scenery which, as a sailor, he had observed. Hannay, moreover, combined with a style at once graceful and terse wide historical as well as literary scholarship, and a fresh, breezy humour which gave all his work a distinction of its own and a ready market. To anticipate for a moment his later literary course, there may be recalled here the late Frederick Greenwood's remark to the present writer, that, in the *Pall Mall Gazette*, Hannay's articles were those of whose immediate effect on the public he seldom failed to find some definite proof. Frederick Greenwood himself, indeed, though never a sojourner in it, as one of Vizetelly's staff, had seen something of the Bohemia which, if it could afterwards boast him for its greatest journalist, might reasonably be proud of Hannay as one who produced the two best nautical novels since Captain Marryat, *Singleton Fontenoy* and *Eustace Conyers*.

With Vizetelly's paper there is connected a name more famous than any of those already given as a newspaper maker. Herbert Ingram, founder of the *Illustrated London News*, made that venture a world-wide success not from any special genius for newspaper management, but because, better perhaps than any man then living, he saw the popular opening for a journal of essentially domestic interest. To bring contemporary events home to English households, so that they might be realised exactly as they happened, without the need of long descriptions, was his object in starting the *Illustrated London News*. He took no counsel with literary or artistic experts. His own experience of daily existence in all its aspects among the middle-class families of the kingdom showed him what was wanted. His business sagacity proved a safeguard against every loss. He forestalled, too, the latter-day policy of the newspaper proprietor in buying up rivals, actual or possible.

Therefore he purchased the *Illustrated Times,* incorporating its happiest features into his own scheme. Vizetelly, however, survived his paper for many years. In the second half of the Victorian Age he still proved himself an active newspaper runner and impresario. During the sixties, Mrs. Lynn Linton's title in a *Saturday* article, *The Girl of the Period,* became the same sort of catchword as did George du Maurier's *Trilby* in the next generation. Vizetelly was not slow to make newspaper capital out of the idea. *The Girl of the Period,* published at an office he had taken in Catherine Street, at once suggested a journal anticipating by a couple of decades the society prints of a later day.

That day was lived into by several if not most of the cleverest and strongest men in Vizetelly's company. These in their turn left behind them still extant memorials equally of their own ability and the serviceableness of Vizetelly's training. Nothing need be added to what has been already said about G. A. Sala and the part played by him in the evolution of the " leader." Frederick Greenwood occasionally did some of the editorial supervision for Vizetelly's paper ; he afterwards became successively editor and founder of the *Pall Mall* and the *St. James's Gazette.* Among his other pupils Vizetelly himself saw Sutherland Edwards the first editor of the *Graphic,* and Edmund Yates the creator of an entirely new journalistic departure in the *World.* The Bohemia itself, which has to-day no more of a local existence than Atlantis or Utopia, had, therefore, in real life, as well as in Thackeray's *Pendennis,* not only its Bludyers, Finucanes, and Costigans, but its Warringtons and the vigorous and capable writers for the press who owed much of their subsequent success to the Warringtons of real life that, happily for the journalistic craft, were a good deal more plentiful than in the novel. With those good personal influences, the advance of trade and the multiplication of events and interests co-operated by introducing demands which the pamphleteer, even had he not gone out, could never have satisfied, and the regular supply of which was to move up the Grub Street wage, to send to the rear the now-discredited survivor of the eighteenth-century bookseller's hack, and at the same time to banish the rider who had sweated that hack to death.

Among other beneficent agencies following the liberality and enterprise of the newspaper proprietors already mentioned, a foremost place must be given to the most ancient of morning journals in the last chapter of its history, and the newest of weekly papers in its opening phases. The *Morning Chronicle* and the *Saturday Review* in point of time over-lapped each other. But though the venerable daily sheet had a nominal existence after its youngest progeny had sprung into birth, the *Saturday Review* in 1855 not only grew out of but absorbed the brains and the capital which had re-created, as a Peelite organ, the *Morning Chronicle* in 1848. In or about 1860 Peel's political heirs and trustees, Lord Cardwell and Lord Stanhope, were relieved of the *Morning Chronicle;* it was bought up by Mr. J. M. Levy to remove a possible rival to the *Daily Telegraph*. If, under the Peelite dispensation, the service rendered by the *Chronicle* to its party fell short of the money paid, the conduct of the paper at this time appreciably raised the standard of political writing throughout the press. The period then opening saw leader-writers more liberally supplied than they had ever yet been with early news to embody in their articles. They then also had not to write under the same pressure as, a few years later, continental wires in the editorial room, and mechanical improvements in the printing process too numerous and complex for mention, placed them under the com-pulsion of doing. Not, indeed, that work done under hot pressure ought, or as a fact is likely, to be less thoughtful than that produced at leisure, for the properly, endowed and equipped journalist has beforehand for weeks, months, perhaps years, meditated on what he commits to paper in a few minutes. He thus finds in the very severity of the conditions under which he puts his paragraphs together an inspiring, a methodising, and a concentrating force at once stimulating and quickening him for his work.

To pass to the men of the *Chronicle* and the *Saturday Review*. During the tenth year of the Victorian Age his powerful friends of the Gordon family furnished with an introduction to John Murray of Albemarle Street a raw youth, John Douglas Cook, who had been through Aberdeen University, and who was settling in London to try whether he could live by his pen. The publisher tested his capacity by at once putting some work in his hands. It was performed so well as to justify an introduction to Delane. The young Aberdonian began with Printing House Square as a parliamentary reporter ; his talent soon secured his advance to the dignity of leader-writer. Fresh promotion awaited him ; for just then (1848), as it has been already necessary to relate, the future Lord Cardwell, with whom was now Mr. Beresford Hope, had negotiated the purchase of the *Morning Chronicle* as a means of securing adequate representation in the daily press for the new and enlightened Conservatism that, pitted against the old exclusive Whigs, often acted in concert with the Tories. Murray's good word, and his own cleverness during his employment on the *Times*, caused Cardwell and Beresford Hope to engage the young Aberdonian as editor. On the *Chronicle* the cleverest pens of the time were engaged ; even these could not revive it. Recognising the inevitable, its proprietors arranged to hand it over to the purchaser already mentioned.

When a little later the paper disappeared, the writers for it remained. Some time before this, however, the *Chronicle* being now visibly *in extremis*, its Peelite proprietors had taken practical steps to prevent the literary talent at their disposal from being turned adrift. The chief part in the Peelite purchase of the *Morning Chronicle* had been taken by Cardwell. The really responsible work of starting the *Saturday Review* in 1855 was borne by Beresford Hope alone. Offices for the new weekly were taken in Southampton Street, Strand. It was, however, understood from the first that these premises would be devoted only to the business of publishing. The editor would live in the Albany, would there see his contributors every Tuesday, and there entertain at his dinner-table the most powerful supporters of the new venture, with occasionally some of its most favoured or effective writers. The occupant of these chambers, more or less the social intimate as well as the occasional host at his Lucullus-like dinners of Lord Lincoln and the Duke of Argyll, was a stout, square, bull-necked, red-faced, apoplectic-looking man in the prime of life, with the taste of an epicure, the literary discrimination of an Aristarchus,[1] and the temper of a fury. At the old *Chronicle* office, so long as it was in existence, there lingered a tradition of his having placed an offending printer on the fire. " A Napoleon among editors indeed, but, mercy on us ! what a temper. Has he not sworn at me? Yes, and actually hit me, if he thought I had not carried out properly any of his commands in the smallest detail." Such was the plaintive reminiscence confided to the present writer by Mrs. Lynn Linton, who had worked for Cook on the *Chronicle* long before she became one of his most effective recruits on the *Saturday Review*. Those who would know more about him may find it in the personal allusions scattered through the occasional writings of its contributors, especially Lord Morley of Blackburn, Sir H. S. Maine, and Sir James Stephen. Maine's introduction of his then pupil at Trinity Hall added Vernon Harcourt to these, the chief of the earliest *Saturday* reviewers. Not one of the men now mentioned but was advanced in the course that led him eventually to fame and power by the fresh element that Beresford Hope and Douglas Cook infused into the periodical literature of their time. On its religious side, Beresford Hope had gone with Disraeli's Young England. The *Saturday Review*, therefore, so far as it did not criticise all religion impartially, was from the first High Anglican in its theological leanings. " Parson Scott," Beresford Hope's special nominee, the Rev. William Scott, of Hoxton, had, together with T. B. Mozley, edited the quarterly organ of the Oxford Puseyites, had proved himself, whether as writer or a critic, an accurate, complete scholar, and sure-footed as a mule. Like G. S. Venables, Harcourt, and Maine in the early days, he seldom wrote less than two articles a week, besides, throughout most of Cook's time, acting as assistant editor, to whom all

[1] It was Sir William Harcourt, one of Cook's earliest writers, who applied to his chief a line from Samuel Foote's *Liar* : " The whole region of belles lettres fell under my inspection. There, sirs, like another Aristarch, I dealt out fame and damnation at pleasure."

troublesome writers or would-be writers were promptly handed over. Douglas Cook had a little house at Tintagel, Cornwall, now belonging to Lady Haversham. Here he passed most of his holidays, as well as maintained all the year round as many fishermen as would furnish forth his luxurious table in the Albany. These aspects of the *Saturday's* first editor are sketched to the life by Walter Thornbury in a novel whose central personage, Greatheart, generally identified with Cook himself, got its author into some trouble. The national part he was afterwards to play makes, however, the Lord Robert Cecil of those days far the most important figure among the early *Saturday* reviewers ; he was equally conspicuous among the *Standard* writers, to whom, under Hamber, till the end of the fifties, he belonged. His deliverances in these two journals form a summary of his political creed during his later career both in and out of office. *Apropos* of Gladstone's famous 1860 Budget, there is the true Salisbury and *Saturday* ring in the criticism of the financial proposals based on Cobdenism. " Farewell," we read both in the *Standard* and the *Saturday,* " to the simple City virtues of slow security, safe investments, and well-balanced ledgers. Everything is now on the grand scale, all-embracing Free Trade, abysses of deficit, mountains of income tax, remissions too numerous to count. As for the Budget's services to industry, there might be those if the duty were only taken off the import of raw materials. When, however, the abolitions include gloves and other Parisian wares, where is the stimulus to industry to be found? Then direct taxation is everywhere substituted for indirect. The latter kind of impost falls on all classes alike. Only the well-to-do classes pay income tax. We have, therefore, now begun the descent of the smooth, easy, sloping path of popular finance, our progress on which cannot stop short of confiscation." On his other particular subject, foreign policy, Lord Robert Cecil hit the popular taste as exactly as on finance. The English danger then came from the second French Empire. The *Saturday* and the *Standard* writer reminds his readers that Napoleon III. is never so silent as when he means to act, and that he fawns up to the last moment before he springs. To recall writing like this to-day is merely to remind a later generation how deeply and widely this one writer influenced the popular feeling of the time, and how truly he struck the note which, first taken up by practically the whole press, rang itself out also in the daily conversations of social and commercial life.[1]

Cook and his men not only made the *Saturday* ; they stamped it with a personal identity which, throughout all subsequent vicissitudes of ownership or conduct, has never been effaced. First (1868) came Philip Harwood, trained by Cook himself on the *Morning Chronicle* ; Walter H. Pollock, who had been born into a *Saturday Review* atmosphere and family, followed. In 1894 the paper passed from the Beresford Hope proprietorship. Its new era was introduced by Mr. Frank Harris ; it is now being continued by Mr. Harold Hodge. The men forming this succession have differed among themselves and from each other as much as was possible in personal temper, literary taste, journalistic antecedents, intellectual quality and calibre. To each and all of them, by the mere force of the Douglas Cook tradition, has there descended the almost instinctive knowledge of the subjects possessing for the moment the public mind, of the treatment best suited to the passing taste of the hour, and of the men it would best pay the paper to employ. The *Saturday's* first editor had passed away before the intellectual atmosphere of the middle class public had felt the quickening influences of Matthew Arnold's literary movement against Philistinism. For Cook's earlier successors it was reserved to reflect and assist that process. Those who subsequently sat in his chair had to recognise that the day of leisurely reading was gone. Further, it was for them to show

---

[1] The present writer had it directly from the late Lord Salisbury himself that, while his regularly supplied articles for the *Standard* ceased during the early sixties, he had occasionally something to do with this newspaper's leaders after that date, and that not till considerably afterwards did he discontinue his active connection with the *Saturday*. Of course, all this time, and indeed till his latest years, Lord Salisbury wrote for the *Quarterly*. Necessarily in his articles there some of his journalistic ideas reappear. The conditions of his newspaper-writing made his daily and weekly comments on the promoters of a policy he disapproved fairer than those to be found in the stately philippics against Conservative surrender, Gladstonian finance, and American democracy on its trial in the *Quarterly*.

that a journal true to its original programme of supplying
not news but comment, might so construct its articles
and arrange its paragraphs as to be an easy coach for
busy men who did not always keep up with their morning paper. For more than half a century no addition
has been made to the weekly press which, in some portion of its contents, did not proclaim the parentage
first of the men whom Cook gathered round him, secondly
of those who were to fill their places after them. Thus
the memory of occasional work for the *Saturday* impelled C. J. Elton and Lawrence Oliphant to give the
excellent Charles Mackay no rest till he had started the
London Review. Mackay objected to the idea of making
his venture a mere mimic of the *Saturday*, and introduced
into it some of the descriptive features with which
Dickens was attracting fresh readers to *Household
Words*. Mackay's colleagues, however, were only
interested in the paper as a medium for their own writing.
Oliphant himself wrote in his best vein some short pieces
that formed the germ of his *Piccadilly*, which influenced
all the lighter journalism of the time, and formed an
inspiring example of style and treatment in a much
later decade for Mr. W. H. Mallock, "Violet Fane,"
and Lady Colin Campbell. The Oliphants and Eltons
of the *London Review* were followed in the paper's later
days by some clever young spirits from Scotland and
the north of Ireland, whose influence in journalism and
works in literature are alive to-day. The leading Scot
was William Black, the novelist, who soon transferred
himself to other Fleet Street offices. His Irish colleague,
who acted as editor, William Barry, continued almost
to its last number, and turned out a sheet that in the
seventies gave Edmund Yates some useful notions for the
World. Clement Scott, the *Saturday* "Parson Scott's"
son, missed in the present century a chance of instituting,
in his *Free-Lance*, what might have been a real rival
to the sixpenny *Saturday*.

Meanwhile, the first serious opposition to the *Saturday*
came in 1861 from the two men who re-created the
Spectator, first started in 1828, and was associated with
the Benthamite movement in the press. The Benthamite
propagandists, helped by Bright and Cobden, founded
the *Morning and Evening Star*, with Samuel Lucas for

its first editor. After him came Mr. Justin McCarthy, Leicester Buckingham, and finally the future Lord Morley of Blackburn. Thus its connection with philosophic Radicalism gave the *Star* a place in the newspaper press not unlike that taken by the *Westminster* among the great magazines. Here, however, our only concern is with the personal aspects of the weekly journalism whose foundations had been laid before the *Saturday Review* came into being. The leading spirits of the (Sunday) *Atlas*, first heard of in 1825-6, were the men who sometimes found a parliamentary leader in Joseph Hume. Their initiating guide, philosopher and friend was, however, in reality Jeremy Bentham. The Benthamite owners of the *Atlas* soon found themselves at the most unphilosophic loggerheads with their crack writers, most of whom had rival crotchets of their own. As a consequence Fonblanque joined the *Examiner*, then recently purchased by a somewhat opiniated politician, but far-sighted man of business, Dr. Fellowes. Rintoul, believing he had a mission to humanise and educate Radicalism, started the *Spectator* as a means to that end.

Leigh Hunt's work on the *Examiner*, as elsewhere, makes him one of the great newspaper men who turned journalism into literature. That, too, was pre-eminently to form the distinction of his most brilliant successor. Albany Fonblanque's humour, sarcasm, instinct for literary form, and sustained finish of style give to all his *Examiner* writings a value which resembles that attaching to Leigh Hunt's in that it is independent of their subject. These qualities, admiringly noticed by his most discriminating contemporaries, caused Bulwer-Lytton to speak of him as the " English Paul Louis Courier." Undoubtedly they constituted gifts partly to be explained by his French descent. His eighteenth-century ancestor had founded a successful London banking house. His father, a well-known equity lawyer and M.P. for Camelford, had attached himself to Liberalism in its darkest days. The Revocation of the Edict of Nantes had made the Fonblanques, like so many other French Huguenots, an English family. Its earliest settlers on this side of the Channel transmitted to all their descendants a hatred of kingcraft and priestcraft. That, however, had not prevented John Martin Fonblanque, Albany Fonblanque's father, from standing well with the future George IV. when, as the patron of Sheridan and Fox, he was supposed to favour the Whigs. Albany Fonblanque himself, a brilliant talker and finished scholar, came into much social request during the Regency period. By nature shy and sensitive, he had no ambition to shine in drawing-rooms or at dinner-tables. Suffering from chronic ill-health and domestic unhappiness, he found the only real solace in his pen ; as a writer he reflected his social temperament and habit. Self-repression, literary and social, formed his chief characteristic. No journalist of the time more strongly impressed his personality on his articles ; he could be detected in almost as few lines as Thackeray himself. Yet when he felt most strongly, he always expressed himself the most temperately ; as a consequence, he conveys the reader to a sense not merely of strength but of power in reserve. His negative bent made him naturally a critic and a censor rather than a champion, but Cobbett's influence with the masses found its parallel among the more educated sections of society in the driving power of Fonblanque's highly-wrought attacks upon the abuses, anomalies, scandals, official and personal, in the period of obscurantism and privilege, against which his working life was one long war. Eventually Fonblanque gained not only an editor's but an owner's control over the journal which, as generally happens in these cases, helped as much to make his fame as did his genius to create the prosperity and power of the paper. Fonblanque's influence upon the contemporary press showed itself most noticeably in the case of Douglas Jerrold, whose deserved reputation for sarcastic humour and biting wit, for puns, pleasantry, and plays, did not militate against the soundness of his Liberalism as a writer. His principles and his more serious writings, especially in *Lloyd's Weekly* newspaper, were indeed exactly those of Fonblanque, between whom and John Forster Jerrold supplied a personally connecting link. Like Laman Blanchard, who superintended the literary department, John Forster, in the interval since his *Daily News* experiences, had worked for a little sheet, the *True Sun*. From the *True Sun* Blanchard, the fairest and most grateful reviewer of his time, went to the *Constitutional* ; Forster transferred himself to the *Examiner*. Here he continued his theatrical critiques till his strong brain and wide knowledge found a fitting exercise in articles dealing with the whole range of public affairs. Thus in his case, as in that of Fonblanque, to whom in journalism he rendered much the same services as he afterwards did to Dickens in literature, the way opened itself to supreme control and ownership. No wiser use of literary position and ability was ever made than by Forster in his *Examiner* days. Ever ready to play a conciliatory and peace-making part, he was keen in discovering new literary talent. Thus he was the first to find out Anthony Trollope, and to publish the earliest productions of his pen in the shape of some *Letters from Ireland* during the famine of 1846. But though few departments of journalism or literature were not affected for the good of their writers by Forster, he could not transmit to his own paper anything of his own intellectual vitality and distinction. The name of the sheet on which he showed himself the worthy successor of Hunt and Fonblanque appeared in the newspaper list for some years afterwards. Never, even when owned by Lord Rosebery and managed by his clever Oxford private tutor of other days, Robert Williams, did it regain its former pride of power and place.

Robert Stephen Rintoul's Scotch deliberateness and self-possession of manner presented a contrast to Fonblanque as complete as that between the different views taken by the two men respectively of their newspaper mission. Rintoul troubled himself less about securing reforms than about educating the reformers. The one great movement which he had deeply at heart was that for improving the condition of the working classes in their domestic life even more than in their political status. The next aim with which he stamped every number of the *Spectator* was to make it, by an economy of space and by symmetry of arrangement, a complete record of contemporary events and a model of technical excellence in its " make-up." As a consequence, the journalistic offspring of Rintoul may, like that of Douglas Cook, claim to have been throughout all its changes [1]

[1] The correspondents who are always ready to testify their gratitude to the *Spectator's* editors and writers have often seen a symbol of their favourite paper's

the educated Englishman's lay preacher and instructor on all the higher interests in ethics, theology, as in society and statesmanship of the time. The flowing of such consequences from the squabbles of the Benthamite publicists in 1828 is due to other influences than the happy conjunction in the Victorian Age of Meredith Townsend and R. H. Hutton. When, in 1861, Mr. Townsend bought the paper, its sellers were represented by the editor then in charge, George Hooper, whose name has been already mentioned in connection with the *Daily Telegraph*. R. H. Hutton's capital was added afterwards. In the successful partnership that followed, Townsend's special department was political, Hutton's literary. But both men had come strongly under the influence of F. D. Maurice. That divine, indeed, had scarcely less to do with giving the paper its special *cachet* than had the proprietors themselves. So, too, in the case of the twentieth-century *Saturday*, Mr. Harold Hodge carries on the traditions and reflects the influences quite as much of the experiences he gathered after Oxford as he does those of Douglas Cook, Philip Harwood, or Walter Pollock. The cosmopolitan knowledge of affairs, the aptitude for the philosophy of politics, the literary genius and insight that belonged to Meredith Townsend and R. H. Hutton, were communicated by them to their paper. During the second half of the nineteenth century, Oxford undergraduates reading for honours in " Greats," and perhaps too prone, as their tutors thought, to take for their essay models the " middle " articles which Douglas Cook had trained a long succession of writers to produce for the *Saturday*, were admonished carefully to examine and endeavour themselves to reproduce the political analysis, the closely-linked chains of argument that were to be found in each successive number of the *Spectator* and, in the English press, nowhere else. As a rule the very best of party writers in the press intensifies and sets upon an intellectual basis his readers' opinions already formed rather than converts them to his own. The intellectual power, the moral earnestness, and the capacity of

adherence through all dispensations to its original programme in the fact that its publishing office, Wellington Street, ha always been the same, the premises on which Rintoul not only worked but lived with his family.

apposite and world-wide illustration possessed by Hutton and his colleague have descended to their successors with no diminution of the best *Spectator* traditions, and this to such a degree that, where other periodical writers only secure readers, those who have followed the re-creators of the Wellington Street journal make converts.

CHAPTER X

FROM FREDERICK GREENWOOD TO HENRY LABOUCHERE

A new power—The evening press and its real founder—Frederick Greenwood's
early course—Projection of the *Pall Mall Gazette*—Writers and writing that
made the paper—The "Amateur Casual"—Greenwood's editorial methods
and journalistic beliefs—Attempts to "nobble" the *Pall Mall*—Remarkable
work in foreign and domestic affairs—Holt Whyte's memorable ride from
Sedan—The union of literature and journalism—Foreign writers on the
Pall Mall—Greenwood and his company "smoked out"—He establishes
a rival *St. James's Gazette*—Further extension of the evening press—The
Westminster Gazette and its founder—Sir George Newnes's newspaper
career—Society journals and their creators—Edmund Yates—T. G. Bowles
—Grenville Murray—Henry Labouchere.

THE men who early in the nineteenth century's second
half stand out in the strongest relief from the other
newspaper figures of the time would not have found
the opportunities they were to turn to such good account
but for the general agencies that, after the fashion
already described, had brought the periodical press to
a higher place and greater prosperity than could have
been predicted, even some years after journalism had
outgrown the disrepute which made it a byword in Walter
Scott's day, and not entirely reputable in Thackeray's.
The nineteenth century's beginning had been of great
promise to the journalist, especially the evening one ;
its fourth decade brought a relapse, and almost robbed
of his occupation the post-meridian daily writer. Then
came a revival. Newspaper enterprise had whetted the
public appetite. From 1850 onwards there once more
seemed no reason why the evening journal should not
successfully compete with the sheet spread before the
suburban citizen on his breakfast table and studied during
his subsequent journey from Caterham to Cannon Street.
The matutinal prints clearly did not admit of addition to

their number.   No practicable improvement could have
been suggested on the freshness or universality of their
world-wide intelligence, or on the literary style, knowledge, and common sense of their comments. Even then,
the most cool and sagacious of writers might be thrown
into confusion by a sudden piece of news. But whatever
the political event, it could not fail of being related to
past or present occurrences well known. The able and
trained journalist became proof against the shock of
surprise even when he heard the unexpected had
happened, and was told off to write about it at an hour's
notice. That hour, denied alike to the journalist's and
public's loss to-day, saved the situation then, and ensured
the production of a well thought out, carefully expressed
composition on the latest issues of the hour. As a
consequence, the individual writer never before or since
enjoyed such a chance as in the sixties ; while Cabinet
Ministers considered him almost of as much importance
as the editor himself. Not that, it may be said in
passing, he necessarily then brought more knowledge
or thought to his work than does to-day his successor
of the better sort whose " copy " goes up to the printer
in tiny slips, and is prepared amid a storm of " wires "
pouring in from every quarter and to be incorporated in the text. The second half, however, of the
Victorian Age had not advanced far when the latest
developments of steam printing and telegraphic communication concurred with a restlessness on the part of
newspaper managers visibly to bring nearer and nearer
the day when the morning paper's political criticisms
would, like its dramatic, have to be dashed off at hot
haste. If, therefore, measured and thoughtful estimates
of contemporary events and their makers were to be
given, they must be found, not in the sheet read by the
Briton with his loins girded before he rushed off to the
City, but in some afternoon print that he could con
at ease on his homeward train, during the intervals of his
domestic after-dinner nap, or at his club.

As usually happens, the man needed by the hour
appeared in the most quietly determined, variously resourceful, and least self-advertising of those who had
learned the rudiments of their craft on Vizetelly's *Illustrated Times*. To good purpose had Frederick Green-

wood made two different observations. On the one hand he saw journalism attracting to itself as a power more and more bright, strong, scholarly minds. Daily it extended its advance on ground that had been well prepared by the *Saturday Review* ; with this weekly he had never been intimate. Even its editor he had only seen once, and that when Cook edited the *Morning Chronicle* in the premises nearly opposite Somerset House. Here he had, indeed, received Greenwood only less roughly than he had already dealt with his printer, whom he had put on the fire for a typographical error. Next to the educating agencies of the *Saturday Review*, Frederick Greenwood was struck by the place manifestly existing for a journal whose publishing hour should be that rather of luncheon than breakfast. In 1865 it was known only to a few that the Tory Protestant M.P., Charles Newdigate, owned the *St. James's Chronicle* ; indeed, the fact of its existence was a secret shared by its proprietor with his printer. The *Globe*, indeed, was in vigorous evidence, and had a few thousand subscribers who never read anything else. Some years later it made a fresh start under the editorship first of Marwood Tucker, then of Captain, afterwards Sir George, Armstrong ; he, with Mortimer Granville for his assistant, Mortimer Collins in his purple velvet coat, Byronic neckgear, most musical and scholarly of Bohemians, for his occasional bard, R. E. Francillon, Thomas Purnell for his prose writers, made the paper a valuable and politically influential property. But in 1865 the afternoon ground had not, even to this extent, been occupied.

Frederick Greenwood did not delay his operations for making the opportunity his own. He confided his plans to the most personally amiable and popular of publishers who then adorned the Strand. This was the once well-known " Johnny Parker." He immediately beamed approval of the project ; he was going into details and considering premises when his father died. A new capitalist had therefore to be found. As Thackeray's successor in editing the *Cornhill Magazine*, Greenwood had already access to George Smith of the Smith and Elder firm. " The kindest gentleman I have had to deal with " was to be J. E. Millais's deathbed opinion of George Murray Smith. His generosity and kindliness to all the men of letters with whom he had to do made him, when once their employer, their friend as well. A single evening's after-dinner conversation on the subject with Greenwood resulted in the decision to bring out the *Pall Mall Gazette* as soon as the necessary preparations could be matured. To-day Greenwood is remembered, if at all, as a practical newspaper man of wide experience, shrewd insight, and first-rate judgment. Could he have chosen his circumstances, he might have taken pure letters, rather than journalism, for his career. Notwithstanding a certain sub-acidity, due chiefly to his surroundings, his mind was traversed by a gentler vein than had an opportunity of declaring itself in the drive and clash of newspaper editing. The reputation won by his *Essay without an End* and his novel *Margaret Denzil* in the *Cornhill* formed the later evidence of powers that had secured his promotion to the *Cornhill* editorship in 1863. Since then he had saturated himself with the terse and telling fluency of Addison, Swift, Steele, the unlaboured dignity of Bolingbroke and others of the Queen Anne period who mark the reaction from the musical and picturesque writers that had preceded them, and who, in their turn, present a contrast to the stately style that had again come in before the Georgian era began. Without the *Saturday Review* there could have been no *Pall Mall Gazette*. But if the new evening paper of the sixties had been run entirely on *Saturday Review* lines, it would have come to grief some time before its sanguine ill-wishers complacently saw signs, not to be fulfilled, of its collapse. Never leaving out of sight the general raising of the journalistic standard by Douglas Cook and his company, Greenwood did not forget the secrets of popular success which he had learned from Vizetelly on the *Illustrated Times*. The heavy guns of his new paper, H. S. Maine, Fitzjames Stephen and of the ultra-radical or positivist division, as occasional contributors during Broadhead's Sheffield outrages in 1867, might have fired away indefinitely without hitting the public between the wind and water. Anthony Trollope wrote some capital short hunting articles ; but they sounded like echoes from the sporting passages in his novels. Lawrence Oliphant's skit on *Ladies at Law* entertained the writer's cronies at the Athenæum. Frederick Greenwood's own *Friends in Council* was newspaper padding of a higher kind than could be found elsewhere. A joint effusion from Charles Austin and H. D. Traill, *Sir Pitt Crawley's Letter on entering Parliament,* was smart but nothing more. Of those two writers, Austin has already been named for his *Saturday* essay on *Jupiter Junior.* Since then he had been attached to the *Times,* both as a writer at home and correspondent in India. Like his elder and ultra-Bohemian brother William Staunton, Charles Austin had the West Indian temperament, and his work, though often admirable, was not easy to get. He fell out of favour in Printing House Square, and so, like many another, disappeared from the newspaper world. One entirely new feature and writer had, indeed, already been secured by Greenwood. This was Maurice Drummond, who, if he did not actually invent the " occasional note," now the common property of the whole press, brought it to a perfection and invested it with a flavour entirely fresh in the *Pall Mall Gazette.*

In Greenwood's own words, however, the craft was still waiting for the breeze which no amount of whistling on the skipper's part seemed likely to bring. Just then were visible the first signs of the polite interest in the welfare of the poorest classes which was afterwards to develop into the fashionable form of " slumming." The condition of workhouses throughout the kingdom had recently disclosed many scandals. Especially had much been heard of the horrors amid which the penniless vagrant passed his night if he sought free shelter in one of the London or provincial unions. The *Pall Mall Gazette's* editor had a brother who wrote most effectively about that half of the world of which the other half knows nothing. To James Greenwood, therefore, Frederick betook himself, with the result that James achieved notoriety for himself as the " amateur casual," and by doing so for the first time put the paper in everyone's hands. " Have you," was the question asked at the time of a charming and since then a famous actress, " heard that one of the *Pall Mall* men has been passing a night in a workhouse? " " Do they," was the demure rejoinder, " pay them so badly as all that? " The words were uttered in a tone which at the time may seem to have meant more than was actually said, because of a recent *Pall Mall* criticism

of T. W. Robertson's *Caste*, just brought out by Miss
Wilton's Prince of Wales company. The writer, stated
at the time to be an ex-cavalry officer, Captain Alfred
Thompson, but since known to be Dutton Cook, particularly condemned the then Mr. Bancroft's impersonation
of a heavy dragoon, Captain Hawtree. The two Greenwood brethren between them had, however, now made
the fortunes of the paper. James Greenwood's experiences were given in his own strong, simple words. The
effects, due to a clever arrangement of light and shade
that made the piece a really artistic composition, were
entirely the adroit contrivances of his brother Frederick.
Exhausted by the fatigues, by the evil sounds, sights,
and smells of his nocturnal adventure, the " amateur
casual " concluded with a description of the welcome
sight awaiting him outside the casual ward in the shape
of the editorial brougham and the saving refreshment
presently administered from the editorial *pâté-de-foie-
gras* sandwich box and silver sherry flask. The addition
of touches like these was a knack Greenwood had learned
from Delane, and often enabled him to improve the
general impression which an article gave by a few
syllables of felicitous and forcible finish.

Still in the prime of life, the freshness of youth just
mellowing into middle-aged maturity, Frederick Greenwood during these years was in his intellectual and
imaginative prime, and really inspired as well as directed
the clever pens whom he had invited to help him in
his work. The sport made in his columns by the passages between Arminius and Adolescens Leo owed as
much to Greenwood's after-suggestions as to Matthew
Arnold's originating impulse. Greenwood also at the
Pall Mall broke with the traditional practice of retain-
ing a regular staff of leader-writers. Men like Fitzjames Stephen and H. S. Maine were, indeed, ever at
his call. On the other hand, he always kept a keen
look-out for rising talent in London clubs, in the Inns
of Court, and even in University common-rooms, in case
it should give any sign of journalistic usefulness.
Literary experience or skill he did not ask for in his
recruits, but only a practical knowledge and a habit of
clear, fresh thinking about subjects which some special
interest had caused them to make their own. He did

not, indeed, commission these to write a leading article ;
he invited them to submit to him their ideas, as they
might do in a letter to a discriminating friend. If
what the promising neophyte thus sent him had really
good stuff in it, it might be elaborated into the leading
article of the day. In this way Professor Lewis Campbell's brother Robert, a Chancery barrister, first made
his appearance, and afterwards often repeated it, in
" leader " type. Years passed on ; having secured the
Pall Mall's present and future, in the interests, as he
believed, of English journalism generally, Greenwood
used his paper for practically illustrating the ideas of
how to make the press more readable, and so more
powerful, first formed by him in his *Illustrated Times*
days. By this time he had his pick of regular correspondents all the world over, in every European capital, and
at whatever continental crisis. Percy William Smythe,
George Smythe's brother of " Young England " fame,
both before and after he became the eighth Viscount
Strangford, was the man who most helped Greenwood
to give the *Pall Mall* something of a European position.
Neither he nor his well-placed friends in every continental centre whom he carried with him had ever before
been much concerned with pen and ink. They now sent
Greenwood not only the exact news, which was most
valuable, but prepared in the precise way he had prescribed. They did not, that is, with a little care or
a vast deal too much, as Greenwood put it, write for
a public which went wild twice a week over sensational
telegrams. Their *Pall Mall* letters were made up of
observation rather than comment ; they consisted for
the most part of paragraphs containing concrete news,
affirming, explaining, correcting or denying, as the case
might be, what had been published elsewhere. Greenwood's editorial course formed one long protest against
the growing tendency to confuse the functions of the
news-collector and the leader-writer. The old ways of
simple and straightforward reporting, he insisted, should
be those of the foreign correspondent. He would have
nothing to do with, and never printed, what he called
long screeds of speculation such as then began to elbow
out the often bald, but ever-informatory and business-
like despatches of Reuter's Agency. Because they were

telegraphed, contended Greenwood, these screeds took in the public, which did not see, and perhaps did not wish to see, that the wired messages, so far from conveying new facts, were apt to be evolved from the sender's agility in jumping to a conclusion, and coloured by the fancy, the prejudice, it might be even the interests, of himself, or more probably of others. Greenwood's insight and precaution in these matters gradually won for the *Pall Mall* in every European Court and Chancery a reputation that stung even Bismarck with a desire to " nobble " it. More than once the German Chancellor sent his emissaries from Berlin to the editorial room in Northumberland Street, where the *Pall Mall* then lived. Greenwood, however, was not once even nearly being got at. " Whenever," said Lord Beaconsfield, " I read Greenwood, I feel myself in the grip of a statesman."

During one memorable year (1875) of his editorial course, the journalist was to give the Prime Minister a lead through an operation in high finance and diplomacy that was to do for his paper's European position what the " amateur casual " had done for its English circulation. The widely-ramifying connection with authentic sources of foreign news had in the first instance come to Greenwood mainly through the good offices of the already-mentioned Lord Strangford. Thus it was that, six years after Strangford's death, Greenwood learned the French intention to dominate the Suez Canal. Elsewhere [1] the present writer has stated the separate steps taken by the *Pall Mall Gazette* editor on making this discovery. Here, however, it may be briefly repeated that Greenwood had no sooner conceived the idea of forestalling France than he mentioned it to Mr. Henry Oppenheim, who, in his turn, imparted the notion to Baron Lionel Rothschild, with whom, at Gunnersbury, the Prime Minister sometimes spent his Sundays. It may, indeed, well be that, before his return to power in 1874, the project had shaped itself in Disraeli's mind, or had been breathed by him to New Court. Should, however, this have been the case, the present writer has Mr. Greenwood's authority for saying that no suggestion of the sort had ever reached him from the City. In the

---

[1] *British Diplomacy: its Makers and its Movements*, pp. 330-1.

middle seventies, therefore, the originator of the scheme was considered by Mr. Oppenheim and others to be no one but the then editor and founder of the *Pall Mall Gazette*.

Nor was it only by feats on this heroic scale that Greenwood glorified his apostleship ; by his diligence, perspicacity and care exercised on homelier sides, he rendered services not less meritorious alike to the community and to his own calling. He had in him a good deal of the detective as well as of the diplomatist. Private knowledge had excited his suspicion that many seemingly innocent advertisements offered to his own paper and widely published elsewhere came in reality from habitual child murderers. A courageous, good-hearted, clever woman, whose name he never disclosed, assisted him in the inquiries he set on foot. She first brought him a bundle of letters which laid the business open to him more plainly than he had ventured to think possible. He had thus a strong foundation on which to base his appeal against publishing all baby-farming announcements. The woman who had been the chief advertiser in this way was soon after brought to justice and hanged. That formed the speedy and conclusive proof of the wholesome influence exercised by Greenwood on his craft, as well as of the obligations under which he had placed the public.

The *Pall Mall Gazette's* founder and first editor showed as much acumen in finding out new and unknown contributors of the first rank as in taking international initiatives or in bringing the most slippery and cruel of criminals within reach of the law. The feats of W. H. Russell during the Crimean Campaign and of Archibald Forbes in the Franco-Prussian War made them not only newspaper celebrities, but national heroes, to whose familiar laurels no fresh leaf remains to add. In the struggle that brought down the second French Empire with the crash of Sedan, Greenwood was represented on the battlefield, among others, by Mr. Holt Whyte ; in choosing him when an untried and almost known man, Greenwood had acted on an instinctive lief that a calm, resolute manner concealed journalistic fts of the rarest and best kind. At any rate the correspondent's performance justified the editor's boast that he would hold his own against all rivals. Take the following instance of the young Oriel graduate's culminating achievement as the military historian of the hour. Holt Whyte was with the Prussian King's staff on the heights above Sedan when the French Emperor's letter of surrender came in. Night was near ; Holt Whyte lost not a moment in riding down the hill, straight across the battlefield. Then he took his route over the Belgian frontier, ; with great ingenuity of resource and strength of nerve that never failed him even when his bodily power almost gave out, he made his way to London and to the *Pall Mall Gazette* office two days before any account had been published in England. The short narrative which Holt Whyte had brought ready written with him of course appeared in the next issue ; it was supplemented by a longer narrative in a later edition. Even that more deliberate record conveyed to the general public the first knowledge of what had happened.

Roughly speaking, Holt Whyte, if in years their junior, was the pen contemporary of Archibald Forbes and George Henty. These again were lineally descended from Antonio Gallenga, the oldest of the race, W. H. Russell, his Crimean colleague, W. H. Stowe, and another *Times* man, an unjustly forgotten master of his craft, " Nick " Woods, chiefly a describer of home events, but equally competent for dealing with scenes of war and peace at any point of this planet. These had for their successors, in one or two cases perhaps their coevals, men not below them in literary power, their equals in seizing the essential features of a dramatic panorama and of tersely and picturesquely condensing them into fewer words than might have sufficed for the masters from whom they had learned their art. For example, to Godfrey Turner, who had his first great chance in the Jamaica disturbances of 1865, succeeded Mr. Bennett Burleigh on the *Daily Telegraph;* after Forbes came MacGahan on the *Daily News.* As regards active service, Charles Williams may be said to have outlived George Henty on the *Standard*, and then transferred his industry to the *Daily Chronicle,* to mention only one of his latest outlets. While owing something, it may be, to hints that suggested themselves in reading what came from the pens of those now named, Holt Whyte, next to his own faculty of quick, clear observation, and of drawing in his mind correct conclusions from what his eyes saw, found that, in his editor's counsel and proof correction, he had the best help towards forming a style whose naturalness, apparently spontaneous finish and point made it a speciality of Greenwood's paper.

Leigh Hunt, Fonblanque, and others already named had but followed the best of seventeenth or eighteenth-century periodical pens in vindicating, by precept and practice, the claim of journalism to be considered a branch of literature. Greenwood arranged his daily bill of fare with an eye to making his journal the political or literary mouthpiece and leader of the cultured class. His own style may have been influenced by the study of Swift, but really grew from his logical mind and his habit of vigilantly watching for, and tenaciously storing with a view to future use, whatever struck him as specially good and wise in well-bred and intellectual company. The pamphleteer, the journalist's progenitor, had fallen into a copyist of what were not the best qualities either in Johnson or in Junius. Even so late as the middle of the nineteenth century, newspaper-writers had not shaken themselves free of a tendency to a stilted heaviness of phrase. They were perpetually lapsing into a diction at once formal, artificial, and hackneyed. Some of the best known and even effective *Times* contributors, such as " S. G. O. " (Lord Sidney Godolphin Osborne) made no effort to rise above it. No one did more than Greenwood to substitute for it a style idiomatic, familiar, in short the natural good English, spiced with humour, that, in their letters and conversation, always remained in fashion with clever and educated men. Thus for the first time the reproach of " newspaper English " was in a fair way of becoming obsolete. To encourage that mode of expression stands to the credit of the new journalism, not only as in Greenwood's hands it was, but as it still remains in the extraordinary access of newspaper enterprise which he lived just long enough to see was coming, and which now marks an entirely fresh dispensation in Fleet Street.

At the same time it will be remembered that Greenwood represented only one among several literary forces, visibly affecting for good the journalistic style of his day. With the sixties Froude had begun to be recognised as a master of simple, nervous, flexible prose. Froude's style had been formed upon the same models as J. H. Newman's and Benjamin Jowett's. Each of these teachers showed at its very best Oxford culture in its influence upon the literary taste of the clever young men who, not by one and one, but by half-dozens, were trooping from the Isis to the Thames, and, instead of schoolmastering at Rugby or curacy-taking at the East End, were gradually struggling into a livelihood on the press. Add to this the magnetically educating charm of Lawrence Oliphant's *Piccadilly* or other writings, of his master's, A. W. Kinglake's, *Eothen*, as well as, nor less important than either, the revived popularity of Eliot Warburton's *Crescent and the Cross*, and of all George Borrow's volumes. Such, in brief, is the sum of the intellectual agencies with which, following Douglas Cook, Meredith Townsend, and R. H. Hutton, Greenwood's editorial methods and opportunities cooperated to make the newspaper, more than ever it had been, the literary mirror of the talk, and therefore of the mind, of the average intelligent and educated Briton.

Others than those whose names have now been given worked nct less certainly than Greenwood in the new and better direction. He had been among the earliest of his generation to find out that the intelligent foreigner with any linguistic turn may be as useful in an English newspaper office and in the leader columns as the most versatile and vigorous of native scribes. One of his most useful writers had long been the *Kolnische Zeitung's* London representative, Max Schlesinger, much resorted 'ɔ and esteemed by diplomatically minded M.P.'s and othɔ:rs with an appetite for authentic foreign news in the sixties and seventies, to be followed in the English correspondence of the same paper by Mr. Schneider during the next decade. Another foreigner who did excellent work for Greenwood, as he did elsewhere, was the present Ambassador of the French Republic at Rome, H.E. Camille Barrère, then a refugee in London, who had mastered an English style free from all traces of a foreign authorship. One of M. Barrère's compatriots named Thieblin, a bright, cheery little gentleman, first won Greenwood's heart by some particularly vivid descriptions of the excitement at Luxemburg on the eve of the Franco-Prussian War. Thieblin afterwards, under the signature " Azamat Batuk," published *A Little Book about Great Britain*, embodying a good deal of what had first done duty in the *Pall Mall Gazette*. Peace had been restored some time when Thieblin, striking an entirely new vein, supplied sketches of French metropolitan or provincial life which appeared during many months, and were so uncommonly and naïvely telling as to make many even of the experts think they could come from no other pen than Grenville Murray's. About him there will be presently something to say.

The general election of 1880 brought with it Gladstone's premiership and Greenwood's deposition from the place of power in the press he had held for fifteen years, scarcely less eventful to journalism generally than to himself. George Smith had made the *Pall Mall Gazette* over to his son-in-law, Mr. Yates Thompson, a gentleman long identified with official Liberalism. During the *Pall Mall's* earlier days James Hannay, having noticed in it something that jarred on his Tory prejudices, asked Greenwood to name the politics of his paper. " Philosophic Radical," came the reply. " I see," was Hannay's comment, " the Radical." Both the man who put the question and the man who answered it had indeed worked on the same paper as the democratic Robert Brough. Greenwood, however, had never been more touched than Hannay himself by the democratic tar-brush. As a fact, he had learned to " think imperially " in his paper, and was always laying a compulsion upon his readers to do the same long before Joseph Chamberlain had formulated the precept. Chamberlainism, as it was known in the seventies, was held up daily by the *Pall Mall* as the one enemy which the nation had to fear. The secret of Greenwood's power was, of course, his independence. Yet to the Conservatives, while a declared neutral, he had rendered a greater service than had ever been done by their own press when he gave writers of such power as Fitzjames Stephen and H. S. Maine the room in his column for justifying the new imperialism on intellectual grounds.

The Gladstonian triumph in the spring of 1880 gave
the *Pall Mall* an editor even more fervently Gladstonian
than was the *Pall Mall's* new proprietor.   The Greenwood company, as some of them put it, were smoked
out ; Mr. John Morley, occupying the recently vacated
chair, superintended the early movements of the paper in
its new and Liberal career.   Among the comparatively
or quite new writers whom he brought out was the young
Oxford man of that time who had won all the prizes
of his University, and who had still to begin his official
career, the future Lord Milner.   Not more than momen-
tary proved the check thus given to Greenwood's course
on the lines he had laid down for himself.   Before
many weeks were over, with the help of Mr. Hucks
Gibbs, the late Lord Aldenham, as principal proprietor,
Greenwood successfully established the *St. James's
Gazette*.   His new staff consisted of those whom he had
chosen as writers for his old paper.   The future Lord
Morley's retirement from the *Pall Mall* in 1883 opened
to his second in command, Mr. W. T. Stead, the editorial
career which has since connected him with so many of
the most remarkable phases in modern journalism.   The
high-pressure period of the Stead administration did
not extend beyond two years.   The paper then came
under the control of Mr. Henry Cokayne Cust.   Mr.
Stead's mingling of democracy and sensationalism in his
methods had left the *Pall Mall* as ultra-Radical as it
was made by Greenwood's first successor.   Mr. Cust
and his friends at least infused new and strong blood
into the weakened parts of the journalistic system.
There was, too, a certain refreshing breeziness in the
energy and the high spirits that animated and lightened
their toil in restoring the paper to the older Conservative traditions that, when they were boys, Hannay had
so largely helped to establish.

Meanwhile Greenwood had given up the second sheet
of his own foundation, the *St. James's Gazette*.   From
his retirement he began to see effected in it transformation scenes not less startling than those already recorded
in the case of the *Pall Mall*.   The financiers who had
found the money for starting the *St. James's* in 1880
sold it eight years later to Edward Steinkopff, a German
gentleman with many other irons in the fire, one among

them taking the form of a large interest in mineral waters. Mr. Sidney J. Low, Greenwood's right-hand man during the *St. James's Gazette* youth, becoming its editor when owned by Mr. Steinkopff, secured it perfect continuity with its best traditions, until, after some seventeen years, Mr. C. Arthur Pearson, now the owner of the whole Shoe Lane establishment, bought it only to destroy its identity by merging it in the *Evening Standard*. By this time, however, the spirit of newspaper activity had showed itself with startling success in the earliest of those journalistic projectors who were, to the latter part of the nineteenth and the beginnings of the twentieth century, what Greenwood and others already mentioned had been to the second half of the Victorian Age. This was the future Sir George Newnes. From his appearance, and as a result of his propulsive enterprise, must be dated the latest nineteenth and twentieth-century phases of newspaper progress. By birth he belonged to the same social order as that which produced the earliest among the real popularisers of the periodical press. Daniel Defoe, himself in the hosiery business, was the son of a Presbyterian tradesman. Sir George Newnes's father was a Congregational minister, who took the same pains to give his son the best education then known as had been taken more than a century and a half earlier by the Cripplegate butcher to provide with a suitable equipment of youthful learning the clever lad who was afterwards to found the *Review* and to write *Robinson Crusoe*. Born at Matlock, where his father had a pastoral charge, George Newnes learnt his rudiments at Shireland Hall, Warwick, first, at Silcoates School, near Wakefield, afterwards. The finishing touches to his boyish training were given at the City of London School under Abbott. There, while winning few prizes, and not showing marked promise of coming intellectual distinction, he impressed his more observant teachers and schoolfellows by the power of application with which he generally contrived to execute whatever he might once have earnestly taken up. While Abbott's pupil, George Newnes had for his contemporary a future Prime Minister in Mr. Asquith. On leaving the school after having been there not more than three or four terms, Newnes adopted the calling of Cobden before him, and became a commercial traveller. Those are the years during which Dickens, by his *Christmas Stories*, especially as well as by certain passages and characters in his novels, had clothed with something of romance, and with more associations of good-fellowship, the bagman's vocation. Such pleasant pictures of their order tended to make the novelist a prime favourite with the " gentlemen of the road," amongst them George Newnes. He, however, was soon to show a literary turn more practicable and profitable than that of authorship. These newspaper paragraphs with which we beguile our journey contain in them, he reflected, not only the embryonic materials of tragedy, comedy, and farce, but the germs of whole treatises, as well as suggest thoughts which one moment make us roar with laughter, the next feel in the vein for sermons. Why, he asked himself, should these literary odds and ends be allowed to perish within a few hours of their being born ; or what is to prevent one from preserving the choicest morsels in a form detached from the less inviting context for which, as we ply through space, we have no appetite ? He was only thirty-one when the refusal of more than one publisher determined George Newnes himself to execute his project. Leaving Manchester for London, he opened an office in Farringdon Street and clothed in visible shape the notion of which his mind had long been full. *Tit Bits* was not sold through the newsagents, but supplied direct to the street boys by Newnes. During the first two hours of his earliest paper's existence, five thousand copies had been sold. Six months later the capitalist who would not venture £500 in the speculation offered £16,000. Newnes, a born financier as well as newspaper runner, preferred keeping his business to himself, and was soon the sole head of the great concern which, transferred from its first premises to Burleigh Street, finally found its headquarters in the same thoroughfare as the *Saturday Review*. The contents of his new sheet did not form its only novelty. To attract fresh supporters, he originated the idea of newspaper insurances,[1] as well as of big prizes.

[1] Coupons committing the newspaper proprietor to the payment of a fixed sum in case of injury or loss of life whenever the current number of the paper is found about the person.

All this was in preparation for the flight after higher game. Four years from his first start, the proprietor of *Tit Bits* found himself a Liberal member of Parliament. Since the *Pall Mall Gazette's* re-conversion to Conservatism, the party to which George Newnes belonged had been without effective representation on the evening press. This want Newnes was ready to supply. He designed the *Westminster Gazette* in 1893, not as the duplicate of the old *Pall Mall*, but as a paper whose " make up " should catch readers who had been deterred as well as impressed by Greenwood's sheet. First-rate sub-editing was to be a prominent feature. The old three-paragraph " leader " on the front page remained a political necessity. Any other articles were to be short, sharp, pungent, personal, written as little as possible in the regulation journalese, but unconventionally presenting fresh thoughts in crisp language. By this time Newnes had seen more than one change in the rank and file of newspaper-writers. The craft had risen in favour with Oxford and Cambridge dons ever since Townsend's gift of political analysis had given the *Spectator* an educational value, or the author of *Ancient Law* had resumed his early *Saturday* work under Greenwood in the *Pall Mall Gazette*. As many University honour men were now on the look-out for newspaper employment as for masterships at Rugby or chairs in the new local competitors with Oxford and Cambridge. Newnes was fortunate enough to find just the man he wanted for his *Westminster* editor in a Wykehamist, a first-class man, Mr. E. T. Cook, who had begun his journalism in the *Pall Mall* at the Morley period. Mr. Cook's removal to the *Daily News* in 1893 brought on, as his successor in the *Westminster*, Mr. J. A. Spender, himself, like Mr. Cook, a typical specimen of the best Oxford culture. During the same period as Lord Milner, he had formerly held a place among those who served the *Pall Mall* in its Morley days. There can be no more notably successful instance of all that is most enterprising in the new journalism combined with all that was best worth preserving in the old than is afforded by the co-operation of Mr. Spender with such colleagues as Sir F. C. Gould and Mr. C. E. Geake. Not only a shrewd, able, really original man this *Westminster Gazette* founder, but a courteous, thoughtful, kindly, and generous gentleman. Beneficent not as in the longest run the cheapest means of advertising himself, but from a wish to do private good, and to help honest workers over rough places. His countless good works done in this quiet fashion form at least as good a monument to his character, career, and success as the fine town hall built by him at Lynton, his favourite North Devon resort, or the completely equipped library with which he presented Putney. These are only one or two specimens of conduct which made George Newnes the most widely popular as well as prosperous newspaper runner of the new era. One serious mistake only in his business did he make—the attempt, in which he had Earl Hodgson for his counsellor as well as editor during the middle nineties, to establish a society daily called the *Courier*.

Newspaper changes are now accomplished so rapidly that it seems almost ancient history to recall the acquisition of the parent evening paper by the American millionaire, Mr. William Waldorf Astor. The personal associations of the new dispensation now entered on in 1896 by the paper which Greenwood had founded a generation earlier are of extreme interest, because they exemplify the sustained attraction of journalistic enterprise or industry for men of the first position in callings quite outside the literary craft. For some time before acquiring the really historic sheet, Mr. W. W. Astor had been universally known and esteemed not only as the head of the American colony settled in fashionable London since 1863, but as the pattern of an Anglo-Saxon gentleman whose grace, dignity, simplicity of manners, kindliness of heart, easy and finished urbanity were shown alike in general society, beneath his own roof in Carlton House Terrace, as well as his Thames-side palace, Clieveden. Mr. Astor differs from his compatriot millionaires who share his domination of St. James's and Mayfair not so much in having a duke for his son-in-law, the wearer of John Churchill's strawberry-leaf (for that is the common lot of a transatlantic Crœsus), but in choosing the old country for his permanent and regular home. He is, too, the only born subject of the Stars and Stripes whose family history has been written and pedigree traced by the most accomplished of New York prose stylists—to the following effect. Early in the nineteenth century Washington Irving had met at Montreal certain partners of the great North-West Fur Company, who had aroused his interest in whatever related to trappers, hunters, Indians, and the peltry trade. Returning to New York in 1812, Irving had many communications on these subjects with the great-grandfather, John Jacob Astor, of the *Pall Mall Gazette's* twentieth-century owner. Born at Waldorf, near Heidelberg, on the banks of the Rhine, J. J. Astor in January, 1784, took with him from London to the United States some little merchandise suited to the American market. On his voyage out he became intimate with a fellow-passenger and countryman, by profession a furrier, who had much to tell him concerning furs and the fur trade. Accompanying this gentleman to New York, Astor invested in peltries the profits he had made out of the goods taken by him from England across the Atlantic. Rigid economy, an aspiring genius that ever looked upward, a sagacity quick to grasp each fresh detail and convert every circumstance to its advantage, and a never wavering confidence in signal success at last formed his most valuable capital. By 1807 his adventures in the fur trade had placed him in the first rank of American merchants. Such in outline was the course of commercial triumph described by Washington Irving in his *Astoria* ; it made Jacob Astor's descendants great captains of industry among their contemporaries, and more than the rivals of crowned heads in their wealth.

Once resolved on purchasing the *Pall Mall*, Jacob Astor's great-grandson showed characteristic sagacity and independence in choosing his editor. Fleet Street in the nineties was beginning to be overrun by clever young men, often of United States extraction, ready to guarantee their creation of a greater boom than had ever yet been known to the newspaper capitalist who would take them into his pay. Such applications were received by Mr. Astor with noncommitting courtesy. It so happened that in 1892 there returned to London from his Allahabad judgeship a man still in the prime of life who, during his earlier London days, had doubled the part of *littérateur* and journalist with distinguished success. This was Sir Douglas Straight. Like many more, he had found in periodical letters an agreeable and effective stepping-stone to law. In 1865 he had made himself the best known, brightest, readiest, and smartest advocate at the Criminal Bar. Entering Parliament for the borough which first returned Benjamin Disraeli—Shrewsbury—he served his party as well as he had done his clients, and received really less reward than was his due by the place given him, the Indian judicature. Re-established in his native land, he returned to his first literary love ; with the already mentioned Mr. Marwood Tucker as occasional assistant, he became Mr. Astor's earliest editor. Once more the *Pall Mall Gazette* promised to be what Greenwood had left it. Its Conservatism was strengthened by its new conductor's wide knowledge of the world, cheerful courtesy, unfailing tact, clear, powerful brain. Since then Sir Douglas Straight's successor has prosperously run the paper on the lines which Greenwood originally laid down. Mr. F. J. Higginbottom, indeed, was connected with the *Pall Mall* before the Straight editorship began ; he always " took charge " during Sir Douglas Straight's holiday, and on his final retirement was obviously the one man fitted to be his successor.

One of Greenwood's contemporaries on that veritably epoch-making little sheet, the *Illustrated Times*, in a journalistic field widely different from Greenwood's, was to win a place among the newspaper founders that were one of the nineteenth century's most characteristic products, and to make himself in the periodical press, in his particular line, not less of an enduring force than the man who brought the *Pall Mall Gazette* into being. Connected by both his parents with the stage, as well as himself endowed with the histrionic temperament, Edmund Yates had been brought up carefully and devotedly by his mother, and through her efforts secured a thoroughly good education, first at Highgate School, afterwards as a student both at Düsseldorf and at Bonn. Combining great intellectual acuteness with a real love of letters, he had made himself a fair English scholar before, while still a lad, getting a Post Office clerkship. At St. Martin's-le-Grand he showed aptitudes which secured him quick promotion, and eventually made him head of the Missing Letter Department. While thus climbing the official ladder, he picked up a good deal which Dickens found useful for *Household Words* essays, and which gave Yates himself many ideas for the most telling effects in his novels. It has been said that these novels were largely written for him by Mrs. Cashel Hoey. This is pure fable. Intimate acquaintance with Mrs. Hoey and with Yates gave the present writer the opportunity of hearing a detailed denial of the statement from both. No one who had heard Edmund Yates talk can ever have credited the report ; for the best things in his stories had generally come out in his conversation before they were put down on paper, and were of exactly the same kind as few people were long in his company without hearing. Take, for an instance, this from *Broken to Harness, or Running the Gauntlet* : " To pay a trades-man to whom a long account is owing a five-pound note on account is like giving a wet brush to a very old hat. It creates a temporary gleam of comfort, and no more." The one person who had placed Yates under any literary obligation was that smartest and wittiest phrase-maker of the later Cockney school, Albert Smith, whose journalism did not go beyond a feuilleton, *The Pottleton Legacy*, in the short-lived *London Telegraph*, but who left behind him a store of cleverish expressions that remained current in Fleet Street to the close of the nineteenth century, and that Shirley Brooks found he could usefully brush up and improve on for his *Punch* work as well as sometimes for his novels and plays. Between 1816 and 1860 it was Albert Smith who first set going through Fleet Street and the entire newspaper region many droll or happy verbal twists and turns, wrongly attributed to the earlier Douglas Jerrold period and Jerrold himself. In the *Illustrated Times* Vizetelly had assigned Yates a weekly column of gossip, headed *The Lounger at the Clubs*. That was continued by the same pen in a little sheet called *Town Talk*. Here appeared the remarks never, indeed, worth making, but in reality much less offensive than their garbled repetition has caused them to seem, that made Thackeray the young man's enemy. As a fact the novelist would not have pursued the matter but for Dickens's championship of Yates. The authors of *David Copperfield* and *Pendennis* were just then more than usually estranged from each other. They now engaged in a sort of duel over the person, or rather the pen, of Edmund Yates. During the sixties, under Justin McCarthy's editorship of the *Star*, Yates was pursuing his vocation in its columns by a weekly contribution of purely personal talk, entitled the *Flâneur*. In 1865 Greenwood had started the *Pall Mall Gazette*, and had invited James Hannay, then fresh from editing the *Edinburgh Courant*, to join its staff. The occasion, in Yates's view, justified a "drop into poetry" to the following effect :—

> "Then answered the flâneur, the flâneur always right,
> 'The banner of George Smithins comes looming into sight
> And with him shadowy Elder, who never yet was seen,
> And Frederick Margaret Denzil [1] of the *Cornhill Magazine*.
> I hear of blood and culture ; I hear of pleb and cad ;
> Hear men and potent tumblers enquiring "Who's your dad ?"
> That jolly old cock Cicero falls blithely on mine ear,
> And how of Titus Livius some books were lost, I hear ;
> I hear of *or* and *argent*, of real tap and of brain,
> And Jigger of the Dodo [2] comes back to us again.'"

Edmund Yates had wider views, a more comprehensive understanding than to project a mere society paper, or to suppose that disjointed paragraphs of chit-chat, such as he had served up in his *Flâneur*, could form the staple of the weekly that he intended should appeal at various points and with a certainty of success to the general public, which, he justly considered, had not yet been catered for in its lighter tastes. A little weekly to which he had contributed or even edited, the *Court Circular*, had, he thought, missed an opportunity by neglecting suburban or provincial readers and professing to recognise only the polite classes. The youngest of the à Beckett family, Arthur, had, indeed, in the *Tomahawk*, 1866, come nearer to Yates's scheme, which was to combine the best literary features of the *Saturday Review* or *Pall Mall* with original effects of humour, satire, social or official intelligence or rumour that had entertained a narrow circle in the exclusive *Owl*. That little sheet had been started in the middle sixties by Algernon Borthwick of the *Morning Post*, James Stuart Wortley, and Evelyn

[1] *The Adventures of Margaret Denzil* was the title of a novel by Greenwood.
[2] A character in one of Hannay's nautical stories.

Ashley. Lawrence Oliphant wrote only in the first few numbers, Lord Wharncliffe wrote in all, Mr. Thomas Gibson Bowles wrote occasionally. The *Owl* can scarcely be looked back upon as a serious undertaking, for it appeared at uncertain intervals as suited its writers' convenience or whim. Though contributions were not gratuitous, it became almost a point of honour to spend the money thus paid on Greenwich and Richmond dinners, or on presents to friends. Still the paper only dropped when the future Lord Glenesk ceased to be a bachelor, and found his hands full of other matters ; but for that it might, as some of its indirect offshoots have done and are doing, have continued to this day. His co-operation with Frederick Clay on à Beckett's *Tomahawk* and his occasional contributions to the *Owl* inspired Mr. T. G. Bowles with the notion of *Vanity Fair*, the real parent of all subsequent growths in that department of journalism at a date when it seemed as fashionable to run a weekly sheet for one's friends as to endow a theatre for one's mistress. In this venture Mr. Bowles showed the dynamic qualities colloquially comprehended in the word " devil " that, after nearly half a century, cause the paper still to bear the literary and intellectual hall-mark with which he stamped it. In *Vanity Fair* Thomas Gibson Bowles and Carlo Pellegrini formed the same successful conjunction that in opera bouffe was presented by the co-operation of W. S. Gilbert and Arthur Sullivan. The two colleagues in each instance inspired one another. In the case of the newspaper the commentator not only explained the cartoonist, but imparted to his letterpress a flavour then entirely new to the periodical press. Since then the paper has known every sort of change. It has never quite lost the secret of the style first invented for it by Mr. Bowles. He also not only brought in the society journal as an institution : he invented its very name. The two other men who in this department displayed an initiative, a vigour, an originality of pen as of management, were Mr. Henry Labouchere and the consummate stylist who journalistically owed something to his experience under Dickens on *Household Words*, E. C. Grenville Murray. The second Duke of Buckingham and Chandos used to be known as " very duke of very duke." He it was who, at the beginning of his money troubles, consulted one of his own order. The friend, going through the household expenditure, suggested that at least one Italian confectioner might be put down. " What ! " exclaimed his Grace ; " mayn't a man have a biscuit with his glass of sherry ? " In August, 1848, came the crash at Stow, with whose echoes Europe rang, followed by the sale of its treasures. Left with the merest pittance, the ruined Duke's reputed son had gained command of a literary style possessed by no one else and opening to him almost on his own terms the newspaper world. His fifteen years of diplomatic experience and of cosmopolitan vagabondage set him up in literary material for the rest of his life. His novel, *Young Brown*, in the *Cornhill Magazine*, introduced him to Greenwood, and produced the same kind of rare effect as also followed Lawrence Oliphant's *Piccadilly* and Mr. W. H. Mallock's *New Republic*. In the story he caricatured his ducal sire ; in his shorter pieces he lampooned the official personages, at home or abroad, of whom he had fallen foul. Under circumstances so familiar already to those likely to be interested in them that they need not be dwelt on here, the most scurrilous and the least lively print for which he ever had any responsibility, the *Queen's Messenger*, died of a scandal that caused his departure for ever from England, and fixed his residence during the rest of his life in Paris.

He and others now classed with him have been accused of Americanising the English newspaper. As little, however, as the men who started the *Owl* did Arthur à Beckett in the *Tomahawk*, Mr. T. G. Bowles in *Vanity Fair*, or even Murray himself in the *Queen's Messenger*, take any transatlantic print for a model. The newspapers chiefly in the mind of each of these were not those of New York but of Paris. The proceeds of a United States lecturing tour helped Edmund Yates to start the *World* ; some fresh notions were given him for it by the several shrewd friends he had made on the other side of the Atlantic, more particularly Samuel Ward and Henry Weikoff, both of them in their day scarcely less influential with the British press than with that of the United States. The chief lines, however, on which Yates prepared and ran his paper were those laid down by Mr. Bowles in *Vanity Fair*, or were suggested by those former experiences in Vizetelly's *Illustrated Times* which had taught Greenwood not a little for the *Pall Mall Gazette*. Like Murray and Sala a pupil of Dickens, Yates, when preparing his "journal for men and women," aimed at producing a miscellany for suburban and provincial entertainment or instruction quite as much as a compilation of *on dits* from St. James's or Mayfair. In his best efforts he had effective help from, for a time, Mr. Labouchere, as well as from B. H. Becker, H. S. Pearse, H. D. Traill, W. L. Courtney, Ralph Earle, Kosmo Wilkinson, and others. But as commercially the paper made him, so he was indispensable to the paper, nor could it be expected entirely to recover from the shock of his death. If Mr. Henry Labouchere sometimes reached an even wider circulation with *Truth* than Edmund Yates with the *World*, never was public more variously representative than that which Yates appealed to with unfailing success, because he ever had his own finger on its pulse. Grenville Murray's literary gift was so entirely his own, and at the same time so stimulating in its effects upon those with whom he might be associated, that his original interest in the *World* could not but be of as much importance to the writing which appeared in the paper as his capital had been useful to it at its beginnings. The assistance supplied by an American friend named Phythian enabled Yates, at a much earlier date than had been supposed, to buy out Murray's share entirely. Nor was the loss of Murray's pen so serious that its withdrawal was not more than compensated by Mr. Henry Labouchere's sensational City articles, together with his attack upon the West End usurers. These new features owed something of their literary form to the animating example of Grenville Murray's style. As, however, he was soon to show in his own *Truth*, Mr. Labouchere combined with his unique insight into the frauds, failures, fallacies and facts of finance and commerce a command of clear, concise, nervous expression, of which, as the "Besieged Resident," he gave proof in the *Daily News* during the seventies, and which, by its subsequently sustained display throughout successive years in *Truth*, raised him, as a journalistic and literary force, to a place scarcely below that due to Grenville Murray.

CHAPTER XI

A GLADSTONIAN FORECAST FULFILLED

Gladstone on the Paper Duty's Repeal—Forerunners of the English cheap press
—The first London halfpenny print—The founder of the *Echo* and his staff
—The *Morning Leader*—Mr. T. P. O'Connor on platform and in press—
The union of art and periodical literature—Rise of the great newspaper
capitalists—the Harmsworths—Competition with *Tit-Bits*—Work in ex-
tending the cheap press—Methods of the new journalism—All-embracing
enterprise at home and abroad—The Harmsworths as pioneer colonists—
Weeding out—Mr. Pearson in the *Tit-Bits* office—Striking out for himself—
Among the great newspaper owners—The Lloyd press—*Lloyd's Weekly
News*—The *Daily Chronicle* and its makers—The first illustrated "daily"—
The *Graphic's* enterprise.

FROM the newspaper men who made society journalism,
and with whom Gladstone was not generally a favourite,
we may pass to a prediction of Gladstone himself and
to those who have been instrumental in fulfilling it.
"The paper duty is gone. For the full results of its
removal men must wait until we of the nineteenth century
are no more." So said Gladstone to his friend Sidney
Herbert during the July of 1861, shortly after the last
of the "taxes on knowledge" had been repealed.
Herbert died on August 2, 1861 ; had his life been
spared till the following October, he would have seen
the enlightening legislation he had supported followed
by a reduction in price of three great journals. His
friend Gladstone was to have two more years of office
when, as Prime Minister, he saw the beginning of the
further consequences which he had always anticipated
as the sequel of the paper duty's abolition. The
foundation in 1896 of a fresh journalistic dynasty by
the first Baron Northcliffe was preceded in 1892 by the
earliest morning newspaper sold for a halfpenny, the
Morning Leader. This was not the only preparation of the

soil found by Lord Northcliffe and his family in the field of journalistic enterprise that they have made particularly their own. The source and originating inspiration of the society journal in its best shape was, it has been seen, French rather than American. So, too, with the half-penny newspaper. So far back as 1861 the *Petit Journal's* founders had shown in Paris the possibility of producing a daily broadsheet for a sou. Why should there not be at least attempted in England that which had been carried out so triumphantly in France, was the question that T. D. Galpin had begun seriously to ask while engaged with John Francis, of the *Athenæum*, as Mr. Wentworth Dilke's representative, in the attack on the paper duty. John Cassell's fine presence and imposing manner may have somewhat overshadowed his business associates. Galpin, however, was the life and soul of the journalistic experiment to which, on his suggestion, La Belle Sauvage Yard committed itself in 1868. The *Petit Journal*, with its circulation of 840,000, formed only one among several auspicious signs. On his own side of the Channel Galpin had seen Glasgow and other provincial capitals prosperously bringing out their halfpenny epitome of the world's contemporary record from sunrise to sunset. The Ludgate Hill house, which had become to London what the Chambers family had made itself in Edinburgh, carried out their task with the omens all in their favour. Sir Arthur Arnold not only conducted the new sheet ; he made the *Echo* office an instructive and stimulating school of journalism. There he gave their earliest training, in the craft of which they afterwards became masters, to William Black the novelist as well as the great literary pillar of the *Daily News*, Frances Power Cobbe, the æsthetic divine H. R. Haweis, George Byrom Curtis, subsequently editor of the *Standard*, Sir John Macdonell, who had previously worked for Alexander Russel on the *Scotsman*, and who, before reaching his present Mastership of the Supreme Court, had, like his brother James, been a principal writer for the *Times*. Other pens employed by Arnold to establish his success were those of George Manville Fenn and E. D. J. Wilson, who, during Chenery's editorship, denounced, as nearly as might be in the manner of Edmund Burke, the iniquities in Irish policy of the new

Whigs, and, instructed by the then Mr. Edward Gibson and Mr. David Plunket, daily unmasked some fresh phase of the unholy alliance between Gladstonian Liberals and Anglo-Irish separatists. Arthur Arnold's gifts were of the safe, homely kind, but the material brought to his hand by his pupils made him conspicuous among the editors of his time, and associated the *Echo* with almost as many journalistic reputations subsequently great as at an earlier day were struggling to the birth on Vizetelly's *Illustrated Times*. Arnold could command, when he wanted it, the energetic help of one who, in due course, became his successor before, as his right-hand man, he joined Mr. Labouchere on *Truth*—Horace Voules, a memorable specimen of the new journalism in its most practical and propulsive aspects, equally able on an emergency to write printer's copy and to set it up himself. He had been from the first indispensable to, or rather a portion of, Arnold's editorship of the *Echo*. When he left that paper he was called in by Mr. Yates Thompson to engineer the *Pall Mall Gazette's* transition from the Greenwood to the Morley regime. In a word, the most universal utility man known to the press in his day, and as " good at need " as Scott's Walter Deloraine himself. As for the *Echo's* first titular editor, Arthur Arnold, notwithstanding the absence of any kinship with the Rugby Arnolds, he, like his brother Edwin, displayed, as journalistic trainer, much of the didactic power that Thomas Arnold transmitted to at least two of his sons. In other words, both the poetic elder brother, Edwin, on the *Daily Telegraph*, and the more prosaic but thoroughly capable Arthur on the *Echo*, as writers or editors had much to do with the making of at least a dozen of first-rate newspaper hands. Especially were Arthur Arnold's pupils noted throughout a whole generation for the sure-footedness of their advance from paragraph to paragraph in the column or so that they were expected to fill.

This little band of diligent toilers found no successors exactly of their own kind till the unjustly forgotten or ignored group, combining in its members literary taste and business powers, presented the world (1892) with the *Echo's* earliest matutinal successor at the same price. The *Morning Leader* in its beginnings was brought into

contact at one or two points with one of the most noticeable figures in the periodical literature of his time, and
in this way. Mr. Ernest Parke was the foremost member
of a company which owned the *Star*, no relation or
remote descendant from the older organ of that name
mentioned on an earlier page, but that once edited by
Mr. T. P. O'Connor. On the *Star* premises Mr. Parke
and his colleagues originated the *Morning Leader*. This
paper was of Eastern Counties origin ; for its earliest
managing director, Sir F. W. Wilson, knighted in 1907,
had a friend and supporter in J. J. Colman, of Norwich
and mustard celebrity. The Norwich association proved
of happy omen for the paper ; Mr. Colman's son-in-law,
Professor Stuart, of whom more presently, became to
it a source of intellectual strength. Since then its commercial position has received no little benefit from the
interest taken in the *Morning Leader* by the two great
cocoa houses of Cadbury and Rowntree. But in Mr.
Parke's newspaper properties Mr. T. P. O'Connor's successful industry and extraordinary personal endowments
had given him certain rights. At any rate an indemnity
amounting to some thousands was found to be his due
before he and his operations established themselves
beneath a new roof. Since then this gifted Irishman
has continually filled a larger place in the popular eye
than perhaps any other purveyor of the new journalism
or the old. Several of his compatriots crossed St.
George's Channel and established themselves in London
at the same time and with the same ambition as Mr.
O'Connor. In respect of education and aptitudes these may
have been his equals, as well grounded in the Greek and
Latin classics and in historical knowledge as himself,
perhaps almost as well read in French and German
literature. They differed from him, however, in being
without his own mental or spiritual inner life. With him
each fresh subjective experience formed a new crisis.
His adventures in philosophy and metaphysics contained
the materials of a romance which he might have worked
up into something like Disraeli's *Contarini Fleming*, into
the more reflective and less sensuous passages of Bulwer-
Lytton's *Falkland*, or into a new series of the same
romancist's *Student* and *Caxtoniana*. And, indeed, to a
certain extent, this is what he actually did. His best

writing has given him a hold on the public because it is his own individual record transfigured. So far as honest study and downright hard work could contribute to such an end, his successes have based themselves on a solid foundation of intellectual self-discipline, of systematic reading and connected thought. In writing an essay or an article, as in planning and launching a new enterprise, he has formed a distinct and generally fresh idea, complete in all its parts, before putting it into execution. Whether on the platform or in the press, he won the applause of stalls and boxes before he brought down the gallery. His maiden speech at Westminster drew from John Bright not only praise, but a wish to be made personally acquainted with the speaker. It has been the same with his newspaper pen. ' T. P." has long since become more of a popular favourite and even celebrity than " G. A. S." (George Augustus Sala) ever really found himself. At the same time, however, he has combined with a good opinion of the multitude the appreciation reserved by experts in newspaper business for brains that can always turn themselves into capital. With the *Morning Leader* he had nothing to do except receive the already mentioned compensation for disturbance. Of others concerned in that venture, the best known and the most inspiring was Professor Stuart. Returned for Hoxton in 1885, this academical ally of the new journalism had already distinguished himself not only by his services to University Extension, but, as professor of mechanism, by showing that manual industry has a science of its own which may make it the handmaid of the most genuine culture.

The tenth year of the twentieth century saw Mr. T. P. O'Connor in his monthly magazine find a place for art as well as literature. So far back as the sixties something of the same kind had been done for the comic press by the man whose father sang the *Song of the Shirt*. Thomas Hood's son went through Oxford at the college which its most famous product, Samuel Johnson, called a " nest of singing birds." This description, seeing how many minor poets were on its staff in the sixties, was at least as well deserved by the War Office, where, on leaving Pembroke, Tom Hood became a clerk. In 1865 he gave up this position to undertake the editorship of *Fun*,

which, with the idea that it might be lifted out of the
gutter, had been recently purchased by a friend of his
named Wyland, and for which Hood himself found, in
Paul Gray, T. Morten, and Gordon Thompson, artists till
then unknown, whose cartoons or small cuts soon
accustomed the penny public to drawings blending freshness and grace with humour and fun. With not a little of
his father's literary genius, Hood combined much of his
ear for rhythm, for rhyme, and his intellectual refinement
generally. No mean hand himself at serio-comic verse,
he discovered for his new paper several who surpassed
him in such compositions and whose *vers de société* need
not have dreaded comparison with Frederick Locker's
gems. Of that company there survived till quite recently
Sir W. S. Gilbert, who, as a member of Tom Hood's'
staff, wrote most of his *Bab Ballads* and, in Christmas
numbers, presented the germ of Dr. Dulcamara [1] and
perhaps other burlesques. Hood himself, having before
this brought out Artemus Ward, Arthur Sketchley as
" Mrs. Brown," and W. J. Prowse as " Nicholas," introduced in an essay Bret Harte to the English public.
Never writing down to *Fun's* earlier purchasers, he
really initiated in his paper something of the educational service to be rendered afterwards by Mr. T. P.
O'Connor.

From the actual literary guides and ornaments of the
existing press, or their forerunners, the transition is now
to the giants and the capitalists, whose operations on
it the present generation has witnessed. Of the two
brothers, Alfred and Cecil Harmsworth, the younger is
naturally the less known. Neither in ability, courage,
nor resource need he shun comparison with any of his
line. Each, indeed, from the first has been the com-
plement of the other. Their co-operation has combined
the qualities of thoughtful prescience, careful provision
for possible risks, guarantees against failures not certainly
to be foreseen, and an intrepidity of enterprise based on
the principle that nothing succeeds like success. Had
they wanted a motto, they might have found it in the
Virgilian aphorism that to create the impression of power

---

[1] First produced in 1866 at the St. James's Theatre, under Frank Matthew's
management, on the same night that Henry Irving played, with Miss Herbert,
in *Hunted Down.*

is to master the secret of success. In a word, both the Harmsworth brothers have shown themselves the two first living masters of newspaper business in all its departments. George Newnes, it has been seen, from much the same beginnings as Daniel Defoe, actually adapted Defoe's tactics to modern conditions. The Harmsworths found their most stimulating exemplar in the man who was Defoe's latter-day analogue. The two brothers were still youths when they emulated their predecessor's *Tit-Bits* with their own *Answers.* This soon achieved such prosperity, and struck out its roots in so many different directions, that it seemed the natural thing to turn it into a company. At this time, too, the *Echo,* as an evening paper, sold for the twenty-fourth part of a shilling, then belonging to Passmore Edwards, of public library fame, practically was without a rival in its own field · and the *Echo's* continued popularity arose from its being a little print, largely composed of short paragraphs. Its one competitor, the *Evening News,* had, from its founder's point of view, fulfilled its mission when it secured him the promise of a baronetcy, though death prevented him from ever himself wearing the title. Coleridge Kennard, to whom the *Evening News* belonged, knew nothing of journalistic management, and had to think of his parliamentary constituents as well as of his paper. Meanwhile the *Echo's* circulation became so languid that it might at any moment have stopped. The Harmsworths saw their first great opportunity. Hitherto theirs had been the day of small things. Their luckiest strokes of newspaper business were with comparatively obscure provincial prints and a great variety of trade journals, of which the general public knew nothing, but which to their proprietors had been veritable gold mines. In 1896 came the first great opening that was to unite for them fortune and fame. Coleridge Kennard lay sick unto death ; his journal's condition seemed scarcely more hopeful. The Harmsworth brothers bought the *Evening News* practically at their own price. That formed the earliest of the family feats on a great scale, but was only one among the many proofs given of keen insight into the needs and opportunities offered by the humbler section of the middle class. Their little papers, the *Sunday Companion, Home Chat,* served as stepping-stones to the greater venture of the *Evening News*. Their smaller enterprises appealed to an immense, and so far a largely neglected class. Following the example set by the houses of Chambers and Cassell, the Harmsworths handled the cheap press as an educational interest. The indefinitely growing multitude of office boys, junior clerks of both sexes, presented a stratum thus far almost untapped. It has been already mentioned that the *Daily Telegraph* owed something of the vogue created by its leading articles to those compositions into which was skilfully condensed the latest knowledge about natural science, English history or literature. That hint had not been thrown away upon the whole class of periodical projectors. The Harmsworths now attracted a more variously composed crowd of searchers after knowledge than had as yet been considered by any literary caterers for the million.

In doing this, they incidentally created a novel branch of literary employment. They supplied on their own premises an answer, partial, indeed, but so far as it went practical, to the chronic parental question, What are we to do with our boys? In any direction and of any kind required by their newspapers, the Harmsworths could of course successfully bid for the best literary talent in the market. At the same time they contrived to utilise the industry of a legion of well-educated lads who, with wits sufficiently sharp, combined a certain amount of literary taste. These were glad to find an employment not of the merely mechanical kind, which would prove not less pleasant and perhaps profitable than electrical engineering or the wine trade. The processes of transforming ox carcasses into diminutively nutritious tabloids supply an army of workers with their livelihood. Homeopathic doses of useful knowledge cannot be scattered broadcast in paragraphs through the land without the preliminary co-operation of many different staffs, each performing different functions in abstract making, précis writing, distributed among them, and cognate tasks, however insignificant, allotted to each individual worker. For the first time in the history of the periodical press the Harmsworths did parents and guardians a good turn by taking on youthful out-of-works as hands in the manufacture of the literary pemmican that formed a whole section of their journalistic establishment.

From the halfpenny *Evening News* to a morning sheet of the same price would, many experts predicted, prove a short and sure stride towards bankruptcy. By the time it had turned out a success beyond precedent, death had removed Gladstone, who had always foreseen and believed in halfpenny newspapers on the same principle that he advocated universal third-class railway carriages. The Harmsworths, however, have done a great deal more than bring literature and the latest intelligence to every workman's door. In October, 1910, they delighted their polite admirers by the zeal with which they forestalled their contemporaries in some details concerning the Portuguese Revolution. The price, one halfpenny, may indeed have made their sheet the joy and teacher of the millions. Their tactful, if occasionally tempered, support of Tariff Reform, and their instinctive advocacy of much that smacks politically of reactionary Toryism have secured their daily print as warm a welcome in the most modish of suburban parlours and West-end boudoirs as at the breakfast-tables of industrial breadwinners in latitudes less fashionable. So with the Bank Holiday makers, with whom the seaside outing would lack its true flavour if the inhalation of the sea breeze were not alternated with glances at the *Daily Mirror*, the earliest and for long the only illustrated halfpenny sheet, with which the Harmsworths even outdid themselves. Where the Harmsworth ownership did not extend, the Harmsworth influence was to permeate ; it made itself felt on the greatest daily paper the world has ever seen, the *Times*, and on the best of the Sunday papers, the *Observer*. Meanwhile the Harmsworth capital had brought into the family what was once known for the most considerable of the society press, the *World*. In the provinces, too, these gentlemen have acquired journals so long identified with private interests and hereditary owners as, not long since, to be considered beyond the possibility of outside purchase.

Considerate or generous dealing with the rank and file of their workers is a well-maintained tradition among the capitalists of the English press. It has not suffered in the hands of those who have most recently entered that body, and with that Northcliffe combination which has already gone some way towards dividing with the Pearson firm sovereign control over some two-thirds of the entire press area. During the sixties the *Daily Telegraph* had a graceful and accomplished writer, already mentioned, W. J. Prowse. The manifestation or threat of lung disease caused his proprietors to send him to the Riviera. This example has been followed more than once by the owners of the *Daily Mail*, who, when one of their workers, falling sick, has been ordered to the Engadine, have made the prescription practicable by presenting the invalid with a return ticket for Davos Platz and a cheque for his hotel bill. Mr. John St. Loe Strachey himself and his *Spectator* disciples have not been more strenuously patriotic than the Messrs. Harmsworth in supporting the rifle club movement and in sending it recruits from their own premises. Neither that, however, nor the unfailing imperialism of their newspaper constitutes the only claim of these gentlemen to be considered pillars of the empire. The overseas dominions of Great Britain have, like its newspaper system, been built up and consolidated largely, if not entirely, by private enterprise. Even Mr. Joseph Chamberlain's concern for the territories which he officially administered between 1895 and 1903 had drawn strength and fervour in the first instance from his own and his family interest in some of our Pacific Islands.

Mr. Chamberlain himself had ceased to be Colonial Secretary when the Newfoundland Government desired to open up for commerce, if not for cultivation, the waste or unused grounds. Effectually to do that capital on a large scale had to be introduced. The Newfoundlanders were, therefore, in the position of men who had informally addressed an advertisement to capitalists generally throughout the world, but not to any particular combination. The Harmsworths were as those who had seen this advertisement. To answer it and to turn the opportunities it offered to the best account lay in the regular business path of newspaper men who wished to buy in the cheapest market material for their papers. The Lloyds presently to be mentioned were the first newspaper owners to employ the cheap paper made of

esparto grass. The Harmsworths were conversant with
the art of making paper out of wood pulp. Newfoundland abounded in trees suitable for that purpose. It was
thus primarily as paper manufacturers that the men of
the *Daily Mail* first thought of establishing themselves
in Newfoundland. The conditions under which they
obtained leave to do so were sufficiently stringent as
well as protective of native or other rights. On a lease of
ninety-nine years, the land received by the Harmsworths
amounted to two thousand square miles, held at an
annual rent of a trifle under £800, and upon terms not
less advantageous to the Newfoundlanders than to the
Harmsworths. The privileges of the new tenants were
the power compulsorily to acquire such fresh land as
might be necessary for opening their way to the sea,
or for securing internal communications, freedom from
municipal taxation, the importation of the mills and
plant used in manufacturing wood pulp and paper free
of duty. Whenever it became necessary to renew the
old machinery, the fresh plant was not to enjoy any
exemption from impost. At every point precautions were
taken against the lessees' abuse of the benefits they
received. They were to make a yearly return of the
trees they cut down, as well as of the specific results in
pulp or paper obtained. Local interests and a healthy
stimulus to native industry and commerce were insured
by a clause providing against any wholesale export of
Newfoundland timber, and providing that the entire yield
of the Newfoundland forests should be manufactured
into paper or pulp upon Newfoundland soil. Stringent
measures were also taken to prevent excessive or
dangerous deforestation. A right of way through the
Harmsworth lands was guaranteed for all who had
occasion to use it. From this it will be seen that the
Harmsworths really entered into an industrial partnership
with the natives and inhabitants of the island.[1]

Such are the facts and such the explanation of the
Harmsworth activities in the North Atlantic. At home
their capital and energy, when employed in buying up,
partially, if not entirely, established journals, have seldom

[1] *See* Cap. 10 of 1905, confirming a lease, dated January 12, 1905, of a great
portion of the Exploits River basin to the Anglo-Newfoundland Development
Company.

been prompted by a wish for the advancement of any political propaganda. They have chiefly or entirely aimed at clearing the ground of sheets that, as has happened chiefly in the case of their provincial enterprises, they think it well to weed out from the soil selected for their own journalistic extensions, or that, as happened with the *Evening News*, they propose galvanising into life and success. In certain contingencies it is as natural for a newspaper to change hands, and in doing so to undergo a transformation more or less complete, as it is for a ship to be wrecked or a theatre to be burnt. A broadsheet with a history yields a steadily increasing, or at least not diminishing, income and influence to its owner. Under these circumstances it is not likely to find its way into the market. The men who gave the paper its character and influence disappear. Their methods have gone out of date ; the journal itself can only be preserved if it is wholly or in part re-created by new capital and by new minds as well. For in a mechanical age like the present there comes over the conditions of daily life and the political ideas of men some change to which the past affords no parallel. It is as though the descendants of a great newspaper's founders seem to have lived into not only a new epoch but a new world, wherein no guidance or safety can be derived from the principles which once formed the pole stars of the print. Unless the old stock have among its latest representatives a really great, courageous, and original intellect, capable of adapting old traditions to new emergencies, the journalistic heirloom becomes a kind of white elephant, to be disposed of to the highest bidder. Such were the conditions actually realised or in course of fulfilment by the *Standard* when, in the nineteenth century's closing years, the third of the great newspaper powers still flourishing, that of the Pearson name, surpassed all former achievements by annexing Shoe Lane to its empire.

Among the most regular purchasers of *Tit-Bits* in the Wimbledon district during the eighties was a City clerk, living with or frequently the guest of his father, who had a Surrey benefice not far from Wimbledon Common. This clergyman had given his son a public school education at Winchester, where he had done well, learning something of books, but a great deal more of human character and life. The lad had gone into business, not from any special aptitude for the work, but because there presented itself an opening too good to neglect. His future career, however, was to be decided and directed by his most frequent purchase at the suburban bookstall before taking the train for town. He found a special attraction in the various competitions that his favourite paper had, as already said, been the first to introduce. Many years before then, indeed, during the early youth of the penny press, a casual correspondent of the *Daily Telegraph* named Kelly displayed such extraordinary vigilance in detecting petty errors in each impression that the proprietors engaged him as one of their proof revisers. Mr. Cyril Arthur Pearson's score in the part of Œdipus to the Southampton Street Sphinx stood so persistently high that Newnes determined to give him a berth on his paper. The time, however, of course came when Mr. Pearson saw no reason why he should not set up for himself. With less difficulty perhaps than had been done by Newnes before him, he found the funds for starting *Pearson's Weekly*. Some time later the *St. James's Gazette* vicissitudes already recounted were ended by its becoming Mr. Pearson's property, and it was, of course, incorporated into the *Evening Standard* on the Shoe Lane property's acquisition by the gentleman whom Mr. Chamberlain dubbed the "champion hustler." Since then Fleet Street has heard many periodical predictions of Pearson or Harmsworth collapse. A reversion, it was from time to time and perhaps is still said, to the old regime must eventually prove inevitable. Writers, reporters, even printers, were either openly rebelling against the organisers of the new journalism, or were secretly disaffected towards them. Here one's concern is with facts as they are. The great majority of the public which the *Standard* made its own when held by the Johnstone family, so far not only clings to it, but sees no reason to be shocked by the transformation that the paper is said to have suffered. Under the Pearsons, indeed, as under the other latest Fleet Street dynasties, a clean sweep has been made of any remnant of the old staffs ; the work has been and is being done by fresh hands and in a new as well no doubt, as a better way.   Abroad and at home Our Own Correspondents or article-writers are altered as frequently, or moved with as little warning from one spot to another, as pastors on a Wesleyan circuit or the recipients of a call to a Congregational church.   The sole practical test of merit in a newspaper is the payment of a handsome dividend. So long as that is forthcoming, it would be an impertinence to criticise the modes of editorship or management employed.   Quick changes of the sort just described formerly would have been considered fatal to the individual journalist's chance of achieving distinction in his calling or influence with the public.   Being, like Tristram Shandy's scullion, here to-day and there to-morrow, he may now entirely miss the opportunity afforded, under the old and anonymous system, of making himself of as much importance in his readers' eyes as the proprietor or conductor for whom he worked.   Even, however, with newspaper proprietors of such antiquity as the Lloyds, he would find himself no better off than with those who started only the day before yesterday.

Here to the list of newspaper families, of whose members enough has already been said, an addition must be made in the latest members of the line which has so long had its quarters in Salisbury Square.   There seems no connection between the Edward Lloyd who, in the seventeenth century, opened the City coffee-house that has given its name to the whole system of ship assurance and the Surrey farmer's son who, some hundred years afterwards, founded *Lloyd's Weekly News*, with, according to the traditional fiction, Douglas Jerrold for its first editor. That distinction really belongs to one named Ball, the wielder of a powerful pen, that won him early nineteenth-century fame with the vehement articles signed " Censorius " in the *Weekly Dispatch*.   Douglas Jerrold first filled the position at the age of forty-nine in 1852; between him and the first editor had come William Carpenter, a very notable figure among pamphleteers and minor authors, whose *Peerage for the People* long remained a democratic handbook, and who, with a courage equal to his convictions, suffered much in person and purse under the old press laws.   Two years after the beginning of Douglas Jerrold's editorship began the connection with the paper of Mr. Thomas Catling.   This journalist, when both Jerrold and his son William, who succeeded him as editor, had passed away, himself became responsible for *Lloyd's Weekly News*. Before his retirement, he raised the paper's circulation to close upon a million—the highest figure probably ever touched by a weekly print. On his death in 1890, Edward Lloyd settled all the newspaper properties in his own family, leaving the chief management to his four sons, of whom two, the eldest and the youngest, survive to-day. Meanwhile, while yet with fourteen years of life before him, Lloyd had bought in 1876 the *Clerkenwell News*. It was one among the innumerable sheets of purely local importance to be found in various metropolitan districts, and was at one time the organ of the watchmakers, long numerous in the Clerkenwell region. A clever, genial, upright, and able Irishman, Robert Whelan Boyle, had begun his London training in the sub-editor's room of the *Daily Telegraph*. Thence he went to the *Hour*, of which and of whose workers enough has already been said. On the death of that paper in 1876, he became the first editor of the *Daily Chronicle*, into which he had rendered Lloyd valuable help in improving the *Clerkenwell News*. While that journal has steadily advanced in credit, enterprise, and prosperity, Mr. Catling will be remembered as a journalist not less distinctly representative of the Victorian Age than his successor, Mr. Robert Donald, represents the workers and the system which characterise the present period. Colonial universities like to catch their professors young. The twentieth-century newspaper owner, whether he be a Lloyd or another, fights shy of a labourer who has lost the gloss of youth. Other times, in a word, other manners. In its peremptory gradations of centurion-like power and responsibility there is something of military precision characterising the distribution of command among those who, whether on *Lloyd's Weekly* or the *Daily Chronicle*, have taken literary service in the family that once employed the author of *Mrs. Caudle's Curtain Lectures*. At the head of the whole system the travelled and cosmopolitan Mr. Robert Donald, encircled by aides-de-camp, transmits his orders to commanders of divisions, and through them to the junior captains of the host, each within a minute's call. As generalissimo of the Messrs. Lloyd's entire force,

Mr. Donald, still, according to the ancient Roman compu-
tation, little more than a youth, unites in himself the
authority before his time divided between Mr. Catling
and Mr. H. W. Massingham. The latter, as editor of
the *Nation*, is one of the three or four newspaper men
on the Liberal side whose word counts for as much with
the extremists of their party as does that of Mr. Garvin
among the more thoroughgoing Conservatives. Mr.
Massingham, however, will also go down to posterity
as one of the very few journalists who appreciably influenced the formation of a Government. That was more
than half a generation since, and happened in this
manner. In 1894 Gladstone's retirement was known
to an influential few long before its public announcement.
Loyalty and respect to the great chief abdicating his
office caused the matter scarcely to be mentioned in
the press. If it had been, the succession must certainly
have gone to Sir William Harcourt, whose supporters
would then have been able openly to co-operate for
establishing his claim to the vacancy. As it was, the
Harcourtians were unorganised and unprepared. Meanwhile Mr. Massingham, then conducting the *Daily
Chronicle*, declared against Harcourt, and convinced a
powerful section that the best arrangement for
Radicalism would be a peer Premier with a lieutenant
in the House of Commons, whose staunchness to the
advanced cause should be as much above suspicion as
his ability. Sir William Harcourt, indeed, could not
be kept from the Chancellorship of the Exchequer. That
Lord Rosebery filled the first place, and that the Liberal
rank and file began to see their eventual chief in Mr.
Asquith, was due entirely to Mr. Donald's predecessor
on the Lloyd establishment.

To produce "process" blocks in a single night for
printing next day was a feat unaccomplished, probably
unattempted, before 1890. The idea, however, of an
illustrated daily paper had occurred quite in early days
to Henry Vizetelly. That prolific and resourceful projector submitted the notion to the first Sir Charles Dilke.
His adviser, John Francis, did not then consider the
various processes connected with engraving had reached
a point at which the experiment could be made with a
fair chance of success. Nothing, therefore, was done

till 1890. By that date such improvements had been effected as even the acute and prescient Vizetelly could not have foreseen. Still, however, the immense advances in rapid reproduction of pictorial design might not have been turned to practical account but for the remarkable man who had found in the Franco-Prussian War of 1870-1 'the opportunity for securing success to the only real competitor the *Illustrated London News* had ever known. William Thomas was fortunate enough to interest in his project the most active of those concerned in the direction of the *Graphic*. This was Mr. Porter, of Redhill. At that time also there still lived the weekly *Graphic's* earliest editor, H. Sutherland Edwards. He, too, quite apart from his earlier connection with Vizetelly, believed a daily pictorial sheet to be possible. Some at least of the money support given to the new venture was forthcoming on his recommendation. Henry Blackburn, himself equally accomplished with pencil and pen, in his books about the Normandy coast and the Oberammergau Passion Play, had given some practical hints about the utilisation of art as an accompaniment to letterpress in the daily newspaper. His expert advice encouraged Mr. Porter and his business colleagues to regard the scheme with fresh favour. Henry Blackburn lived long enough to witness the harvest borne by his suggestions in the *Daily Graphic*. Itself resulting from the initiative of not more than half a dozen men, the new paper had scarcely been established when its growing acceptance by the public set the conductors of one or two other sheets on decorating their columns with pictorial designs after their own fashion.

CHAPTER XII

NEWSPAPER MAKERS OUT OF LONDON

AMONG the great operators of the newspaper system, some, like the Harmsworths, have carried their enterprise from the metropolitan into that provincial field where the twentieth-century journalist has done greater things even than in the capital for himself and for his craft. During mid-Victorian days (1846), instead of the two hundred and two "dailies" of 1910, the United Kingdom possessed only fourteen, of which the metropolis supplied nine. London thus supplied all England with its morning journal. The singular number is correctly used because, at the point now looked back upon, that morning journal was practically always the *Times*. Not that the provincial reader, whose opinions the mighty organ did so much towards forming, was himself a regular subscriber to it. At most he saw it beneath his own roof for a fixed time on hire on the first, or more likely the second day of publication. If he lived in or near a country town, he looked at the day's news as it issued from Printing House Square in an inn coffee-room or at the local stationer's, where, before the club system's development out of London, clergymen of various degrees and county magistrates used to congregate, not only to read the Blackfriars broadsheet, but to discuss among themselves the problems which it proposed. Country prints of course there were, epitomising the week's doings throughout the world, and reporting local incidents at full length. These were regularly taken in by the well-to-do gentry or clergy, not so much for reading as by way of patting an indigenous industry on the back, just as they might have encouraged any other manufacture 'on the spot, whether it were something to eat or drink or to wear. By degrees things improved. Local competition insured better writing, wider, as well as earlier news. The journalist out of London began not to fear comparison with his metropolitan rival. In 1881 the last disadvantage under which he had laboured was removed by his admission to the full privileges of the press galleries and the lobbies, on the same footing as the most favoured of his London brethren, at Westminster.

The man who first made the English newspaper a national institution, in his *Kentish Petition* and *Legion Memorial*, did something towards creating the germs of a provincial press ; he went, however, much further than that. While a fugitive and a wanderer through all parts of the United Kingdom, Daniel Defoe found himself almost as much at home in the local centres on which he descended as in his native Cripplegate. Before winging his flight further, or being moved on by law officers to fresh cities of refuge, he had a way of leaving his mark where he had once alighted in the shape of a few periodical columns for supporting the Revolution Settlement which his pen had served so well. Amongst the local capitals where now or afterwards Defoe established himself was Edinburgh. Here, as has been already shown in the chapter dealing at length with his career, he made himself the literary life and soul of the negotiations for the Anglo-Scottish Union of 1707. By that time there had already come into existence a newspaper called the *Edinburgh Courant*. It lapsed in consequence of its owner's death. In 1710 it was revived and reorganised by Defoe for the purpose of overcoming the Northern partner's sentimental dislike of incorporation into the unity of Great Britain. Having served or attempted to serve that end, the *Edinburgh Courant* had done its real work. The Scotch national products were once described by Lord Rosebery as oatmeal and Liberal members of Parliament. Notwithstanding the lavish contributions of Scotch Conservatives and the literary efforts of the distinguished and accomplished men successively concerned in its management, the *Courant* never became a popular paper. About the year 1850, indeed, as regards circulation, it took a start, and began running the *Scotsman* close. But it failed to seize the heart and mind of the multitude. It therefore did not penetrate, as the *Scotsman* did, into every nook and corner of the country. At this time Alexander Russel's paper, further particulars about which presently will be given, published in each issue one or two editorials interpreting, with the searching insight of familiarity and power, the inarticulate sentiment, social, religious, or political, of the most curiously varied and complex public in the kingdom. Russel himself was a personality better known to his fellow-countrymen and in closer touch with their most cherished prejudices, partialities, or convictions than could have been the case with Delane of the *Times* in England. James Hannay, whose name is not now mentioned for the first time in these pages, and who began to edit the *Courant* in 1860, had a higher literary reputation than the other editor against whom he was pitted, and, on his return after some years of adventurous absence to his native land, was welcomed as clever novelist in the Captain Marryat vein, a *Quarterly* reviewer of sound literary judgment, of great illustrative power, and a lecturer who had done for satire and the satirists what had been done by his friend and teacher, Thackeray, for the seventeenth or eighteenth-century sovereigns and wits. The two men in private life were friends and associates ; in their respective newspapers they were perpetually crossing swords. Hannay was a hard hitter, never more pleased than when what he gave was returned, and excited much amusement in a certain controversial episode by his description of his adversary's manners and methods—" invective brandished as recklessly as the writer's own dinner-knife when peas are in season." On his migration in 1865 from Edinburgh to London, Hannay gave up the *Courant* to Francis Espinasse, a Scot of Gascon descent, who remained at the paper till its purchase by Charles Wescomb, the purchaser also, about the same time, of the London *Globe*. In James Scot Henderson, Wescomb found a thoroughly capable, cultivated, clever, and kindly successor to Espinasse, and in Dr. J. P. Steele, a writer also for the *Yorkshire Post* and the *Lancet*, a really consummate master of the leader-manufacturer's art. Meanwhile the earlier promise of better days had not been maintained. The *Courant* steadily fell rather than grew in favour. Years earlier Russel's just description of it as a kept paper while the *Scotsman* was everywhere had drawn from Hannay the retort : " Better to be kept than to be on the streets." Now its protectors were falling away. Presently there came a rally ; the hat was sent round to the Conservative lairds, with the result that the *Courant* struggled on a little longer under the conduct of James Mure, a younger son of that William Mure of Caldwell who, between 1850 and 1857, wrote the well-known and still read *History of Greek Literature*, and who had relieved his pen's severer labours by occasional contributions to journals which appreciated classical learning, and which allowed him to make his animadversions upon the economic fallacies of democratic Athens the occasion for telling backhanders at the financial blunders of English Radicalism. Like the most distinguished among his predecessors, James Hannay, James Mure had begun life in the Navy, but had from time to time, when on shore, revived under his learned father's eye the knowledge he had picked up at Westminster, and received from him the continuation lessons that were in themselves a little journalistic training. He also resembled Hannay in having, after his nautical days, served his newspaper apprenticeship on the London press. The Edinburgh Blackwoods had long been the *Courant's* most generous and sanguine supporters ; James Mure, their personal friend, took over the paper practically as their nominee. Never had it been more thoroughly Scotch in the personnel of its management than during Mure's short editorship ; for in those days its business arrangements were looked after first by a Macdonald sprung from the ancient Skye stock, afterwards by James Somervell of Sorn, who first connected the office in the Scotch capital with the London headquarters by a special wire, giving up nearly the whole of every night to the superintendence of despatches, so that he at least was free from blame if the *Courant* in this respect were not kept up to the *Scotsman's* mark. So things went on to 1886, the year of political chaos following the Gladstonian conversion to Home Rule.

Ten years had now passed since the *Scotsman's* reins fell from the strong hand of Russel, who died in 1876, and whose temporary successor, Wallace, inheriting his statesmanlike wisdom, preserved the newspaper's Liberal traditions while keeping it out of the Home Rule quag-mire. Russel himself was so much of a national person-age, as well as a newspaper celebrity, that he claims a few final words now. An Edinburgh solicitor's son, he had received a good classical grounding at Ross Kennedy's school, St. James's Square, in his native city. Leaving it while still a boy, he was bound over to serve his articles with a printer ; here he had for his fellow-apprentice the bearer of a name destined afterwards to become famous in newspaper narrative. This was John Johnstone, less noticeable for his future con-nection with the *Inverness Courier* than for his kinship to the family of the same name that produced the re-creator, and, as it exists to-day, the real founder of the London *Standard*. Russel's earliest berth was the *Berwick Advertiser*, which at the age of twenty-five he edited for a yearly wage of £70, paid every week. Then, after a short control of an obscure Kilmarnock sheet, he fell in with one among the shrewdest and most far-seeing of the *Scotsman's* founders.

The triumph of personal enterprise signalised by this paper from the first calls for a few details about the little group of remarkable men who made it. In the autumn of 1816, James Ritchie, of Edinburgh, desired to publish his views concerning the conduct of the Royal Infirmary. Fear of offending the " little great men " then locally supreme closed against him all exist-ing newspaper doors. " Surely," he said, when taking counsel of his friend Charles Maclaren, " there must be room in this North British capital of ours for a free organ of public opinion." To that end the two men at once set to work. Professional business with clients abroad took Ritchie to the Continent, and kept him there for some months. Maclaren, a State servant in the Edinburgh Custom House, was visited with misgivings about the policy of connecting himself with an opposition journal. Confiding in John Ramsay M'Culloch, a common friend of himself and of Ritchie, he secured that acquaintance's help in starting the new paper, and induced him to become its first editor.

James Ritchie had keenly watched his movements but a short time when he decided on getting Russel into his own office as assistant to the chief editor, Maclaren. Whatever might be the farthest limit of success in the line on which he at once received a start, Ritchie for one felt no doubt of Russel's reaching it. He had entered the *Scotsman's* office in 1845 ; in 1848, at the age of thirty-four, the ex-printer's apprentice was promoted to its supreme control. That position during twenty-eight years proved his capacity for being to the *Scotsman* all that not only Delane but Walter was to the *Times*. For wide experience, keen perception of life and character, and personal acceptability in all circles, the Scotch editor did not come after the English. A canny, clear talker, with much dry wit, and a memory that never paused or slipped, at the dinner-tables of his native land he had no conversational superior. He was, too, a sportsman, who, as he could fish or describe fishing against any, so could bring down a grouse or a capercailzie against most. Altogether a guest universally welcome for as long as he liked to stay, equally beneath the feudal roofs on the border or in the spick-and-span new châteaux on the Clyde. Working gradually upward from his creditably humble beginnings, he knew his countrymen on every level so thoroughly by heart that he could play upon popular feeling like a Highland musician on an old set of bagpipes. As a consequence, he had so impressed his personality first on his paper, secondly on the uncritical thousands who swore by it, that everything which they found of special interest was put down as coming from his pen. The true secret, however, of his universal ascendancy, whether in print or out of it, was the faculty which must be found among the one or two great men, without whom neither a newspaper nor a Cabinet can long carry on. This was the power of judging and interpreting public opinion by an instinctive process, just as some men know all about the wind and weather on first waking from sleep, before they have scanned the horizon from the window. Nor had a greater effect on the popular mind been produced by Russel's remarkable gifts than by those testimonials to his national position that formed the unsolicited acknowledgments of his fruitful connection with the national story of his time. Macaulay had more than completed his brilliant parliamentary reputation by his Reform speeches, and had held the highest offices of his Cabinet career when he lost his seat for Edinburgh in 1847. During that year Russel's position on the *Scotsman* was subordinate only. His good offices for the writer and orator whose genius he admired and whose views he shared could, therefore, be but limited. A little later, in 1852, Russel, as editor of the paper and to some extent the first man in Edinburgh, threw his opportunities and influences into the scale. Macaulay was returned not only at the head of the poll, but by a majority of considerably more than a hundred over the next successful candidate of his own party. In this year, too, the unsuccessful candidate on Macaulay's own side brought an action for libel against the *Scotsman;* Russel and his paper were cast in £400 and costs. The entire sum was paid by public subscription. The greatest proof of the public appreciation he had won was, of course, the wide sale that, in 1855, had enabled him to reduce the *Scotsman* to a penny. No ebb followed in the tide of compliment that had thus set in. Instead of sending a special correspondent, he attended in his own person and described with his own pen the opening of the Suez Canal in 1869. During the three days' festivities, Ismail Pasha, then Khedive, singled out Russel among all press representatives for nearly as many marks of distinction as if, like the great official guests of the occasion, he had been a crowned head. The Austrian Emperor personally initiated him into the mysteries of Balkan politics. The then Queen of European beauty and fashion, the Empress Eugénie, claimed him as a fellow-countryman on the strength of her own descent from the Belfast trader,

William Kirkpatrick, whose daughter, by a Belgian marriage, eventually became the Marquis of Montijo's wife
and the Imperial Eugénie's mother. Three years later
the rising generation of his own country paid him
the greatest compliment in the Scotch gift to bestow
—candidature for the Aberdeen Lord Rectorship ; he
made his refusal even more impressive than would have
been his acceptance by a few well-chosen words in the
nolo episcopari sense that could soon be repeated by
all from Cape Wrath to the Clyde. One reason for
declining the offer may have been the conscious failure
of health, shortly afterwards obliging him to pass the
winter in Southern France. Before, however, in 1876,
the curtain finally fell, he had been specially elected to
the Reform Club, Pall Mall, for his distinguished public
services ; about the same time his fellow-citizens presented him with a service of silver plate and £1,600.
Alexander Russel not only gratified Scotch patriotism
when he created a newspaper respected and loved by its
readers throughout the world as a mirror of national
feeling and a monument of national enterprise, but
founded an editorial succession perpetuating from stage
to stage his own wisdom and methods. Among the
newspaper-writers whom he trained, and who, on the
strength of that preparation, took the highest places in
London journalism, were James and John Macdonell ;
both on the *Times*, and both as closely representative of
himself as first-rate gifts and original genius could allow
any disciples to be. At the *Scotsman* office he had
formed the man for filling the chair vacated by
himself. This was Mr. Cooper, the shrewdest and
most determined of men—in mere literary capacity
perhaps Russel's inferior, but absolutely unrivalled in
the aptitude of doing without it. The editorial interval
between Russel's death and Mr. Cooper's formal succession was filled by the Rev. Robert Wallace, D.D., who
left the chair of Church History in Edinburgh University, as well as the ministry of Greyfriars Church, for
editorial work on the *Scotsman*. Dr. Wallace, however,
had on the paper a resolute and able rival, Mr. C. A.
Cooper, himself an aspirant to Dr. Wallace's position,
and presently favoured by a little incident which may
be briefly mentioned. Visiting the Strangers' Gallery in

the House of Commons, Dr. Wallace found himself listening to the speech of another Scotch editor—of the *Glasgow Daily Mail*, who was also M.P. for one of the Glasgow divisions. It seemed a tedious harangue, and provoked Dr. Wallace's dissent at every point till he could contain himself no longer, and gave vent to his feelings by breaking the absolute silence imposed on strangers. The Speaker showed no pity ; Dr. Wallace had to leave the building. Meanwhile, of course, what had happened was telegraphed to every provincial news-paper, the *Scotsman* included. Dr. Wallace was far too good a writer to be lost to the paper. But his fine sense of the becoming and the honourable left him with no wish to retain the editorship, the way to which now lay open to Mr. Cooper. As for the clever, kindly, and universally popular gentleman whom Mr. Cooper replaced, after having qualified for the English Bar, he successfully stood for East Edinburgh against the then Mr. Goschen in 1886, held the seat with the good wishes of the entire Chamber [1] till 1899, when, while speaking against the South African policy that led to the Boer War, he dropped down dead, leaving with all who knew anything of him a keen sense of personal loss. For thirty years Mr. Cooper enjoyed the fruits of his personal conquest. Before in 1906, he retired into private life, he had not only justified by an unbroken course of success his original triumph ; he had engraved his personality, in characters as clear and deep as had been done by Russel before him, upon the minds of his public, and, like Russel, too, had become the hero of countless achievements, some perhaps legendary, though not on that account the less historically significant of his own remarkable idiosyncrasy.

Mr. Cooper's place began in 1906 effectively to be filled by Mr. J. P. Croal. The *Scotsman's* present editor

---

[1] "The most delightful of companions and entertaining of speakers" was the social verdict of St. Stephens on Dr. Wallace, who brought down the House by the description of his Radical colleagues, at the command of their wives, engaging in a wild chase for titles to the cry of "Knight, lord take the hindmost"—a jest ruined by the reporters, who wrote it "devil." In the same speech Wallace was even merrier at the expense of the increase in peers of humble birth. These, he said, reminded him of the Spanish proverb, "The higher a monkey climbs the more he shows his tail."

belongs to a distinguished newspaper family. Trained
for his life's business in his father's office at Haddington,
he worked for the *Liverpool Albion* before, in 1872,
being promoted to the *Scotsman,* and at once making
his start there with an inquiry into the condition of the
crofters. Next came a transfer to the *Scotsman's* London
office. For twenty-five years without a break, Mr. Croal
managed its parliamentary staff and its London correspondence. Consequently he entered upon his editorship
with as full and practical knowledge of political men
and matters as had been Alexander Russel's when his
career closed.

Of all provincial capitals, Liverpool is that in which
individual newspaper reputations of national distinction
have been most conspicuously or frequently achieved.
During the nineteenth century's first half, the great city
on the Mersey knew no more striking representative of
the craft than Michael James Whitty, father of the
E. M. Whitty already mentioned more than once in the
course of this narrative. A maltster's son of Wexford
birth, he was one of the most gifted among the clever
Irishmen who in the twenties found a place on the
London press, and soon made famous friends—among
them Sir James Bacon and George Cruikshank ; Cruikshank, indeed, illustrated those sketches of Irish life
that had given Whitty name and fame in authorship
before he became powerful as a journalist. His Lancashire connection opened in 1830 with the *Liverpool
Journal's* editorship. The abilities displayed by him
in that office won recognition from his fellow-citizens in
his appointment to the post of Chief Constable. After
twelve years (1836-48) of that employment, he returned to
his earliest pursuits by purchasing the *Liverpool Journal.*
Having acted as correspondent to the London *Daily
News,* he promoted the newspaper stamp's abolition by
his evidence before the Parliamentary Commission of
1851. Other newspaper men examined at the same time
as himself were Russel of the *Scotsman,* Mowbray Morris,
manager of the *Times,* and Knight Hunt, on the staff of
the *Daily News.* Michael Whitty's twelve years' control
of the Liverpool police had not only made him a larger
number of well-placed friends than his newspaper opportunities alone might have secured, but had presented

him with a retiring gift, raised by subscription, of a thousand pounds. It was not so much that modest capital as the substantial supporters who flocked round him that, on the abolition of the newspaper stamp in 1855, enabled him to start the first penny paper established in the United Kingdom, the *Liverpool Daily Post*. Of this, Whitty himself took the reins. Edward R. Russell during six years was his chief assistant ; he then went to London, and from 1865 to 1869 became one of the chief writers on the *Morning Star*, under Justin McCarthy, at the same time earning a great reputation for the delicacy and skill with which, in the interests of the paper, he conducted his frequent interviews with W. E. Gladstone, John Bright, W. E. Forster, Lord Clarendon, and other political leaders, whose good opinion of his sagacity it concerned a journalist to cultivate. In 1869 Sir Edward Russell returned to Liverpool as the *Daily Post's* full editor. That position he still retains. During the forty years covered by them, his editorial experiences knew only one change or break , from 1885 to 1887 he sat in the House of Commons for the Bridgeton division of Glasgow, winning from both sides golden opinions for his debating power. No provincial editor has handled more judgmatically the most disturbing questions of the day, notably in Church as well as State, or has given a better tone to literary and theatrical criticism, and that in a city whose dramatic tastes are as universal as its critical appreciation is intelligent and quick.

Among other makers of the Liverpool press in Sir Edward Russell's time has been John Maitland, of the *Mercury*, now incorporated in the *Post*, founded by Egerton Smith, and associated with memories of Sir John A. Willox, M.P., a notably strenuous representative of Lancashire's journalistic interests. The qualities most distinctive of Lancashire enterprise were also personified in Hugh Shimmin. During the shirt sleeves and long clay stage of the Savage Club's development, Clement Millward, one of the club's earliest habitués, established a literary link between London and Liverpool Bohemianism in the *Porcupine* ; that paper's tendency to the frivolous and the comic went on growing till it received an entirely different bias from its new proprietor,

Shimmin. Acquiring decisive influence with the permanent officials of the civic body, he made the paper the organ of the most advanced progressives, and the pioneer of sweeping changes, social, sanitary, and municipal.

There is a story which may be repeated here, but which must be taken only for what it may be worth, about the correspondent of a great Lancashire journal deceiving himself during the Franco-Prussian War into an account of a battle that was never fought. Taking his ease in an upper room at his hotel, he was startled from a reverie by, as he supposed, the thunders of a cannonade proceeding from a quarter where he knew an engagement to be expected. Here he saw a chance of forestalling his colleagues of other papers, though they might be on the field of action and he was not. He at once began a report of the engagement, trusting to pick up fresh details for filling in and finishing as he went along, and perhaps encounter communicative stragglers from the fray. He reached the nearest frontier station, and with great secrecy by good luck contrived to get his despatch on the wires at once. That done, he reappeared for dinner at his hotel. Preserving a discreet silence on the feat he had just accomplished, he learned from casual informants, diners and waiters in the coffee-room, that the distant volleys of artillery whose reverberations on the heavy air he had just so graphically described came from the kicking and plunging of some frightened horses in an adjacent shed.

The vivid account of the imaginary fight which his zeal had prompted him to send home did not detract from the sustained excellence with which the real charges, counter-charges, assaults, sieges, and all the pomp, shock, and circumstance of war were described by representatives of the Lancashire press, especially the *Manchester Guardian*. These, in the seventies, were doing for the provincial press the same work as was done by Forbes for the London *Daily News*. Not only Manchester, but other great North of England centres presently to be mentioned had been fortunate in obtaining for their cheap papers men of the same stamp as those who, like Mr. Andrew Lang and Mr. J. A. Spender, have quickened and adorned journalism with the best variety of the Oxford touch. With these is to be associated Mr. C. P. Scott, as not only editor but governing director, and the leading spirit of the *Manchester Guardian*. Like another Lancashire editor already mentioned, Sir E. R. Russell, Mr. Scott combined during some years (1895-1906) of his journalistic service a parliamentary with an editorial seat, and, as member for the Leigh division of Lancashire, proved himself the most useful committee-man of his time. Among others bearing famous names or representing great positions who have served under Mr. Scott was, some time since, Matthew Arnold's nephew, in his day the best dramatic critic, perhaps, out of London.

The *Guardian* has not had even the Liberal field entirely to its own. Provincial journalism could not show a better representative of its rugged strength than Henry Dunckley ; he it was who, from his editorial chair in the *Manchester Examiner's* office, discovered Benjamin Disraeli's sinister and secret design of unconstitutionally reviving the monarchy's lapsed prerogatives. First the office of Lord High Admiral was to be recreated to fill it with Queen Victoria's second son, the Duke of Edinburgh. Many more machinations of the same kind were brought to light by the *Examiner's* editor in the pamphlet which, under the signature of " Verax," he published during that nineteenth-century period in which Disraeli was charged with an attempt to convert fact into fiction by realising some of the dreams of his own Fakredeen in *Tancred*. Let it be remembered, urged Dunckley, that in this novel had been suggested the substitution of Delhi for London as capital of the Empire. And now had not the first step towards that been taken by bringing Asiatic troops into England's European possessions? As for the next step in Orientalising the United Kingdom, time alone could show. Meanwhile Verax more than hinted that Queen Victoria's infatuation for the Disraelian statesmanship might cause her to accept its author's hand and heart as well as counsels. On that suggestion, when repeated to him, Disraeli's characteristic comment was : " Impossible ; there are two objections. The first is John Bull, the second is John Brown." The other competitor with which the *Manchester Guardian* has had to reckon is the *Courier*, the product of the enterprise and energy which two remarkable brothers, James and Thomas

Sowler, dedicated to journalism, less as a business speculation than because, honest and ardent Conservatives,
they believed they had a mission to stem the torrent of
subversive thought and democratic writing then poured
forth from so many sources in their native county. The
Sowlers of an earlier generation are represented at the
Manchester Courier to-day by a descendant of their name,
Mr. Harry Sowler, whose antecedents, social or political,
literary and academic, are much those belonging to his
rival, the already mentioned Mr. Scott, of the *Guardian*.

Till the eve of King Edward's accession, the ,most
notable and interesting among provincial journalists north
of the Trent was Joseph Cowen, the creator, practically
the editor, of the *Newcastle Chronicle*, and quite capable,
had it been necessary, of daily filling, with his own
vigorous pen, its chief columns. The public temper
and the international events connected with the Imperial
Titles Bill of 1876 brought Cowen, as they also did
Dunckley, into sudden fame and made himself and his
paper a politico-literary school, the most apt disciple in
which is still a force on the twentieth-century press.
In foreign politics David Urquhart's pupil, Joseph Cowen
entered the House of Commons a decade after his master
had done so. In the debate on the Disraelian measure for
improving Queen Victoria into an Empress, Cowen found
an opportunity for expressing the same distrust of Russia,
of her policy, and of the English statesman whom her
influence had blinded, that had been so often manufactured by Urquhart, with Chisholm Anstey for his
supporter, during the Palmerstonian period. So eloquently was the whole thing done, in such terse, telling,
antithetical Anglo-Saxon phraseology were the well-knit
and closely coherent sentences delivered, that, for the first
time in the five years of his parliamentary course, Cowen
found himself cited on both sides as an instance of the
invaluable training for House of Commons eloquence
which a well-conducted newspaper office might prove.
The mass of pamphlets, magazine articles, and other
serials brought together by Urquhart was enormous.
From the *Pillars of Hercules* to the *Diplomatic Review*
and the *Portfolio*, they had all been mastered by Cowen.
The traditions in foreign policy which the acceptance
of Urquhart's views imported into his paper have found

continuous expression, since Cowen's death, not merely in the Tyneside journal but elsewhere, and from a pen whose vigour and knowledge are largely due to himself. But for his early connection with the *Newcastle Chronicle*, Mr. J. L. Garvin might scarcely have rendered services so valuable to the *Daily Telegraph* as he still does, to the *Fortnightly Review*, or have been in a position to make his own *Observer* the mouthpiece of Cowen's statesmanship, and to-day the one organ in the English press, the founder of whose political philosophy is as much David Urquhart as if that remarkable man were amongst us now. Some of the personal associations attaching to the Sunday paper edited by Cowen's twentieth-century representative are so striking that no apology is needed for passing reference to them here. Mr. Edward Dicey had made that journal a well-informed critic of the less known diplomatic movements both before and after its acquisition by Julius Beer, himself a man of much intellectual subtlety and keen interest in foreign affairs. On his death it was conducted by his son with such help as he found necessary from professional literary advisers. The son died, but the daughter-in-law remained. Mrs. Beer gradually found that, in undertaking its sole management, she had essayed a task beyond her power. Fond of writing as well as editing, she always for choice did her "leaders" herself. Her powers gave way ; her final appearance in her own columns was the fragment of an article, her inability to finish which was pathetically testified after what should have been the second paragraph by the words, "To be concluded in our next." His detestation of "Little Englanders" in every guise did not prevent Joseph Cowen calling himself a Radical to the last. His imperialism and zeal for the Turk against the Russ were explained, no doubt inaccurately, by the alleged identity of his own name with Cohen. It was, one heard, the Hebrew strain in his blood which impelled him, as it then did so many of Semitic connections, to rank for the moment among the partisans of the Crescent against the Cross. Urquhart's political propagandism was a triumph of organisation covering the northern half of the United Kingdom. That it remained a force long after its deviser's death was due chiefly to the Northumbrian journalist just described.

Cowen was still busy at this work when a neighbouring county suggested itself as a promising field for journalistic enterprise in the Conservative interest. The Yorkshire squires of the North Riding had long talked of a rival newspaper to the *Leeds Mercury*. Neither their desires nor their capital would have borne fruit but for the organising brain of the most experienced Conservative writer then living, T. E. Kebbel, a name now mentioned not for the first time in these pages. While the business managers were arranging premises, plant, and other preliminaries, Mr. Kebbel was getting together capable writers, to start at least under his conduct. Tied to London himself, he edited the new sheet from his Temple chambers ; soon afterwards he recommended a resident successor, the able and accomplished John Ralph, with Mr. E. J. Goodman for his chief assistant. There were plenty of Conservative Yorkshiremen ; but, though politics may have had the first place in their affection, horses were something more than a good second. In that part of the world the Liberal press severely ignored the racecourse. As became a paper so many of whose best friends, being Tories, were also sportsmen, the *Yorkshire Post* cultivated the interest systematically let alone by the Liberal organs. The turf news of the newly established sheet recommended it to its political enemies as well as friends, and fairly started it on the road to the great success which it soon achieved and has ever since maintained.

The journalistic activities belonging to the early sixties in the North extended also to widely distant parts of the kingdom. In West Anglia two brothers-in-law, Edward Spender and William Saunders, established the first daily sheet issued from the Plymouth press. One, at least, of the West Country journalists in the pre-*Western Morning News* era forms a personal landmark too interesting entirely to be omitted here. A Plymouth man by birth, Mortimer Collins took successfully to newspaper-writing and to mathematical schoolmastering in the same casual breezy fashion that he did to versifying. His best articles were not political pieces but random fragments of picturesque essay-writing, with something of the same grace and jauntiness that showed themselves in the lilt and the music of his poetry. Previously to the

Saunders-Spender operations, the seaport city of the West had three local weeklies ; of these the two most important were the *Plymouth and Devonport Journal*, done by Mr. Isaac Latimer, and the *Plymouth Mail*, edited and largely written by Collins. The normal relations between the two prints were those of the *Eatanswill Gazette* and *Independent* described in *Pickwick* :—

> "Isaac the editor, Isaac the ass,
>   The sayer of things that don't come to pass,"

was the opening of a skit chiefly directed by Collins at his rival. The gentleman thus pleasantly described in his enemy's by no means best metrical form retaliated with a catalogue of the various processes for debt in which his adversary had figured, but was subsequently caricatured as Ridley in a novel written by Collins for *London Society*. So the war went merrily on till Collins transferred himself to the cottage, Knowl Hill, Berkshire, where, in the intervals of short pieces in the London *Globe* and magazine versifying, he produced such really clever and melodious jeux-d'esprit as the *British Birds* and a *Letter to Disraeli* in heroic couplets, as well as, on a prolonged South Coast holiday, endowed Brighton for a season with a vivacious little sheet, exclusively his own manufacture, called the *Rapier*, whose memory still amusingly lingers in some South Coast newspaper offices, but which, during its brief and bright existence, attempted no rivalry with such first-rate specimens of local enterprise as the *Sussex Daily News* and the *Brighton Herald*. The poem addressed to Disraeli and in the manner of Bulwer Lytton's *New Timon* and *St. Stephens*, described the parliamentary personnel :—

> " Flashy directors, birds of evil omen,
>   Enormous fellows of immense abdomen,
>   Stockjobbers, gorgeous with their diamond rings—
>   Such form the sum of our six hundred kings."

Altogether it was a fresh, musical, and, in its way, stimulating current of thought and phrase, turned on by Collins into the journalistic channel of his day.

To resume the more sober theme of the new Western

daily that, in 1860, began to leave no place either for Collins or his antagonist. During some years a great portion of the *Western Morning News* was sent down daily in stereotype from an office in Hatton Garden, managed by Edward Spender, with William Hunt and J. F. Hitchman, subsequently of the *Manchester Courier*, for his assistants. Mr. Spender's keen and nice perception of local newspaper wants and possibilities was equalled by his literary aptitudes and high sense of duty. Such qualities might have made him independent of other counsel. Mr. Hunt's advice, however, he instinctively regarded as too valuable to be neglected. Hunt therefore merits a place in the little group which presented the two Western counties with a morning print that soon became the household name it has ever since continued, from the Exe to the Tamar, and from Mount's Bay to the Land's End. Other associations of lasting interest cling to the names of these Western journalists. William Hunt exercised his journalistic activities far outside the limits of his native county. He was one of those whose advice had been asked and taken by the founders of the *Yorkshire Post*, whose editorship Hunt, at a later date, himself was offered and refused. He was, however, too good a man finally to avoid editorial responsibilities in another direction. In 1863, taking Hull as the basis of their operations, the indefatigable Edward Spender and William Saunders organised an *Eastern Morning News* ; its conduct was entrusted to the best available man they had, none other than Hunt himself. Edward Spender raised another lasting memorial of his journalistic knowledge and energy in the Central Press—a news agency whose usefulness, if first felt by the Spender papers, soon communicated itself to the entire comity of the provincial press. Not the least noticeable adventure of the Saunders-Spender combination was one across the Scotch border, which brought about the *Caledonian Mercury's* transformation from a weekly into a daily paper. The net result of reviving this ancient hebdomadal as a quotidian print, less at the instance of Edward Spender than of William Saunders, was the *Scotsman's* ultimate acquisition of the *Mercury's* plant. Meanwhile Edward Spender himself, having personally laid the local foundations of the *Western Morning News* by 1862, had moved his residence from Plymouth to London. Here, in the Lobby at Westminster, in one or two Pall Mall clubs, and at some of the best houses in town, he achieved a reputation, of which any newspaper man might be proud, for conscientious excellence of workmanship, for skill and discretion in employing the news, always trustworthy and often exclusive, that he contrived to pick up. The London Letter that formed a feature in most of or all his papers was written always by himself, never hurriedly or at the last moment, but at the rate of a few deliberate paragraphs daily throughout the week. Compositions with this title were commoner then than they have since become. Edward Spender's came to be considered a model of its kind. This remarkable man, indeed, may accurately be described as an instructor in his craft of others as well as a capital performer himself. No man could give better hints about effective newspaper diction or sounder warnings against the pitfalls into which haste often betrays those who are far from being neophytes. Thoroughly literate, to quote Thackeray's word, himself, both by the closeness of his general supervision and the practical details of his proof correction, he did his best to impart that distinction to all who came under him. William Hunt was, of course, a colleague in the quality of whose writing and the wisdom of whose action entire reliance might be placed. Among his London helpers, J. F. Hitchman and Rowe Bennett both testified to the advantages they consciously received from their co-operation with one who knew his trade so thoroughly as their chief.

Time went on ; in accordance with its growing tendencies, less of the important work was done in London and more at the Plymouth offices. Gradually even the despatch of the " stereos " was given up. The Plymouth men increasingly justified Edward Spender's teaching ; sometimes they were able to show that the provincial as well as the metropolitan press might keep well ahead of the Government in the receipt of early and authentic intelligence or important news at anxious times. That proved conspicuously the case during the Ashantee War, when day after day the *Western Morning News*, in advance of any official despatches, enlightened the public as to what was going on ; while questions asked in Parliament of Ministers in charge elicited a practical confirmation of the newspaper's account.

What has here been said about local newspapers specified by name is applicable to many other forces in provincial journalism not so particularised. The truth is that in no forward movement illustrated by the London journalist has his provincial brother been without a share. Of late years the Foreign Office as a whole has profited much from the progressively frequent interchange of the London and foreign members of the diplomatic service. Something of the same sort has taken place in the relations between the London and the provincial press. The best men from the country find their way to Fleet Street permanencies. On the other hand no important provincial post falls vacant without attracting many first-class metropolitan applicants. Some notion can be formed of the trend and results of this movement from its most modern instances. Nor should these be confined entirely within the United Kingdom's limits. The men of the English newspaper, as the world has been reminded by certain journalistic hospitalities on a grand scale held in London early in the present or late in the last century, are not only national but imperial personages, in whom the British dominions beyond the seas, as well as on this side of the English Channel, have a share. During the fifties or the sixties, soon after H. E. Watts was exchanging for the post of leader-writer in Shoe Lane the editorship of the *Melbourne Argus*, a paper, for its ability and influence, second only to the *Times* of that date, A. P. Sinnett, an important manufacturer of *Standard* editorials in the Hamber and Johnstone epochs, was on his way to Allahabad as editor of the *Pioneer*. Even before that, shortly after his first London start at the *Globe*, he had learned something of Asiatic newspaper control from conducting the *Hong Kong Daily Press*.

Passing to purely domestic instances, the recent list opens with Mr. W. T. Stead, who, from the Darlington office of the *Northern Echo*, in 1883, came to assist Mr. John Morley with the *Pall Mall Gazette*. On the other hand, Mr. James Nicol Dunn has moved to and fro between the metropolis and the provinces so as to belong almost equally to both. Beginning with the *Dundee Advertiser*, he was then transplanted to the *Scots-*

man. Thence he came to London for controlling the Anglo-Scottish gifted and defunct sheet, the *National Observer.* After that successively he made his mark at the *Pall Mall Gazette*, then as editor first of *Black and White*, afterwards of the *Morning Post.* His return to country pastures followed. To-day he is not only editor of the *Manchester Courier*, but the prolific projector of ingenious newspaper combinations throughout the whole region beyond the Trent. Prominence has been given on an earlier page to one of the most remarkable figures among the journalistic stalwarts on the Tory side. Mr. J. L. Garvin is now giving the *Observer* a new lease of life and power. It was not in the Strand nor near it that he gathered the experience which has equipped him for his present work. The pupil of Joseph Cowen, and therefore one among the very few disciples now existing of David Urquhart, Mr. Garvin wrote much and after a fashion indistinguishable from his present mature style in the *Fortnightly Review* on foreign politics, in the *National Review* on fiscal matters, before he exchanged the *Newcastle Chronicle* for the *Daily Telegraph*, or, a little later, made one of the happiest newspaper hits of the time with the *Outlook.* The *Observer's* registered owner is, of course, Lord Northcliffe, with those about him. The sole director of its policy and source of the extraordinary influence it now wields is Mr. Garvin ; he, to conclude the present references to him, has, on his own political side and in his own department, been, among writers, without a rival except, perhaps, the late Iwan Muller, who, from the fullness of his varied knowledge and natural strength, drove his points home, paragraph by paragraph and sentence by sentence, as with a literary sledge-hammer. Muller, too, like Mr. Garvin, started from a provincial basis, and had become a power of the first magnitude on the *Daily Telegraph* before giving fresh *éclat* to Mr. Cust's brilliant dispensation at the *Pall Mall Gazette.* Before Mr. Garvin exchanged the *Newcastle Chronicle* office for Fleet Street, Joseph Cowen, desirous of dissuading him from, as he thought, an unwise step, clenched his protest with : " You are a great person with us ; you will be lost in London." This, if properly understood, shows not only Mr. Garvin's place in the shrewd Northumbrian expert's estimate, but also the practical homogeneity characterising the best organs of opinion in the capital and in the country.

Absolutely the oldest representative of the relations subsisting between these two sections already appears in the remarks about the *Yorkshire Post*. Mr. E. J. Goodman, now a retired but hale and hearty veteran, left Leeds for London in 1874. Previously to becoming the first Lord Burnham's right-hand man on the *Daily Telegraph*, he had started a daily venture of his own, then entirely novel both in conception and in execution, called the *Circle*. This stopped at the very moment of its turning the corner and entering upon the path which would have led to commercial success.

CHAPTER XIII

THE JOURNALIST IN IRELAND

The Irishman in exile—American influence on the press across St. George's Channel—The Franco-Irish alliance—Young Ireland movement and its organ—Young hearts and hot heads on the *Nation*—John Mitchell starts the rival *United Irishman*, which is suppressed—Famous men of the *Nation* —Ireland's earliest "dailies"—Foundation of *Freeman's Journal*, 1763— —Amateurish writing—Some notable contributors—The *Freeman* of the present—Other South Ireland papers—*Saunders' News Letter*, the eminently "respectable" print, becomes Ireland's leading journal—An Irish newspaper king—The Murphy papers and their rivals—In the North—The *Northern Whig*—From press to parliamentary and official life.

In its newspaper manifestations, the Irish genius, like the Scotch, has so widely permeated the English press as of necessity already to have received more than passing attention in these pages. Jonathan Swift could not avoid the admission of having, as he himself put it, been "dropped in Ireland." With perfect truth he could insist on his purely British ancestry. He was, however, as Lecky has recognised, forced into being a leader of public opinion in Ireland ; nor could he divest himself of the Irish influences and connection which, from his day to Edward Sterling, and from Sterling to Delane, have been shared by so many among the chief personal forces in our "fourth estate." This, indeed, is but another way of saying that Irish brains have generally found the most prosperous and brilliant fields for their display elsewhere than in their native land. Charles Lever's later writings in his maturer and best vein draw illustrations of this fact from diplomacy, politics, and society, just as his earlier instances of the same truth were those suggested by the adventures of war. The historian Froude gave more circumstantial testimony to a like effect in his solitary novel, the *Two Chiefs of*

Dunboy, with its moral that, once removed beyond St. George's Channel, and, if possible, the Straits of Dover, no one is more qualified for harvest reaping in commercial enterprise than the astute exile from the " distressful country."

Not, however, that the Irish journalist at home has failed to attain an authority and success that, for exactly one hundred and thirteen years, uninterruptedly from 1797 to the present day, has made him a power in his native land from Giant's Causeway to Cape Clear. He has also been a conspicuous landmark in the modern Irish record, and has not infrequently in his own person epitomised the events and tendencies of his time. Moreover, during the earlier stages of his development the Irish journalist was more appreciably influenced than any other penmen of the United Kingdom by the wise thoughts, expressed for the most part in stately phrase, of the statesmen and publicists who gave periodical writers and students of political philosophy a model for all time in the *Federalist*. Edmund Burke was about contemporary with the *Federalist's* leading spirits, Madison and Hamilton. His political summaries for the *Annual Register* may occasionally suggest that he had himself read them. He can, however, scarcely be claimed as a father of Irish journalism, even on its literary side. The best of the working Irish journalists frequently modelled themselves on the *Federalist*. If Burke cannot be claimed for a practitioner of the newspaper craft, he showed himself at least its prophet when he said that cheapness of production and progressive freedom from State censorship would provide both the Old World and the New with a rival and controller of Cabinets and Parliaments. The traditional connection between England's disaffected dependency beyond St. George's Channel and her nearest continental neighbour had specially prepared the Irish mind to accept and exult in such a prediction. For the seventeenth-century French journalist, Rénaudod, of the *Gazette de France*, had been a personage with a literary following on the Liffey while as yet he and his print scarcely received the compliment of quotation in Fleet Street. So was it, too, with the print, named the *Mazarine*, of Richelieu's successor. Before the seventeenth century closed, Isaac Disraeli's fathers of the English newspaper, Birkenhead, Nedham, and L'Estrange, had done their life's work. The Irish journalist was not, therefore, in advance of his British brother when, between 1686 and 1690, he blossomed out into the *Dublin Newsletter* and the *Dublin Intelligencer*. His literary ancestors of unrecorded name had, however, sat at the feet of French teachers, and acquired, for transmission to their descendants, a style of their own long before the occurrences of 1797, followed by those of 1848, inspired the nationalist rhetorician of the pen with the arguments or aspirations they clothed in diction, Anglo-Saxon as to its words, but Gallic or Celtic in respect of its rhythm and finish.

Both in his own country and when a subject of the Stars and Stripes, the Irishman took as naturally and as conspicuously to newspaper-writing as did the Gaul himself. He had, indeed, while as yet Massachusetts had not shaken off allegiance to King George, given Boston its own *Newsletter*. By the middle of the eighteenth century, in the person of Benjamin Harris, he had done the same thing for New Hampshire. Harris, coming in 1704, prepared the way for Benjamin Franklin and his pupils. In this way were brought into being the personal forces which, having created the press of the United States, at once reacted, with consequences scarcely less productive, upon Ireland. Individual initiative and ideas received indeed help at once timely and indispensable from the general trend of historic events, personally manipulated as these were to the prejudice of England and the strengthening of the Franco-Irish *entente*. By 1797 the Anglo-French negotiations at Lille for peace had finally failed ; Austria had come to an understanding with Napoleon. The great war which followed the Revolution had, for the moment at least, reduced itself to a duel between the second Pitt and the " Little Corporal." Bonaparte at Paris was marshalling an army intended to begin the subjugation of Britain by invading Ireland. Grattan and his friends were already organising a Convention that was to supersede the Irish Parliament on St. Stephen's Green. It might be a matter not of months but of weeks or even days before the disaffected province should be in a blaze of insurrection from Belfast to Cork. In the spring of the year already mentioned

(1797), the Franco-Irish conspiracy possessed no organ of its own. By the following autumn the movement had equipped itself with far the ablest news sheet that had as yet arisen from French inspiration and Irish money as well as brains. This was the *Press*. Its responsible owner was a small printer named Finnerty. It was run with funds largely supplied by Lawless, and was edited by Arthur O'Connor. Its staff included not only the cleverest pens of the time, but the most popular political leaders, Lord Edward Fitzgerald, Chambers, Jackson, and Bond.[1] For more than half a century after the formidable but futile effort which brought together, under the banner raised by Finnerty in the *Press*, so many capable writers, the typical Irish journalist did little more than play the part of chorus in a Greek play, keenly criticising the party managers and policy on both sides of St. George's Channel, picturesquely hinting at the disastrous consummation that Saxon misrule was preparing for itself. The revolutionary year of 1848 raised Irish hopes of deliverance from Saxon tyranny. Spoiling for a fight, Young Ireland had become angry with itself for entertaining the comparatively moderate counsels advocated by O'Connell. At a little later date, the fine presence and eloquent tongue of Feargus O'Connor marked the point at which Young Ireland prepared to unite with English Chartism. On that union Young Ireland's journal, the *Nation*, says little. Nor did the two movements possess many features in common. Chartism began in 1838. It was dying out in 1848. The spirit animating the Young Irelanders in that year had been at work ever since 1795, and remained an operative force in future risings long after Chartism was forgotten. Chartism, too, lacked the literary associations, their wealth in which naturally drove Young Ireland into print. It thus connected the Irish nineteenth-century rising with the literature which had inspired the European convulsions amid which the eighteenth century closed. For Voltaire had written, and, while the French monarchy still existed, the courtly audience of the Versailles theatre had applauded the words : "I am the son of Brutus, and bear graven on my heart the love of liberty and a horror of kings."

[1] Lecky's *Eighteenth Century*, vol. vii. pp. 424-5.

Here might be found the keynote of the Young Irelandism of 1848, as of its newspaper activities. It resembled Disraeli's somewhat earlier Young Englandism. The Irish movement had, like the English, largely grown out of disgusted disappointment with the Whigs, and scornful hatred for the official Tories. It also resembled the English in being dependent on patrician patronage. Its leader, Smith O'Brien—did he not trace back his lineage to Celtic kings, as, for that matter, did Feargus O'Connor?—was really a man of good birth, highly-placed connections, and of considerable fortune, the brother of a baron, Lord Inchiquin, the Marquis of Thomond's cousin, with a pedigree going back in a straight line to the royal and national hero, Brian Boru. From his colleagues Smith O'Brien received an absurdly exaggerated homage that so disturbed his intellectual faculties as to disqualify him from giving sane advice about the management of the Young Ireland organ, the *Nation*. Its first editor, Thomas Davis, had written much verse quite up to the highest album standard, and could be trusted to produce elegant prose as well. As pilot of the *Nation* he thought less about keeping together and directing a political agency than about producing a miscellany of general interest. Not that its largely poetic contents failed to derive some variety from an occasional enforcement of the opinions it had been started to proclaim. For O'Connell had split his party by telling its young bloods to stop short of actual violence. On the other hand, the Young Irelanders who had placed Davis in his chair desired to see it frequently and emphatically stated that, as Jefferson Brick put it to the Colonel in *Martin Chuzzlewit*, " the libation of Freedom must sometimes be quaffed in blood." The men who conducted and wrote the *Nation* showed themselves bad politicians, and therefore worse patriots. Smith O'Brien, whose social position and resources made him the " boss " of the business, had less aptitude for affairs or organising power than the average country squire, English or Irish, at that period generally contrived to pick up at Quarter Sessions. Davis himself, an accomplished and amiable rather than an able man, proved the creature of his feather-brained and hot-headed band, as well as the dupe of his own fond and perfectly

groundless hopes. Alphonse Lamartine, the most sentimental of French Revolutionists, became the Young
Irelanders' political or literary idol, and used the opportunity to fool his admirers to his heart's content. A
Republic had replaced the monarchy of Louis Philippe
Lamartine gulled his Irish worshippers into looking for
the new French Government's interference on behalf of
their distracted and oppressed country. In 1797 the
United Irishmen's earlier organ, the *Press*, had misled
its victims in the same way. A like result followed the
efforts of those who took their politics from the *Nation*
in 1848. The closing scene of the Young Ireland episode
only came nearly a generation after the organ of the
movement had ceased to wake many responsive echoes
with its war-notes. Its decline was due to two causes.
First, its capitalists began to weary of an unproductive
enterprise, as well perhaps as to be visited with some
compunctions about a persistent vehemence of abuse,
suggestive rather of the weakness of the cause than of
its strength, and subjecting them at any moment to legal
pains and penalties. Secondly, the most ferocious of its
writers, John Mitchel, having been dismissed from the
paper, started an opposition organ of his own, the *United
Irishman*. The proceedings against Mitchel for incitement to sedition and outrage had ended in his transporta-
tion. While serving his sentence abroad, he escaped
to the United States ; in 1875, while still in America,
he was elected member for Tipperary. The House of
Commons, then led by Disraeli, decided that a convict,
although a successful prison-breaker, was disqualified
from sitting in Parliament. In the same year that the
appearance of Mitchel's name revived memories of the
Nation, another of that paper's contributors succeeded
in actually entering St. Stephens. This was Edward
Vaughan Kenealy, notorious for having been the
Tichborne claimant's counsel. Kenealy had a vague
reputation, entirely undeserved, for scholarship and
literary culture ; he had shown nothing of either
in the weekly journal, the *Englishman*, which he
had started, it would seem, for the special
object of publicly rehearsing the attack that he had
entered Parliament for the one purpose of making
on Lord Chief Justice Cockburn. John Mitchel had

died in 1875, immediately after his second election for Tipperary. Kenealy lived on till 1880. The man whose money had supported the *Nation*, Gavan Duffy, had meanwhile become Prime Minister of Australia, and been knighted by his sovereign. Journalism comes as naturally to the Irishman as politics. The prints whose personal fortunes have now been traced are the chief, if not the only Irish newspaper enterprises that have gone hopelessly wrong.

Between the seventeenth-century projectors of the two Dublin sheets mentioned above and Young Ireland's journalistic escapade with the *Nation*, memories of Swift are revived by the name of the man who owned and printed one of the two earliest Irish daily papers. This was the George Faulkner who, in 1741, published the Dean of St. Patrick's *Thoughts upon the Present State of Affairs*. Faulkner, however, had been anticipated more than a quarter of a century earlier by another speculator in paper and printer's ink ; for Pue, when in 1700 he brought out his *Pue's Occurrences*, made himself the founder of the Irish daily press. A little more than a generation later the Irish journalist had advanced to the same stage of development as had been completed by his English predecessor in 1726. In that year the *Craftsman* had brought the leader-writer full-fledged before the London public. In 1763 the Irish newspaper-man similarly began to show himself not merely as a collector of news but as a creator of opinion. The Irish hatred of the English connection did not prevent the newspaper men of Dublin from finding in it the same kind of inspiration for their enterprise as they had already welcomed from revotionary France and even from America. The year last mentioned was marked not only by the Peace of Paris and the protest of six British colonies in America against the Stamp Act, but by the fall of Bute, by the subsequent rise of Grenville, Egremont, Halifax. This triumvirate's war against freedom of speech generally, and in particular its undignified duel with John Wilkes, produced in England an excitement which soon reacted upon popular feeling across St. George's Channel. The medium for expressing that sentiment had been prepared upon principles and in a manner far more practical and business-like than was to be the case with the already-recounted newspaper adventure of Young Ireland some eight decades after 1763. The men who in that year brought into being the earliest of still existing Irish journals belonged to the same class as the English Woodfalls, the Mallets, the Walters, and others, already mentioned in their proper place, who had widened and deepened the foundations of the English newspaper. The London bookseller had cleared the path for the later advent alike of the publisher and the journalist. The men who in the Irish capital during the reign of George III. profited by the literary example of the English booksellers were not even printers. They were substantial, hard-headed men of business, who had done well enough in their respective trades to indulge a tolerably cultivated taste with a typographical enterprise. One, probably the chief of their number, bore the same name, if he did not belong to the same family, as the first secretary to the United Irishmen, when they aimed at conspiring with Bonaparte for the overthrow of English rule. The United Irishmen, who were not known by that name till 1791, have been misrepresented as lending a hand in the *Freeman's* foundation. Perhaps, however, it may be said that these later patriots were the political heirs of malcontents in evidence at least a generation earlier. At any rate, one of the Tandy name, notorious in the nineties, Edward Tandy, a successful draper, hunted up two or three other partners in the venture. As a result of conferences and efforts, the *Freeman's Journal* came into existence at the sign of the " Mæcenas Head," Bride Street, Dublin, on September 10, 1763. A bi-weekly print, edited by Henry Brooke, it owed immediate popularity not to the merit of its writing but the colour of its politics.[1] Brooke's control was at first exercised jointly with a committee of its proprietors. These, however, once satisfied of his entire fitness for the work, gave him no trouble, left the choice of writers as well as of the paper's policy to this most competent representative, merely stipulating that he should enlist the best pens available, and that its general treatment of subjects should reach the high-water mark of contemporary culture and taste. Among those forming the *Freeman's*

[1] Madden's *Irish Periodical Literature*, vol. ii. p. 374.

early staff was at least one member of the gifted journalistic family of Lucas. Dr. Lucas no doubt served the
paper well with his pen, but was never responsible for
its conduct. Valuing his own services at least at their
full worth, he had a nephew who, in 1772, started in
opposition a *New Freeman's Journal*. This gentleman justified his title on the ground that the idea and
the name of the original *Freeman* sprang from his own
brains, and that its prosperity had been secured by his
uncle's writings alone. However telling his articles may
have been, Dr. Lucas was only one of several from
whom the paper profited, at least as much as from
himself. In truth, however, a good deal of what
appeared in the *Freeman's* earlier issues was very poor
stuff indeed, well meriting the time-honoured journalistic
epithet of " sloppy." The great defects of the *Freeman's*
earlier writers were an amateurishness of form and pro-
lixity of style shared with his contributors by Brooke
himself. The whole paper only filled one sheet ; of
this a single article sometimes occupied four or five
columns. In spite of these defects, the high reputation
belonging to some of the writers redeemed the inferiority
of their work and to the public even invested it with a
value that was certainly not its own. Dr. Frederick
Jebb, the ancestor of Sir R. C. Jebb, the nineteenth-century Cambridge Greek professor, made a hit with his
pieces signed " Guatimozin." " Causidicus " (Robert
Johnson) pleased the public, and largely promoted Henry
Grattan's Irish Volunteers movement. Grattan himself
is said to have written first for the *Freeman* his often-
quoted character of Lord Chatham. The Dublin residence of Sir Hercules Langrishe, the great Kilkenny
landlord, social leader, political pamphleteer, and parliamentary orator, is now the University Club. There in
the room that was its sometime owner's library, Sir
Hercules himself composed the prose and poetical pieces
that at once enlightened the paper and helped his political
chief, Grattan, whose organ the *Freeman* became, and
who, in return, together with Flood, rewarded it with
more than applause for its attacks on the Government.
In 1767 the editor Brooke and his chief proprietors were
agreed that the line taken by the *Freeman* should, though
national, be anti-Romanist—Grattan himself, it must be

remembered, while the champion of Irish independence and of Catholic Emancipation, was a Protestant. Protestant grievances unredressed, the abominations of Poyning's law, the evils of a military administration, arbitrary acts of the Lord-Lieutenant, Whiteboyism, and Captain Fearnought's followers encouraged by Government's slackness in executing the laws against papists, Popery the true cause of all riots, robberies, insurrections—such were the flaming headlines which, in the *Freeman's* daily bill, anticipated the most sensational lines in the American newspaper of a later day. The few genuine specimens of Irish wit and humour sometimes secured by Brooke came in a column headed the *Copper Alley Gazette*, were chiefly rhymed squibs and now and then a smartly-written, short prose lampoon on the English parliamentary leaders at Westminster, with whom Grattan, Flood, and their friends were at perpetual war. For the rest, Brooke, like his whole editorial and sub-editorial staff, was at least careful not to shoot over the heads of his public. The invective said by Grattan to form the staple of contents was watered down copiously with paragraphs of the lightest chit-chat, as well as with long or short dissertations to which exception could only be taken on the score of their didactic dullness. Flood was another of the public celebrities who became a figure on the *Freeman*. Though a failure afterwards in the Westminster Parliament, he had won high distinction less for his oratory than his debating skill in the Irish House of Commons, and was considered good enough with his pen for a claim to be put forward by his admirers to the authorship of the Junius Letters.

The passing phase in the *Freeman's* existence now glanced at has, of course, long been forgotten in its modern position as a leading Nationalist organ, distinguished equally for patriotic sagacity in its politics and adroitness of literary expression. To-day its managing director is one who, in the Gladstonian House of Commons, delighted even his opponents by his ready gifts of brilliant speech, and impressed the coolest of parliamentary experts by his mastery of the Assembly's rules, as well as of the phraseology and technicalities which so often confuse or conceal its legislative procedure. The elective Chamber still misses Mr. Thomas Sexton. Irish journalism generally and the *Freeman* in particular are gaining every day from the transference of his rare powers to the work of newspaper control ; at the present time of writing (1911), he is a tower of strength to the *Freeman* not only as its managing director, but as himself a writer chiefly on subjects connected with railway amalgamation and land purchase. One of Mr. Sexton's former contemporaries at Westminster, Mr. M. M'D. Bodkin, was one of the *Freeman's* most regular and effective pens till his public services and his legal experience secured him a County Court judgeship. Among other journalists contributed by Ireland to the Legislature is Mr. T. M. Kettle. The *Freeman's* London correspondent, Mr. J. M. Tuohy, combines to-day the national quickness of brain and neatness of diction with an insight into parliamentary and social situations un-impaired by the growing tendency to substitute hurried telegrams for the carefully-knit narrative of the London letter. From the distant nineteenth-century days when " Father Prout " (Frank Mahony) represented the *Globe* in Paris to those in which Mr. Tuohy performs a like function for the *Freeman* in London, Cork has been prolific of newspaper men.

Southern Ireland, too, has ever been rich in the essen-tially national union of newspaper and parliamentary gifts. Of that an illustrious instance has been supplied by Mr. Justin McCarthy, now living in retirement from politics and journalism alike, and happy in a son who has inherited not a few of his father's qualifications for both careers. The *Cork Examiner*, on which Mr. McCarthy began, still remains the property of the old Irish family, Crosbie. Mr. William O'Brien has before now, by acting as its London correspondent, varied his articles for the *Freeman's Journal* and relieved his parliamentary labours. Like Mr. Justin McCarthy a Cork man, Mr. O'Brien continues a prominent figure in the journalism of his native province. To-day he is perhaps the one newspaper M.P. who copiously writes for and owns a journal, the *Cork Free Press*, bearing his constituency's name. Mr. O'Brien's paper has proved a formidable rival to the sheet whose already-mentioned owners are the Crosbies. Its editor is Mr. Herlihy, an incisive and prolific journalist, at one time a power on the London

Standard. From what has been already said it will be seen that at one time or another most of the Irish newspaper-men have had to do with the *Freeman's Journal*. Under its existing control by Mr. Thomas Sexton, this paper, during the last twenty years, has had for its editor Mr. William Henry Brayden. Its chief and most useful writers are the already-mentioned Mr. Kettle and Mr. Skeffington, both men who impart to their work scarcely less of individuality than Mr. Sexton infuses into its management. These gentlemen are also seen in the halfpenny journal, the *Telegraph*, that supplements the morning *Freeman*, and that, like it, is heart and soul for the Nationalist cause.

The *Freeman's* founders, though not printers by profession, differed only in the detail of the business they carried on from the typical tradesmen, for the most part calling themselves booksellers, who figured so prominently among newspaper projectors on the British side of St. George's Channel. Before passing on to those who at a later date emulated the *Freeman* enterprise, some notice must be taken of a working printer who, without, it would seem, much help from any partners, contrived to start, eighteen years before the *Freeman* began, the chief journal which may be called that paper's contemporary. Just two decades before the little group of traders on the Liffey co-operated to produce the paper that Mr. Sexton to-day controls, a Dublin printer and bookseller, who had learnt his trade with George Faulkner, brought into being a broadsheet modelled, it would seem, upon those which served Daniel Defoe for the English newspaper's foundation. Some political trouble into which his vocation as a general printer had brought the man now referred to, James Esdall, compelled him to flee the country. He transferred his paper to Henry Saunders, who thus, in 1755, became personally instrumental in giving Dublin what was long its most reputable, and what to the middle of the nineteenth century remained its most prosperous and widely circulated sheet. *Saunders' News Letter* aimed neither at cleverness, originality, nor any partisanship except for the official side ; its staple of news was English, its information, domestic or foreign, had generally done duty elsewhere before appearing in its own columns. The paper's politics were those of Dublin Castle. It was, therefore, in favour with the ruling class and with all those who took their ideas from the official order. An entire generation has passed since its last number appeared. When in its prime it gave not only intelligence of passing events, but comment on them ; its columns were enriched by the most incisive and philosophical writers of the day, at whose head was the still famous Dr. Shaw of Trinity College. Ireland has not to-day, and never had, a paper holding the same position as the *Times* in England. *Saunders' News Letter* during the Shaw period was the nearest approach to an Irish *Times* ever witnessed.

Ireland, too, may still lack any predominating jour-nalistic presence like Lord Northcliffe, but Mr. William Murphy, ex-M.P. for Dublin, is at least a very consider-able newspaper personage. Mr. Murphy has, too, other irons in the fire which justify his fellow-countrymen's proud and fond comparison of his national services to those performed by Bianconi, of coaching fame, between the years 1815 and 1875. Chairman of the Dublin Tramways Company, as well as railway contractor in East Africa, this gentleman has laid down the chief tram-lines not only in Ireland at Dublin and Cork, but in Belfast, Paisley, and in the Isle of Thanet. Mr. Murphy also owns the most widely circulated of Irish papers, the *Independent*, price one halfpenny, edited by Mr. Harrington, notable, perhaps, even more for his business powers than for his literary tastes. Mr. Harrington has always shown a quickness of editorial sense almost amounting to an instinct in manning his paper with political leader-writers like Mr. Lehane, and bright and ready masters in the art of paragraph such as Mr. Cox, of the Civil Service. Another of the Murphy papers, the *Evening Herald*, has for its chief Mr. Joseph A. Rice. Both of these prints are carried on in the moderate Nationalist interest. Their managers con-form to the growing English practice of giving their most important utterances not as editorials but as signed articles. Mr. Murphy completes the circle of his sway by owning, if not managing, the *Irish Catholic*, the one Irish paper authoritatively expressing the ideas of the Roman Church.

Irish journalistic talent is, however, equal to much more than the maintenance of a Nationalist press at a high political and literary level. Father Healy, the wit, gave Charles Lever hints not only for more than one of his most amusing characters but for some of his most telling incidents and best contrived scenes. He has bequeathed to Conservative journalism a thoroughly capable custodian and ornament in his nephew, Mr. Healy, whose Protestantism does not make him less racy of his native soil as an exponent of Conservative principles. The chief director of the company owning the *Irish Times* is the son of Sir John Arnott, a fine, breezy representative of the picturesque old Munster Toryism. The proprietorial influence thus co-operates with the editor's tact and knowledge, not less of his country than of his craft, to make the *Irish Times*, with its circulation of some thirty thousand, a thoroughly popular exponent of Irish thought as well as a literary stronghold of anti-Nationalist conviction. Mr. Manders, sprung from a good old Irish legal stock, is a typical member of the staff which Mr. Healy has gathered round him. Consequently the paper is read by moderate Catholics not less than by Protestants, while its editor also finds time to do the Dublin correspondence for the *Times* itself. As might be expected, the descendants of the man who did his country the service of restoring St. Patrick's Cathedral have invested their energy and wealth in the press that upholds their faith in Church and State. Sir Benjamin Lee Guinness's eldest son, Lord Ardilaun, has successfully organised and effectively equipped the more advanced Conservative organs of his native capital. Here he has found an indispensable colleague in Mr. McPeake, his adroit and able chief editor. From the premises supplied by Lord Ardilaun are issued the (matutinal) *Express*, and, later in the day, the *Evening Mail*. Mr. McPeake's position is the more useful as well as pleasant, and his work the more easily, agreeably, and therefore effectively done, because he serves under a single most capable master. Sir Edward Carson, indeed, and one or two of his way of thinking, may have a small interest in Mr. McPeake's papers. But the one actively managing proprietor is Lord Ardilaun alone. Mr. McPeake, too, is fortunate in possessing for his right-hand man and chief writer one who, like Mr. Longworth, has in him not a little of the great Dr. Shaw's superlatively good material.

What has already been said about the Conservative scribes at work on the press of the Irish capital is enough to show that first-rate journalistic brains are not a Liberal monopoly. So, too, it naturally is in the northern stronghold of constitutional principles. Mr. Frank Finlay, during most of the nineteenth century, lived in London, and, while having an interest in the *Northern Whig*, was seldom compelled by his Belfast connection to desert the little Reform Club coterie, including James Payn the novelist, Sir J. R. Robinson, and Mr. J. C. Parkinson, to which he belonged. To-day the renowned Ulster organ belongs to Mr. Smylie, whose duties as M.P. for Antrim help rather than hinder him in his general supervision of Orange Protestantism's chief but not only exponent ; for the Henderson family carry the Orange principles beyond even the *Northern Whig* in the *Belfast News Letter*. On the other side, Belfast is indebted to the energy and resources shown by Mr. Joseph Devlin, the representative of West Belfast, as well as Secretary to the United Irish League and the Hibernians, for the counter-blast to the Orange screeds which, as its editor, he supplies in the *Irish News*.

The resemblance between the typical French and Irish journalists, still as actual and as close as ever, is, to anything like the same extent, unknown in England. Just as much in Ireland as in France has the newspaper proved the stepping-stone to Parliament. It is doing so to-day. The successive stages in the process are few and simple. Beginning as a reporter, the aspirant wins promotion to the editorial room. If his work be well done there, entrance to the Bar follows as a matter of course, and all is clear for Parliament after that. Some notable instances of advance on these lines may now be given, in connection with the different newspapers from which the start has been made. Among the *Freeman's* contributions to Bar, Bench, or other official posts are the ex-M.P. Judge Bodkin ; Mr. T. P. Gill, now Vice-President of the Agricultural Department and trained on the *Freeman* for the *Daily Express* editorship ; Mr. J. G. McSweeney, promoted from the

Weekly Freeman's chair to a Local Government Board inspectorship ; Mr. George McSweeney, who left the *Freeman* to conduct the *Evening Telegraph*, and whose rise in the legal profession has since then been unbroken ; Mr. Muldoon, whose legal notes in the *Freeman* formed the first rung of the ladder, and who, having been Crown Prosecutor for Cork, is now Mr. John Dillon's confidential law adviser.   Other cases were Mr. Linehan, who made his way direct from the reporting staff to the position of the Attorney-General's " devil," and Mr. Robert Donovan, whose present goal, however, is neither legal nor parliamentary, but professorial, in the new University.   Mr. Redmond has found a confidant and the party that he leads a wise adviser in Mr. Clancy, for many years one of the *Nation's* editors before being called to the Bar.   Notwithstanding Viscount Morley's former journalistic co-operation with the late Sir William Harcourt on the *Saturday* and the essays as *Quarterly* or weekly reviewer, remarked upon in an earlier chapter, of the Marquis of Salisbury when Lord Robert Cecil, there has not often been in England such a direct line of advance from the newspaper office to public eminence as this, though in France it has been and may still be as common as in Ireland.   The Irish and French politico-literary developments also resemble each other in certain changes that have almost equally come over Irish and French diction, whether written or spoken, since the years when Lamartine's emotional eloquence in denouncing the Orleanist regime inspired much of Young Ireland's invectives against the English connection.   Whether in the Press or in Parliament, the Irishmen of 1797 set a literary fashion that was exactly reproduced by their descendants of 1848, and that has not even to-day quite gone out.   Still, since 1848, notably with Irish writers, perceptibly even with the rank and file of Irish speakers, there has set in a tendency towards a businesslike reserve and terseness of expression such as marks increasingly the Parliament men and publicists of the third French Republic.   Mr. John Dillon's, and at times even Mr. Redmond's more impassioned passages may not only recall Young Ireland's periods in the mid-Victorian epoch, but may be resonant with the eighteenth-century ring.   Their picturesque old-world stylism finds no echo in their party press, and the heats of parliamentary declamation have not perhaps more effect upon the paragraphs of the *Freeman* or the *Northern Whig* than the dithyrambs of the French Tribune upon the wary, vigorous, but disciplined pens who ply the art of their historic master Courier in the *Gaulois* or the *Temps*. The truth is that C. S. Parnell set the example of the terse and severely uncoloured diction which in the seventeenth century John Pym and John Eliot introduced at Westminster. Still, as on the platform so in the assembly, Celtic argument and imagination are not always to be bound by Saxon fetters. In *Pendennis* Mick and Morgan agree that the taste for eloquence was going out more than half a century ago. Yet to-day not only Mr. Dillon but even Mr. Redmond and Mr. Joseph Devlin are eighteenth century itself compared with Mr. Arthur Balfour and Mr. Bonar Law. In France the already-mentioned Paul Louis Courier combined with Emile de Girardin to give the French journalist a new birth. Something like that, it is no exaggeration to say, resulted for the Irish newspaper-writer from the exercise which Dr. Shaw, of Trinity College, found in *Saunders' News Letter* for his fine Irish brains, for his potent and sternly self-disciplined pen. As a fact, though the historical accidents of the time may have given it a greater prominence, the relationship of the Irish journalist to the French is not probably closer than that of the English, who, often at the instance of individual teachers like the late James Macdonell, began systematically, rather more than a generation ago, to derive profit from the study of French masters in his craft. Whether in the future he will find his vocation the same natural pathway to State service and promotion as it has proved to his brethren on the other side both of St. George's Channel and the Dover Straits is a point belonging not to history but to speculation.

CHAPTER XIV

THEN AND NOW IN FLEET STREET

The journalist in social life—Upward struggle of the penny press—Friends of the country papers—Literary influences in the early Victorian Press—When was the journalistic golden age ?—True significance of Delane's and others' " lionising "—The journalist still a cipher in party wire-pulling—Hard fate of budding writers in army and society—Wearing down the opposition—Then and now in the press—No real decline in the English newspaper—The pressman's relation to the public—The stormy petrel of contemporary history—Riding in the whirlwind—Disquieting effect on international relations—Expert opinion on newspaper influence.

THE progressive fortunes of the provincial journalist interweave themselves at innumerable points so closely with those of his London colleague that the two have an equal claim to a place in the same narrative. The same personages, too, as has been already seen, often belong almost equally to the metropolitan and provincial portrait gallery. From the social point of view also the newspaper-men in the capital and in the country resemble each other in the serviceable friends they have each at different times found among their more important and representative readers. The editors and writers of the penny press, promoted if not actually created by the abolition of the " taxes on knowledge," first became known to the outside world beneath the roof of the man who had led the battle against the paper duty, Mr. Milner Gibson, at his clever wife's weekly parties. They had never been included with Delane and a few of his occasional contributors, like Hayward and King-lake, at Lady Palmerston's Cambridge House receptions. The sixties had advanced some way before the prejudice against the " penny press " showed many signs of wearing off. The despisers of the popular price could not deny that the news was often accurate as well as

early, and the writing of the articles very often good.
" Ah, yes ! " they added, " but then consider the standing and resources of the *Times*. Its writers, too, are
drawn from such a superior class, and so thoroughly
know what they are talking about. This is what you
cannot secure on your *Telegraphs* or *Standards*." Facts
are not wanting circumstantially to prove that all this
was mere conventional prejudice and ill-informed fancy.
During the eighties a distinguished leader-writer for
the *Times* occasionally furnished the *Standard*, personally to oblige his private friend, Mr. W. H. Mudford,
then editor, with an article on a subject he had made
particularly his own—politics in the Balkan Peninsula.
Upon one occasion both the papers now mentioned, the
Times and the *Standard*, published on the same day
articles from the same writer on the same topic, so
skilfully treated, and from a point of view so appropriately different in each case, that the identity of authorship could have been neither seen nor suspected. An
acute outsider, however, prepossessed with a conviction
that whatever appeared in the threepenny print must be
essentially superior to anything in " price one penny,"
in Mr. Mudford's hearing triumphantly compared the
Balkan leader of the *Times* with the " shallow, flimsy
stuff " on the same matter issuing from Shoe Lane.
" Strange," drily remarked Mr. Mudford, " such difference there should be 'twixt tweedledum and tweedledee,
and all the stranger because this particular tweedledum
and tweedledee were both written by the same man."

Probably this experience, coming from the present
writer's personal knowledge, could be paralleled by other
instances of the same sort in connection with the *Times*
and other penny papers than the *Standard*.

While, after the fashion already described, Mr. and
Mrs. Milner Gibson's good offices were removing the
mists of prejudice from the men of the penny press in
the capital, they were found scarcely less useful by the
journalist in those parts of East Anglia and Lancashire
with which Milner Gibson himself had a parliamentary connection. That, too, was the period during
which another personal influence was operating towards
the same end. William Shirley Brooks, Mark Lemon's
successor in the editorship of *Punch*, had, like

Dickens, though not as reporter but leader-writer,
been on the staff of the *Morning Chronicle*; he
had also the same experience as an earlier *Punch*
man, Gilbert a Beckett, of being an occasional writer
for the *Times*. He condescended to show an
interest in Mr. and Mrs. Milner Gibson's literary
protégés, and really did the sheets for which they wrote
a good turn by bestowing on them what he deemed
the patronage of recognition by Mr. Punch. A Shrop-
shire man by birth, he patriotically remembered that
his native place was really the chief of Salopian market
towns. While the laurels won by *The Naggletons* were
still fresh upon him, he occasionally found, in a short
and perhaps generally satirical paragraph, an opportunity
for acquainting the world with the existence of the
Oswestry Advertiser.

Meanwhile the Fleet Street atmosphere had been
refined by contact with quite another set of intellectual
agencies more widely, subtly diffused, and more healthily
stimulating than any of those already mentioned. How
comes it, was the question once put to a person of
consideration in the councils of Printing House Square,
that the *Times* articles read every day as if they had all
been written by the same person? The answer of course
is that, on the *Times*, as for that matter on any other
paper, there is invariably some pen so masterful and
so intellectually contagious in its touch as to become
the object of almost unconscious imitation by other contributors. In the case of the journal on which Mr.
Buckle to-day carries on exactly in their way the work
of Barnes, Delane, and Chenery, inferior to none of his
predecessors, the individual writer, it may well be
without knowing it, is too much subject to that coercive
abstraction, the policy of the paper, and by its literary
usages, to show himself affected by those models of
thought and diction which it would not be beneath the
dignity of his craft to imitate. Elsewhere in the Fleet
Street region, the pens manufacturing for the printer
his daily supply of " copy " are readily receptive of the
external influences which the *Times* writer contracts the
habit of ignoring. The journalist who, outside the Walter
establishment, began to address himself to a new and
wider public during the later sixties, found himself valued

by his employers and readers in proportion as he reflected
in his work the dominating intellectual and literary forces
of the hour.   George Borrow, while collecting on the
spot materials for the *Bible in Spain*, had occasionally
acted as *Times* correspondent.   In the office of the
paper which published them, his letters may not have
seemed an extraordinary event.   Half a generation or
so later, they became the manuals and the patterns
not only of Peterborough Court's " young lions," as
Matthew Arnold called them, but of those whom James
Johnstone had set to work in Shoe Lane.   During
Hamber's editorship, a young writer named Hertford,
who, had he lived, would probably have done great
things, had so steeped himself in Borrow's pure and
easy phrasing that some of the disciple's *Letters from
Corsica* were mistaken by experts for the master's own.
By this time, also, the journalistic rank and file had
become students of a more ancient master than Borrow,
the late George Meredith's father-in-law and classical
tutor, Thomas Love Peacock.   Next a fresh literary and
intellectual current, making its way under Temple Bar,
triumphantly entered the whole line of newspaper offices,
carrying on with it some fresh votaries from each.   In
other words, between 1860 and 1870 the journalist,
however much his language might conceal the fact, had
drunk deeply of Carlyle. Almost simultaneously, the taste
and authority of one or two leading Fleet Street workers,
particularly Tom Hood, as well as Beatty Kingston and
W. J. Prowse, both of the *Daily Telegraph*, did much
towards introducing their follow-craftsmen to the masters
of thought or style, then at the height of their fame ; and
Robert Browning's poetry with Matthew Arnold's prose,
profitably conned by discriminating students, had a share
in helping forward a perceptible reaction against the
commonplaces of journalism, and the conventional use
of the epithets and substantives once known to juvenile
Latin verse-makers as "otiose."   All who saw anything of the inner life of Fleet Street during the
earlier struggles of Gladstone and Disraeli for political
leadership will recall J. A. Froude, George Eliot, and
another novelist of the same sex, Miss Rhoda Broughton,
as Fleet Street favourites, almost insensibly stimulating
Fleet Street writers to shun " sloppiness " of phrase

as they would the plague. Throughout all the time, too, now looked back upon, the Universities were daily increasing the number of highly equipped recruits which they had begun systematically sending to the London press, largely through Jowett's influence, during the later sixties ; for the remarkable man who, long before he became its Master, had identified himself with Balliol, not satisfied that his College should produce an un-broken succession of illustrious citizens and imperial rulers, thought that it should be the nursing mother of their public critics as well.

The Greek myths, one has been told, represent a past which was never a present ; so probably, too, is it as regards the halcyon epoch so fondly looked back upon by the panegyrists of the past who, with respect to its exact date, differ among themselves in everything except that we have travelled hopelessly beyond it in the present. The journalist's golden age is still very generally thought not to have lasted beyond Delane's domination of Print-ing House Square. It therefore had for its exact date rather the first than the second half of his career. Delane magnified his apostleship, no doubt, to the advantage of, as he himself used to call it, the whole comity of journalism. His rise in society was in the first place due much less to his historic editorship than to high favour with one or two of the great ladies who swayed the very select company of which society then con-sisted. The great political friendship of Delane's life, that with Palmerston, did not grow out of his command-ing position in John Walter's company. In fact, when Delane went to Printing House Square he found that his predecessor Barnes, so far back as 1839, had inspired Palmerston with a disgust of the *Times* by its satire on the " juvenile old Whig nicknamed Cupid." Palmer-ston's self-love and vanity were wounded at a tender point. He visited his wrath against the *Times* by com-pletely ignoring it, and making the *Morning Post* his organ. The feud between the statesman and the " organ of the City " only began gradually to heal when Lady Molesworth, acting as she had done in many other cases, decided that Delane and Palmerston must be good friends, helping each other, and sealed a treaty of personal good-will and peace between them at a series of little dinners she gave for the purpose in Eaton Square. As for his later intimacy with Palmerston, it would never have happened had not Delane been used from his youth to the kind of society from which Palmerston chose his acquaintances, and been visibly stamped with its hall-mark. The Princess Lieven and the Duchess de Dino had both reached their zenith before the Delane period. Each, however, lived into it, and each wrote her memoirs. Neither in the one book nor in the other does there occur a passage that can be said to form a tribute to the influence of the press. And yet even in those far off days, in advance it might be not only of Delane but of Barnes, there were newspaper personages not less indisputably commanding than Daniel Stuart, John Perry and William Black. If there be any date at which the journalist first came into marked demand with fashionable hosts and hostesses, it must be fixed well within the limits of our own time. As regards society and politics the journalist was then much more in evidence than he had been twenty years earlier. During this, the twentieth century's second decade, the fierce light of the notoriety due to power beats on him much more strongly than it did within any previous experience. Mr. Garvin, of the *Observer*, for instance, is a power of a magnitude seldom or never approached by any of his predecessors.

Not that the newspaper man's influence is always to be measured by the aggressive visibility of his power or presence. Delane was by nature as much of a diner-out as Abraham Hayward, and really liked evening parties, provided the hostess resembled Lady Palmerston in not being one of the " stair-head " order, and in getting the right sort of people together. So, too, the late Lord Glenesk while, as Algernon Borthwick, he handled the reins and whip of the *Morning Post*. Delane's immediate successor, Chenery, kept as much as possible to the Theodore Hook table at the *Athenæum*, and for choice would have been every night of the company that included Gallenga, Lawrence Oliphant, and Kinglake. Mr. Buckle has long since renewed and extended Delane's fashionable prestige. Other newspaper chiefs, nearly or quite the contemporaries of these, have proved guests less easily caught. Lord Burnham, Greenwood, Mr. Edward Dicey and Mr. W. H. Mudford, in their more journalistically strenuous days, were scarcely less economical of their presence in general society than the Irish leader of their time, C. S. Parnell, himself.

To-day, at least as much as, if not more than at any previous date, the best doors in town and country still fly open to the journalist with any real message or marked personality of his own, and to the editor who carries heavy guns, as well as knows how to point and when to fire them. If, as it has been sometimes said, newspaper names of real distinction appear less frequently than they did thirty years ago among the guests of ministerial or opposition chiefs, that, so far from being significant of the journalist's social decline, is really a tribute at once to his still-growing consciousness of power, and a cautious sagacity infinitely creditable to the men themselves, as well as conclusively demonstrating a steady growth in the importance of their craft. If the names are not seen, no one supposes it is due to lack of invitations or, for that matter, positive importunities. Politics and society, when a certain class of public questions fill clubs and drawing-rooms, get mixed up together. The whole thing tends to resolve itself into a medley of petty personal or pettier social rivalries. The word " genteel " has gone out of use ; the reality remains. The only way for the newspaper man, whether one in authority or not, to secure at such a juncture self-respect and a chance of escaping boredom to death is by retiring into his shell. Thus, and thus only, he will avoid at the outset the entanglement in associations that, before he is quite aware, will have gone some way towards committing him to support the political idol of one among the various competitive coteries to which circumstances may give the best chance of winning the editorial ear or of engaging the active pen. Any lingering notion that, during the two electoral periods respectively at the opening and towards the close of 1910, the journalist was less in social request than half a century or three-quarters earlier, may be disposed of by contrasting the methods in favour with the fashionable wire-pullers to secure their own ends at the two dates. Between 1830 and 1835 Lord Lansdowne first spoke of retiring from the Cabinet in which Lord Brougham also had a place. The Duchess de Dino and some great English ladies decided that this should not be allowed. Had a movement of this kind been started in 1911, its authors would have begun with giving an exceedingly bad half hour to some gentlemen of the profession and in the position then of Mr. St. Loe Strachey, Mr. Buckle, or Mr. Spender to-day. No thought of any such thing crossed their minds. Instead, the Duchess de Dino and a few more went, not to a favourite editor, but to the detested Brougham, and asked him whether he knew what Lord Lansdowne represented, only to be told : " Oh, yes. All the old women in England." A certain gentleman more than suspected, in the parlance of the day, of writing for the papers, actually volunteered the grand stateswomen a paragraph or an article. " Thank you," was the reply. " We can do very well without the press." And they did ; for Lord Lansdowne retained his office. Nor did he throw it up before, in 1841, together with all his colleagues, he went out in the natural order. During the first year of King George V., certain wearers of Whig titles of both sexes, also calling themselves Liberals, have hoped that the Cabinet might shed Mr. Lloyd George and Mr. Winston Churchill. There is no rumour of their having gone with such a suggestion to Mr. Asquith, but from time to time at least one influential newspaper monitor has been moved to an argument that the Prime Minister would be lucky if he could shake himself free from two such firebrands and marplots. Again, in 1910, if personal friction between a Foreign Secretary and a foreign ambassador threatened international irritation, the ministerial press would receive a hint to apply soothing treatment. How, by way of contrast, let it be asked and shown, did they manage these things on the eve of the Victorian Age? In 1834 the lordly game of Government-making was being played after the grand old manner between the great houses, not, on this occasion, on opposite sides, but within the sacred pale of Whiggism. By the tacit consent of both parties popular opinion was particularly consulted in the Postmaster-General's appointment. When Melbourne rose to the first place and formed his earliest Ministry, he gratified William IV. by putting in as the Duke of Richmond's successor and as Postmaster-General the head of a much favoured Court family, Lord Conyngham. The Holland House set expressed their dissatisfaction by a private movement to cancel the nomination. They would have been only following the Whig precedent, in the case of the Post Office above all other departments, had they tried to enlist the journalist on their side. The omission to do anything of the sort shows how little, even two years after the Reform Act, the privileged classes recognised the journalist as a power. And this within the decade that witnessed Delane's succession to Barnes at the *Times* ! Just four years earlier Brougham had taken on himself to give, as he put it, Barnes a wigging for an article about the Duchess of Kent's absence from William IV.'s coronation. The writer turned out to be Henry, afterwards Lord, de Ros, which, as Brougham said, only showed how easily the press autocrats could be " got at." If throughout the nineteenth century's first half the journalist was, as one sometimes hears, so much more considerable a personage than a generation or two later, the foundations of that superior authority would have been visibly laid by the end of the Georgian Age. But it was exactly then that we see the great ladies never condescending to use the newspaper men whom they knew, at least by name, but sending more of their own number to deal with the highly placed men of whom they disapproved, or otherwise to fulfil their behests. The truth is that, throughout most or much of the nineteenth century's first half, the queens and princesses of Mayfair only knew just enough of journalism as at once to despise, distrust, just a little dread, all those really or reputedly connected with it, and spoke of newspaper-writers generally as reporters, in the same way that they classed every grade of medical man under the head of apothecaries. The presiding divinity and Egeria of Toryism, the consummate Countess of Jersey, the magnificent Zenobia of Disraeli's last novel, *Endymion*, had, at one time or another, penned, on the superfine, wire-woven post of the period, a paragraph or two which, getting into print, she thought might serve her against her dreaded and detested rival, the Duchess of Sutherland. That great lady, however, had her satellites also in the various Mayfair strongholds. The next time her rival entered a drawing-room whose occupants were engaged in a friendly chat, one of the fair ducal retainers

said in a very audible whisper : " You must be careful
what you say before Lady Jersey. She reports for the
papers." And this of the magnificently severe Almack's
patroness, who, a few nights earlier, when the hero of
Waterloo reached the famous rooms in King Street, St.
James's, a quarter of an hour late, and made his way
through the half closed doors, accused him of leading
a mob—actually made this charge against the august
personification of reactionary Toryism, who so loathed
newspapers, as well as everything and everybody to do
with them, that his particular world, the grandest and
most exclusive of all, had not then forgotten, but often
proudly recalled, an instance of his short way with quasi-
journalistic intrusion during the peninsular campaign.
Major-General Sir Charles Stewart, afterwards Lord
Londonderry, while serving under the then Lord
Wellington, had been in communication with the *Morning
Chronicle*. " Now, Stewart," was the form taken by the
great General's reprimand, " though your brother Castlereagh is my best friend, to whom I owe everything, if
you continue writing letters to the *Chronicle* or to any
other newspaper, I will send you home."

Even then, however, nothing daunted the journalist.
In the Anglo-French fashionable slang of the period,
he was *impayable*. As the modish Yankee dialect of a
later time might have put it, his cussedness caused him
to penetrate everywhere, to discover all the secrets he
wanted, and to indulge whatever might be his tastes in
his comments on them. *Improbus* in the peculiarly
Virgilian sense was the epithet applied to this irrepressible, ubiquitous being of pen and ink. No public re-
prisals against him were possible now. A summons to
the Bar for contempt of Parliament, and an order that
meekly on his knees he should ask pardon for lightly
speaking of his betters—these penalties could no more
be meted out to him than could the pillory, the whipping
at the cart-tail, the ruinous fine, the slitting of the nose,
or the cropping off of the ears. But whatever his virtues
or genius, he remained as much as possible the reverse
of a *persona grata* even with the politicians whom he
was ready intelligently to commend, and whom his own
personal predilections might make him anxious to serve.
His relation, indeed, alike to Government and Opposition,

might best be understood by comparison with a common street experience. A husband and wife are violently quarrelling ; an exchange of blows seems inevitable when, failing a policeman, a private peacemaker stands between the would-be combatants, and implores them to make it up. In a moment the two set upon the philanthropic pacificator with tongue and gesture, if not with tooth, nail, and fist. So during the years sometimes regretfully recalled as the journalist's Periclean period, his efforts at intervention in a quarrel between politicians, even though prompted by a wish to serve his party or his personal benefactor, was really apt to secure him at least a snub from both of the two political adversaries. Thus it occasionally continued to be throughout much or most of the leisurely time during which, instead of having to feed the press with diminutive slips between midnight and sunrise, he received his subject from the editor on the afternoon of one day, and was expected to have the article ready for the printer the next morning.

As with the journalist, so with the journal. Both have undergone, and are still undergoing, great changes. The quality and position of neither have made any really downhill movement. Much less, it may at once be granted, than formerly is heard about the " policy of the paper." That used to be something more than a mere phrase throughout most, if not all, of the Victorian epoch. The traditions handed down from a long line of predecessors, who had written for the same journal very likely on the same premises, seated at the same table and in the same chair, were almost as much present to the leader manufacturer as the instructions of the editor under whom he was working. Those, too, were the days when the editorial " we " was no conventional or meaningless syllable. That, indeed, to a great extent has gone by.

The newspaper system as it exists to-day has, in the foregoing pages, been seen to have resulted from a long series of personal forces, operating in the same direction, but impelled by a great variety of moral and mental attributes. From time to time the manifestations of this progress have varied. To-day the men whose pens or management produce the oldest and best known of morning newspapers conduct their operations in as nearly as possible the same manner as was done by those who filled their place nearly half a century ago. Even, however, with the *Morning Post*, the *Standard*, and the *Daily News*, as with the *Times* itself, the earlier methods, if still pursued in principle, have been modified in detail. But it is a hurried age. The old triple paragraph article—exordium, discussion, and conclusion—has been largely elbowed out by the sprightly tripping leaderette and the ever-encroaching occasional note. Official information is no longer exclusively given to the world through the medium of double-leaded compositions running, as they sometimes did, to a column and a half. " Don't give your essays a porch," was Benjamin Jowett's advice to the long-windedness of inexperience and youth. And the present tendency towards condensation and brevity may be traced back in its beginnings to Jowett's former pupils, now widely pervading the new journalism. Concurrently with this, the editorial " we " has dropped a time-honoured prerogative in often entrusting a correspondent, anonymous or bearing an expert's, perhaps a known politician's name, to flash on the world, in the editorial column, some State secret, recently discovered national danger, or whatever else may thus be for the first time communicated to citizens and electors, their common country's friends or foes. The individual, eminent or otherwise, chosen for that duty as often as not now receives the formerly unknown compliment of not finding his announcement emphasised by the professional leader-writer. When those who to-day are generals of division in the journalistic army were junior captains, nothing was known of this usage. It results, however, from general causes which had even then begun to operate on many branches of periodical literature ; these brought with hem a general rising against the anonymous system. The reaction towards giving every writer the open credit for his work set in with the monthly magazines. Within the last few years it has extended in one direction to the *Quarterly Review* and in another to several of the weeklies. The change had been inevitable from the moment that the publication from being, as hitherto it always had been, an organ transformed itself into a platform. Of that change one consequence is the member of Parliament's increasing readiness to dispute the professional journalist's claim to a monopoly of the printed column. To-day there is no sheet, daily or weekly, whose editor could not quite respectably fill his space with amateur " copy " from Westminster legislators, who believe they can reach the public ear more widely and effectively by the journalistic pen than on the floor of Parliament or of the provincial town hall.

So, too, with the news columns ; the paragraphs that make up these, domestic or foreign, are no longer of the old stereotyped form. In the record of everyday events the chronicler is allowed greater room for freshness of form and individuality in the presentation of common-place details. Sir Donald Mackenzie Wallace or Valentine Chirol at the *Times*, Mr. Goodman at the *Daily Tele-graph*, or other " foreign editors " equally of journals new and old, like their domestic colleagues—though in these departments, as elsewhere, the literary manner, if scope for it ever existed, has gone out—have secured European recognition for their neatness and pithiness. Even he who runs while he rea   is seldom in such haste that he does not notice this a: ie summary writer's prevailing characteristic. Never certainly were higher intellectual qualifications and better social antecedents than to-day possessed by newspaper-writers of every kind. The prestige of the *Saturday Review*, as explained on an earlier page, was among the earliest of the attractions to Fleet Street for successive companies of young men combining good position with high university record. The movement which began then has gone on con-tinuously ever since. Whether in the case of the old journalists or the new, the competition for entrance into the number is equally keen on the part of aspirants belonging exactly to the same order as those who, on leaving college, formerly qualified themselves for a country gentleman's duties first by the Grand Tour, afterwards by a call to the Bar. Pliers of the newspaper pen may occasionally suffer from the abuse of their professional designation as much as the artists of the stage. The lady of loud dress and golden hair who figures in a nocturnal altercation with the police often describes herself as an actress. The strayed reveller whose name is on the charge sheet at Marlborough Street is called a journalist. As a fact, newspaper men of every department have shared the leader-writer's rise in antecedents and quality. The parliamentary staffs in particular consist largely of university men educated for the Anglican, Scotch, and Roman Churches, or men not unfrequently qualified as physicians and surgeons not less than barristers-at-law.

Such being the journalist's modern equipment for his work, what are his relations to the public he is supposed to influence or instruct? The one English satirist, Jonathan O'Dell, who has had anything to say bearing directly or indirectly on the Anglo-Saxon press, summarises its general tendency, and service in some vigorous couplets generally unfamiliar enough to be quoted here as follows :—

> "When civil madness first from man to man
> In these devoted climes like wildfire ran,
> There were who gave the moderating hint,
> In conversation some, and some in print ;
> Wisely they spake—and what was their reward?—
> The tar, the rail, the prison, and the cord."

The moderating hints mentioned here, followed by any reduction of the popular temperature, must always have been journalistic rarities. The newspaper man's task as he has conceived it to be prescribed by passing events has, under all dispensations, been rather to stimulate than control popular feeling. Even the great Delane, the exact counterpart in journalism of Palmerston in statesmanship, with the august traditions of his predecessors behind him and the cool counsel of John Walter at his side, was, as has been already, shown, throughout the Crimean War episode, carried onward by the wave of excitement just as much as the man in the street, whose oracle, indeed, he became. What the editor then felt, that he instructed his contributors to write. And this has proved, as probably it ever will, the general rule. The collective omniscience of the press prides itself on not fearing comparison with the corporate smattering of Parliament. Both the one and the other echo rather than make much real show of restraining or regulating popular sentiment in its more excited moods. The journalist, indeed, if he happen also to be a proprietor, can never have an interest, as he is falsely accused, in a desire for war as a means of increasing his circulation and filling his pockets by a

multiplicity of special editions. To begin with, the
chief source of his income is his advertisements rather
than his sales. To secure those auriferous announcements, he must indeed be able to guarantee the amount
of publicity that a large circulation only secures. But
that condition once forthcoming in a sufficient degree,
he is not greatly concerned for the exact number of issues
sent forth each morning to the newsagents. When the
Daily Telegraph, for instance, had achieved the " largest
circulation " and had become the most paying advertisement medium in the world, it used to be said that the
paper lost rather than gained on every unnecessary copy
that its machines turned off. That may have been a
figure of speech. The cost of maintaining an army of
special correspondents, and the immense sums paid for
the columns transmitted daily to headquarters by the
telegraph wire, leave, it may certainly be said, very little
profit on the additions they secure to the normal
returns of the publishing department. Nevertheless the
journalist has long been, and will probably always
remain, a stormy petrel, a fisher in troubled waters,
one whose activities tend to excite, not moderate,
the popular passions. Like the angel to whom
Addison in his poem compares Marlborough, he may
" ride in the whirlwind " ; he seldom, however, even
attempts to " direct the storm." His readers expect him
to emphasise and intensify their own prejudices or convictions, resent it if he makes a show of contradicting
or correcting, and at the utmost only allow him to flatter
their vanity by discovering, as the more thoughtful
of newspaper men do, an intellectual basis for their
emotional preferences and antipathies. Who, they are
apt rather impatiently to ask, is the individual writer
that he should sit in judgment on a jury of his fellow-
countrymen? The journalist therefore may inflame, may
even instruct public opinion ; he does not create it.
Nor on great public questions at home or abroad does
he often, save by stimulants, influence it. He may, however, and in the case of party papers does, sometimes
affect the line taken by the party managers. That was
conspicuously done just before the general election of
1910 by Mr. St. Loe Strachey, of the *Spectator*, who,
having long appealed to the Conservative chiefs not to

divide and weaken the party through pledging it too unconditionally to Tariff Reform, had the satisfaction of finding Mr. Balfour exactly respond by declaring that it was for the nation, not its statesmen, to decide its fiscal policy. Mr. St. Loe Strachey thus supplied an interesting proof that a newspaper is strong precisely in proportion as it is independent ; for his journal is not, and never has been, conventionally partisan.

The concentration of newspaper properties into comparatively few hands is not likely to produce any new departure, but rather to extend and deepen the tendency now mentioned. The journal, indeed, we have already made it abundantly plain, was never primarily designed by its promoters as an educational or philanthropic agency. It has always been a business enterprise whose success has depended on its supplying, as the halfpenny papers conspicuously have done, a real want, and in giving day by day information and entertainment of the kind which the masses appreciate. The individual writer may be of less importance in the new system than formerly. He may, perhaps, complain that he has less fixity of tenure than he would like. He has probably not his former chance of becoming a literary power on a particular sheet before he is moved off to another owned by the same employer. On the other hand, he is not without substantial compensations. Never was he allowed freer play for his own particular turn of fancy, humour, or wit, provided only that these qualities are backed by brain power, and have in them enough strength really to make their mark. That condition demonstrably fulfilled, he may now indulge his literary idiosyncrasy after a manner he could never have done before, and exactly in the shape which he considers most effective. In other words, he need not restrict himself to the conventional leader form. He is free to choose the exact variety of composition which suits him best. Whether it be narrative, allegory, or dialogue, the more novel the shape he has given it, in the present day, the better. Interviews, conversations, real or imaginary, between interlocutors alive or dead, short copies of satirical or serious verse—if he can put really good wine into these new bottles, he has in twentieth-century journalism a dozen chances of making his personal mark where, under the old regime, he would not have had one.

To pass from the journalist himself to his relation to
the Government under which he lives : it was a French
newspaper hand of the highest order, Emile de Girardin,
who called all writers for the press "mischievous and
mutable," declaring they only repeated what their purchasers liked to hear. Better, he exclaimed, than a free
press in a free State a despotism instructed by a few
trained statesmen, who are much more likely than the
newspapers to tell the tyrant what the other side thinks.
That to some extent has been the opinion held by more
than one English authority, with something of an expert's
knowledge alike of journalism and politics. Internation-
ally, once said Sir Charles Dilke, the press almost or
quite invariably does and must do more harm than good.
Hear what another authority has to say about the same
subject. "The diplomatists and Foreign Ministers of
Europe would get on perfectly well together, and settle
their own differences comfortably, but for the new
journalists' intermeddling and stirring up international
jealousy and spite. It is a disgusting spectacle, which
makes me feel thankful that I am seventy years of age."
So, in a letter to the present writer, in the last year of
his distinguished life, Sir Mount Stuart Grant-Duff.
Recent years have habituated the public to the idea of
international press conferences, and the periodical interchange of hospitalities between the newspaper men
of different European capitals. But one must remember
that it was not the journalist who did much to help
forward the mediatorial mission discharged by King
Edward VII., and that, as Bismarck said of the Parisian
Globe or *Patrie* before Napoleon III.'s *coup d'état*, as
regards recent Anglo-German relations the mutually embittering influence proceeds as often as not first from the
journalist, who increasingly seems to think that his duty
to his paper requires the discovery of a new crisis or
a new era.

CHAPTER XV

THE SUB-EDITOR—"THE VERY PULSE OF THE MACHINE"

Another side of journalistic life—The sub-editor: his work, influence, and importance—Newspaper reputations made or marred in the sub-editorial columns—Characteristics of American sub-editing—Have editorials any real influence?—American reaction on the English press—The science of "writing up" as demonstrated by the Yankee—Humble imitators in England—Training the newspaper writer for his work—All roads lead to journalism—"Time's whirligig"—The press supplants the patron as literary critic and bread-giver—A modest offer of ten-guinea "leaders" has no taker—Nothing new under the sun—Newspaper runners and writers reflect all the forces which are the mainspring of the nation's life.

So far the journalist with whom we have had to do has been an occupant of the editorial chair or a leader-writer. Incidentally, indeed, mention has been made of his work in the Westminster Galleries, as well as of his varied acquaintance with life and character not less than with books. The journalist, however, has many readers who know him best, not as a parliamentary reporter, political or social lecturer, but as one who collects a diurnal miscellany of news items. These judge him and his paper's tone much more from the sub-editing than from his original comments. As a fact, a newspaper's character and circulation practically depend more upon the sub-editor, his methods and his men, than on the Sterlings and Edwin Arnolds of a bygone day, or the Humphry Wards, W. L. Courtneys, A. G. Gardiners, G. K. Chestertons, P. W. Wilsons of the present. So practical an authority as the late Frederick Greenwood held that with the Bulgarian Atrocities agitation of 1878 the English sub-editor first began to be "Americanised." The policy of the paper was a consideration more powerfully present to a journalist of an earlier generation than in these days when, after the fashion already explained, the newspaper tends increasingly to transform itself from an organ into a platform. The importance, therefore, of the leader-writer or the occasional contributor,, honoured with wide-spaced type, diminishes rather than grows. But while the value of the original pen thus varies, the necessity of paste and scissors remains always the same. The sub-editor, in fact, is he who may have even more to do than the editor himself, from the public superficial point of view, with stamping, by what issues from his department, its social and moral character upon the entire sheet. The articles, leading or headed, are thoroughly read and meditated on by a comparative few. The news paragraphs, if sometimes stowed away in rather obscure corners, are seldom missed by thousands and tens of thousands. An unsavoury epithet, a printer's error involving some suggestion repulsive or ridiculous, may do a newspaper more harm than the noblest sentiments, expressed in corresponding language, can accomplish of good. The sub-editor's work is often called mechanical. He, however, it is who more than shares with the editor himself the custody of a newspaper's reputation for adaptability to household reading, for general entertainment, and above all things for the absence of whatever might bring the blush to the young face. On the country press no single journalist ever did more than the already mentioned Edward Spender to raise the sub-editorial standard. In London the earliest influences in the same direction were exercised by none more powerfully than by the *Daily Telegraph's* creators. Thus it is that by degrees it is now the exception to find any member of a sub-editorial staff unequal to responsibility for the good taste, and even the good grammar, not only of mere paragraphs, but of whole reports and other items of late intelligence. Editors-in-chief, therefore, have always aimed at reading every small print entry before going to press. Though in theory that may never be left undone, it is physically impossible that the rule should not have exceptions, tending greatly to increase the sub-editor's responsibility and importance. It is through the miscellaneous matter of the sub-editorial columns, arranged to suit each issue's particular make-up, that libel for the most part finds its way into print.

Technically, assistant editor and sub-editor, if some-

times used indifferently, are not really synonymous. As
a fact, however, in addition to the more prosaic routine
of his department, the sub-editor may often be called
upon to discharge duties strictly speaking editorial. In
England his qualifications were never higher than to-day
for such calls. The *Daily Chronicle's* first editor, R. W.
Boyle already mentioned, a man of much cultivation and
literary taste, began as sub-editor on the *Telegraph*
first, on the *Hour* afterwards, and in all the other posts
he filled did a work and set an example that still live to-
day. On the other side of the Atlantic, the sub-editor
has become a still more important personage than here,
and the selection of news that he makes decides to which
of several classes the journal itself belongs. It all
depends on the tendency and contents of the sub-editorial
columns. The yellow press editor devotes some twenty
per cent. of his space to crime and vice. Sometimes
he contrives to satisfy his employers while reducing it
to five per cent. He is then called a conservative sub-
editor, and exposes himself to the charge of squeamish-
ness. The American newspaper owner or manager boasts
of being a tradesman who supplies his customers with
unhealthy as well as healthy news if they come to his
shop to ask for it. He does not keep a preaching house
but a store, and is free to sell any poison they ask for,
provided he does not infringe the law. " If you complain
of this,'' he adds, " go to the police-station, but don't
come bothering me."

The English sub-editor, metropolitan or provincial,
seldom, probably never, has to do with an employer who
puts it quite as cynically as this. But if his proprietor
cannot command the success of political influence he
must sometimes make the most of the profits that come
from scandal. To-day the public has ceased to lament or
even notice the absence from any leading columns or
elsewhere of the journalist who wrote the literary style
of the nineteenth century. The leader itself, it is said,
can be demonstrated an imposture ; for in 1906 the
London editors almost to a man published Unionist
leaders ; but, as the Unionist rout which at once followed
showed, with no advantage whatever to the party. Again,
in the provinces, for the best part of half a century, the
sustained and rare ability of the *Manchester Guardian's*

Liberal championship did not lose the Lancashire Conservatives a single vote. There is never any lack of quick
returns for the sub-editorial muck-raker who, in crisp
and highly coloured phrase, throws the flashlight upon
the nauseating and poisonous mysteries of crime after the
fashion of the sixpeny shocker or the penny novelette.
While these lines are being written, Mr. Moberley Bell,
the *Times* manager, is said to have made a move in the
right direction by stating that if a certain class of police
reports and divorce cases were kept by law from newspaper publication, his own feeling and that of others
besides his proprietors would be only one of relief.
But in England, it must be remembered, the Blue-Skin
paragraph monger flourished long before we could boast
any disciples of that American master described as the
sub-editor's best exemplar because he " knew. exactly
where hell would break out next and had a reporter on
the spot at once." A Chicago estimate fixes the present
total of the world's newspapers at sixty thousand,[1] and
claims a third of this amount for the United States. These
figures, no doubt substantially accurate, serve at once to
remind one of, and to explain, the progressive closeness
of journalistic and literary as well as social intercourse
between the Anglo-Saxon race on both sides of the dividing ocean ; and the Britisher would be ungrateful if he
ignored that to Yankee inspiration may be referred most
of those colossal newspaper fortunes whose acquisition
by his own countrymen he so greatly admires. The
preparation of a striking bill has always been the English
journalist's last business before going to press. James
Gordon Bennett, of the *New York Herald*, became his
earliest instructor in the manufacture of startling headlines. Then came several other journalistic masters from
the Far West, including Samuel Ward (" Uncle Sam "),
boss of the Lobby at Washington and king of *bon
vivants* at Delmonico's, the Chevalier Wikoff, who once
passed for one of Palmerston's secret agents, and the
editor first, from 1875 the owner, of the *New York
World*, W. H. Hurlbert, already before his arrival well
known to and much thought of by those shrewder
journalists here who saw there was something more to

[1] *The American Newspaper*, by James Edward Rogers, p. 17.

be learned from America than scare and sensation-mongering in print. Till then there had been no newspaper man from the other side whose opinion went for more in our own Fleet Street, or who, when an English paper needed a little financing, was more responsibly, consulted by the British capitalist before the cheque was given. Not less of an oracle with the peers and publicists of Mayfair was Mr. G. W. Smalley, so long the universally popular and admired *New York Tribune's* correspondent before he represented the *Times* at Washington. To the same order as Mr. Smalley belongs the American scholar and philosopher, Mr. E. S. Nadal, who in the *Nation* gave his countrymen something between a New York *Saturday Review* and *Spectator*, not much below either British model. Mr. Okey Hall, of the *New York Herald*, was in the eighties another of those who convinced not a few journalistic Britishers of the superiority of American notions to home grown ideas.

In traversing the United States from the Atlantic to the Pacific, one passes through several distinct newspaper zones ; the American visitor will find nothing of the same sort here. At no stage of his journey will the traveller through the States see a journal able to turn out an American President during his term of office any more than the London *Times* can eject a Lord Mayor. He will, however, find no spot where the journalist fails to be the dominating central force—the acknowledged teacher and oracle of the whole community, supplying it not only with its opinions on public affairs, but its ideas of life generally, of the arts and graces of society and, by systematic extracts or references, with an insight into the literature of all ages as well. In an address delivered by him to a purely journalistic audience at Cambridge in August, 1894, Professor R. C. Jebb dwelt on the American newspaper as a universal educator, without an exact British equivalent. May it not be said that in our own land the latest conductors of cheap newspaper enterprise, with their Universal Educators, and other varieties of omniscience tabloids, are making the journalist not less ubiquitous in England than in America ? Both countries are newspaper ridden rather than newspaper ruled. In both, too, the journalistic babel created by the multiplication of sheets on the same side or on different sides has resulted in a confused din, deafening the public to the journalist's voice, and so far subversive of the journalist's influence.

To some extent in London itself, but generally throughout the provinces, the popular demand is for increasingly full details of sport, cricket and football, as well as racing, among the latest news which may come in while the sheets are going through the press and the editor has left the premises. This inevitably increases the subeditorial power, and in practice makes the chief of the news department the most important person in the place. The more recently established and the fewer the restraining traditions of the London or country journal, the greater the sub-editor's inducement to find his model ready-made in the notoriously successful, the eye-compelling and the purse-opening contents bills and news paragraphs which line the entire route from Long Island to San Francisco. The arts of working up the tamest item of news into thrilling narratives of misery, crime, of clever gallows-cheating, or of the accumulation of more than Monte Cristo's millions are, it must be admitted, as yet only in their English infancy. Still, we are getting on, and the British newspaper " boss " sees at every stage fresh signs of his own resources and power. As he steams out of Euston Square, he throws back a lingering glance on posters announcing his day's wares in type that would stare out of face a circus bill or a new patent drug advertisement. From the railway carriage he may witness the blazonry of his own bills proudly triumphant over such petty competitors as Oxo, Wincarnis, and Beecham's Pills. On descending at Manchester the " boss's " eyes are dazzled by local placards of his own sheets typographically quite eclipsing those on which his eyes last rested at the metropolitan end. Thank heaven, he piously murmurs, for a " sub " who knows his business ; and indeed all these things are the sub-editor's handiwork.

The course of literary ambition was neatly said by James Hannay to begin with aspirations for high poetic renown and to end with promotion to a sub-editorship. And even to-day the sub-editor purely British bred and trained has not always divested himself of his literary prejudices and associations sufficiently to suit the newspaper magnate who thinks that literature and journalism ought to be kept as distinct from each other as science and theology. The American tongue, indeed, is now known by the English journalist of every degree, and for many expressive phrases, such as " going strong," is useful enough. But not all the reputedly newest tricks of the journalistic trade are Yankee novelties. Thus telegram exploitation had been known in Fleet Street as long as telegrams themselves, and in fact earlier. Later improvements in this direction are now described in the vernacular of their native land as " playing-up " news, doctoring news, and falsifying news. All this may be done with greater smartness in the Far West, but in some form or other it was all known and practised in London as soon as in New York. Hence the sub-editorial obligation of the Old World to the New has probably been somewhat over-rated. There is room for a good deal of casuistry in any attempt to estimate the true character of these refinements in journalistic practice. One cannot help speculating how far they may come within the ken of the Chair of Journalism which at least one English University has been credited with the thought of founding. That, however, might only set one on wondering how far the Professor of Moral Philosophy might always approve the lessons taught by his journalistic colleague.

To confine oneself to accomplished fact, what is the machinery already at work for improving the supply of skilled hands in every section of the newspaper mill? The Prime Minister's nursing mother, the City of London School, has not only opened a class of journalism, but gives a travelling scholarship to the best pupil. King's College, London, and Birmingham University both train newspaper reporters and writers of every kind in the way they should go. In Tudor Street, Blackfriars, is the Institute of Journalists, established with the idea of being a trade union for newspaper men. It has, however, since been captured by the newspaper masters. Among its earlier Presidents was Lord Glenesk, succeeded at the present time by Mr. Harry Lawson. Its programme includes periodical meetings in the great provincial centres, with much hospitality from municipal bodies and local big-wigs of every degree. The discussions which vary the social functions are seldom without much real interest, if perhaps, also, too abstract or general in their tone to serve a very practical end. The Institute of Journalists will, however, be of real service to the working journalist if only because it often acts as a benefit society by granting money votes to newspaper men and their families who have fallen on evil times. The soundness and prudence of its administration are beyond suspicion, but the complaint is sometimes made that the conditions on which help is doled out may be often such as to prevent the self-respecting journalist from being an applicant. The Institute of Journalists had existed some time when its social and economical methods were charged with not being sufficiently parsimonious or severe. The censorious and frugal northerners therefore started a National Association of Journalists which, not dissipating its energies on the Institute's conferences, devotes itself entirely to the journalist's professional welfare. Amongst several of the eminent and amiable wealthy interested in newspaper men's well-being was Baroness Burdett-Coutts. The charming little villas built on her Highgate property for the clerks in Coutts's Bank, but not entirely utilised in the intended way, might, the good lady thought, be available at a nominal rent for journalistic occupants. The idea, however, while both considerate and picturesque, proved no more practicable than Bulwer-Lytton's scheme many years earlier for grouping those who were to form the Guild of Art and Letters in nests of model dwellings under the shadow of Knebworth Park.

Enough has been now said to show that the journalist in this, the first year of the new Georgian Age, is the subject of two diametrically opposite movements. On the one hand his energies have carried professional organisation to an extreme point. On the other, the gates of his craft were never opened more widely to newcomers quite independently of qualifications ; nor was so much passably good newspaper work ever before done by the outsiders who have preferred the press to the wine trade or governessing. And this for a wage that is at best but nominal, and in reality only from a wish for a start in connection with the mighty engine concerning which Thackeray made Warrington apostrophise so eloquently in *Pendennis*. One who, in his time, had been journalist as well as Parliament man and author, " Eothen " Kinglake, used to say that the literary difference between his own earlier days and those into which he lived was that everyone now hurried to print what nobody thought it worth while to say then If one does not exclude those who send letters to the editor, it will be scarcely an exaggeration to say that the hundred and twenty-two years of existence now completed by the *Times* have witnessed the growth of almost as many newspaper writers as there are readers. This process is likely to increase rather than diminish. In the first place, throughout much of the Victorian Age, when married and research fellowships were yet unknown, the majority of the cleverest men who turned their backs on their university still took up active work in education or in the Church. To-day these often begin by being professors at the new local universities or university colleges. When their term of office expires, they may find themselves without anything fresh to say concerning the Latin poets of the Silver Age, or the unsuspected references to modern democracy in the poets of the Italian renaissance. They are forced, of course, into any hack work they can find, and for literary hacks, if they are worth anything, the newspaper pace and pay are at least six times as good as the average publisher's terms. In the second place, scarcely a year passes now without the retirement from Westminster of someone who has either achieved Cabinet rank, or who is well on his way to it, not because of any false step which may have marred his career, but for the simple reason that he has wearied of the exasperatingly inadequate results yielded by the expenditure of physical, intellectual, nervous, and pecuniary force at Westminster. Of Parliament men who have exchanged politics for book-writing, newspaper-writing, or for both, no one has done so with more public distinction or satisfaction to himself than Sir G. O. Trevelyan ; he, with intellectual vigour and even freshness still unimpaired, while yet on the right side of threescore years and ten, obeyed Nature's earliest warning, and, before being quite exhausted by the "nights of endless talk " that he has mentioned in his own *Ladies in Parliament*, sought repose that has enriched English letters with his *American Revolution*, and has been brightened by his son's fulfilment of the best Trevelyan traditions at the Education Board. Another Harrovian, Sir George Trevelyan's junior, Mr. G. W. E. Russell, was only forty-two when he gave up his seat for North Bedfordshire, and produced, in addition to an immense and regular supply of good newspaper material, the best monograph of which so far Matthew Arnold has been the subject. The latest instance of a like retirement is that of Lord Fitzmaurice ; he, indeed, had always kept his pen pretty free from the journalist's ink. Now, in the intervals of political biography, his interest in newspaper work to-day more than compensates him for retirement from business at Westminster. Thus does Time's whirligig work its revenges, and Wisdom justify herself of her children. The journalist, as we have seen, began by stirring up against himself Parliament's persistent jealousy and scornful hate. He criticised or even observed its proceedings almost with a rope round his neck. He knew the ascent to the pillory as well as he did his own doorstep. In the near distance stood the common hangman, in one hand holding the whip which was to flog him at the cart-tail round the town, in the other displaying the shears that were to crop his ears before the day's programme was finished. A restless, unconscionable, irrepressible kind of being, he was, in the natural order of providence, suffered to spit his lies, libels, venom of all sorts abroad, and generally to infest the earth just as a like tolerance was granted to beasts, to birds of prey, and to other noisome creatures. Before the eighteenth century was out, the mightiest and most philosophical intellect in the Parliament of his day, Edmund Burke, had found out that this generally distrusted, detested, but inextinguishable person had laid the foundation of a Fourth Estate. So things went on. The future Prime Minister who, ten years before the Victorian Age, worried poor Mr. Murray into starting the *Representative*, found, in the episode of that luckless print, some hints for the Carabas episode in *Vivian Grey* ; eleven years later it was as a " gentleman of the press " that Benjamin Disraeli won his election for Maidstone. After another seven years, in the novel which made his literary fortune, he represents Sidonia as satirising to Coningsby the "imperfect vicariate of the House of Commons," and more than hinting that the only real representation of the English people since the destruction of so many ancient franchises by the Grey Reform Bill must be found not at Westminster but in Fleet Street. The doubt as to the journalist's power to create or even in great national crises profoundly and permanently to influence the issues of the hour is, it has been seen, not a thing to be taken for granted. In the social province the case is very different. Here there is no domestic reform which has not been directly delayed or hastened by the newspaper-writer, no abuse or evil in the everyday life of his readers which his pen has not helped to rectify or remove, no miscarriage of justice his comments on which have failed to awake popular echoes of demand for the scandal's termination. The twentieth century may almost have been said to open with a striking proof of the journalist's power to right wrong in the release which crowned the *Daily Mail* agitation for the wrongly imprisoned Adolf Beck.

Writing their pleasant and instructive autobiography some time before the Victorian Age had brought the journalist into prominence, Mary and William Howitt complained of everything in London literary work being done by favour and connection. William Howitt himself practically testified the truth of these words by only being able to turn the corner with a little sheet called the *Constitutional* when he had found a patron for his paper and himself in Daniel O'Connell. In 1820, seven years before he had made a success with *Philip van Artevelde*, Sir Henry Taylor, when beginning on the London press, found far less help in Gifford, the *Quarterly* editor for whom he had already written, than in the present Lord Knutsford's father, Sir Henry Holland, the famous physician, whose acquaintance with great peers and equally great commoners first opened Paternoster Row to his young friend. The Howitts attributed the difficulties of their literary start to their Quaker descent. Irrespectively of Church or station in life, Samuel Johnson, fresh from his visit to Lord Chesterfield, foresaw the day when the first care of writers would not be to know peers, when scholars, historians, and essayists would experience none of his own difficulties in receiving the moral or material support denied to workers of the pen in his own day, from patrons more generous and less difficult than the titled rich. With that prophecy's fulfilment the journalist has associated himself in more ways than one. In some of his capacities he has superseded the patron as the awarder and arbiter of literary reputation. To writers of every degree it is a clear gain of literary self-respect that the tribunal sitting in judgment upon them should no longer consist of well-placed individuals with a taste for pen and ink among the nobility or higher gentry of the land, but of men who have for the most part been professional writers themselves, who are critics not, as *Lothair's* Gaston Phœbus said, because they failed in literature or art, but who have been retained for the journals to whose staff they belong because they have given proof of their competence to record responsible and trustworthy judgments on literary performances.

During the last year of his life, Matthew Arnold, in conversation with the present writer, touched on the striking increase, as he called it, in the output of far more than passable verse in the evening journals, and on the highly capable criticism that he never took up a daily or weekly journal without noticing. For that, in the weekly organ so long the possession of their house, few have done more than successive members of the Dilke family, each entitled to a place among the latter-day fathers of the press. A word, however, of recognition should not be withheld also from one who, as proprietor, editor, and to a large extent writer of the long-departed *Reader*, was in one sense their competitor, but in another their colleague. Most of the men formerly employed by Thomas Bendyshe, such as Francis Drummond and Joseph Knight, wrote regularly for the daily press as well. Bendyshe failed, indeed, as has been done by several others before and since his day, in making the *Reader* a rival to the *Athenæum*. He had, however, a knack of dealing, after an original and scholarlike fashion, with literary subjects and personages of all periods. The best of his writers caught some of his freshness and inspiring intolerance of the commonplace. These qualities were not without an educational value of their own, and may, indeed, reasonably be connected with the great improvement shown by the journalist as literary critic towards the close of the sixties.

The author, however, has to thank the journalist for something more than sound practical advice about securing and keeping the goodwill of the public. That in these latter days he escapes so many of the miseries and degradations that broke the spirit of the book-seller's hack in the eighteenth century, and throughout the first half of the nineteenth, is chiefly or entirely due to the fact that the employment he can generally find as journalist prevents his being entirely at the mercy of the publisher, who, in this age of literary overproduction, finds himself, really through no fault of his own, obliged to sweat his writers rather than pay them.

If, recently remarked to me a clever and accomplished novelist of the Victorian Age who still retains her earliest favour, things go on at this rate, we shall soon be looking back upon the Grub Street period as the Augustan Age of authorship. If one may dismiss this rhetorical figure as a wise warning rather than a literal prediction, it is to a great extent because the author has long since realised the expediency of turning journalist also, and does not exclusively depend upon the royalties on sales by which work done for publishers is very generally remunerated. Some half a century ago, the late J. C. Jeaffreson, the *Athenæum* critic as well as a novelist and miscellaneous author, finding that he had some time on his hands, rather thought he would amuse, himself and make a little pocket-money by bestowing it on the newspapers. His modest offer of writing as many leaders as were wanted for ten guineas each was received with less universal avidity than he had expected ; in fact, to his keen disappointment it did not, if I rightly remember, find a single taker. Incidentally, how-ever, it has already been seen that the leader-writer's wage had long tended to fix itself at something like from two to three guineas a single article. No one journalist ever was or ever will be indispensable to his sheet. Jeaffreson soon recognised the fairness of the ordinary market terms, and, once having obtained some very occasional leader work, after a time discontinued it with more than regret. Special rates, now that the signed article has so widely supplanted the anonymous, may sometimes be secured by a star writer, an acknowledged and perhaps unapproachable expert on his particular subject, and so the bearer of a name which, it can be almost proved mathematically, will make the paragraph subscribed by him the sensation of the hour. Save in entirely exceptional circumstances like these, he has about as much practical chance of making " fancy " terms as of inventing a series that will make him the breaker of the bank at Monte Carlo. The pace and the quality all round are too good, the supply of men each equally effective with his pen, and with an equal claim to be considered a master of his art and his subject, is too great, the public demand for journalistic delicacies that are " caviare to the general " is too slight, and experience shows it to be so entirely a toss-up whether the abnormally paid contributor of world-wide notoriety sells a single extra copy, that even a titled convict who has just done fourteen months for forgery has no better chance than the most plebeian and obscure criminal of realising, from the columns in which he condenses his experiences, enough appreciably to help him in getting a new start.

About the journalist's past and present, there remains nothing more to be said. There are, however, bearing on his future one or two remarks which may be ventured on with reasonable confidence. Whether he be master or man, he will continue, in the personal training for his life's work, and in its close association with the movements of his time, to represent not so much a single order or a limited number of interests as all the tendencies, issues, concerns and problems of his time. His energy may discover new forms of enterprise, and divert itself into fresh channels ; but the point has now been reached when experience seems likely to place its veto upon the repetition of undertakings already proved to be impracticable. The late autumn of 1910 witnessed the issue of a new halfpenny evening paper. That is a comparatively small affair. The scale on which an effective and permanent addition can alone be made to the morning dailies of the established type is too vast and costly to invite many competitors.

That was practically settled by the attempt in 1906 with the *Tribune*, which had every kind of high desert, and ended only because the public that commended and might have bought it was sufficiently supplied already. Scarcely less desperate seems the effort to invent any journalistic devices or methods of literary presentation so unknown to existing ingenuity, so essentially unanticipated in substance or shape, as not to come under one or other of the heads into which existing newspaper contents divide themselves in the posters of to-day. No stratum of the world's actual or potential reading public is now untapped. From the philosopher to the felon, from the Primate's palace to the casual ward, there is nothing said, done, or thought which escapes the journalist's daily record. There is no idiosyncrasy on any human level, famous or infamous, which, if it will catch a single eye, is not trotted out by the journalist in charge, to outdo earlier feats of the newspaper *manège* in the performing columns.

The high finance, the unostentatiously accumulated millions handed down from generation to generation in Lancashire mills, cotton stores, or family banking houses, every order of the aristocracy of cash as well as of land—not one of these national forces is unrepresented in the proprietary of the great newspapers. To-day, therefore, the journalistic interest, using the word in a commercial sense, has diffused itself as widely through the body politic as the railway interest or the brewing interest. While newspaper boards are thus becoming as familiar as any in the *Directory of Directors*, the journalist himself, in *Who's Who* or other reference books of the period, appears increasingly under other than a literary heading. Society knows him as a man about town, as an ornament of the liberal professions, or as one who stands high in the fighting services. Fifty years ago he would have employed his literary leisure by writing an occasional article for the *Quarterly Review*. To-day at shorter intervals he finds a chance of wielding a more direct influence in a shorter space by taking up the specialist's pen for the *Times*, the *Post*, the *Chronicle*, or the *Daily Mail*. In politics the journalist, whether writing under his own name or anonymously, may not move large bodies of men, and may exercise little weight upon general elections. On the other hand, his appeals to party leaders on his own side were never more eagerly listened to than now, and his arguments, especially if of personal application, never permeated more widely the rank and file to which they are addressed. In an increasing degree, therefore, the journalist prefers the column he controls to the parliamentary seat ; because that would be more likely to mean self-effacement than fame. Consequently, on the civil or military side, in Church or State, the professional journalist has now to hold his own against a growing host of amateur competitors of the most highly equipped and determined kind.

Thomas Arnold of Rugby and the most famous of his pattern pupils, Arthur Stanley of Westminster, may have resembled Sir William Vernon Harcourt in never having taken the *Times* shilling. Both the Churchman and the lawyer derived from their newspaper work advantages greater than those of money. Such as in the twentieth century profit by their example not only receive payment, but stipulate for terms. There may be a show of deprecating publicity. But Parliament men on their probation, and divines not yet installed in a pulpit of their own, are amongst the most persistent advertisers or newspaper employment in the way of gossip paragraphs and descriptive sketches. The novelty is, however, less the presence of these outside competitors than their keenness in driving money bargains. Not, indeed, that the extra-professional pen, ecclesiastical or secular, was, as often as it has been the fashion to suppose, unpaid for the column over which it disported itself. J. W. Burgon pocketed a fee for his *Standard* contributions during the sixties, as well as for his *Quarterly* articles, and found both kinds of composition useful steps towards the Chichester deanery which he reached in 1876. Dean Wace of Canterbury and Dr. Cumming of Crown Court also in the sixties occupied pulpits belonging to their respective communions, and were thought the better of by their congregations because at the same time they were providing Printing House Square with almost a daily leader.

The journalist, too, has been one with the soldier even more than with the ecclesiastic. What one at least of the services, from the official point of view, thought about the officer who, while actively campaigning, used his pen too much has been shown by the passage between the Iron Duke and Colonel Stewart cited some little way back. The Duke of Wellington's short way with the newspaper-writing officer may have found admirers, but never many practical imitators. It was none of Grote's favourites, but one heartily disgusted with the Athenian democracy, the reactionary Tory Xenophon, who, after his service in the army of the Persian king, had retired from public life, civil or military, before instituting the alliance, since so fruitful, of the writer with the fighter. This union finds its earliest representatives in Sir William Napier and Sir Archibald Alison. Each found the periodical pre s an equally convenient outlet. Throughout the Victorian Age the relations between the journalist and the general were on the whole those of mutual goodwill and reciprocal assistance. During the Crimean episode, W. H. Russell and one or two more of the war correspondents at the same time that they performed a national service in drawing attention to, and so mitigating, the sufferings of our soldiers, had been charged with letting the Russians into the secret of the Allies' plans, and so of making themselves responsible for mo e than one strategical miscarriage. For a repetition of that charge no pretext was subsequently given in all the wars after the Indian Mutiny. The writer and the fighter maintained a perfect understanding with each other. In 1871 the abolition of Purchase was followed by the bitterly controverted Bill for the Regulation of the Forces. The Burmese War, the operations before Sebastopol, the Indian Mutiny, the Chinese War and, more recently, the Red River Expedition, had given Lord Wolseley that opportunity of showing his genius as a commander which occasion had denied to Sir George Hamley, to Adye, to Lintorn Simmons, to Lynedoch and to Hill. He now identified himself with the latest military reforms of that Liberal party traditionally distrusted of the soldier. Without avowing himself Gladstonian, he dared to say that the Liberals themselves had not unmade the Army as an instrument of war. The chief officers who had served under or with him could handle the pen not

less effectively than the sword.   The old prejudice against
the literary officer wore itself out.   The war correspondent under sympathetic control was tolerated at
headquarters in the campaign.   The new *entente* between
sword and pen worked in the interests of all concerned.
The Commander-in-Chief and the press chronicler began
to supplement each other.   In peace-time correspondents
like Archibald Forbes read papers on strategy at the
United Services Institution before experts from the Staff
College.   Whether civilian or soldier, the military
journalist at least maintains in the new Georgian era
his position of Victorian days.   Mr. Spenser Wilkinson,
before filling the chair of Military History at Oxford,
had made his mark as military critic of the *Morning
Post*.   Another of the Xenophons of the Isis, Mr. Amery,
wrote the *Times History of the Boer War*.   Nor must
one forget that the widening of the Oxford curriculum
so as to include at least the rudiments of the art of
war has been largely brought about by the military
journalist.   Beginning with the present Sir Henry
Brackenbury, his late brother Charles and the two
Hoziers, John and Henry, each of whom, but especially
the former, was a real soldier of universities as well as
an officer of the land forces of the sovereign, the movement now mentioned was effectively promoted, amongst
others, by an old Balliol man and light cavalry officer,
General F. S. Russell, as well as Lord Roberts, an Etonian
who knew Oxford well.   Thus has there come into existence
on the Isis the delegacy for military instruction which,
in concert with the War Office, selects Army candidates
who, having proved their qualifications by papers on
military subjects set in the Final Pass Schools, receive
twice a year artillery, cavalry, or infantry commissions.
Sir Henry Brackenbury will be remembered not only as
uniting the highest literary accomplishments with the
military critic's professional knowledge, but as, if not
the founder, a conspicuous member of the gifted group
that, now nearly half a century ago, illustrated the then
incipient union of sword and pen.   This company has
included Sir Henry Brackenbury's two old pupils, Sir
Edward Law and Sir John Ardagh ; it has been presided over by his two chiefs, both first-rate writers,
Lord Roberts and Lord Wolseley, and has had among

its ornaments General Sir F. Maurice, Sir Coleridge Grove, Sir Ian Hamilton and Sir Evelyn Wood.

In some of these cases the fame of a book-writer may eclipse that of the journalist. But in none had the author won his laurels except after searching experience of the journalistic mill. To-day, therefore, the two interests concerned in the newspaper industry—labour and capital, master and man—resemble each other in reflecting all the forces, moral, mental, material, chiefly conspicuous in the nation's life. The growth of a private adventure into a public institution, attracting and incorporating into itself the most various resources of successive periods, summarises in a few words the journalist's earliest rise and latest progress. In prose fiction as well as poetry, the twentieth century has already witnessed an innovation upon established modes of expression. That has been exemplified by Mr. Thomas Hardy in his fine poem *The Dynasts: a Drama of the Napoleonic Wars*. His most thoughtful critic, Mr. Henry Newbolt, pointed out some time since [1] that the very novelty of Mr. Hardy's cadences prevented them from at once satisfying the surprised ear. So, too, may it be with much that seems most novel in the diction and methods alike of the journalist who to-day represents most faithfully and forcibly the taste and spirit of his epoch. The change, however, as has been shown in the foregoing pages, is one not of revolution but of development. Between the spirit in which, whether capitalist or writer, he first addressed himself to his work, and that in which he accomplishes it to-day, the continuity, moral and intellectual, has been on the whole without solution.

[1] " A New Departure in English Poetry," *Quarterly Review*, No. 418.

INDEX